I0715400

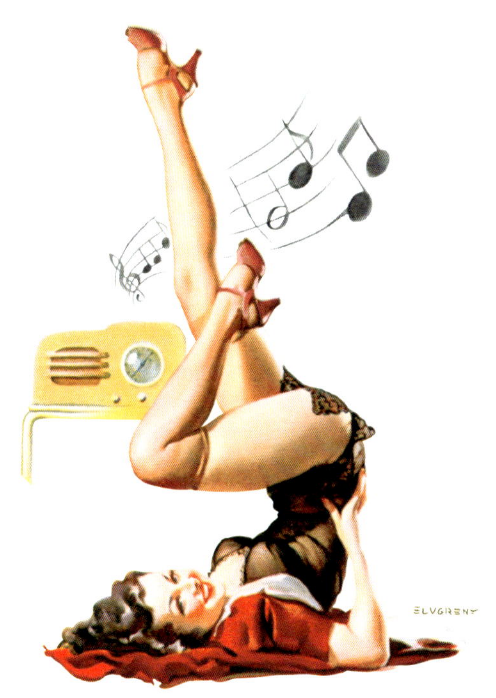
ELVGREN

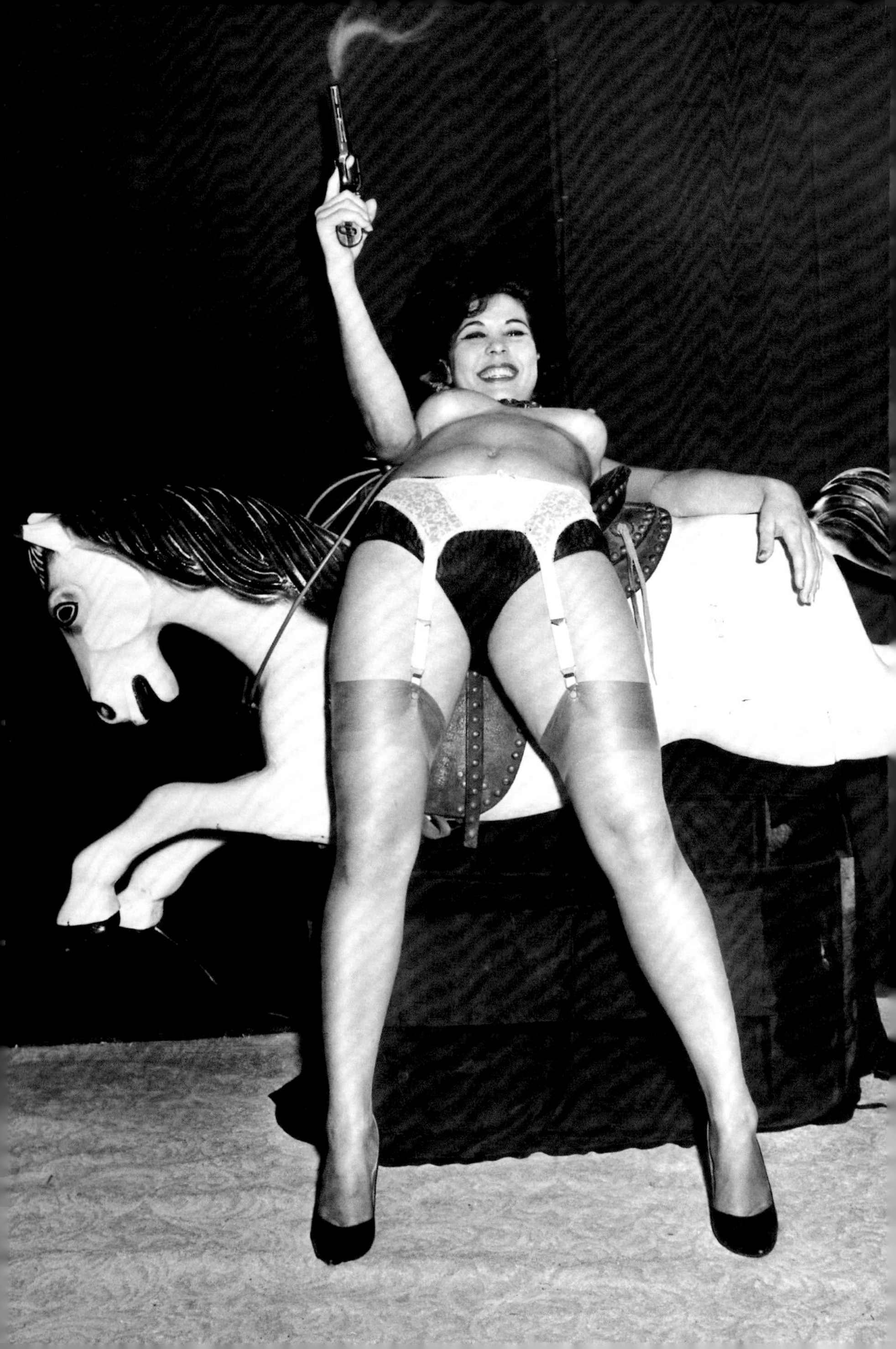

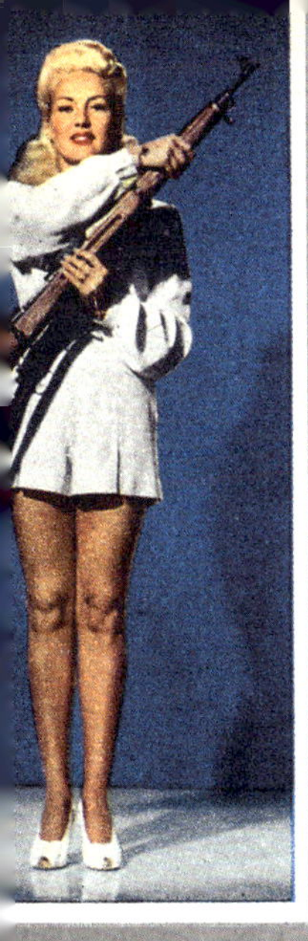
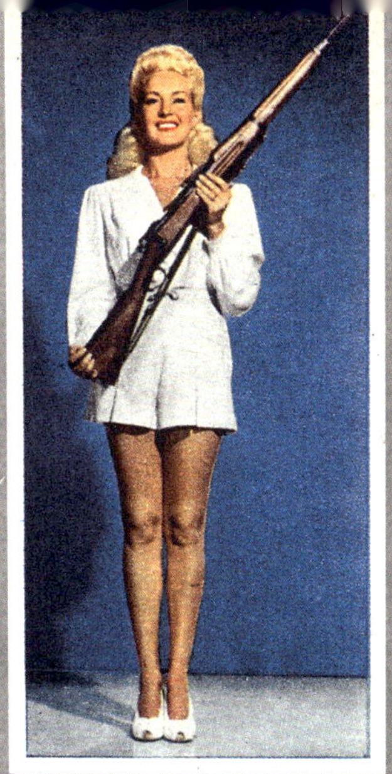
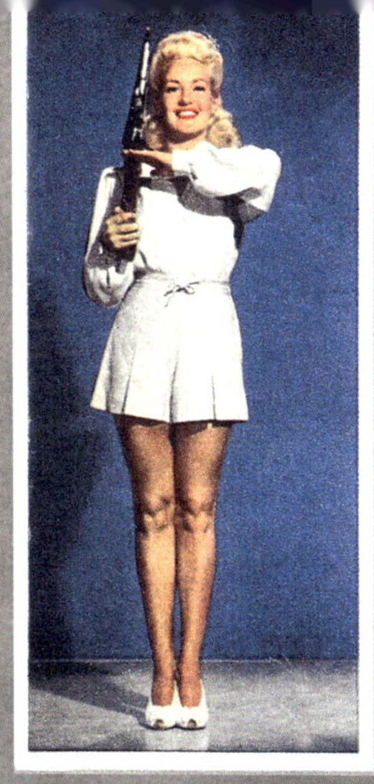
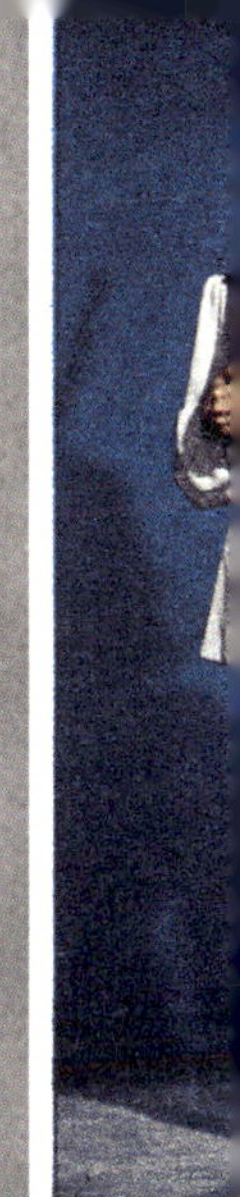

SHOULDER ARMS:
the rifle
ight hand.

Grasp it and balance
With left, steady stand!

Regrasp it, right hand
This time on the butt,

Now pla
At shou

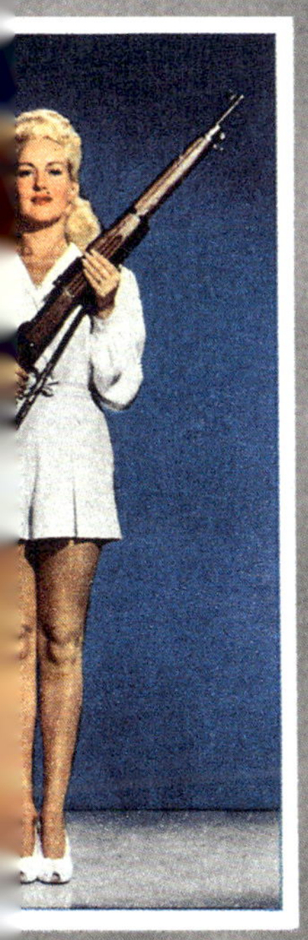
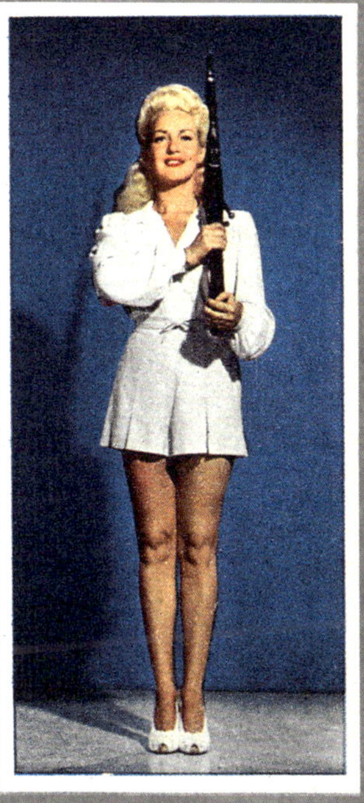
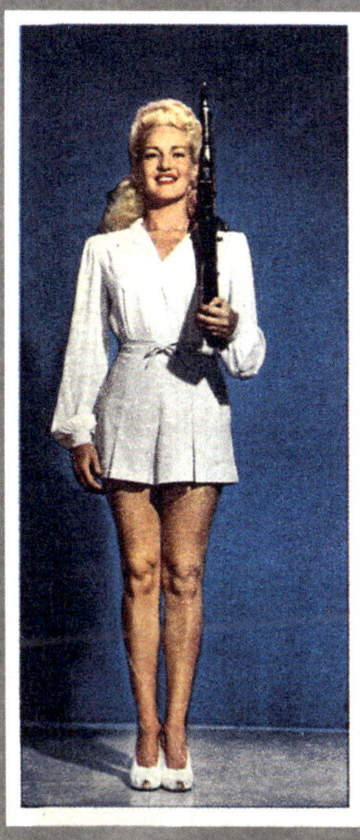
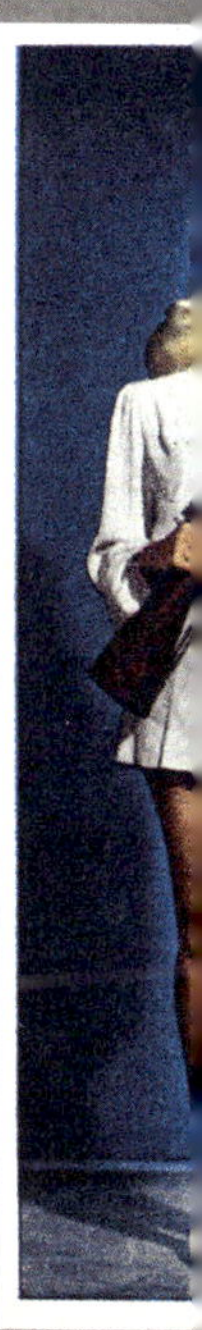

over, up right,
shoulder land!

4. LEFT SHOULDER ARMS:
Now release rifle
With the left hand,

Forearms horizontal!
Drop right. (A command!)

5. INSI
Seize th
Look th

DIAN HANSON

THE LITTLE BIG BOOK OF

Legs

GREAT GAMS IN A PETITE PACKAGE

TASCHEN

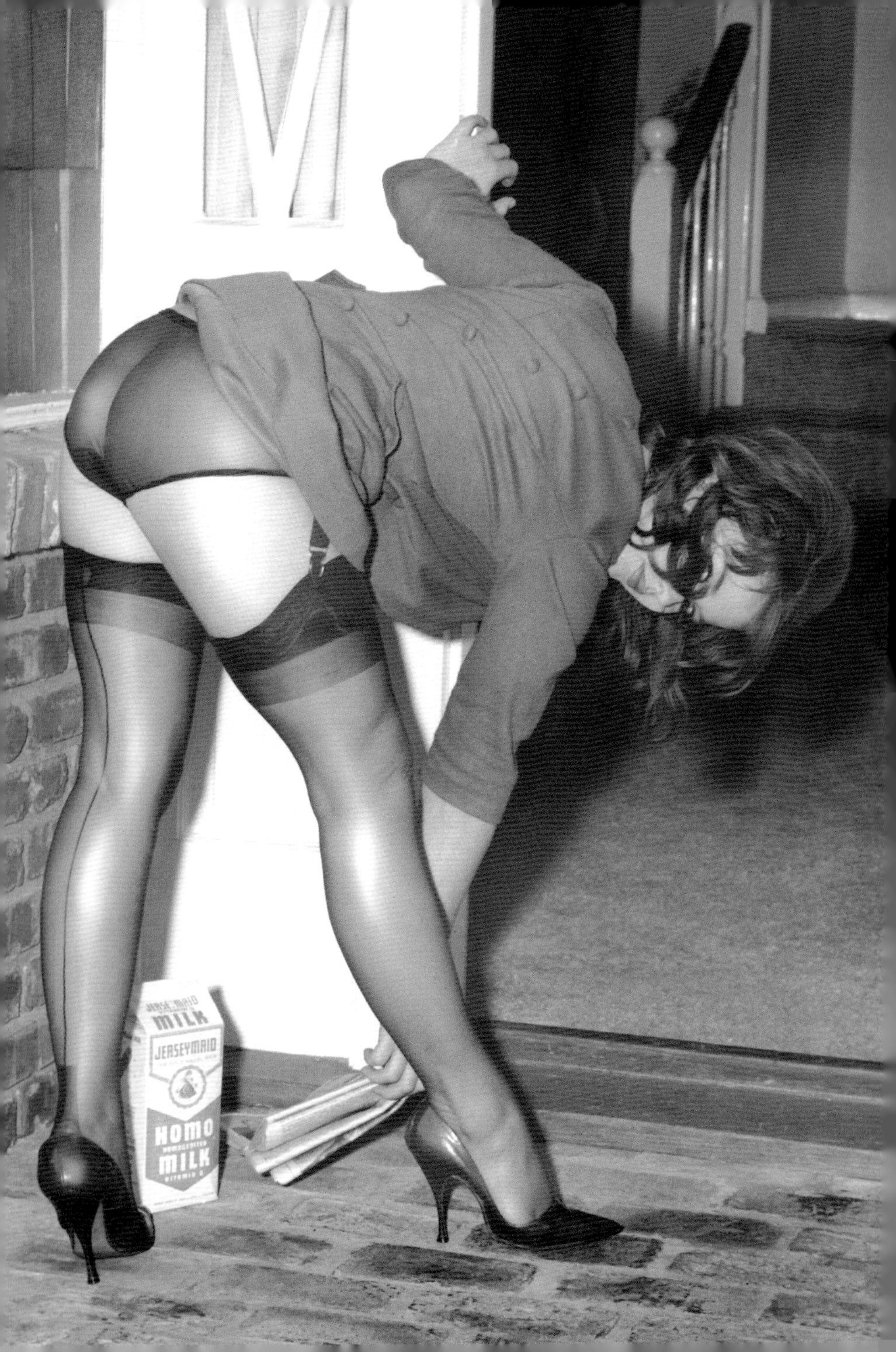

JERSEYMAID
MILK
JERSEYMAID
HOMO
HOMOGENIZED
MILK
VITAMIN D

The Curiously Sexy Leg

BY DIAN HANSON

The female leg is a sexual oddity. Nonerogenous, and nearly identical in structure to its corresponding male part, there is no obvious reason for its allure. Yet, through much of history, across many cultures, women's legs were subject to the same taboos surrounding genitalia, hidden away beneath skirts and petticoats until they became objects of intense sexual obsession.

The fascination peaked in the Victorian era, when one could not even utter the word *leg* in polite society for fear of inflaming male passions. Legs have now been out of hiding for over 80 years, but their appeal remains curiously, and consistently, strong.

What is it about this simple construction of bone, muscle, and fat that makes it so different from the arm, which is seldom, if ever, eroticized? Some claim legs are alluring because of what lies between them; let a man's mind start wandering up ankles and it won't stop until it bumps

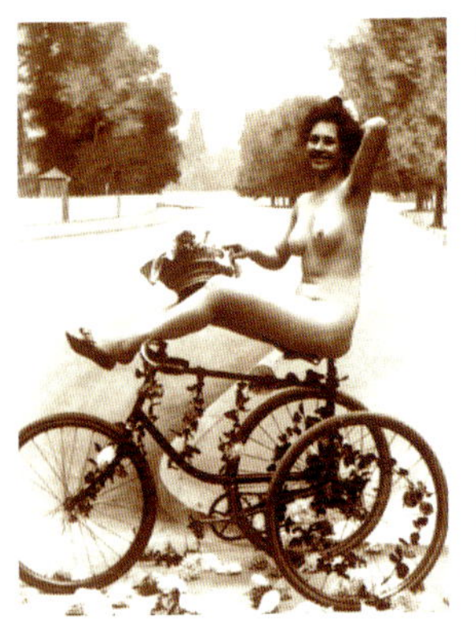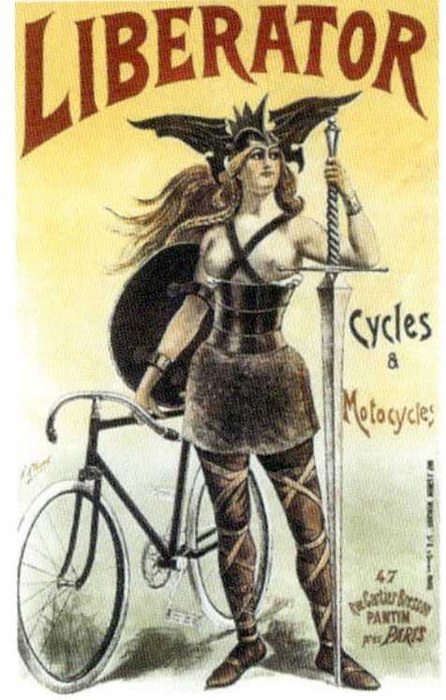

PAGE 4 Mary Ann, circa 1962

FAR LEFT French postcard eroticizing female bicyclists, circa 1920.

LEFT Poster, circa 1900, for French Liberator bicycles by artist E. Clouet.

OPPOSITE French novelty card that opens to reveal cancan dancers, circa 1945.

into that cauldron of sin between the thighs. But if legs were just pathways to the pussy, wouldn't women have covered their groins instead of their thighs all those centuries? Indeed, all underpants, when women wore them at all, were crotchless until the 1890s. No, there is something in the leg itself that concerned the establishment.

Women's legs posed a threat to the moral order because they represented female autonomy. The heavy layers of skirts and petticoats weren't just intended to hide legs, but to hobble them. There was a real, though largely unspoken, fear that if women gained mobility they would run from their housebound lives — a subconscious admission that the comparative freedom enjoyed by men was far more appealing than what was prescribed for "the gentle sex." This is why the first wave of women's liberation was so determined to free the female leg. The unlikely vehicle for change was the lowly bicycle.

In the 1890s many women were determined to straddle what the suffragists called "freedom machines," and adopted sporty outfits including a knee-length bloomer with stockings and high boots. Many were harassed and arrested, but by the 1910s men accepted, and even enjoyed the "new woman."

Once hems began to rise "gams" became the most popular subject of what passed for pornography in America. *Capt. Billy's Whiz Bang*, America's first men's magazine, featured illustrations of leg-baring flappers from 1919, and was joined by *Hot Dog*, *TNT*, and *Smokehouse Monthly* in the 1920s. In the '30s magazines solely devoted to legs appeared, first *Silk Stocking Stories* in 1935, followed by *High Heel Magazine* in '37, and *The Stocking Parade* in '38. In 1942, when the United States entered World War II, a flood of new patriotic pin-up magazines all emphasized legs, epitomized by the "million-dollar legs" of America's #1 pin-up, Betty Grable. Few who admired wholesome blond Betty's pins in *Yank*, the Army's own magazine, stopped to consider that it had taken just 20 years for the female leg to travel from immoral to All-American.

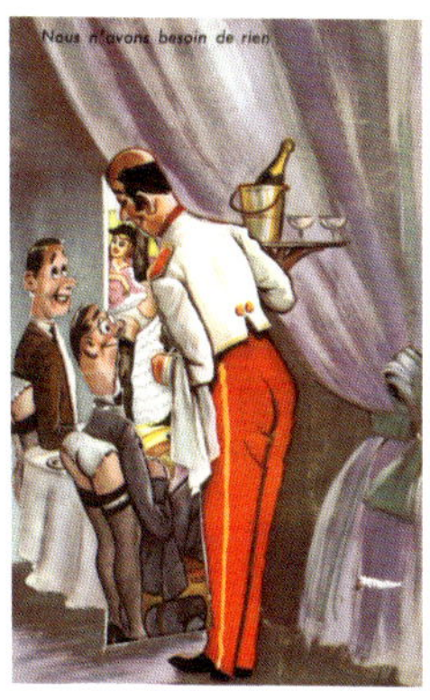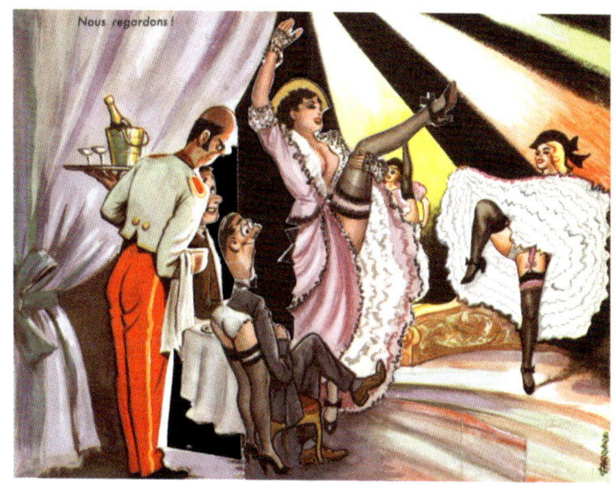

During this same 20 years the commercial leg show had evolved just as significantly. Burlesque split into two distinct camps in the 1920s, with the traditional variety show renamed *vaudeville*, while *burlesque* came to mean striptease, a show that went well beyond the leg.

Undressing to music was first conceived at the Folies Bergere in Paris around 1895. Striptease arrived in New York via Minsky's National Winter Garden in 1917, though the first dancer to remove her clothes onstage reportedly did so by accident. Minsky's was raided repeatedly through the 1920s, but the club, and the public's interest in striptease, persevered. By 1933 there was little objection when Minsky's star Sally Rand was the star attraction of the Chicago World's Fair.

Rand's bubble dance epitomized American burlesque in the '30s and '40s as a tease culminating in a brief flash of nudity, while legs, clad in stockings and high heels, were visible throughout. Thus, even after tits and ass were added, burlesque remained largely a leg show, and for burlesque-loving legmen Betty Grable and *Yank* were a touch too wholesome. These men wanted dames with a whiff of sin about them, the kind of tough cookies dished up by Robert Harrison.

Harrison launched *Beauty Parade* in 1941, followed by *Eyeful*, *Wink*, and *Titter* in '43, *Whisper* in '46, and *Flirt* in '47. Like other leg magazines, Harrison's had no nudity, but there the resemblance ended. The models were top strippers, not starlets, pin-ups, or "girls next door." The magazine covers featured lurid pin-ups of women in stockings and heels by the masters of leg art, including Earl Moran, Billy DeVorss, and most commonly, Peter Driben.

Despite his emphasis on burlesque, Harrison's most famous model was Bettie Page. In 1951, before Bunny Yeager dressed her in leopard skin, before Irving and Paula Klaw put a whip in her hand, Bettie made her magazine debut in *Flirt*. Just four years later, as Betty Grable announced her retirement, Bettie Page was declared *Miss Pin-up Girl of the World* and featured as "Miss January" in the hot new magazine *Playboy*. Page's popularity illustrated the evolving state of leg art, since by 1955 she'd starred in scores of bondage and S/M photos for the Klaws and built a strong following in the new fetish magazines.

Wink magazine introduced John Willie through his *Sweet Gwendoline* comic strip in the mid-'40s. In 1946 Willie launched *Bizarre*, which soon became the world's most notorious fetish magazine. Though bondage and discipline were its mainstays, *Bizarre* made a clear connection between women's legs and sexual power, specifically the potent fetish potential of high-heeled shoes. An accomplished artist, he enjoyed designing his own shoes, and demonstrating the effect of extreme heel heights on the foot. In both his art and photography he laid down enduring standards for fetish wear, including masks, opera-length leather gloves, corsets, tight leather skirts, and black seamed stockings.

In 1957 Elmer Batters self-published *Man's Favorite Pastime* and ushered in the next, and greatest, era of leg magazines. As a leg and foot fetishist Batters knew what his audience wanted and had the photographic talent to give it to them. Once Elmer showed the way, American publishers produced a wealth of leg magazines that would never be equaled, a golden age of glossy nylons, stiletto heels, towering bouffants, black patent eyeliner, cigarettes dangling from thickly painted lips, martini glasses clutched by long red nails, and attitude oozing from every pore. These trashy goddesses vamped from the covers of *Black Garter, Black Nylons, Black Nylons and High Heels, Dandy in Hose, Garter Parade, Hip & Toe, Leg Show, Legs & Lasses, Slip & Garter, Naughty Nylons, Nylon Jungle, Nylon Mood, Silk Seams, Stocking Parade, Tic Toc, Tip Top*, and the dozen magazines Elmer made personally.

The golden age of leg magazines ran 10 years, from 1958 to 1968, when the more adventuresome magazines began showing pubic hair. They all but died in the '70s, wiped out by pussy, which upstaged everything else. Tits? Gone. Ass? Gone. Legs? Way gone. When I started my porn career in 1976 I'd never even heard of leg magazines. I was your standard young sexual revolutionary who went straight from sneaking peeks at my father's *Playboys*

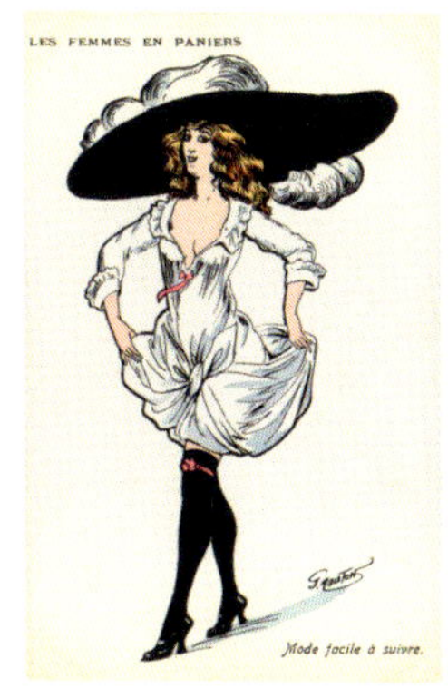

RIGHT This French postcard, circa 1910, references the pannier undergarment of the 18th century, a kind of cage worn to elevate the skirt.

to hardcore pornography by age 18. I encountered the newly reissued *Leg Show* while working at *OUI* in 1981, and couldn't believe there was a market for such an odd, archaic concept. Then in November 1987 I was abruptly laid off from *Hooker* magazine and gratefully accepted the offer to edit *Leg Show*.

By 1992 *Leg Show* was the best-selling leg magazine ever, perfected through reading the thousands of letters I received from its readers and by long talks with Elmer Batters. It continued to grow to a peak of 200,000 copies a month.

When I left *Leg Show* to join TASCHEN in 2001 I'd spent 15 years among the legmen and read approximately 60,000 letters. I learned, among many other things, that men who love legs and feet are unlike those who prefer more obvious erogenous zones. They are, as a whole, better educated, more accomplished, and likely to prefer strong, assertive women, as female strength resides in the legs. As a group they're unusually open to sexual experimentation, reflecting their intelligence, education, and preference for

the body part that most contradicts our ingrained notions of femininity.

This just might be the real reason women's legs were kept covered for so long. The moral certainties of life were imperiled when women hiked up their skirts and gained mobility, leading to freedom. Finding their strength made them question their traditional roles, and many men found this female strength curiously attractive and began questioning the rigid roles they'd prescribed for themselves.

To this day there's something about a long, shapely pair of female legs, preferably mounted on 5-inch heels, that stimulates renegade fantasies, making the female owner feel strong and the male viewer weak in the knees. These symbols of women's sexual strength are a danger to men's morals, but it's much, much too late to get them back under wraps now, and we'll all just have to bear the titillating consequences.

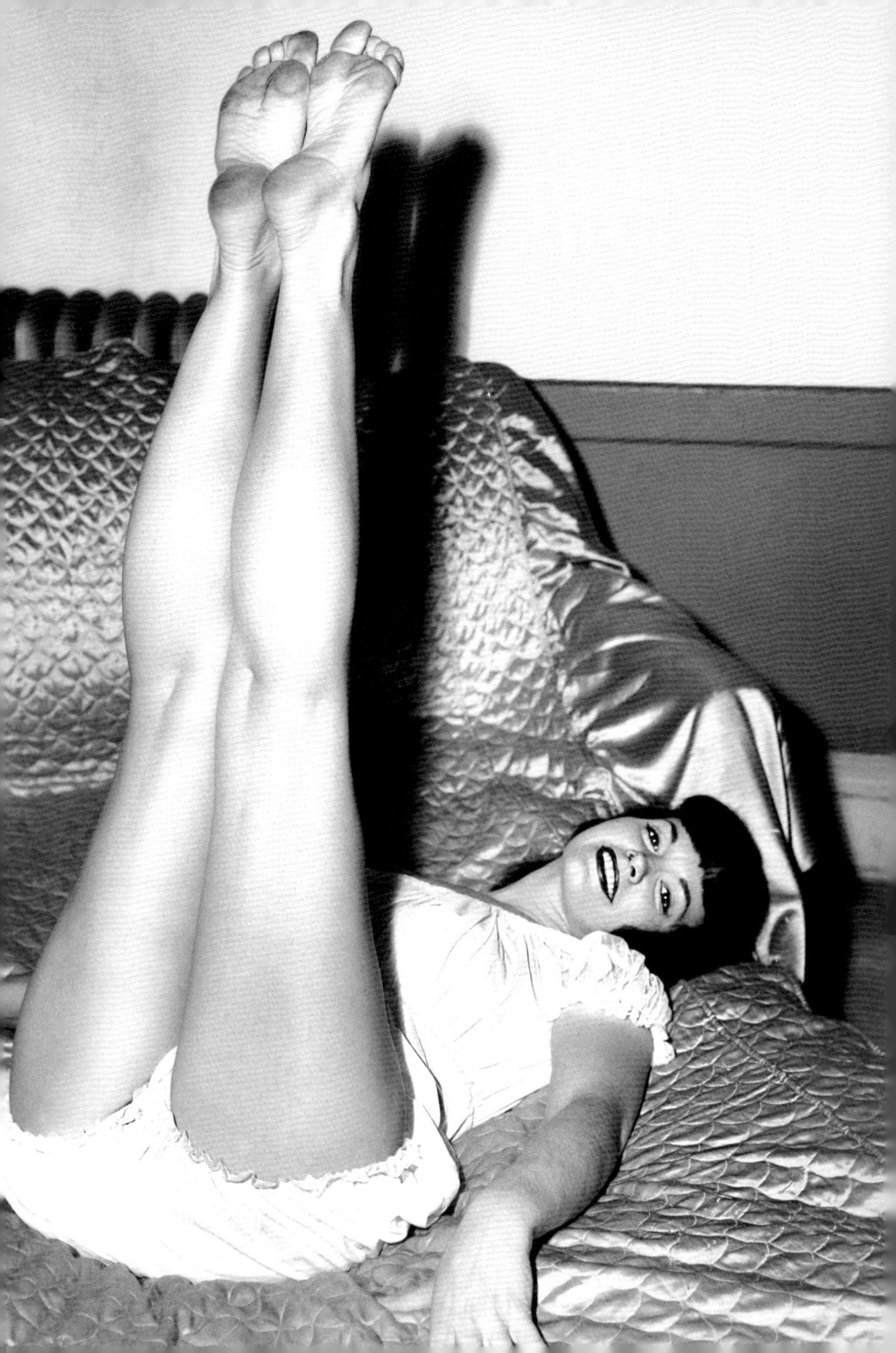

Der Zauber des weiblichen Beins

VON DIAN HANSON

Das weibliche Bein ist ein erotisches Phänomen. Es ist kein Geschlechtsteil, es ähnelt seinem männlichen Gegenstück fast aufs Haar – warum sollte man es also sexualisieren? Und doch wurden quer durch alle Zeiten und Kulturen Frauenbeine bedeckt, versteckt und derart tabuisiert, dass sie sich in Objekte intensiver sexueller Obsession verwandelten. Unter Königin Viktoria war in der feinen britischen Gesellschaft schon das Wort „leg" verpönt, da man befürchtete, allein sein Klang könne Männern vor Lust die Besinnung rauben. Und sogar heute, 80 Jahre nach ihrer Enthüllung, üben Frauenbeine noch starke erotische Anziehungskraft aus.

Was unterscheidet das Bein, eine einfache Konstruktion aus Knochen, Muskeln und Fett, vom Arm, der eher selten erotisiert wird? Manche behaupten, der Reiz von Beinen liege zwischen ihnen; die Gedanken des Mannes wandern von den Fußgelenken der Frau nach oben zum sündigen Dreieck zwischen den Schenkeln. Doch wenn Beine nur Wege zur Muschi wären, hätten Frauen in vergangenen Jahr-

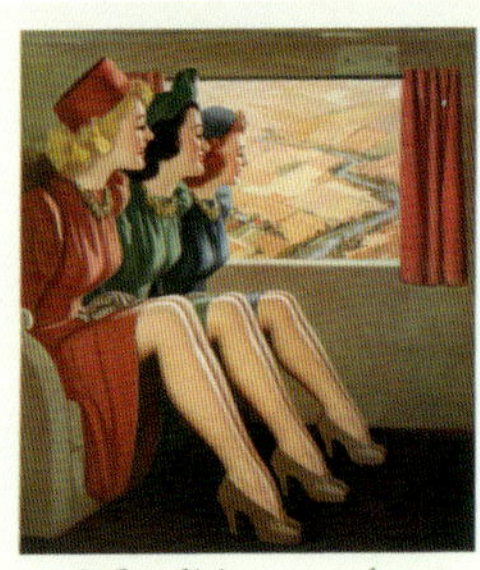

PAGE 10 Bettie Page by Irving and Paula Klaw, circa 1955.

LEFT Magazine ad for Vanette nylons, circa 1948.

OPPOSITE LEFT Fruit of the Loom stocking display, circa 1955.

OPPOSITE RIGHT Actress Marie Wilson poses with a 35-foot model of her leg, erected in Los Angeles in 1949 to advertise nylon stockings.

hunderten nicht eher ihre Lenden als ihre Schenkel bedeckt? Tatsächlich waren aber Unterhosen, soweit es sie überhaupt gab, bis in die 1890er-Jahre im Schritt offen. Nein, es muss etwas am Bein selbst sein, das das Establishment beunruhigte.

Frauenbeine wurden als Bedrohung der moralischen Ordnung angesehen, weil sie weibliche Unabhängigkeit symbolisierten. Röcke und Unterröcke sollten die Beine nicht nur verbergen, sondern sie auch zügeln, denn es herrschte die unausgesprochene Angst, dass Frauen ihrem häuslichen Leben entfliehen würden, wenn sie nur etwas mobiler wären. Das kam einem – wenn auch unbewussten – Eingeständnis gleich, dass das relativ freie Leben der Männer erstrebens werter war als jenes, das dem „schwachen Geschlecht" auferlegt wurde. Deshalb war die Vorhut der Frauenemanzipation auch so versessen darauf, das weibliche Bein zu befreien. Dabei half ihr unerwarteterweise ein simples Transportmittel: das Fahrrad.

In den 1890er-Jahren bestiegen viele Frauen die von den Suffragetten als „Freiheitsmaschinen" titulierten Gefährte, und zwar in sportlicher Bekleidung, zu der knielange weit geschnittene Hosen, die unten mit einem Gummiband zusammengefasst wurden, Strümpfe und hohe Stiefel gehörten. Viele von ihnen wurden beschimpft und verhaftet, doch ab etwa 1910 akzeptieren Männer im Allgemeinen die „neue Frau" und genossen den Anblick.

Sobald die Rocksäume etwas höher rutschten, wurden Beine das populärste Objekt dessen, was in den USA damals als Pornografie galt. Amerikas erstes Herrenmagazin, *Capt. Billy's Whiz Bang*, zeigte 1919 Illustrationen von Damen mit nacktem Bein, in den 1920er-Jahren erschienen *Hot Dog*, *TNT* und *Smokehouse Monthly*. In den 1930er-Jahren kamen dann Magazine auf, die sich ganz dem Bein widmeten: zuerst *Silk Stocking Stories* im Jahr 1935, dann *High Heel Magazine* 1937 und *The Stocking Parade* 1938. 1942, bei Kriegseintritt der USA, überfluteten patriotische Pin-up-Magazine den Markt, die alle auf Beine fokussiert waren, angeführt durch die „Millionen-Dollar-Beine" von Amerikas Pin-up Nr. 1, Betty Grable. Wohl nur wenigen Lesern, die die Fotos der blonden

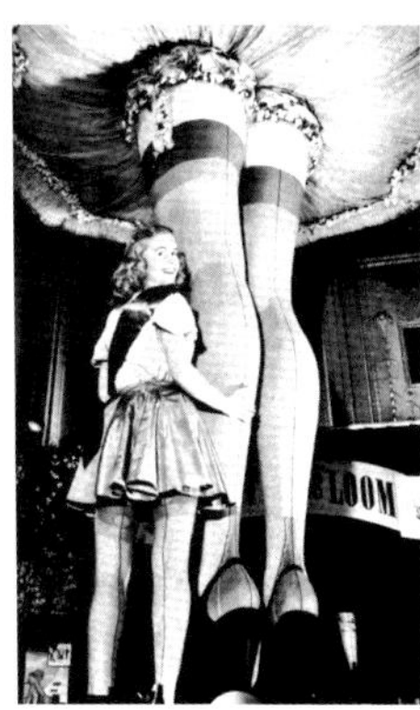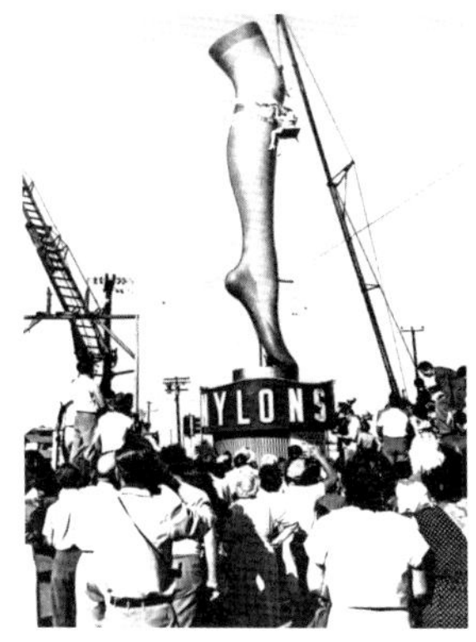

Betty im Armeemagazin *Yank* bewunderten, war vermutlich klar, dass das weibliche Bein innerhalb von nur 20 Jahren von unmoralisch zu uramerikanisch mutiert war.

Im Verlauf dieser 20 Jahre hatte sich auch die kommerzielle Leg Show enorm weiterentwickelt. In den 1920er-Jahren kristallisierten sich zwei Richtungen heraus: das traditionelle Varieté oder Vaudeville und die Burleske, die als Stripshow weit über das Bein hinausging.

Um 1895 zogen sich in den Folies-Bergère erstmals Tänzerinnen zu Musik aus. 1917 kam der Striptease nach New York, zu Minsky's National Winter Garden, wobei sich die erste Tänzerin angeblich versehentlich auf der Bühne entblößte. Im Minsky's fanden in den 1920er-Jahren mehrfach Razzien statt, doch der Klub überlebte und mit ihm das Interesse des Publikums am Striptease. Schon 1933 regte sich kaum noch öffentlicher Widerstand, als der Minsky-Star Sally Rand zur Hauptattraktion der Weltausstellung in Chicago wurde.

Rands Seifenblasentanz war typisch für die amerikanischen Burlesken der 1930er- und 1940er-Jahre. Sie gipfelten zwar in

einem Aufblitzen von Nacktheit, doch nur die Beine in Nylonstrümpfen und hochhackigen Schuhen wurden durchgängig den Blicken preisgegeben. So blieb die Burleske im Wesentlichen auch dann eine Leg Show, als Titten und Ärsche hinzukamen. Für Fans dieser Shows waren Betty Grable und *Yank* einen Tick zu bieder. Sie begehrten Damen mit einem Hauch von Sünde, wie die Girls von Robert Harrison.

Harrison brachte 1941 die Zeitschrift Beauty Parade heraus, 1943 folgten *Eyeful*, *Wink* und *Titter*, 1946 *Whisper* und 1947 *Flirt*. Wie in anderen Leg Magazines wurden auch in Harrisons Blättern keine nackten Frauen abgebildet, doch da endeten auch schon die Gemeinsamkeiten. Seine Models waren keine Starlets, Pin-ups oder „Mädchen von nebenan", sondern Topstripperinnen. Die Titelbilder zierten reißerische Pin-ups von Frauen in Strümpfen und High Heels, gemalt von Meistern der Leg Art wie Earl Moran, Billy DeVorss und vor allem Peter Driben.

Harrisons berühmtestes Modell war Bettie Page. 1951 – noch bevor Bunny Yeager sie in ein Leopardenkostüm steck-

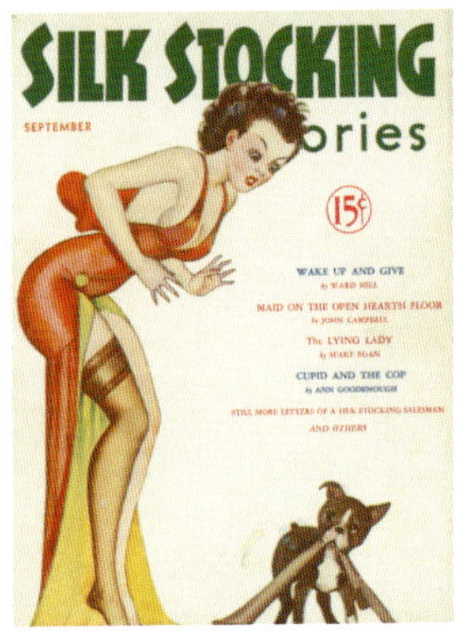

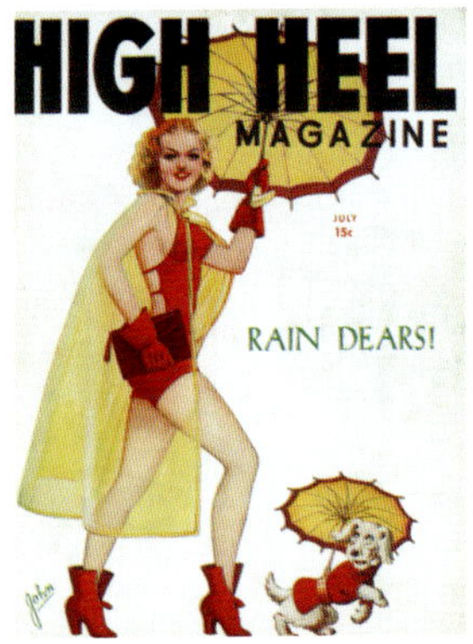

te sowie Irving und Paula Klaw ihr eine Peitsche in die Hand drückten – gab Bettie ihr Magazindebüt in *Flirt*. Nur vier Jahre später, als Betty Grable ihren Rückzug bekannt gab, wurde Page zur „Miss Pin-up Girl of the World" gekürt und war die „Miss January" des neuen heißen Magazins *Playboy*. Ihre Popularität bewies, dass die Leg Art sehr beliebt war. Bis 1955 hatte Bettie bereits für zahlreiche Bondage- und S/M-Fotos der Klaws Modell gestanden und sich über die neuen Fetischmagazine eine äußerst treue Fangemeinde aufgebaut.

John Willie wurde Mitte der 1940er-Jahre durch seinen Comicstrip *Sweet Gwendoline* bekannt, der in *Wink* erschien. 1946 gab er *Bizarre* heraus, das es bald zum berüchtigtsten Fetischmagazin der Welt brachte. Hauptthemen waren Bondage und Züchtigung, doch *Bizarre* zog auch eine klare Verbindung zwischen Frauenbeinen und sexueller Macht, besonders in Form des potenten Fetischs, den hochhackige Schuhe darstellten. Willie unterschied die guten von den bösen Mädchen durch ihr Schuhwerk: Die unterwürfige

Sweet Gwendoline bekam einfache Pumps, ihre dominanten Peinigerinnen trugen hingegen eng anliegende Lederstiefel. Der Künstler hatte Spaß daran, neue Schuhe zu entwerfen und die Auswirkungen von extrem hohen Absätzen auf den Fuß zu demonstrieren. Mit seinen Zeichnungen und seinem fotografischen Werk legte er die klassischen Standards von Fetisch-Accessoires fest, zu denen Masken, lange Lederhandschuhe, Korsetts, enge, figurbetonte Lederröcke und schwarze Strümpfe mit Naht gehörten.

1957 brachte Elmer Batters im Eigenverlag *Man's Favorite Pastime* heraus und läutete damit eine neue Ära für Leg Magazines ein. Als eingefleischter Bein- und Fußfetischist wusste Batters genau, was seine Leser wollten, und er besaß das fotografische Talent, ihnen auch genau das zu bieten. Nachdem Elmer das Eis gebrochen hatte, warfen amerikanische Verleger eine nie zuvor und danach gesehene Flut von Leg Magazines auf den Markt. Es wimmelte nur so von schimmernden Nylons, High Heels, hohen Turmfrisuren, schwarzen Lidstrichen, Zigaretten in rot

OPPOSITE LEFT *Silk Stocking Stories* magazine, September 1936.

OPPOSITE RIGHT *High Heel* magazine, July 1937.

RIGHT *Stocking Parade* magazine, March 1942. Most men's magazines were leg oriented in the 1930s and '40s.

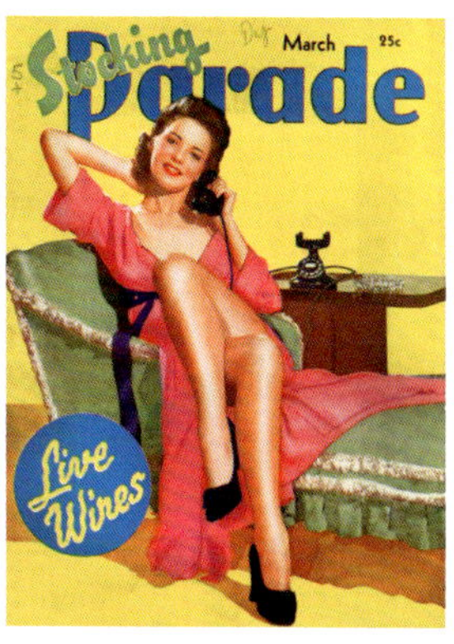

geschminkten Mundwinkeln, langen, rot lackierten Fingernägeln – all das gepaart mit einer gewissen arroganten Haltung. Diese Trash-Göttinnen blickten von den Covern diverser Zeitschriften herab, wie etwa von *Black Garter, Black Nylons, Black Nylons and High Heels, Dandy in Hose, Garter Parade, Hip & Toe, Leg Show, Legs & Lasses, Slip & Garter, Naughty Nylons, Nylon Jungle, Nylon Mood, Silk Seams, Stocking Parade, Tic Toc, Tip Top* sowie den etwa ein Dutzend von Elmer selbst produzierten Magazinen.

Das Goldene Zeitalter der Leg Magazines erstreckte sich über zehn Jahre, von 1958 bis 1968. Dann zeigten die mutigeren Zeitschriften auf einmal Schamhaar, was in den 1970er-Jahren den Untergang der Leg Magazines einläutete – sie wurden schlichtweg von der Muschi ausgelöscht. Titten? Passé! Ärsche? Passé! Beine? Längst passé! Als ich 1976 in der Pornobranche anfing, hatte ich noch nie etwas von Leg Magazines gehört. Ich war die typische junge Sexrebellin, die als Kind heimlich in den *Playboys* ihres Vaters blätterte und von dort mit 18 geradewegs zur Hardcorepornografie überging. Auf das kurz zuvor

relaunchte *Leg Show* stieß ich 1981, während ich für *OUI* arbeitete, und konnte kaum fassen, dass es für ein so seltsames und archaisches Konzept einen Markt gab. Doch als ich 1987 plötzlich bei *Hooker* rausflog, nahm ich dankbar das Angebot an, *Leg Show* herauszugeben.

Durch Tausende von Leserbriefen und lange Gespräche mit Elmer Batters gelang es mir, *Leg Show* zu perfektionieren. 1992 war es das meistverkaufte Leg Magazine aller Zeiten und erreichte schließlich eine monatliche Auflage von 200 000.

Als ich *Leg Show* 2001 verließ, um zu TASCHEN zu wechseln, hatte ich 15 Jahre unter Beinfetischisten verbracht und vermutlich 60 000 Leserbriefe gelesen. Dabei hatte ich gelernt, dass Männer, die Beine und Füße lieben, anders sind als solche, die offensichtlichere erogene Zonen bevorzugen. Sie sind im Allgemeinen gebildeter und erfolgreicher und bevorzugen oft selbstbewusste Frauen, da weibliche Stärke in den Beinen sitzt. Sie sind sexuell experimentierfreudiger, ein Zeichen für ihre Intelligenz und die Vorliebe für den Körperteil, der unseren tief verwurzelten Vorstellungen von Weiblichkeit am meisten zuwiderläuft. Vielleicht ist dies der Grund, warum Frauenbeine so lange verdeckt wurden. Die moralischen Grundpfeiler der Gesellschaft waren tatsächlich in Gefahr, als Frauen ihre Röcke rafften und durch mehr Bewegungsfreiheit auch mehr gesellschaftliche Freiheit erlangten. Sie hinterfragten ihre traditionellen Rollen, und viele Männer fanden dies so anziehend, dass sie anfingen, ihre eigenen starren Rollenmodelle zu überdenken.

Bis zum heutigen Tag regen ein paar lange, wohlgeformte Frauenbeine, vorzugsweise auf 13 cm hohen Absätzen, rollenkonträre Fantasien an: Sie geben der Besitzerin ein Gefühl von Stärke und lassen die Knie des Betrachters weich werden. Diese Symbole der weiblichen sexuellen Kraft bringen wirklich die Moral der Männer ins Wanken. Aber es ist viel zu spät, sie wieder einzupacken, und wir müssen nun alle mit den aufregenden Konsequenzen leben.

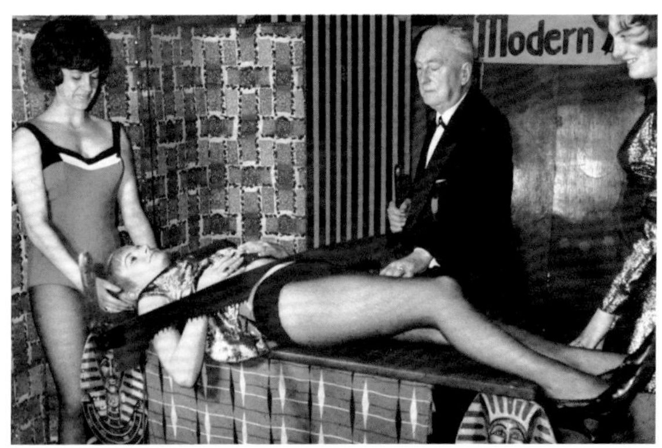

LEFT British magician Frank Baumforth saws a stiletto-heeled woman in half, circa 1965.

OPPOSITE Lilith Anderson by Elmer Batters, circa 1965.

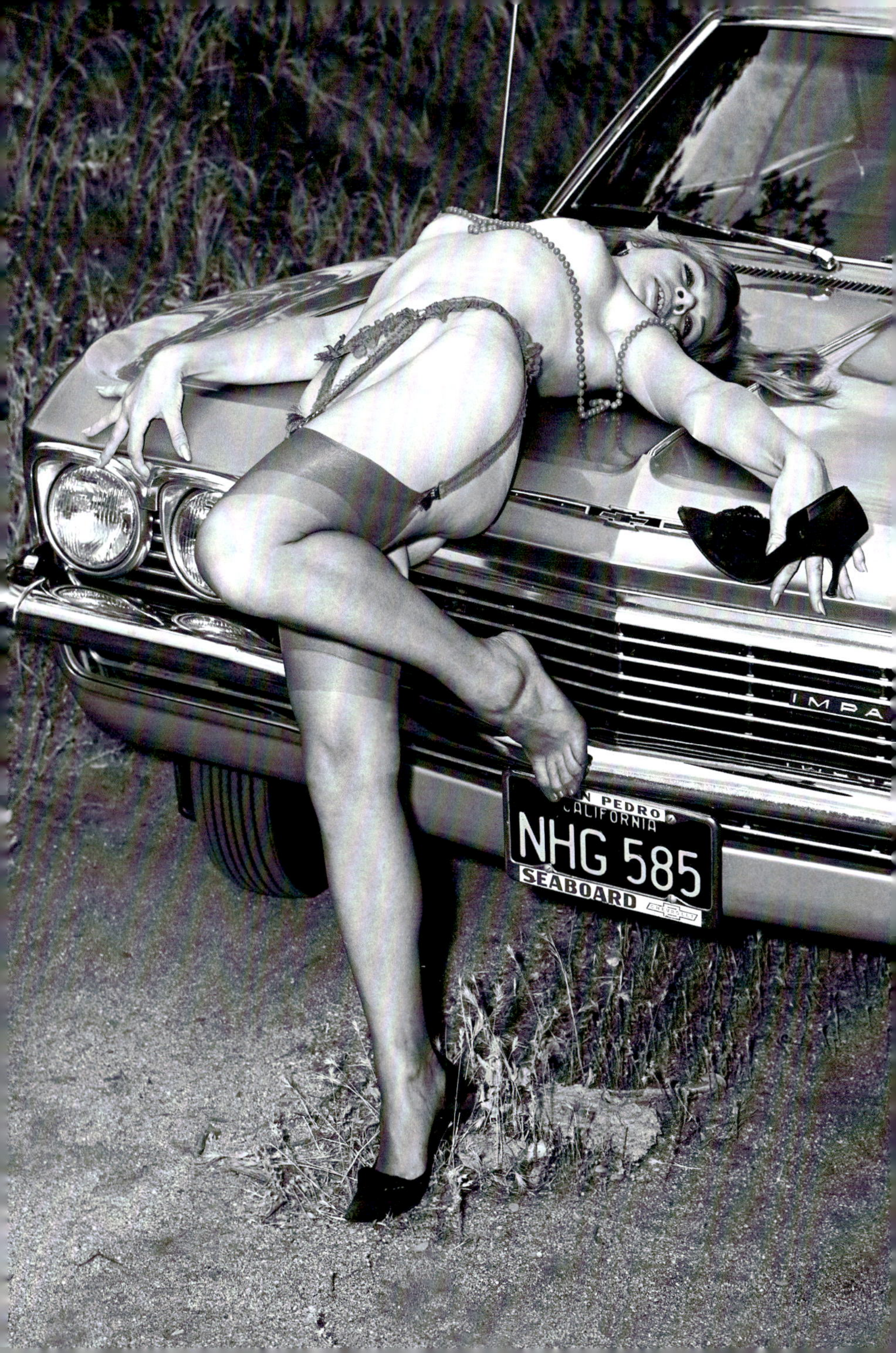
SAN PEDRO
CALIFORNIA
NHG 585
SEABOARD

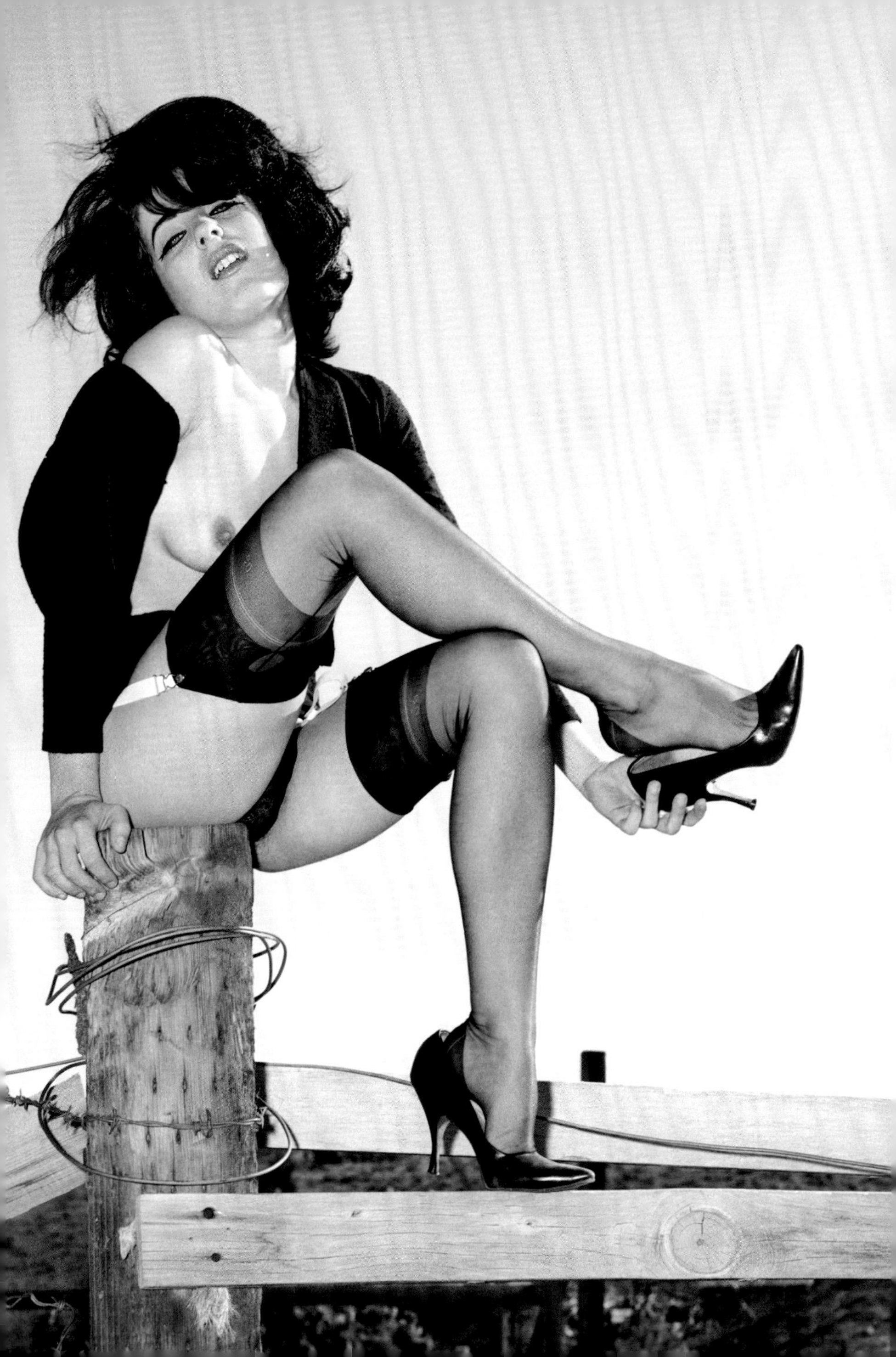

La jambe étrangement sexy

PAR DIAN HANSON

La jambe féminine est une bizarrerie sexuelle. Non érogène et presque identique en structure au membre masculin équivalent, on ne voit pas de raison évidente à son attraction. Pourtant, tout au long de l'histoire et dans de nombreuses cultures, les jambes féminines ont été l'objet des mêmes tabous que les zones génitales, cachées sous des jupes et des jupons, ce qui en a fait des objets d'intense obsession sexuelle. Cette fascination a culminé sous l'ère victorienne, où, dans la bonne société, personne ne devait prononcer le mot « jambe » de peur d'exciter les passions. Quatre-vingts ans plus tard, les jambes ne sont plus cachées, mais curieusement leur attrait reste toujours aussi fort.

Qu'y a-t-il dans cette simple structure d'os, de muscles et de graisse qui la rende si différente du bras, lequel est rarement, voire jamais, érotisé ? Selon certains, c'est l'entrejambe qui expliquerait l'attirance qu'exercent les jambes. Que l'esprit masculin commence à remonter depuis les chevilles et il ne s'arrêtera qu'en arrivant au brasier de luxure niché entre les cuisses.

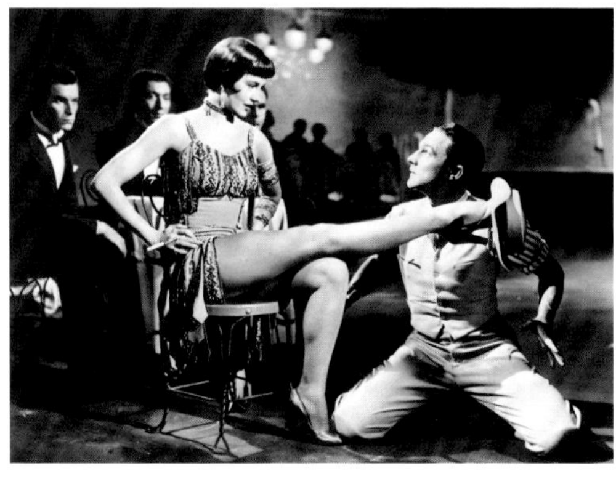

PAGE 18 Cynthia Bond by Elmer Batters, circa 1962.

LEFT Cyd Charisse and Gene Kelly in *Singin' in the Rain*, 1952. The Kobal Collection.

OPPOSITE LEFT Betty Grable's iconic WWII pin-up by Frank Powolny, 1942.

OPPOSITE RIGHT Film poster for *Heartbeat*, starring Ginger Rogers.

Mais si les jambes n'étaient que des chemins menant au minou, pourquoi les femmes ne s'étaient-elles pas contentées durant tous ces siècles de couvrir leur pubis plutôt que leurs cuisses ? Pourtant, toutes les culottes, quand les femmes en portaient, étaient fendues à l'entrejambe jusqu'aux années 1890. Non, il y avait quelque chose dans la jambe elle-même qui contrariait la classe dirigeante.

Les jambes féminines représentaient en fait une menace pour l'ordre moral parce qu'elles incarnaient l'autonomie féminine. Il existait une crainte répandue bien que largement tue : si les femmes gagnaient en mobilité, elles seraient tentées de fuir leur vie cantonnée au foyer, aveu implicite que la vie beaucoup plus libre des hommes était bien plus attirante que celle dévolue une fois pour toutes au « sexe faible ». C'est pour cette raison que les premières militantes de la condition féminine étaient si décidées à libérer les jambes des femmes. Elles trouvèrent un allié inattendu dans ce projet avec la bicyclette. Dans les années 1880, nombre de femmes déterminées à enfourcher les « machines de la liberté »,

surnom que lui donnèrent les suffragettes, adoptèrent des tenues sportives. Beaucoup furent harcelées et arrêtées mais, vers 1910, les hommes finirent par accepter et même par apprécier la « nouvelle femme ».

Quand les jambes ont commencé à se découvrir, elles sont rapidement devenues l'objet le plus convoité en matière de pornographie aux États-Unis. *Capt. Billy's Whiz Bang*, le premier magazine de charme américain à présenter dès 1919 des illustrations de garçonnes aux jambes nues, fut bientôt imité par *Hot Dog*, *TNT* et *Smokehouse Monthly* dans les années 1920. Dans les années 1930 apparurent des magazines exclusivement dédiés aux jambes, le premier, *Silk Stocking Stories* en 1935, suivi de *High Heel Magazine* en 1937 et de *The Stocking Parade* en 1938. En 1942, lors de l'entrée en guerre des États-Unis, une multitude de nouveaux magazines de pin-up patriotiques sortirent, tous obsédés par les jambes, reproduisant à qui mieux mieux les « jambes à un million de dollars » de Betty Grable, pin-up américaine numéro un à l'époque. Parmi les admirateurs des gambettes de Betty dans *Yank*, le magazine officiel de

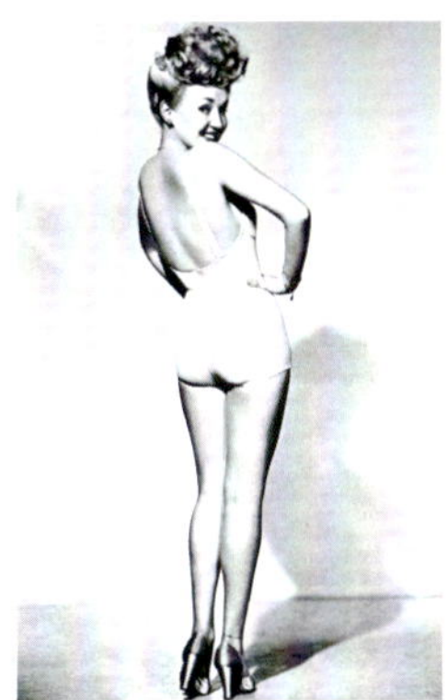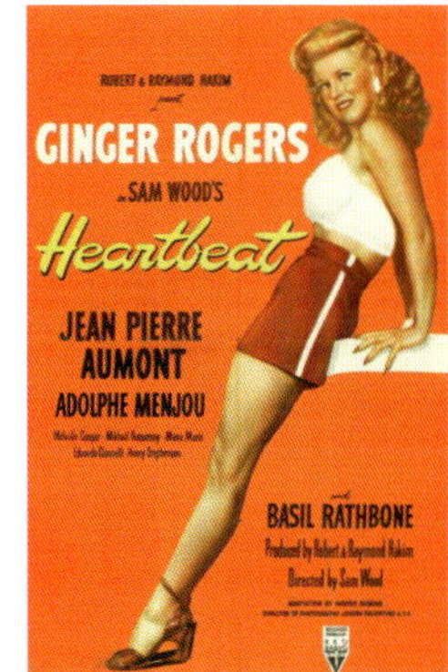

l'armée, peu réalisèrent qu'il n'avait fallu que vingt ans pour que la jambe féminine si indécente devienne banale en Amérique.

Durant ces mêmes vingt années, le spectacle de type « Leg Show » avait lui aussi spectaculairement évolué. La revue déshabillée s'était scindée en deux camps distincts dans les années 1920, d'une part le traditionnel spectacle de variétés rebaptisé « vaudeville », d'autre part le « burlesque » qui évoluait vers le strip-tease.

L'effeuillage en musique avait commencé à Paris aux Folies Bergère vers 1895. Le strip-tease est arrivé à New York via le Minsky's National Winter Garden en 1917. Le Minsky fut régulièrement perquisitionné dans les années 1920, mais le club et l'intérêt du public pour le strip-tease résistèrent. En 1933, les objections furent rares quand la star du Minsky, Sally Rand, devint l'attraction phare de l'Exposition universelle de Chicago.

La danse du ballon (bubble dance) de Sally Rand illustre parfaitement le « burlesque » américain des années 1930 et 1940 : des numéros provocants et sexy qui culminent dans un bref éclair de nudité, tandis que les jambes, revêtues de bas et chaussées de hauts talons, s'offrent au regard. Et même après que les seins et les fesses eurent commencé à se montrer, ce type de spectacle resta pour l'essentiel un show de jambes. Pour les hommes qui aimaient les strip-teases plus corsés, Betty Grable et *Yank* étaient un rien trop convenus. Ces messieurs voulaient des dames auréolées de péché, le genre de jolies filles que Robert Harrison savait dénicher.

Harrison lança *Beauty Parade* en 1941, suivi par *Eyeful*, *Wink* et *Titter* en 1943, *Whisper* en 1946, et *Flirt* en 1947. À l'instar des autres revues fétichistes de jambes, on ne pouvait y voir de filles nues, mais Harrison avait un autre atout en poche. Ses modèles étaient des strip-teaseuses haut de gamme, pas des pin-up ou des « jeunes filles gentilles ». Les couvertures de ses magazines montraient des pin-up tapageuses en bas et talons illustrées par des maîtres du genre, Earl Moran, Billy DeVorss et, le plus souvent, Peter Driben.

Le plus célèbre modèle de Harrison fut Bettie Page, l'égérie du fétichisme des années 1950. En 1951, avant que Bunnie

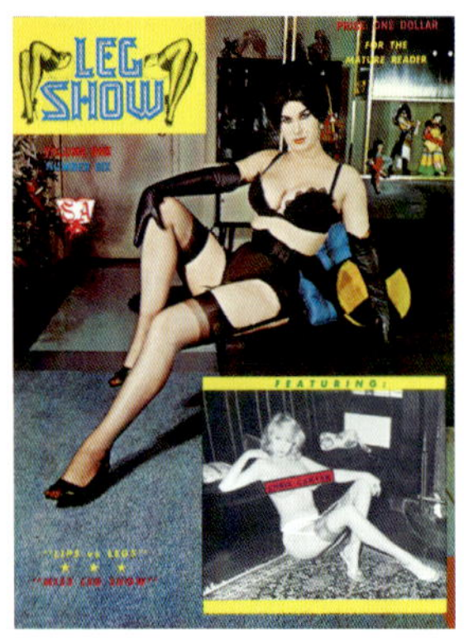
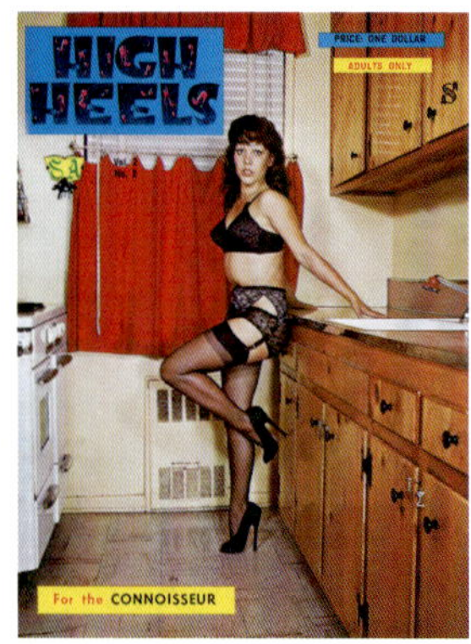

Yeager lui fasse enfiler une peau de léopard et que Irving et Paula Klaw lui glissent un fouet dans la main, Bettie faisait ses débuts de modèle dans le magazine *Flirt*. Quatre ans plus tard, au moment où Betty Grable annonçait sa retraite, Bettie Page était élue « Miss Pin-up Girl of the World » et posait pour *Playboy*, le nouveau magazine porno soft, où elle devenait « Miss January ». Le succès croissant de Bettie Page a suivi l'évolution du leg art ; dès 1955, elle posait pour des photos de bondage et de SM pour Irving et Paula Klaw, style qui allait être rapidement imité par les nouveaux magazines fétichistes.

John Willie a commencé sa carrière de dessinateur au magazine *Wink* avec Sweet Gwendoline au milieu des années 1940. En 1946, il lance *Bizarre* qui devient rapidement un magazine fétichiste de renommée internationale. Si le bondage et la soumission sont ses principaux thèmes, *Bizarre* a toujours associé les jambes des femmes à la puissance sexuelle, notamment avec le grand potentiel fétichiste des chaussures à hauts talons. Willie séparait les bonnes filles des mauvaises d'après leurs chaus-sures : des escarpins ordinaires pour la soumise Sweet Gwendoline et des bottes ou des cuissardes en cuir pour ses domi-natrices implacables. Artiste accompli, il a inventé la panoplie de l'univers fétichiste avec masques, gants longs en cuir gainant le bras, corsets, jupes en cuir moulantes et bas à couture noire.

En 1957, Elmer Batters autoédite *Man's Favorite Pastime*. Fétichiste de la jambe et du pied, Elmer Batters connaissait les attentes de son public et disposait du ta-lent photographique requis pour les lui fournir. Elmer ayant ouvert la voie, toute une série d'éditeurs américains lui em-boîtèrent le pas, lançant des magazines fétichistes de jambes qui ne devaient ja-mais être égalés. Ce fut un âge d'or pour les bas de nylon luisants, les talons aiguilles, les coiffures choucroute, les yeux souli-gnés de larges traits noirs, la cigarette pendant au coin de lèvres lourdement maquillées, le verre de Martini entre des doigts aux longs ongles rouges, autant de détails censés signifier l'agressivité sexuelle. Ces déesses trash faisaient frémir les lecteurs de *Black Garter*, *Black*

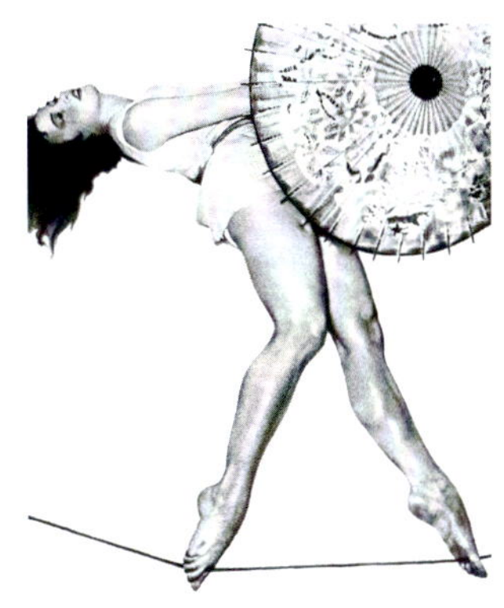

Nylons, Black Nylons and High Heels, Dandy in Hose, Garter Parade, Hip & Toe, Leg Show, Legs & Lasses, Slip & Garter, Naughty Nylons, Nylon Jungle, Nylon Mood, Silk Seams, Stocking Parade, Tic Toc, Tip Top, sans compter la dizaine de magazines qu'Elmer éditait personnellement.

L'âge d'or des magazines fétichistes de jambes s'étend de 1958 à 1968, date à laquelle les revues masculines ont commencé à montrer les poils pubiens. Tous ont périclité dans les années 1970, balayés par l'exhibition de l'entrejambe qui a rendu désuet tout le reste. Quand j'ai commencé ma carrière dans les revues porno en 1976, je n'avais jamais entendu parler des magazines fétichistes de jambes. J'étais le prototype de la jeune émancipée sexuelle passée directement de la contemplation clandestine des numéros de *Playboy* de son père à la pornographie pure et dure vers 18 ans. J'ai découvert la nouvelle version de *Leg Show* en 1981 alors que je travaillais à *OUI*, et je ne pouvais croire qu'il existe un marché pour un concept aussi bizarre et archaïque. Puis, en novembre 1987, j'ai été brutalement congédiée de Hooker et c'est alors que j'ai accepté le poste de rédactrice en chef de *Leg Show*.

Quand j'ai quitté *Leg Show* pour rejoindre TASCHEN en 2001, j'avais passé quinze ans parmi les fétichistes de la jambe féminine et lu approximativement 60 000 lettres. J'ai appris entre autres que les hommes qui aiment les jambes et les pieds ne ressemblent pas à ceux qui sont attirés par des zones érogènes plus évidentes. Ils sont en général d'un niveau culturel plus élevé et ont mieux réussi socialement. C'étaient des médecins, des psychologues, des psychiatres, des ingénieurs, des avocats, des fonctionnaires ; il y avait aussi des prêtres, des pasteurs et des rabbins, des patrons, de hauts responsables gouvernementaux. Ce sont des êtres plutôt attirés par des femmes fortes et autoritaires, car la force féminine réside dans les jambes. Ils sont pour beaucoup ouverts à l'expérimentation sexuelle, ce qui reflète leur intelligence, leur éducation et leur préférence pour la partie du corps qui contredit le plus notre vision si ancrée de la féminité.

C'est peut-être la véritable raison pour laquelle la jambe féminine est restée si longtemps couverte. Les certitudes morales ont été mises en péril quand les femmes ont remonté leurs jupes, gagnant en mobilité et donc en liberté. Prendre la mesure de leur force les a amenées à remettre en question leur rôle traditionnel, et nombre d'hommes qui trouvaient cette force féminine étrangement attirante ont eux aussi commencé à reconsidérer le rôle rigide qu'ils s'étaient attribué.

Jusqu'à ce jour, quelque chose dans une longue paire de jambes féminines galbées, de préférence montées sur des talons de 12 cm, stimule les fantasmes d'inversion et renforce l'autorité de la femme, et le sentiment de fragilité masculin. Ce qui me fait penser que le maire de Chautaqua (New York) n'avait finalement pas tort : ces symboles de force sexuelle féminine représentent bien un danger pour la morale masculine, mais il est tard, bien trop tard, pour remiser les accessoires au vestiaire, et nous aurons tous à en supporter les émoustillantes conséquences.

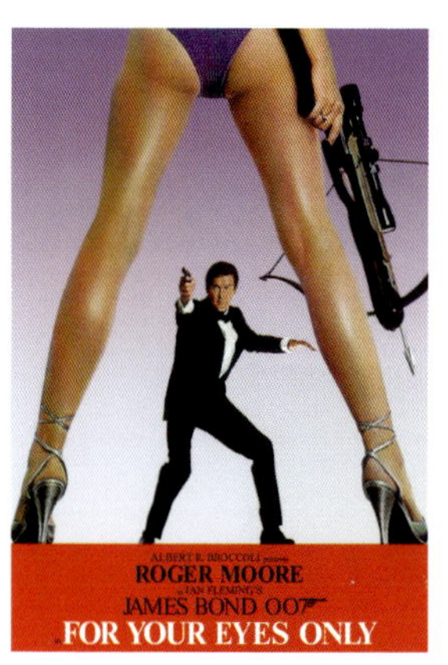
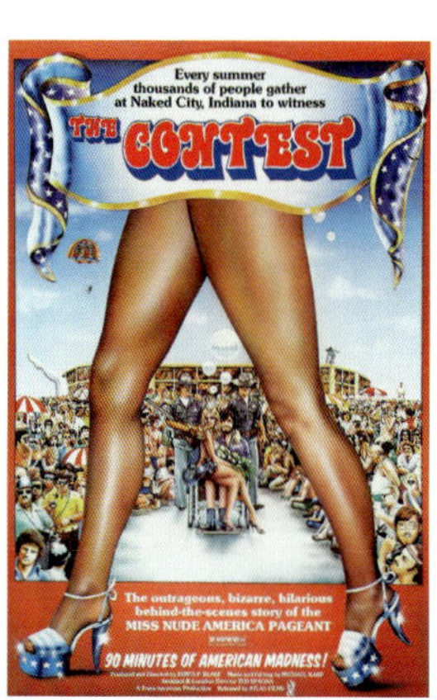

FAR LEFT *For Your Eyes Only* film poster, 1981, United Artists.

LEFT *The Contest* film poster, Atlas Films, 1976.

OPPOSITE © Estate of Guy Bourdin / Art + Commerce.

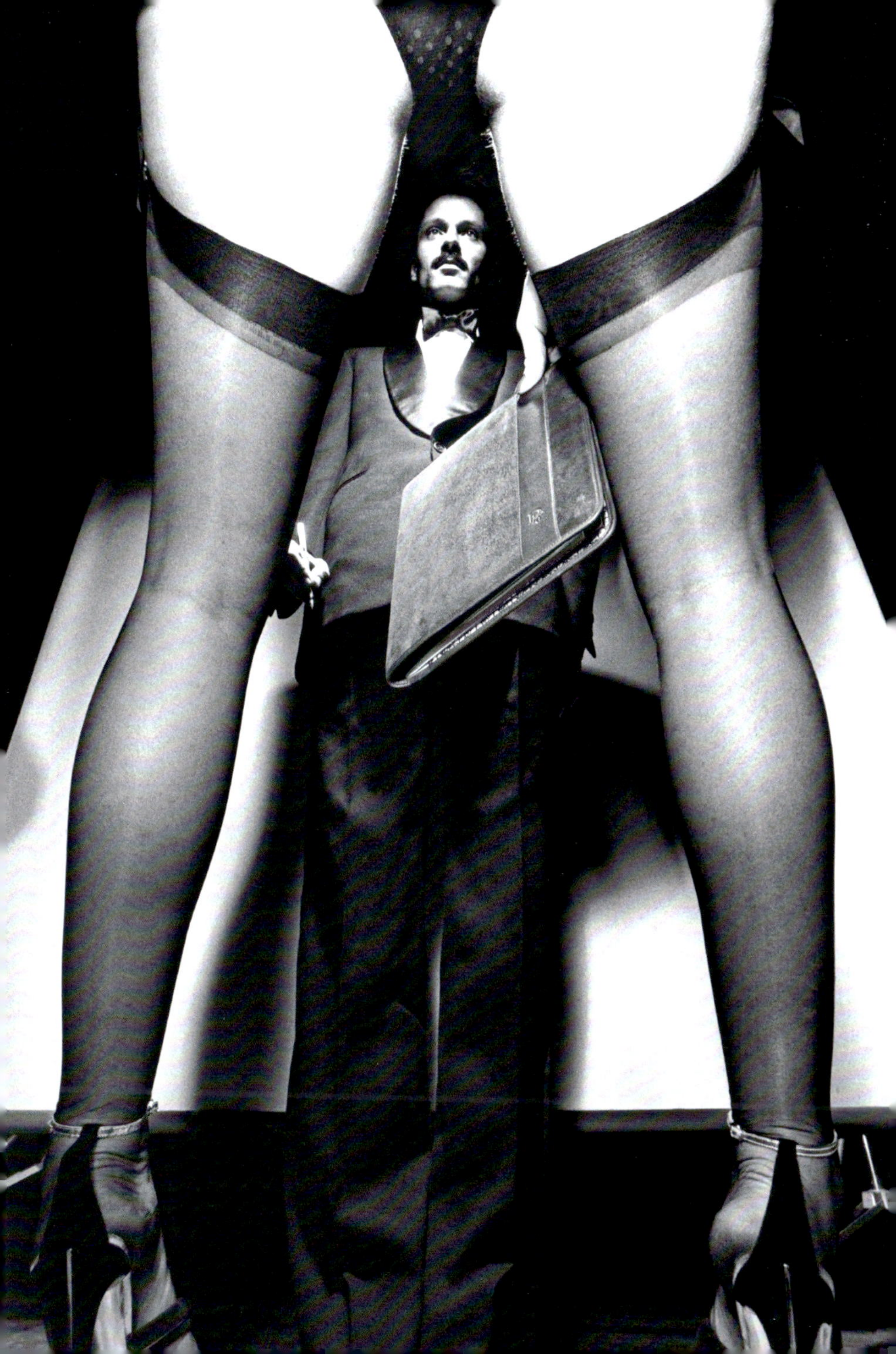

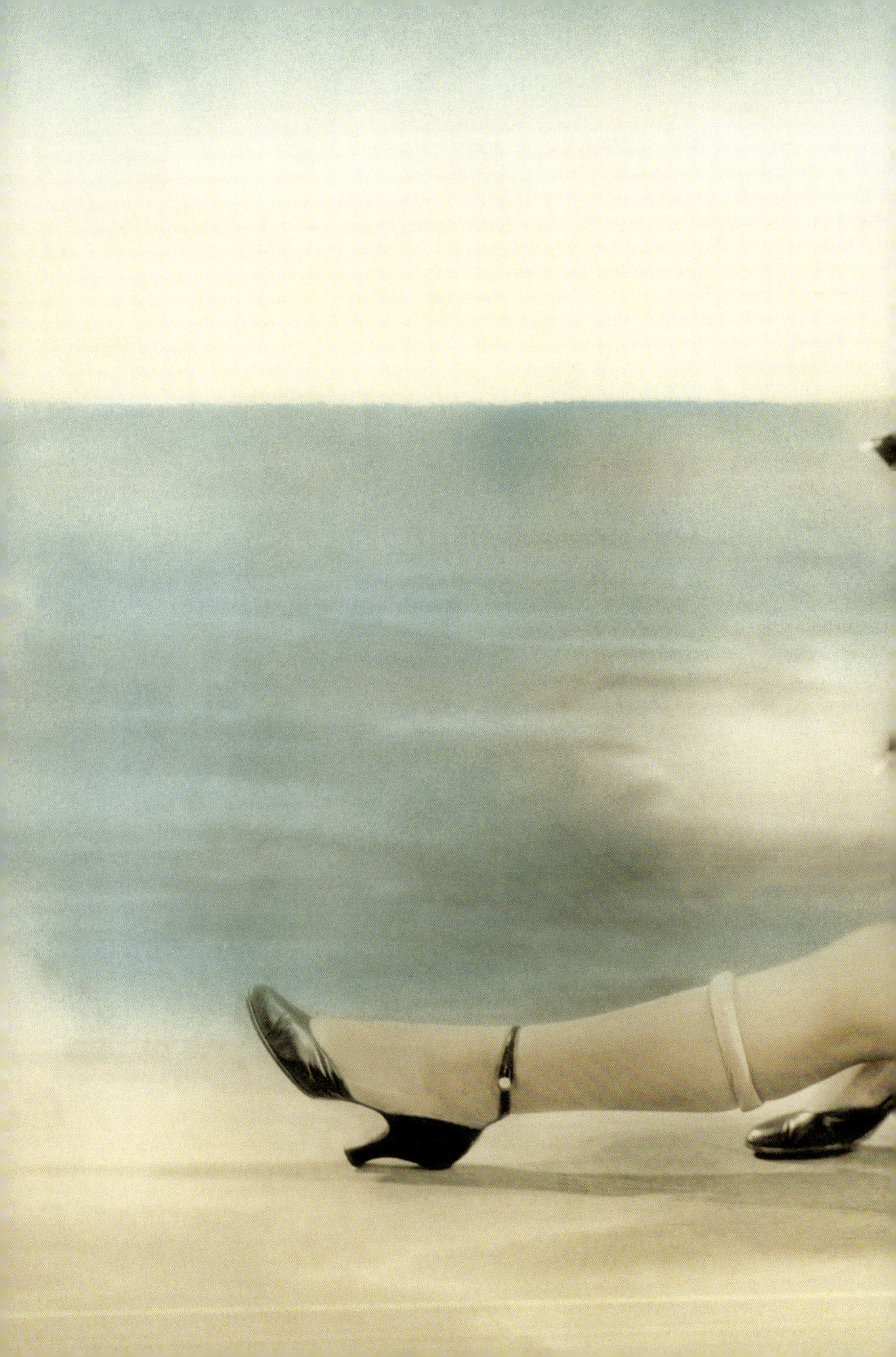

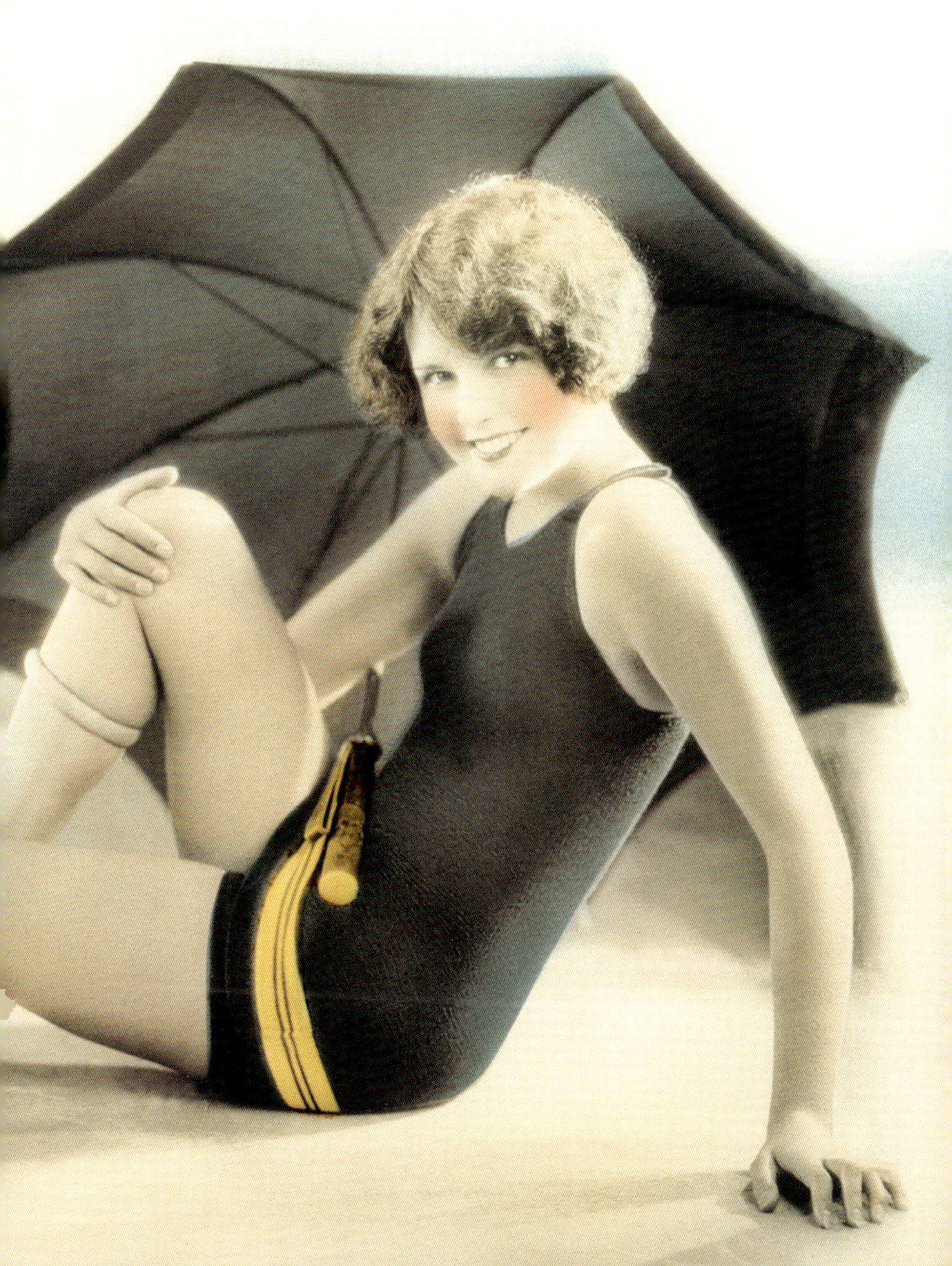

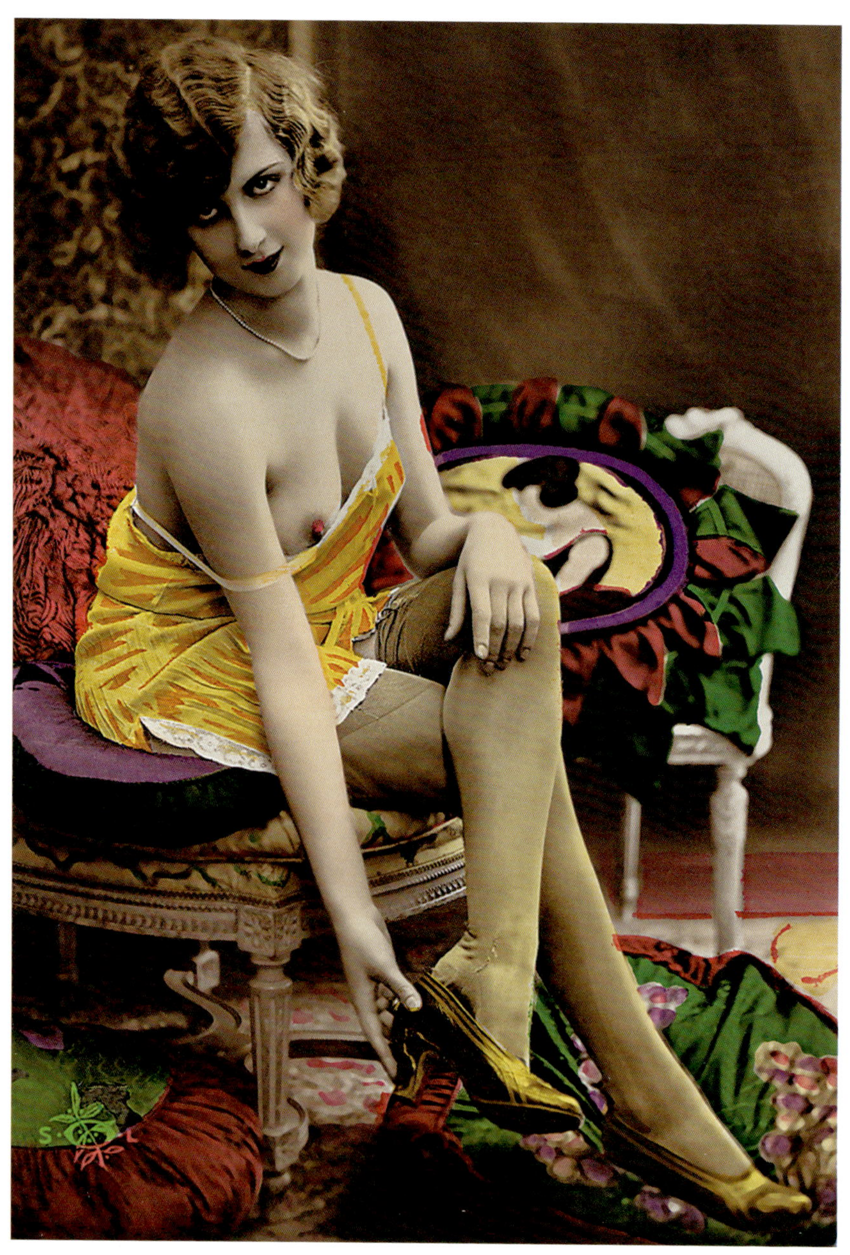

PAGES 26-27 Unknown   ABOVE AND OPPOSITE Unknown

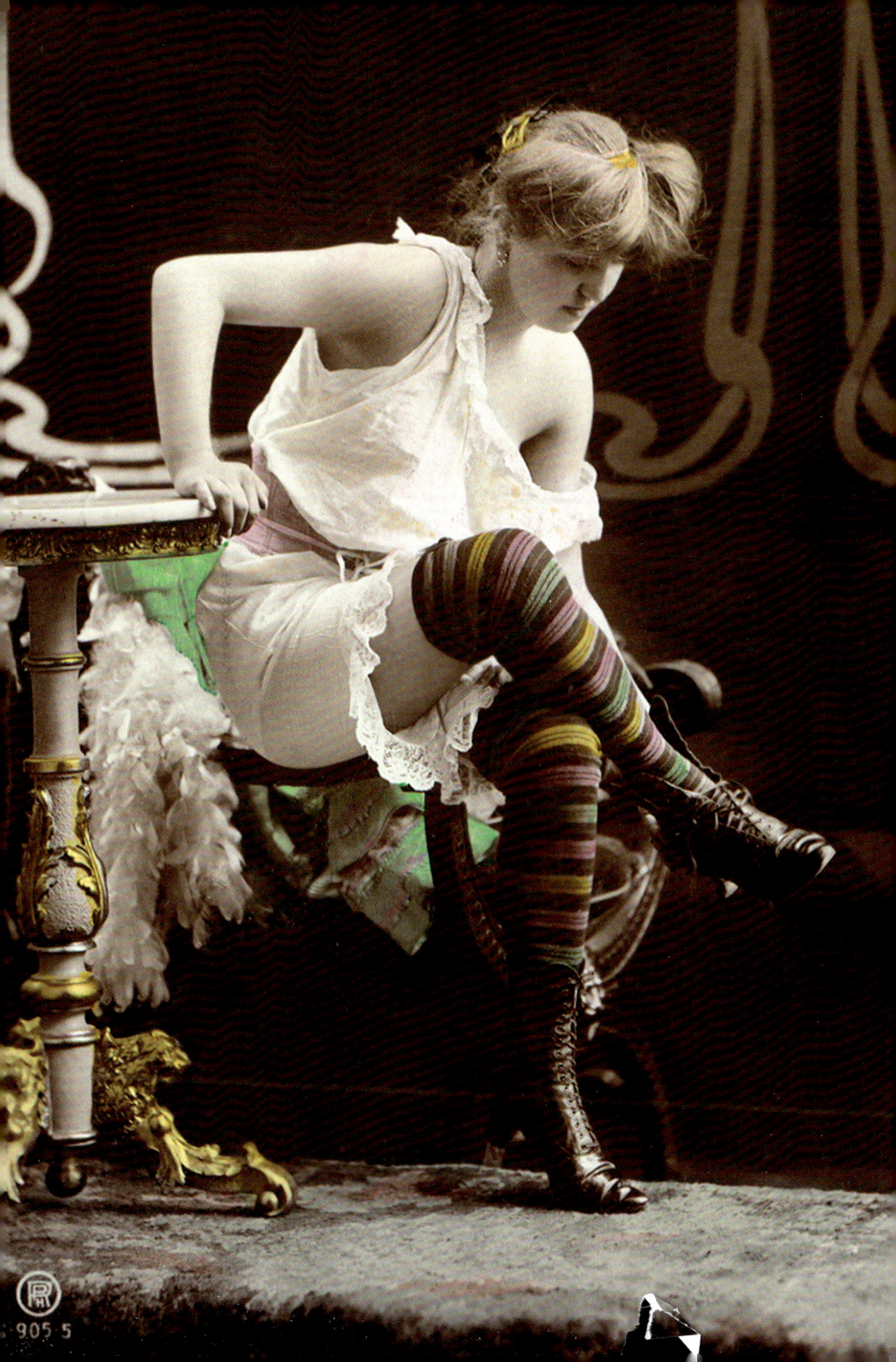

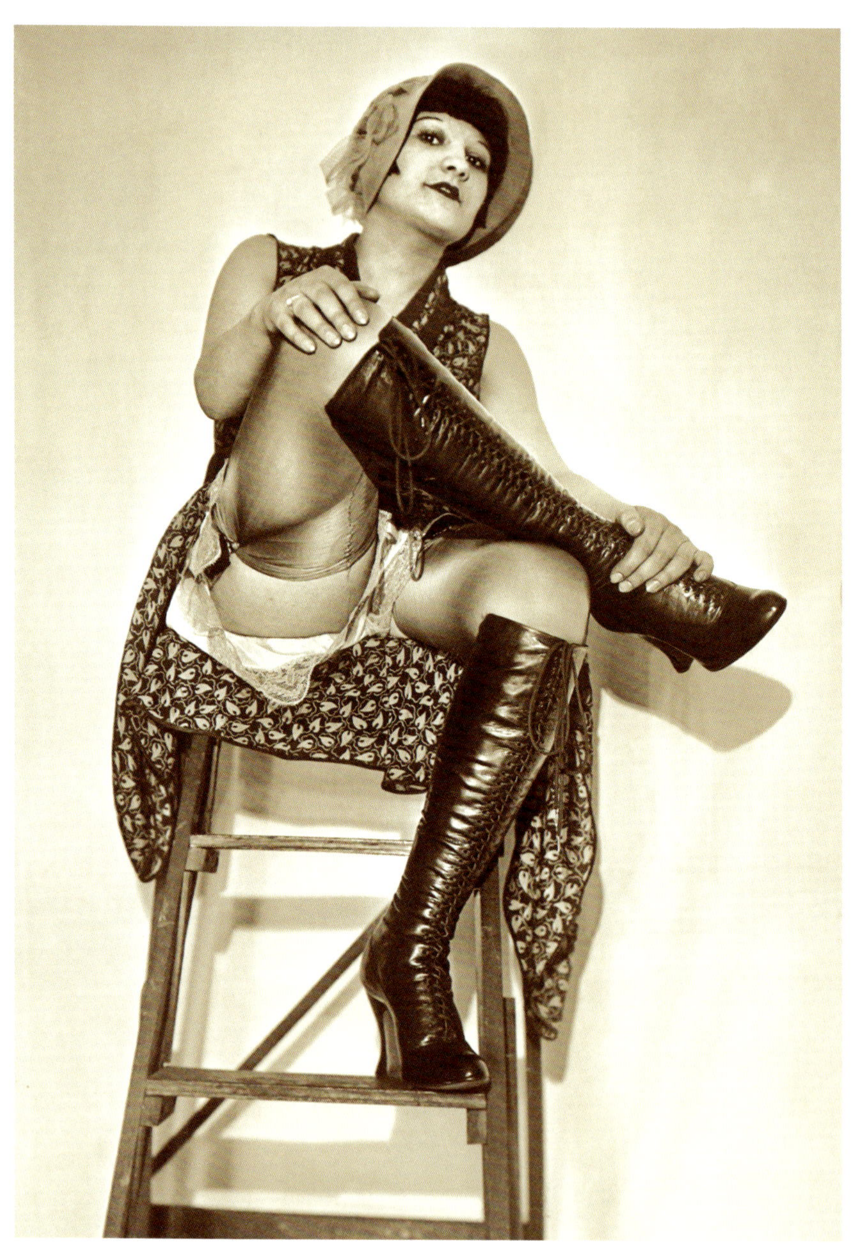

ABOVE AND OPPOSITE Unknown

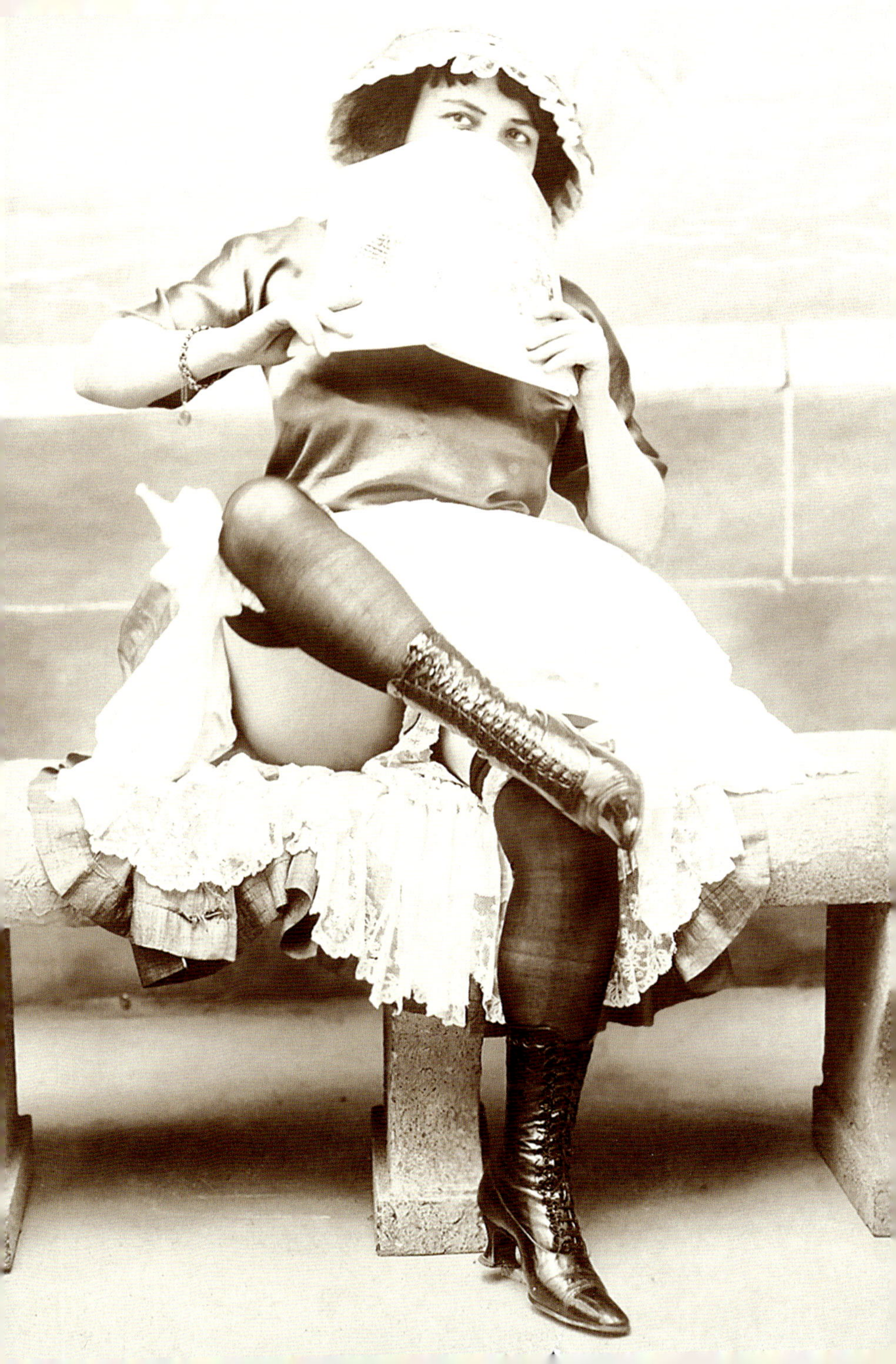

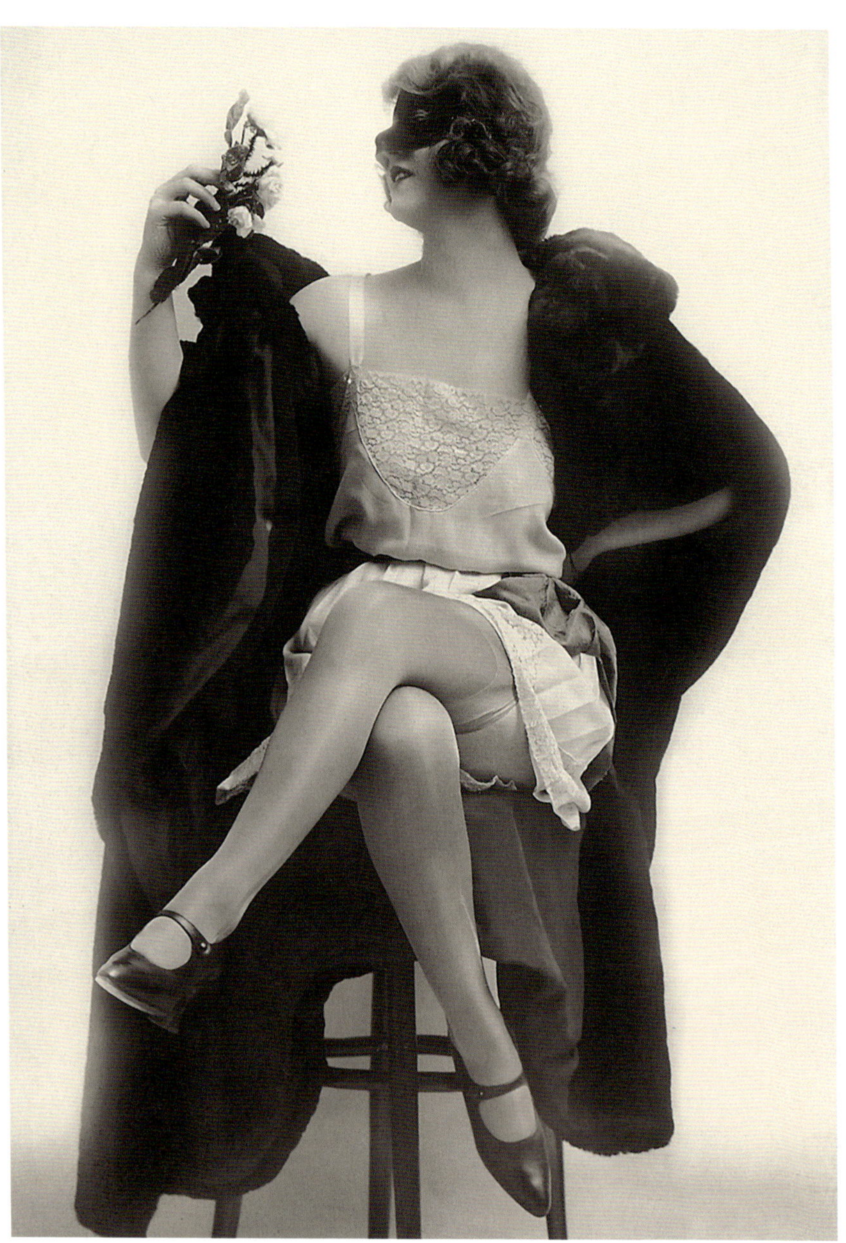

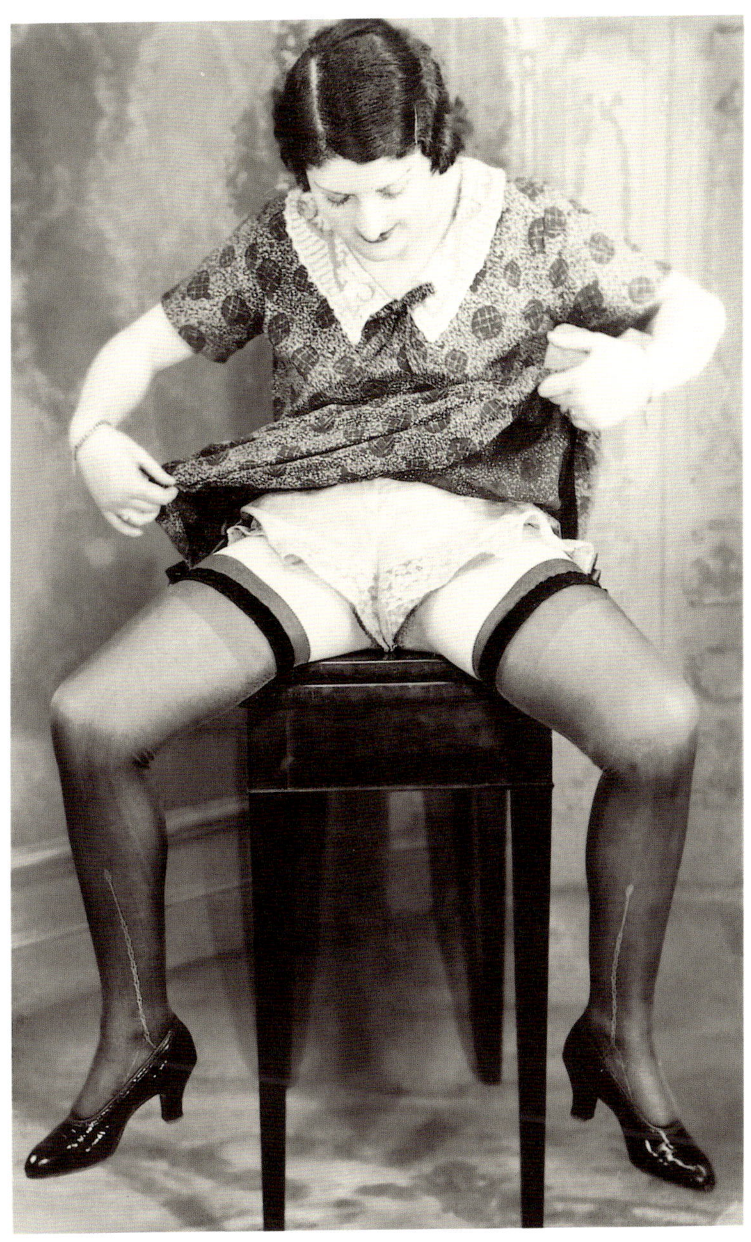

OPPOSITE AND ABOVE Unknown

33

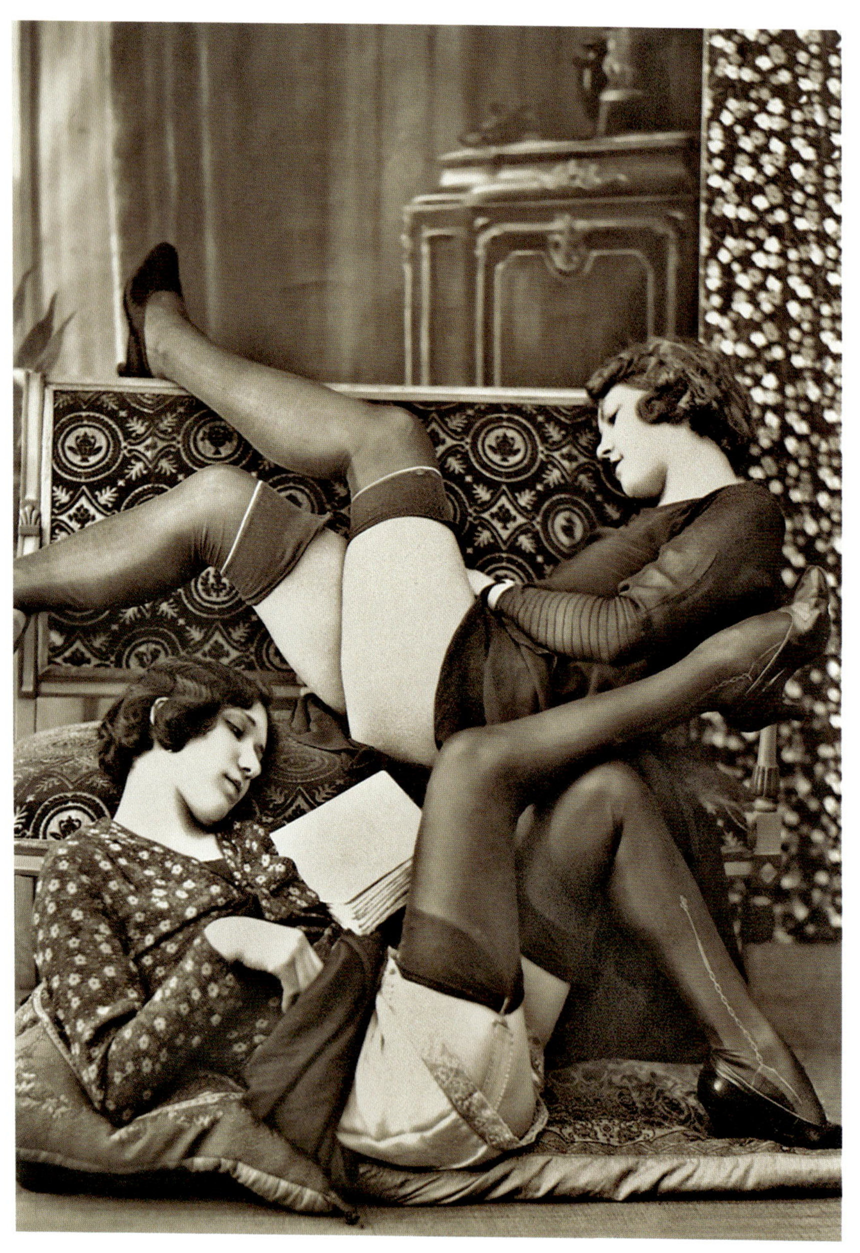

ABOVE AND OPPOSITE Unknown, BIEDERER

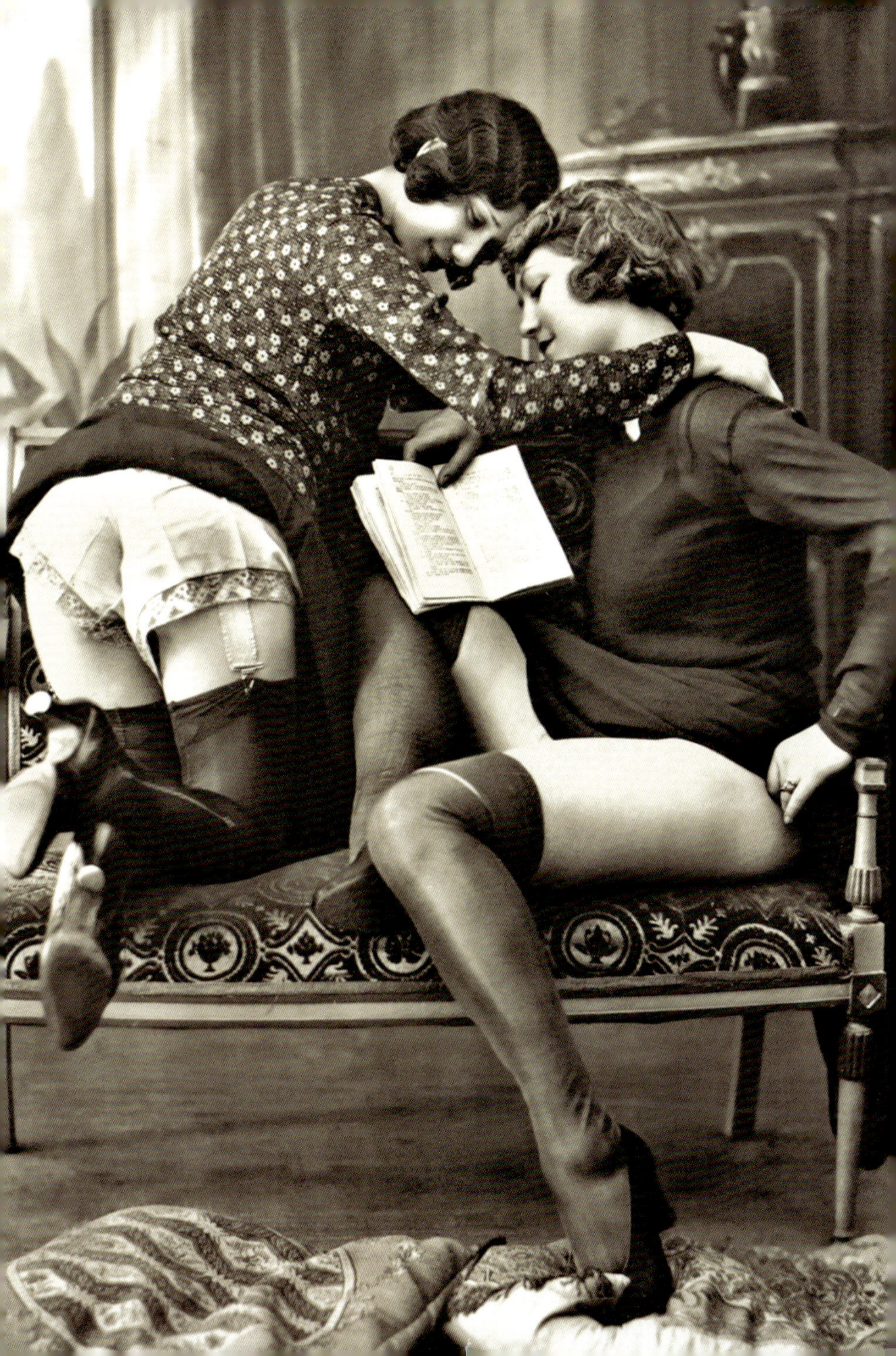

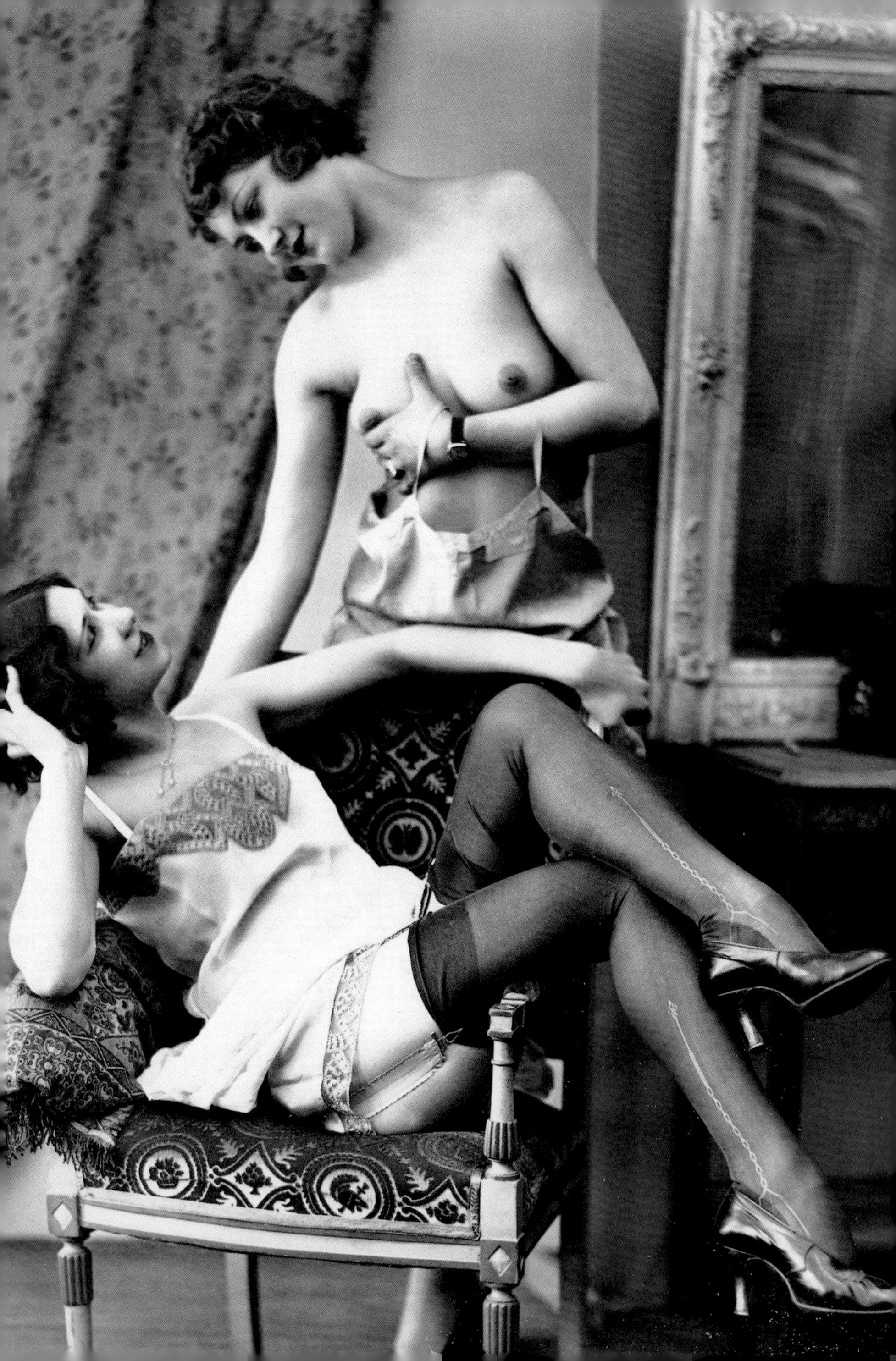

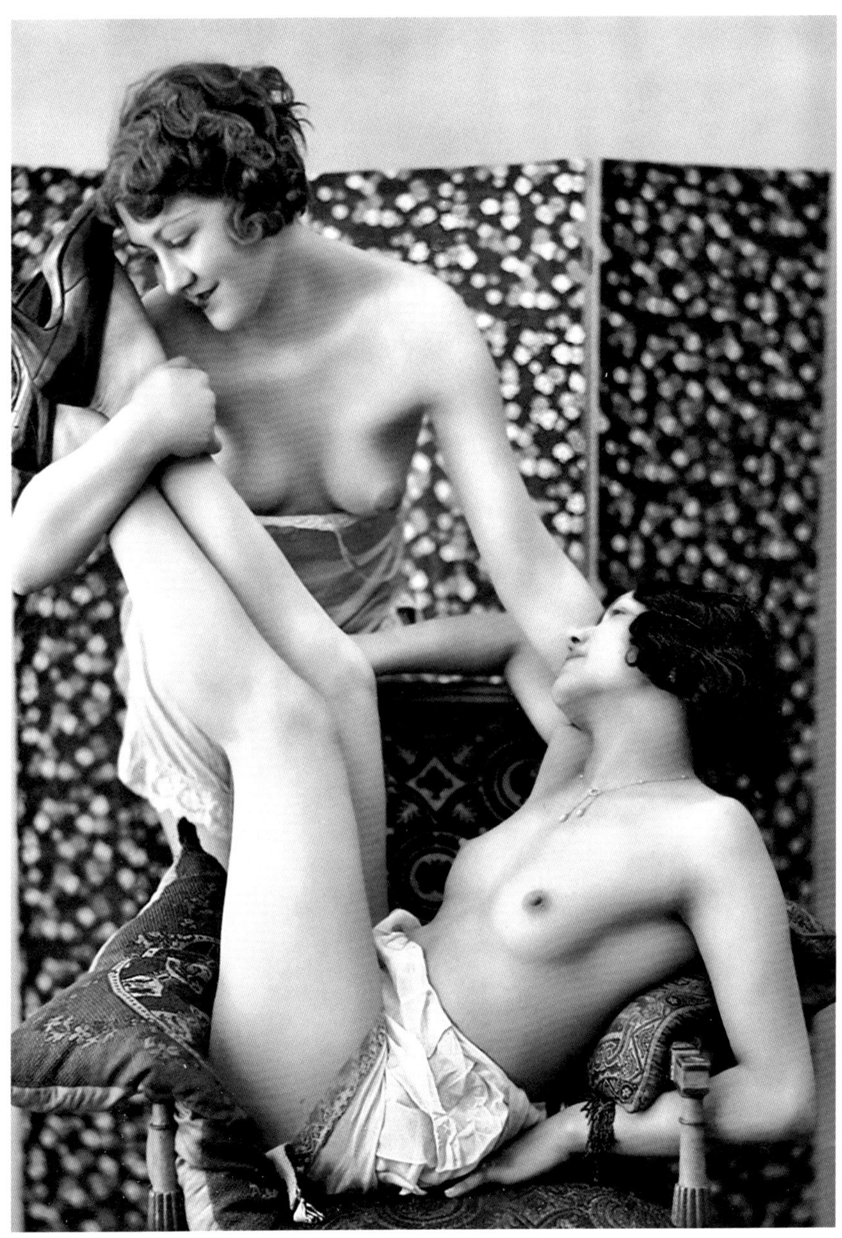

OPPOSITE AND ABOVE Unknown, BIEDERER

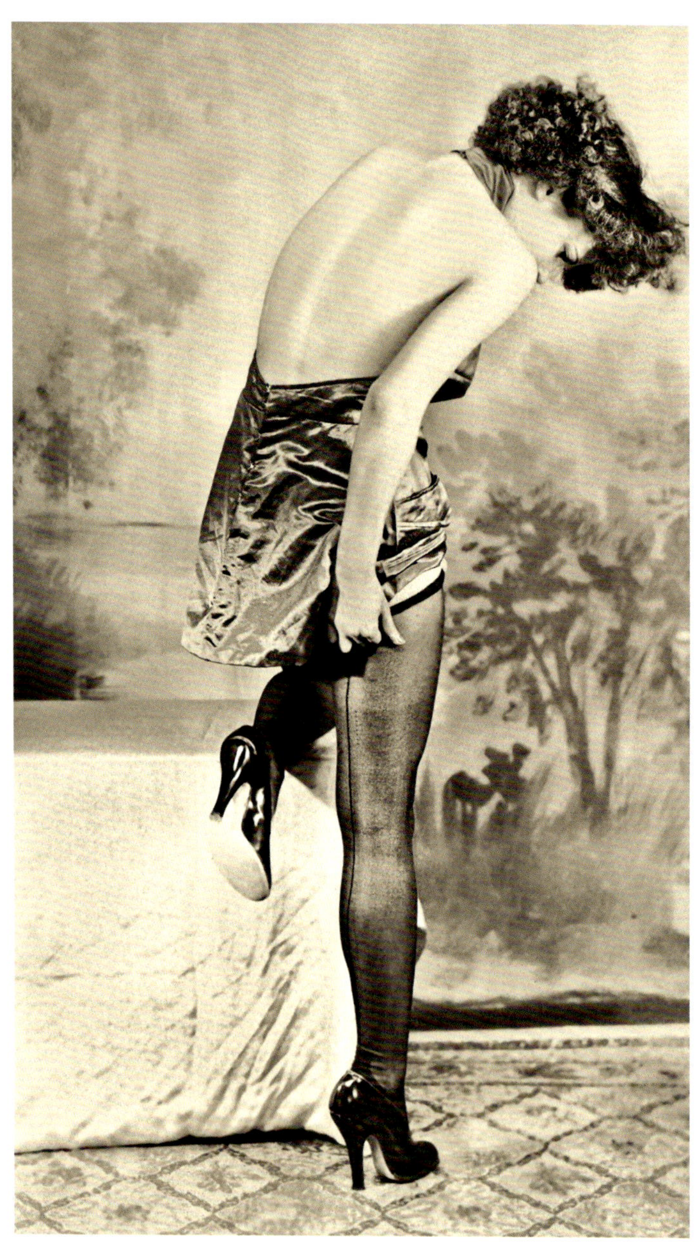

ABOVE AND OPPOSITE Unknown

38

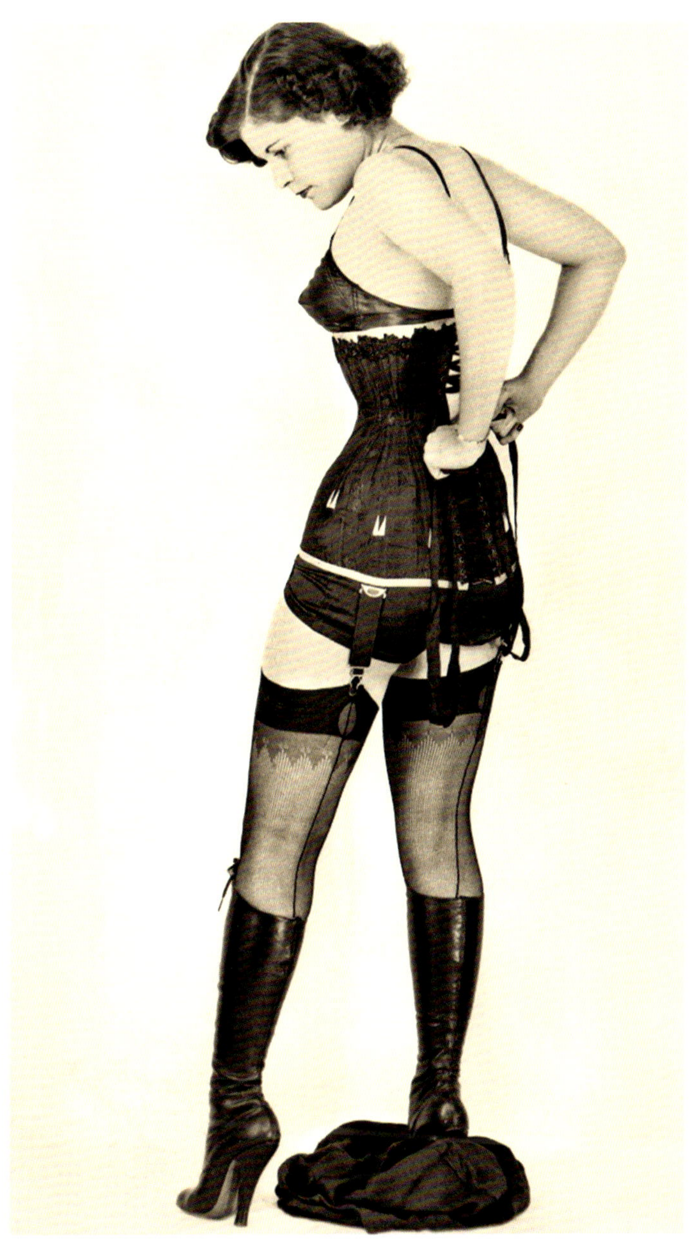

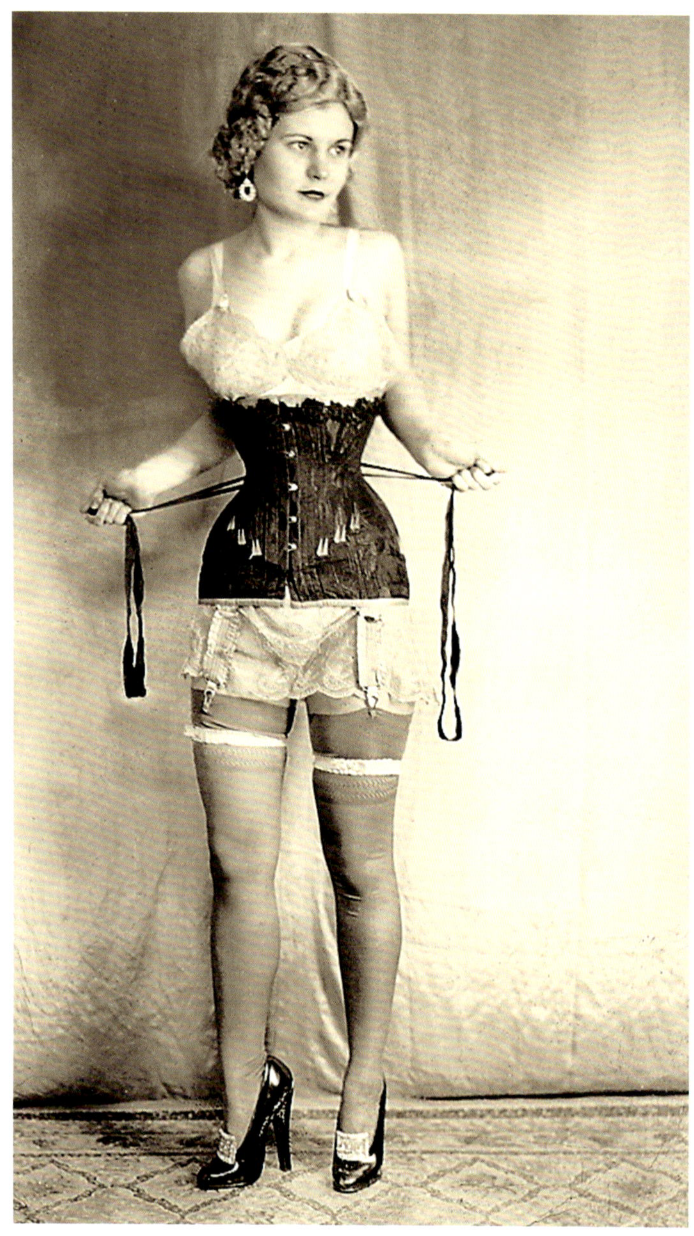

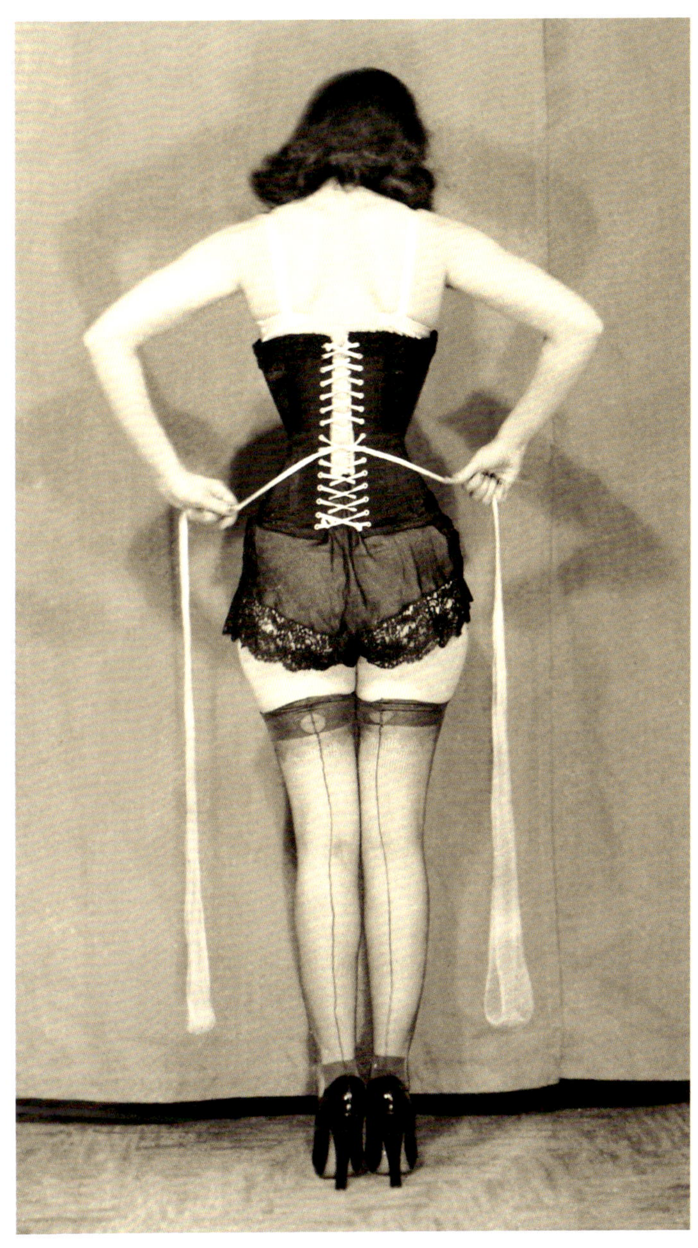

OPPOSITE AND ABOVE Unknown

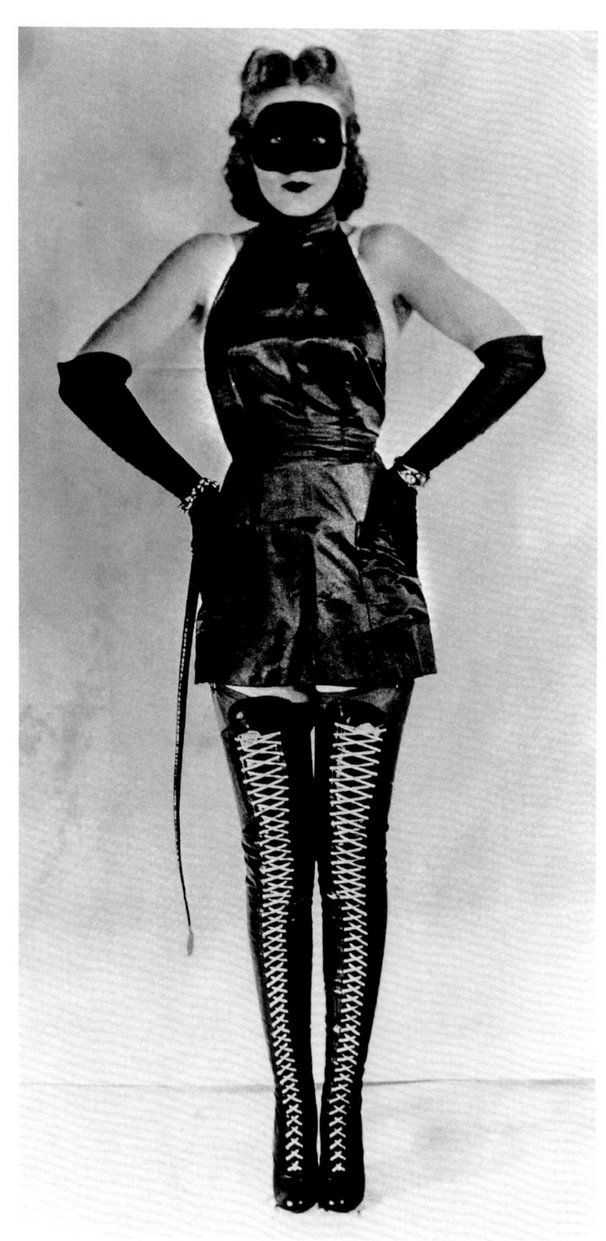

ABOVE Unknown   OPPOSITE Unknown, ELMER BATTERS

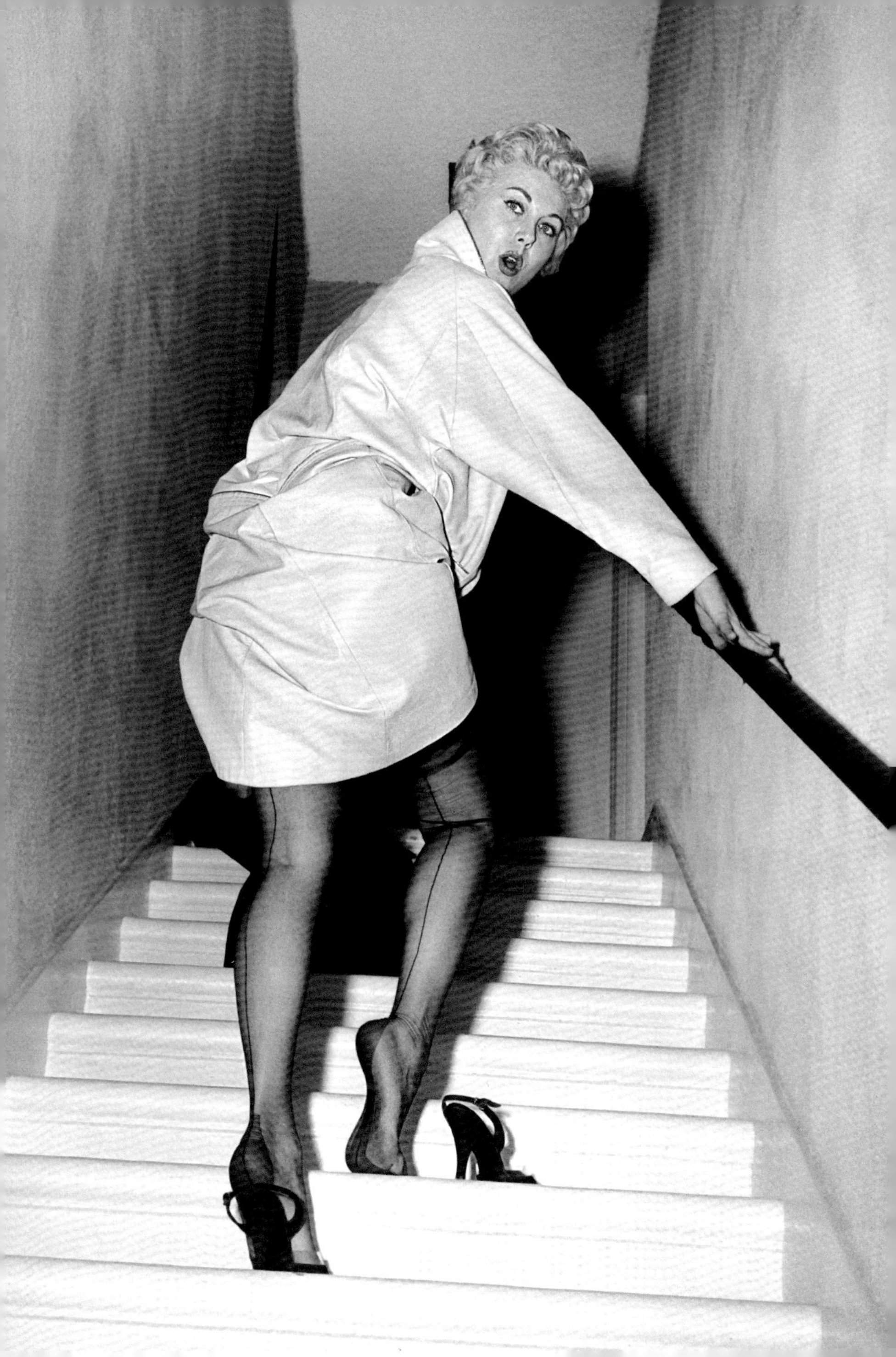

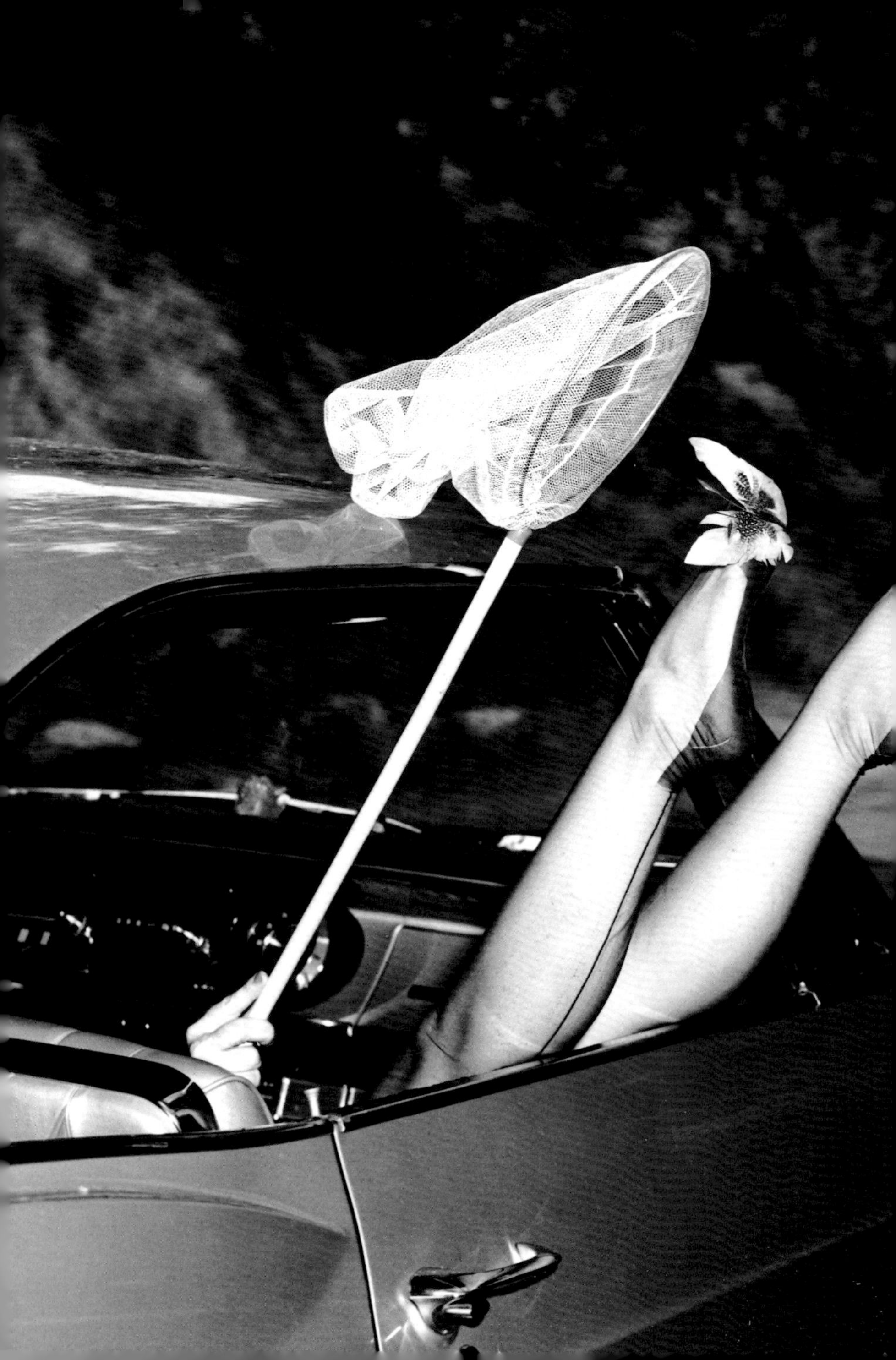

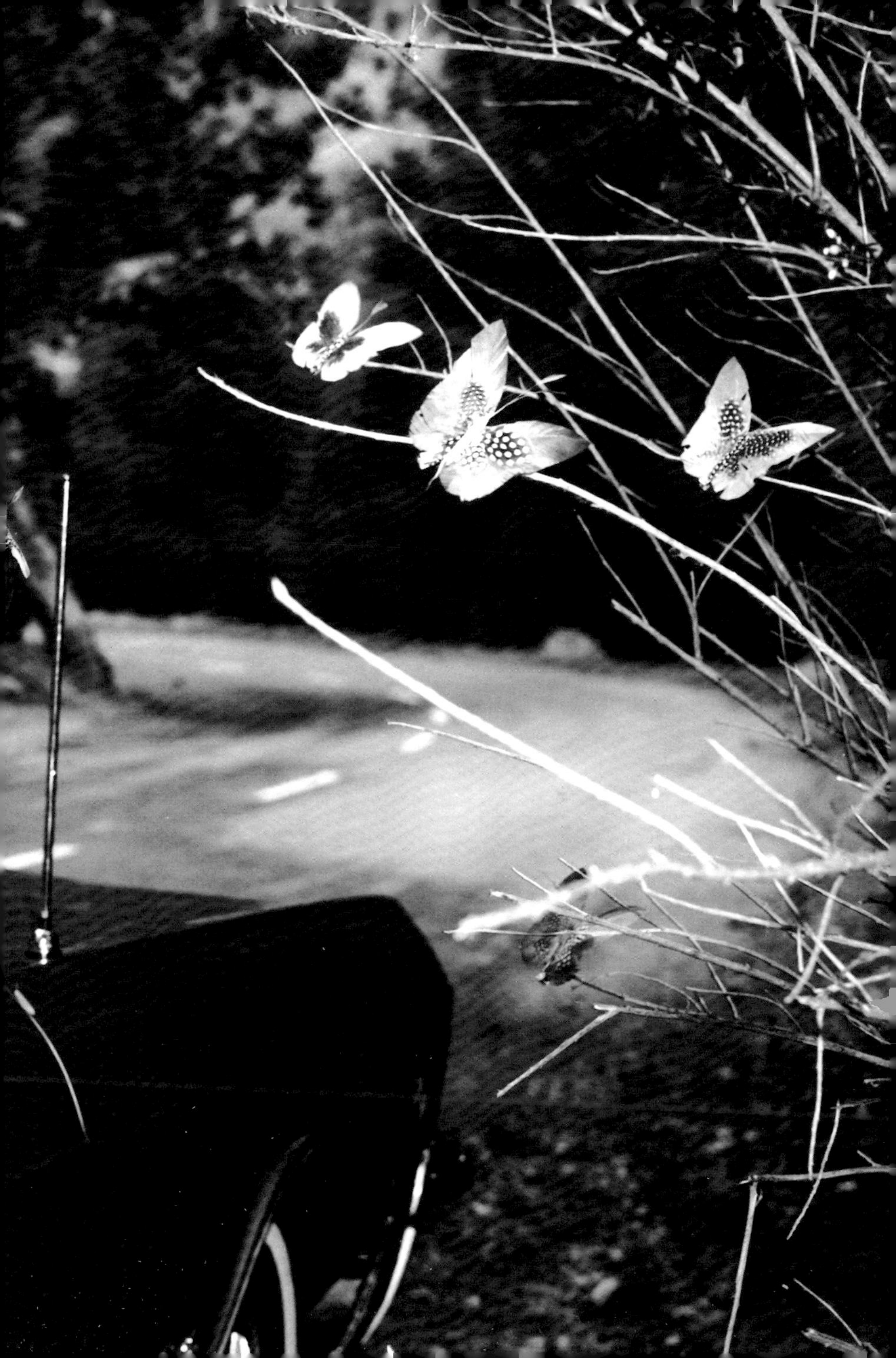

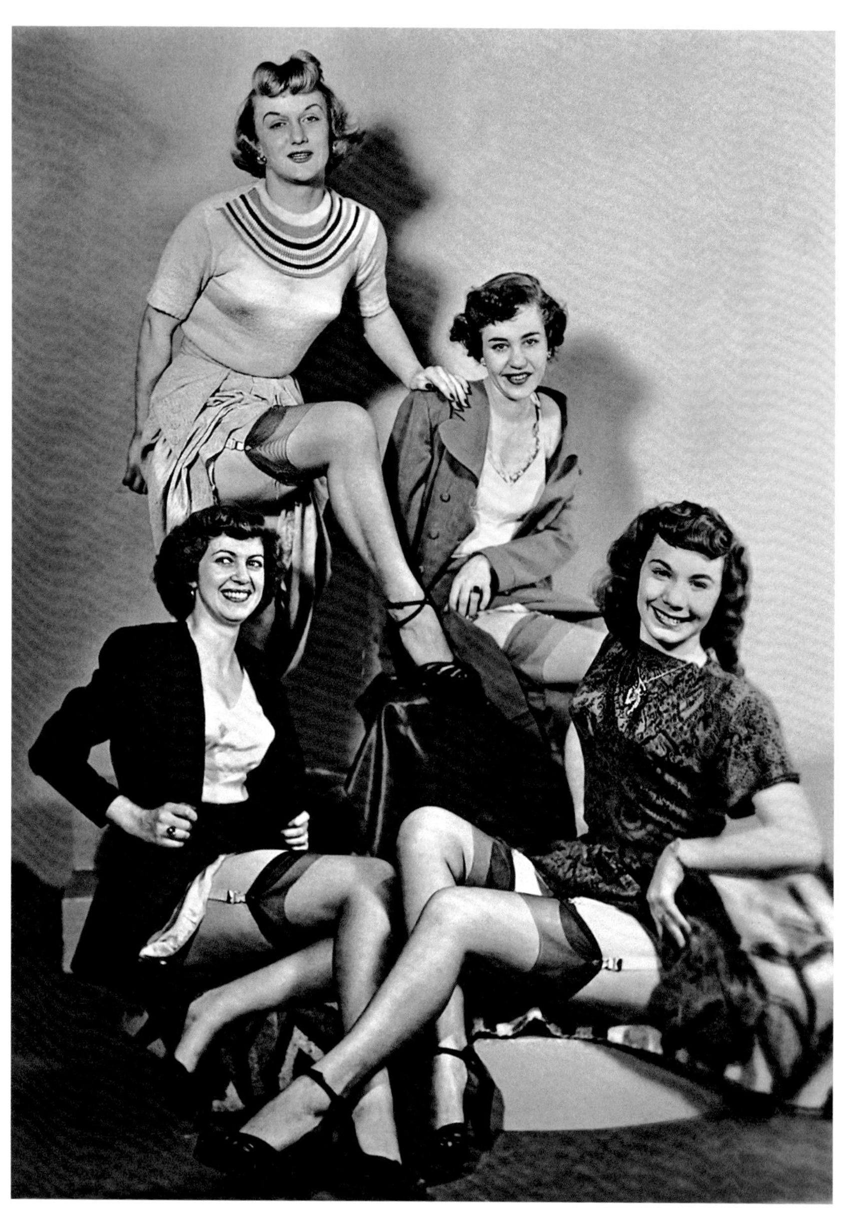

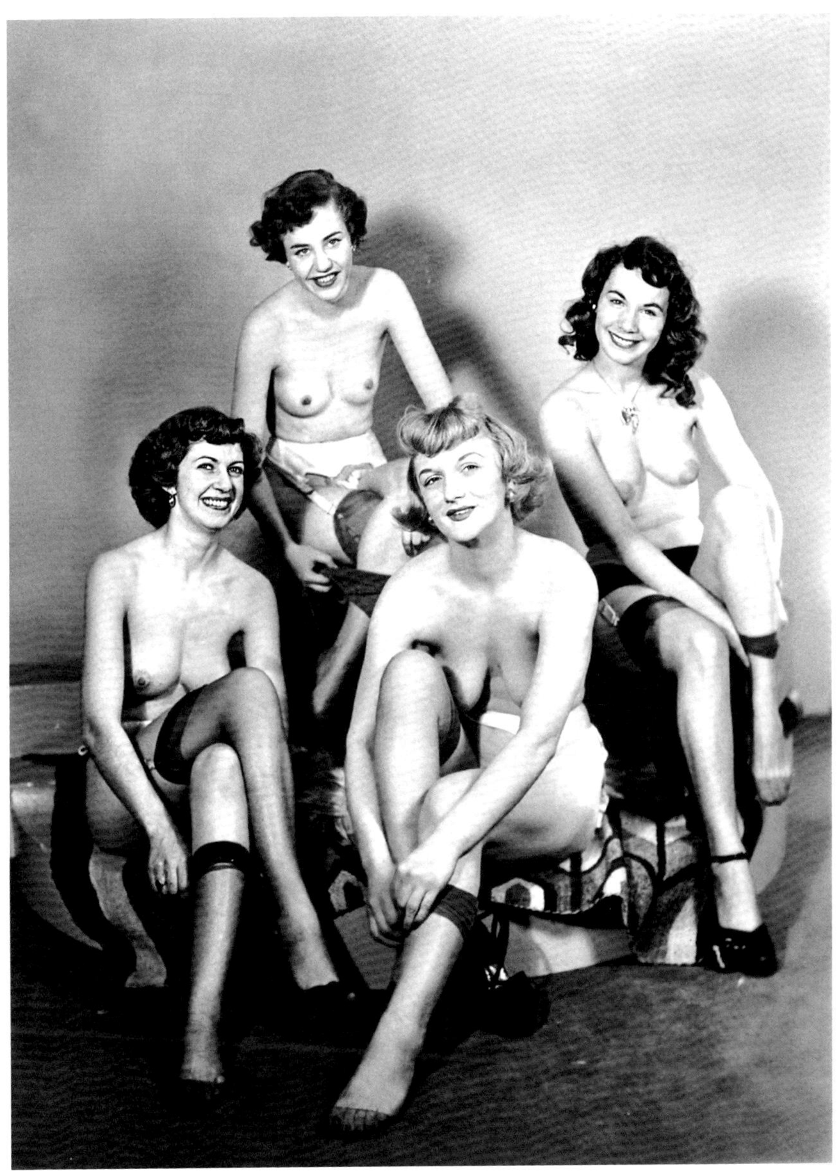

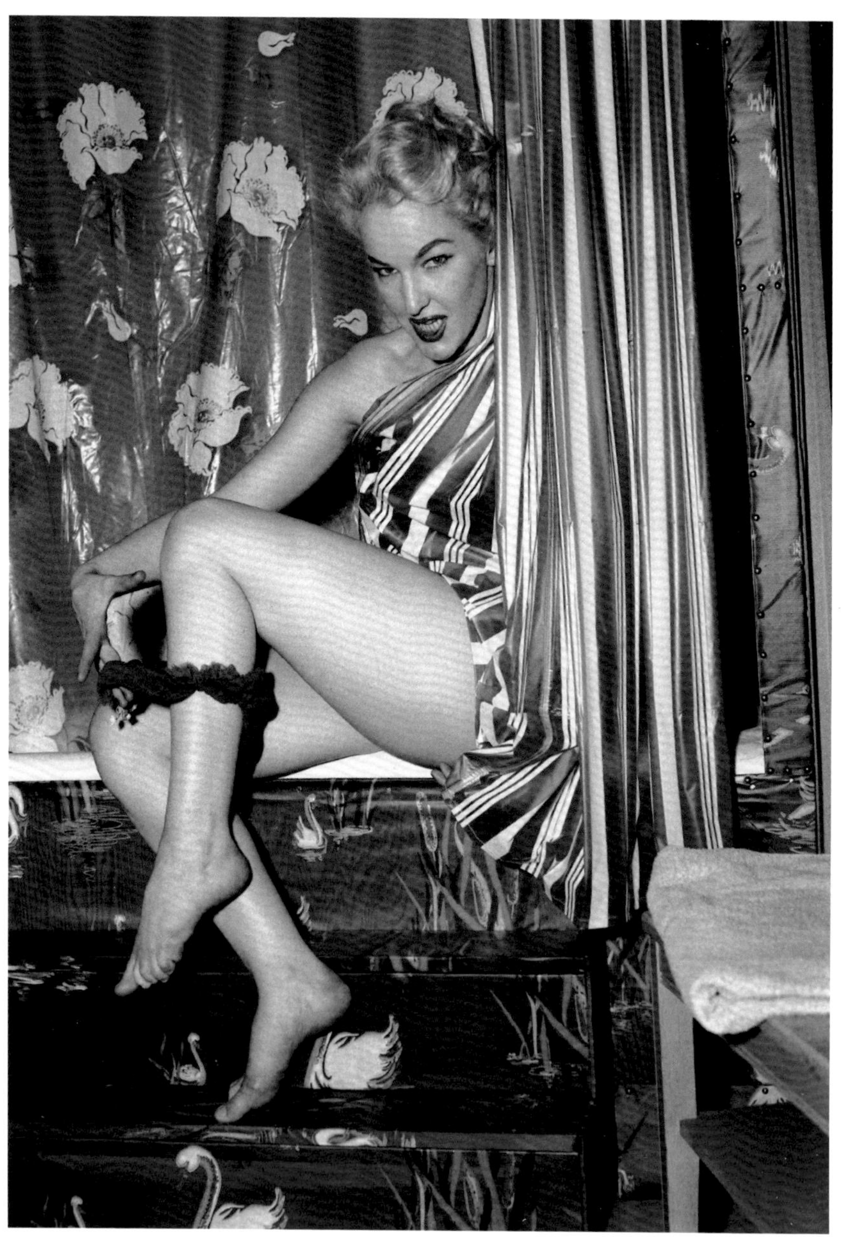

ABOVE Pat Hobson, PAULA KLAW

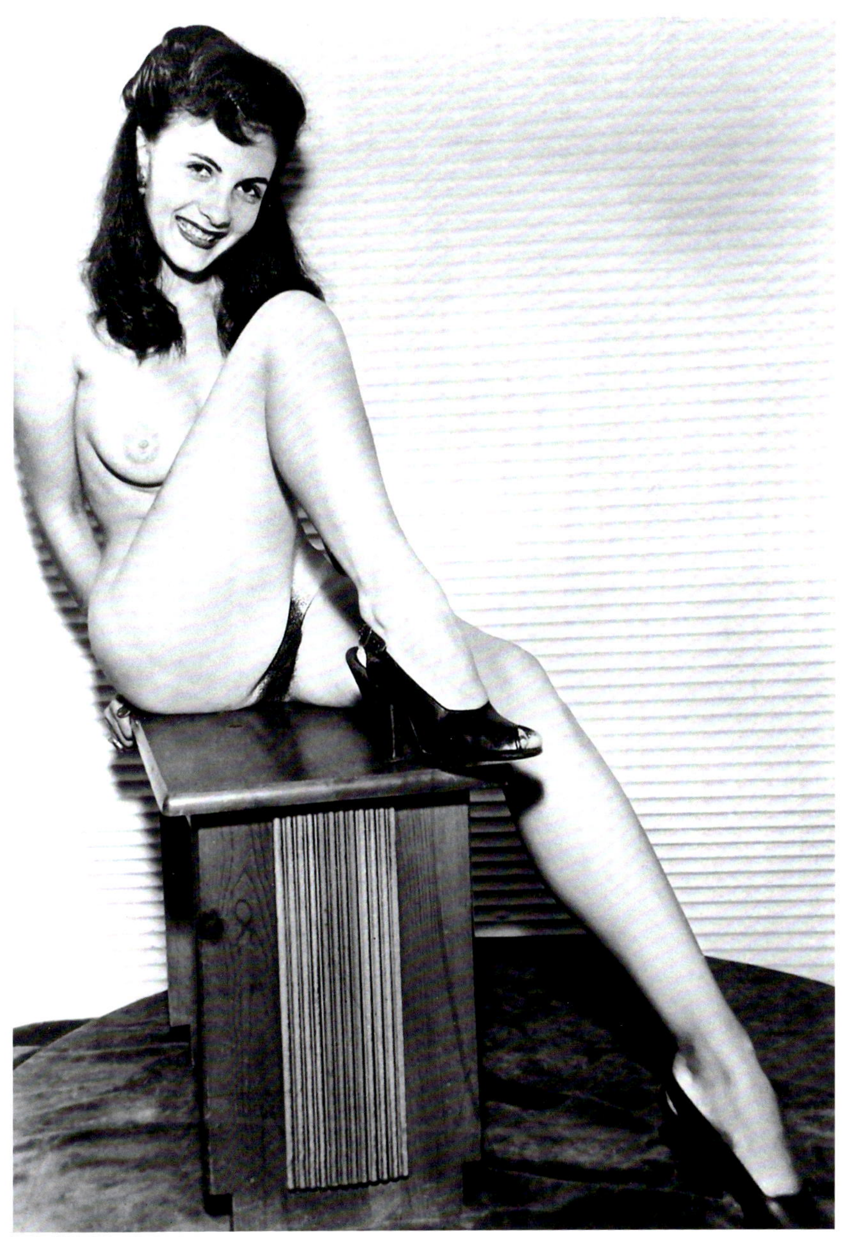

ABOVE Unknown

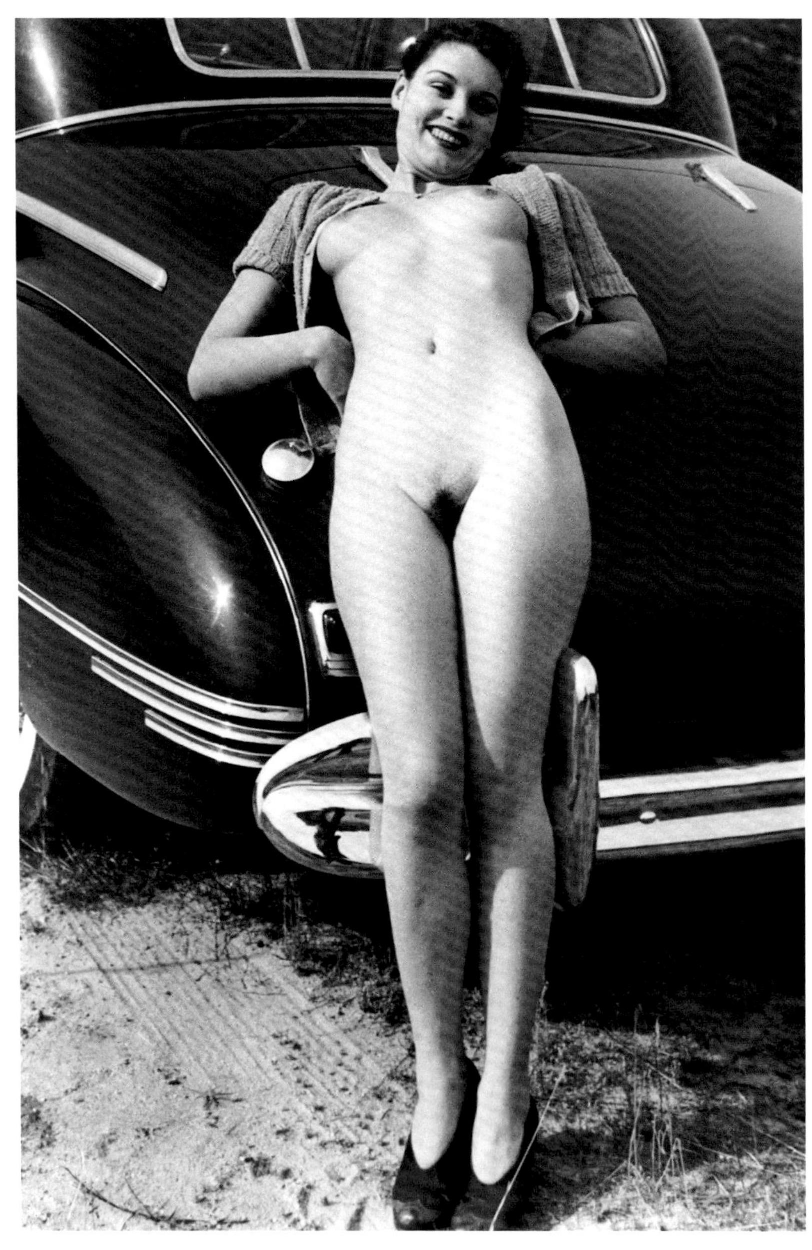

ABOVE AND OPPOSITE Unknown

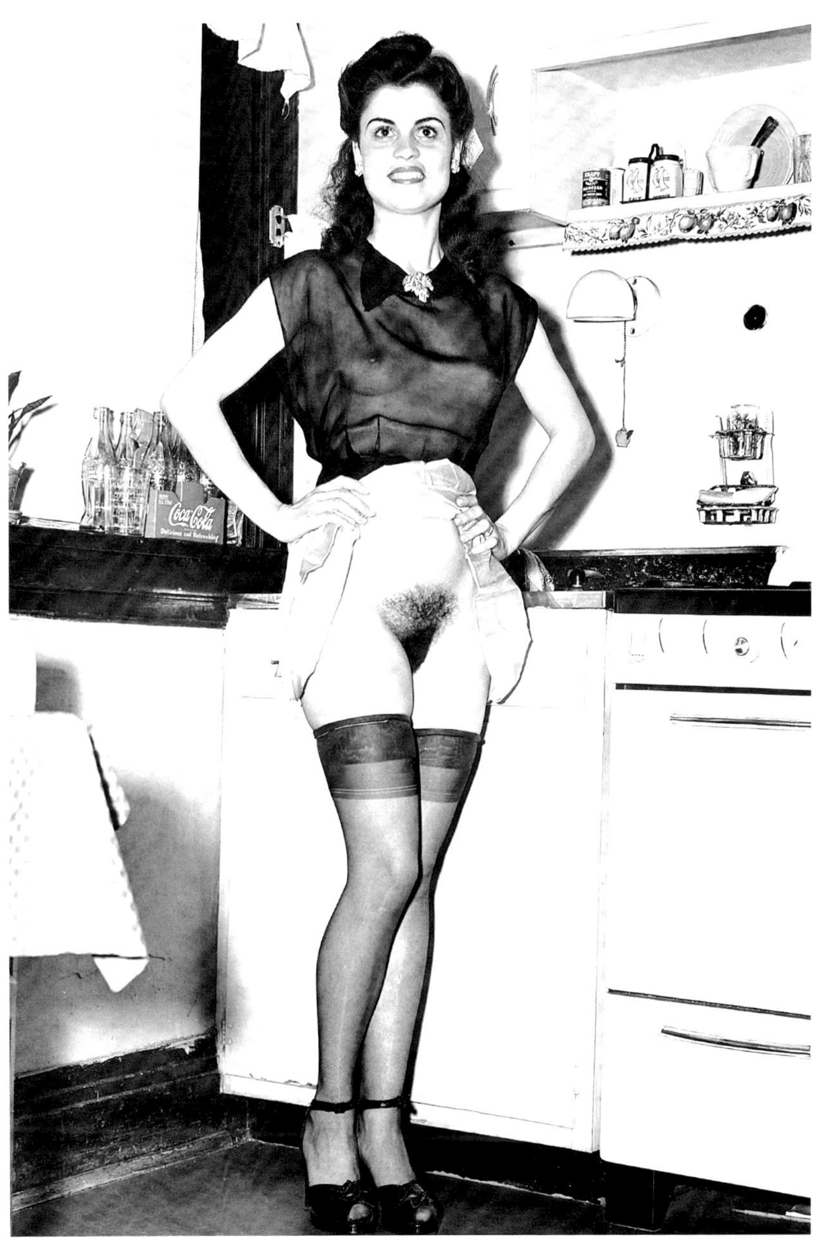

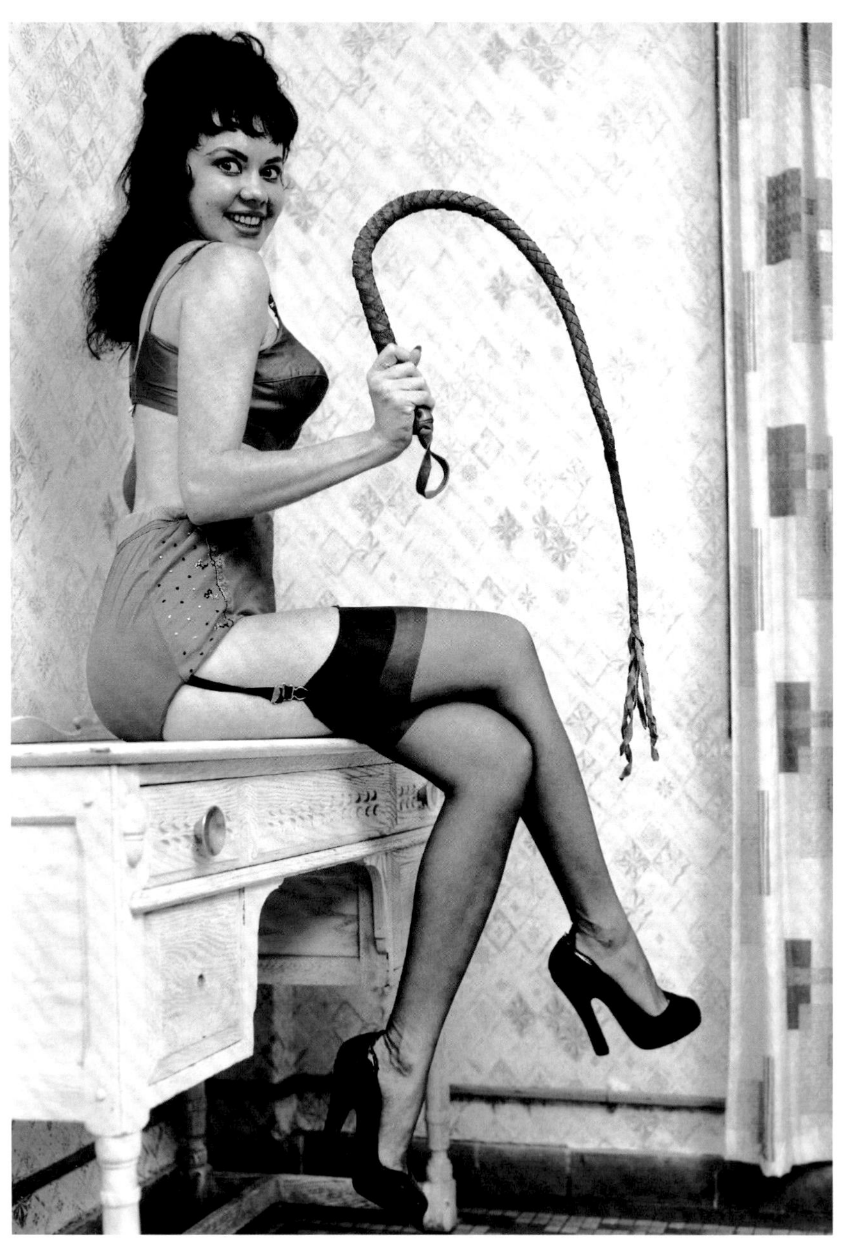

ABOVE Unknown, PAULA KLAW

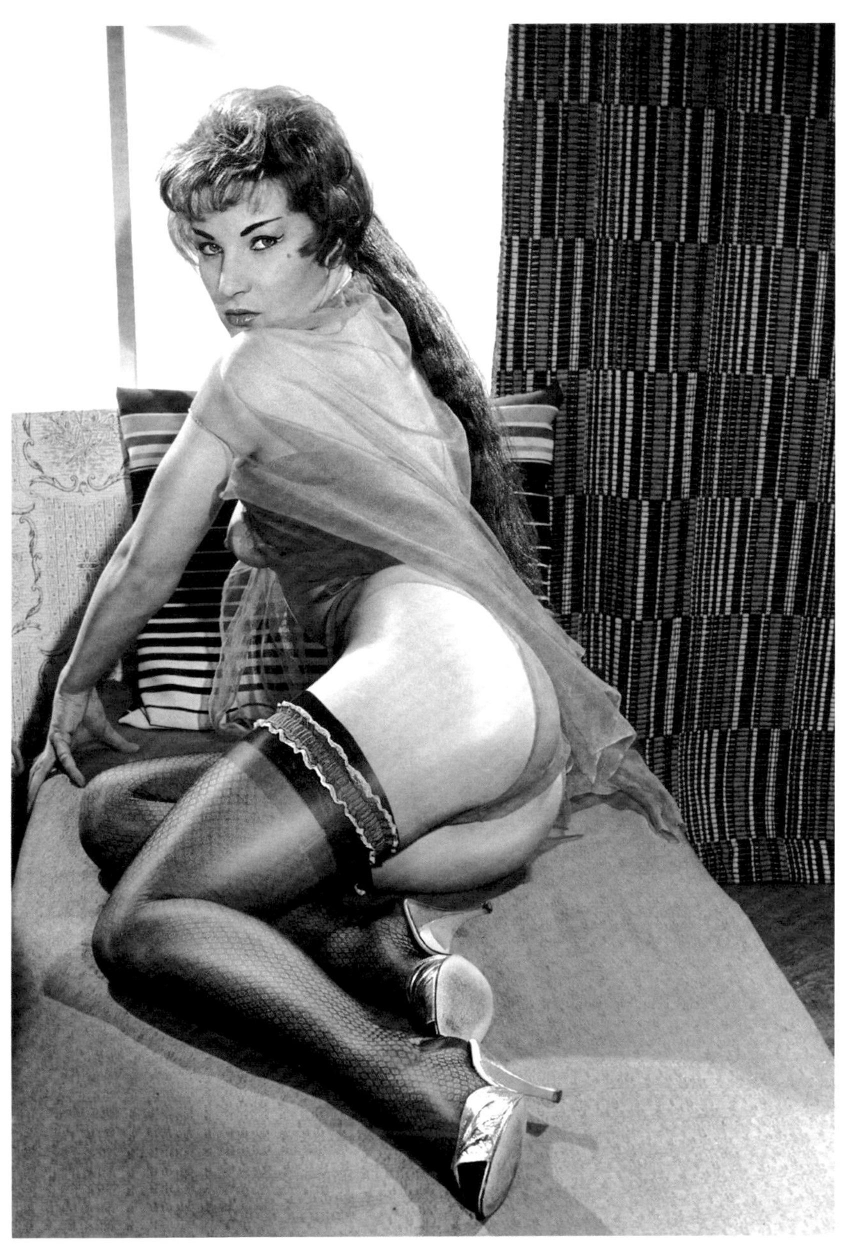

ABOVE **Unknown**   PAGES 54-55 **Bettie Page**, PAULA KLAW

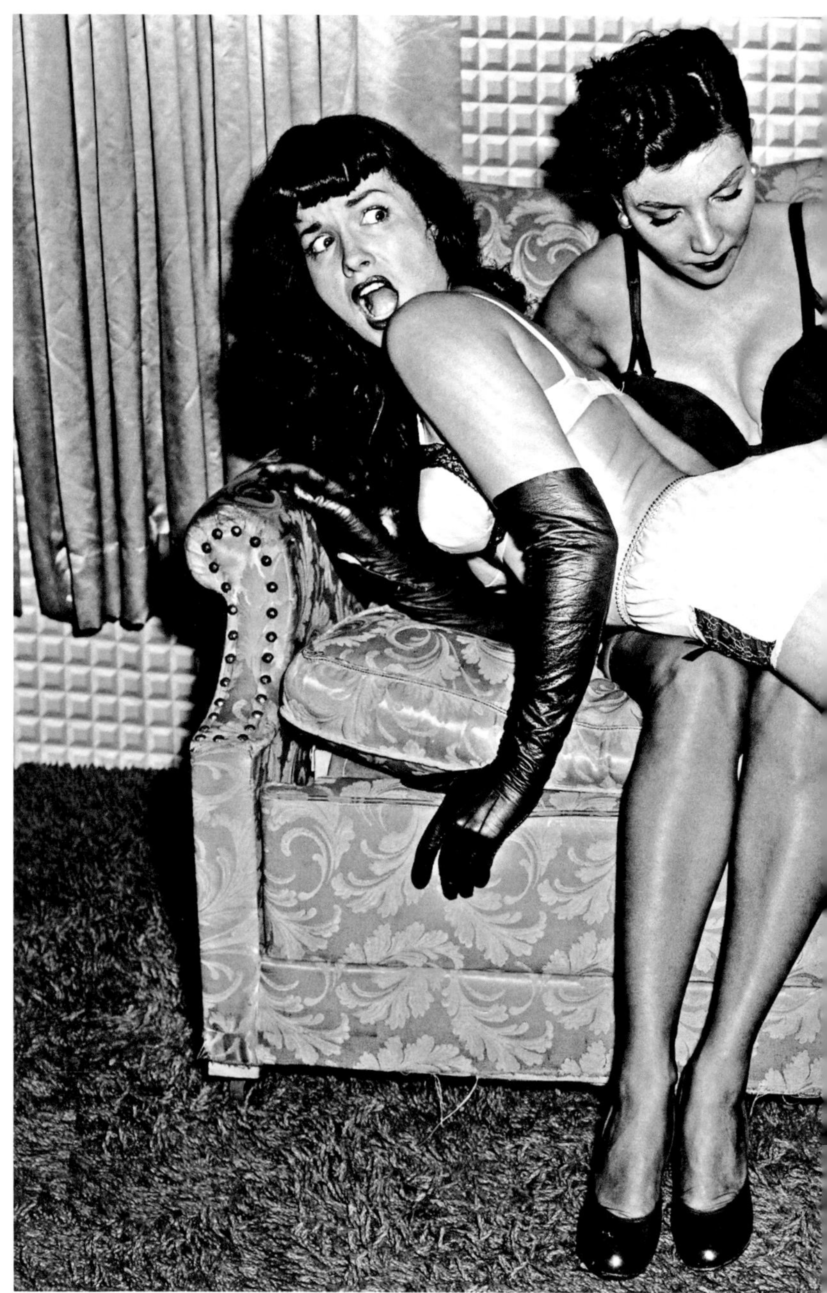

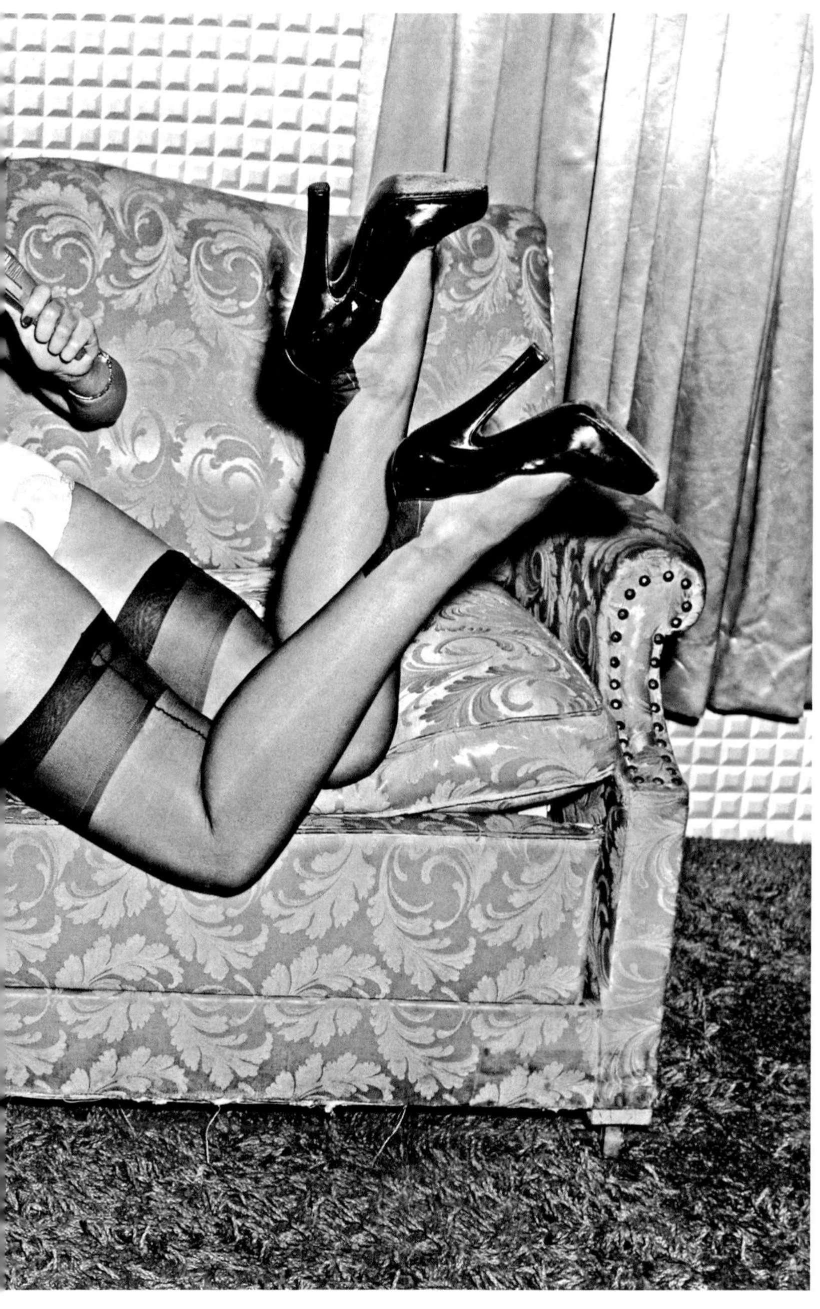

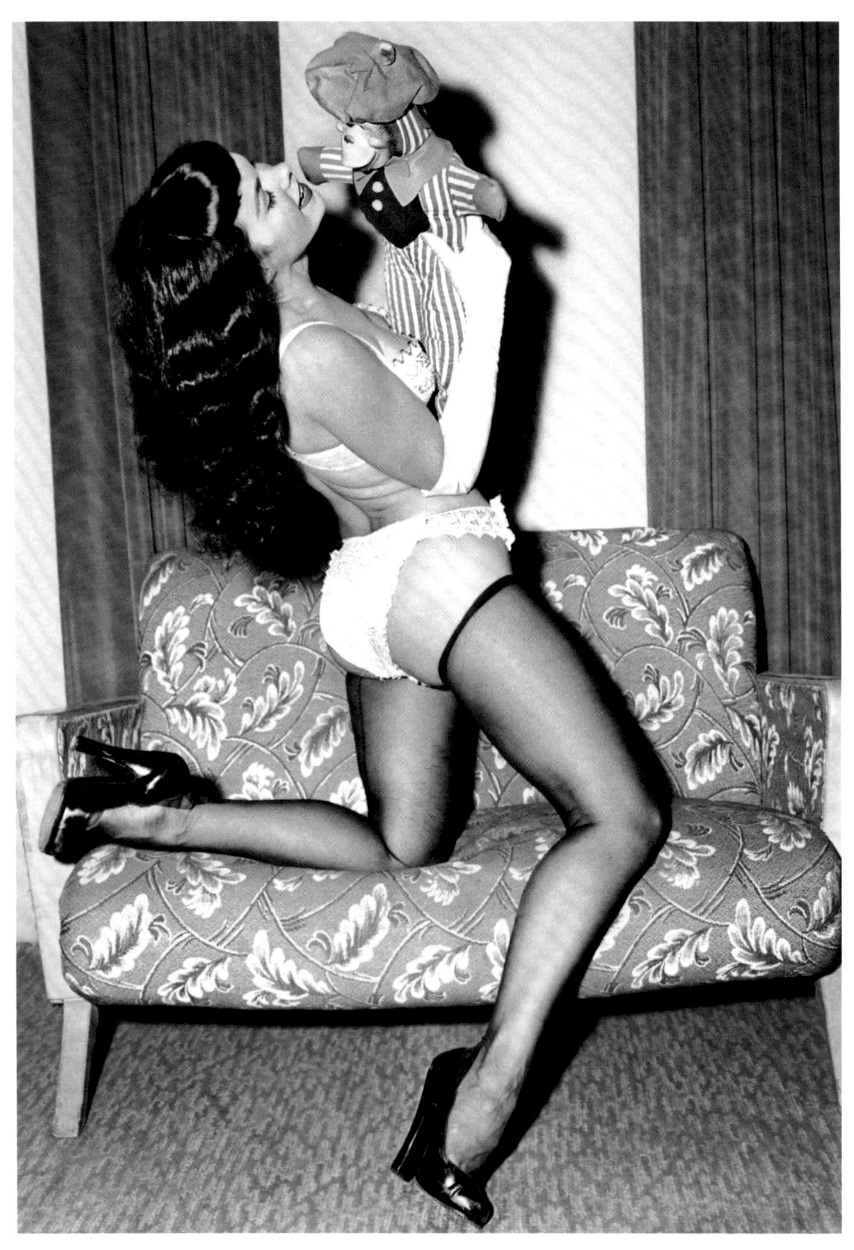

ABOVE AND OPPOSITE Bettie Page, PAULA KLAW   PAGES 58-59 Unknown, ELMER BATTERS

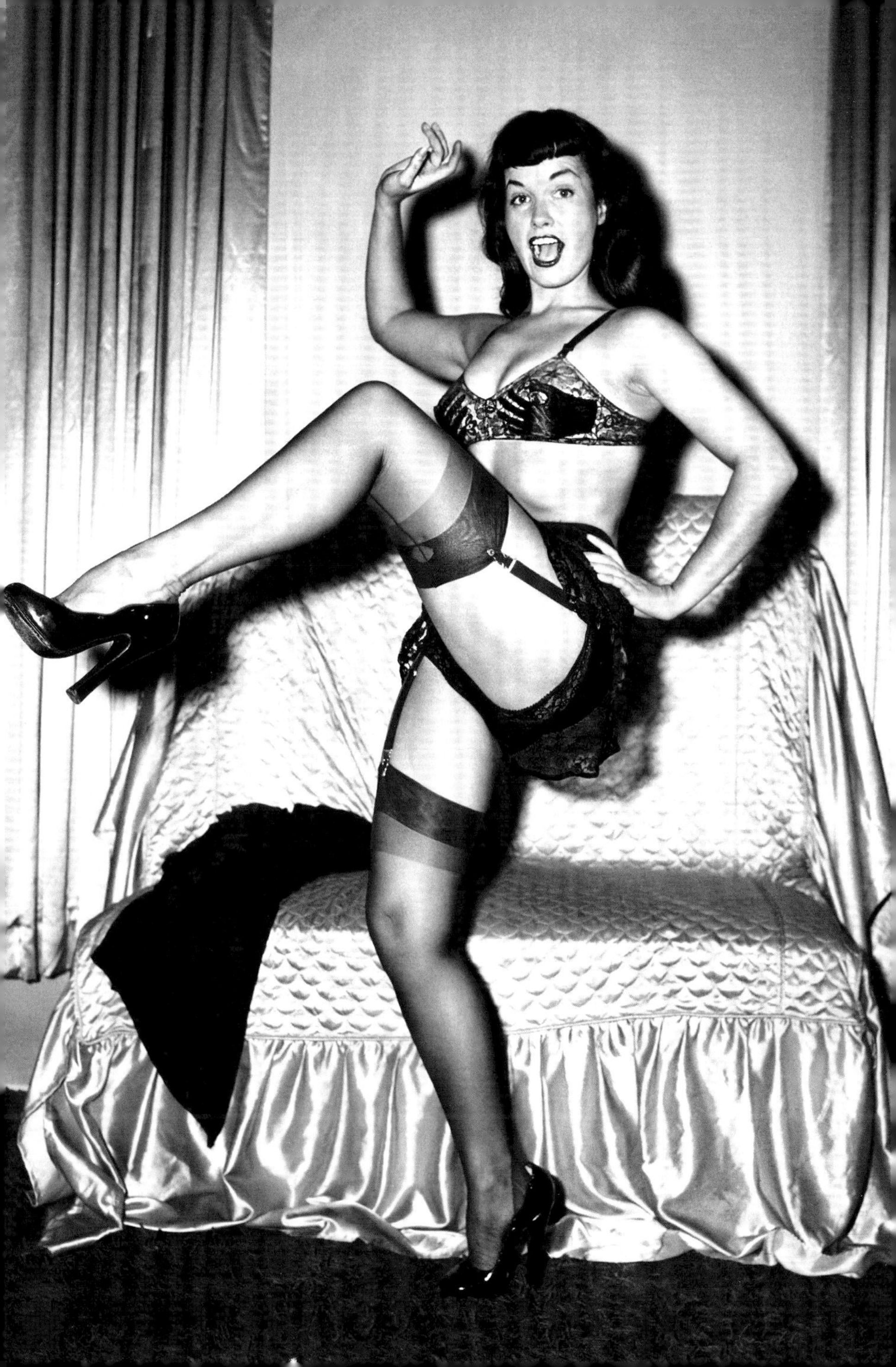

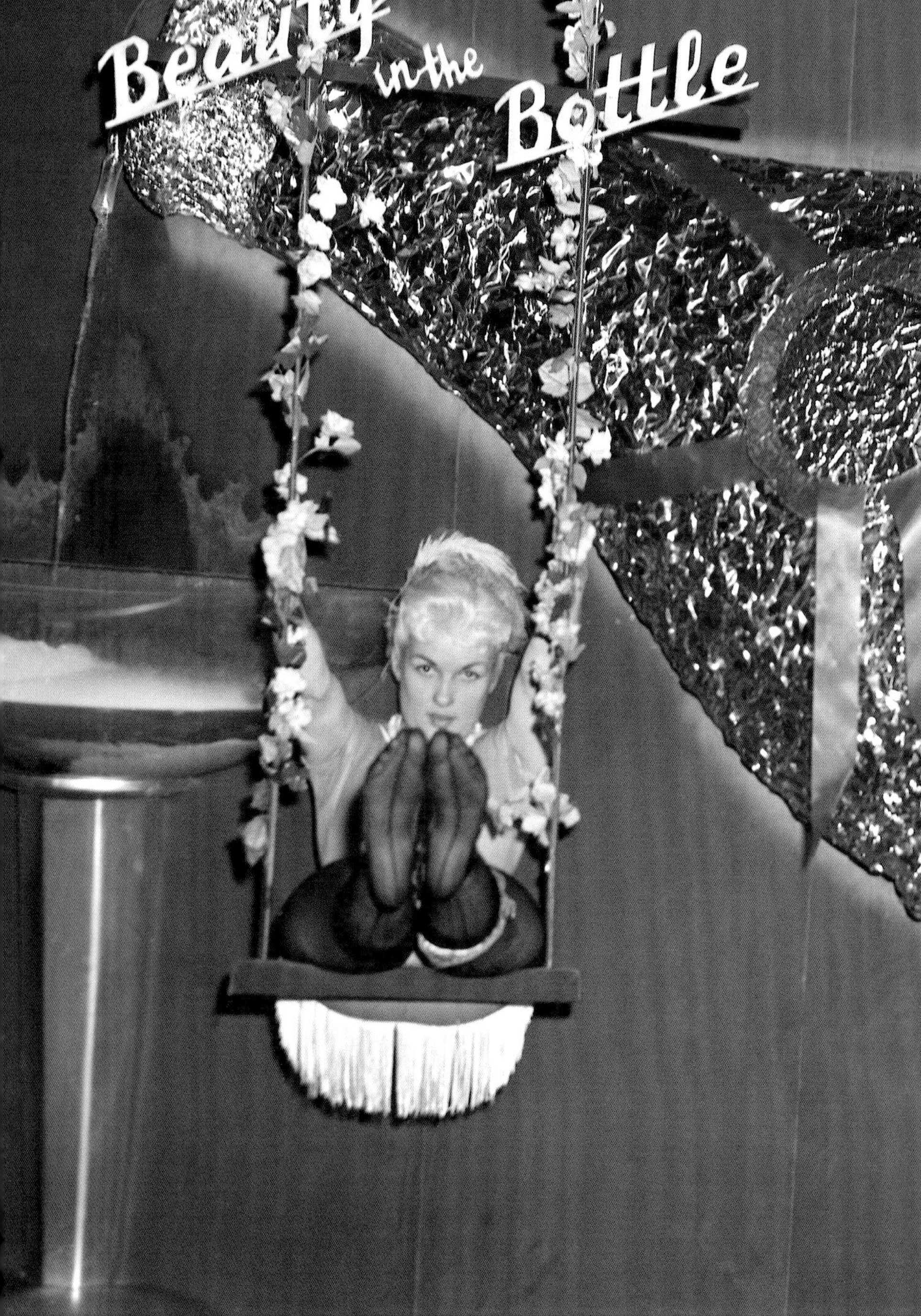

Beauty in the
Bottle

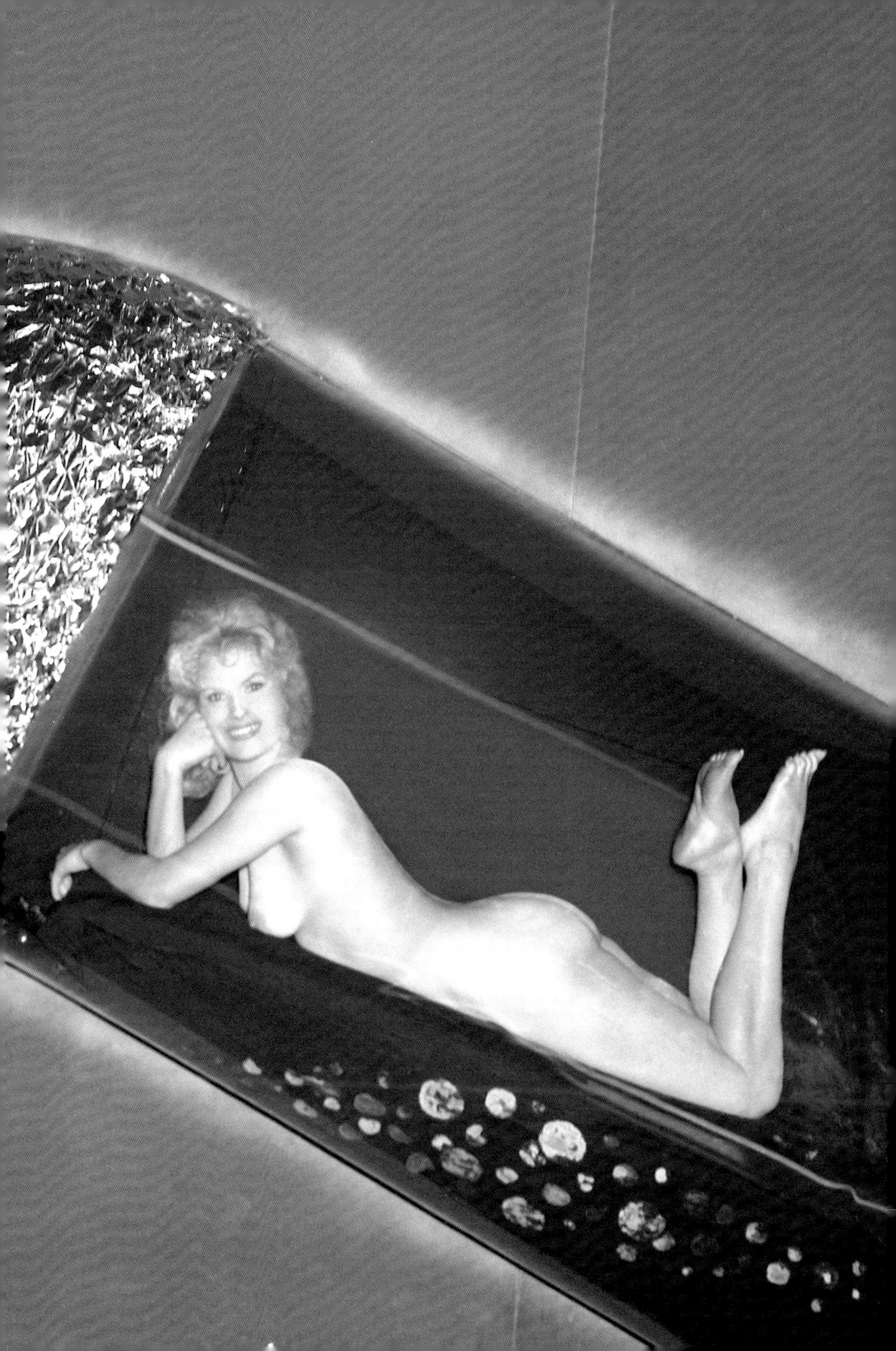

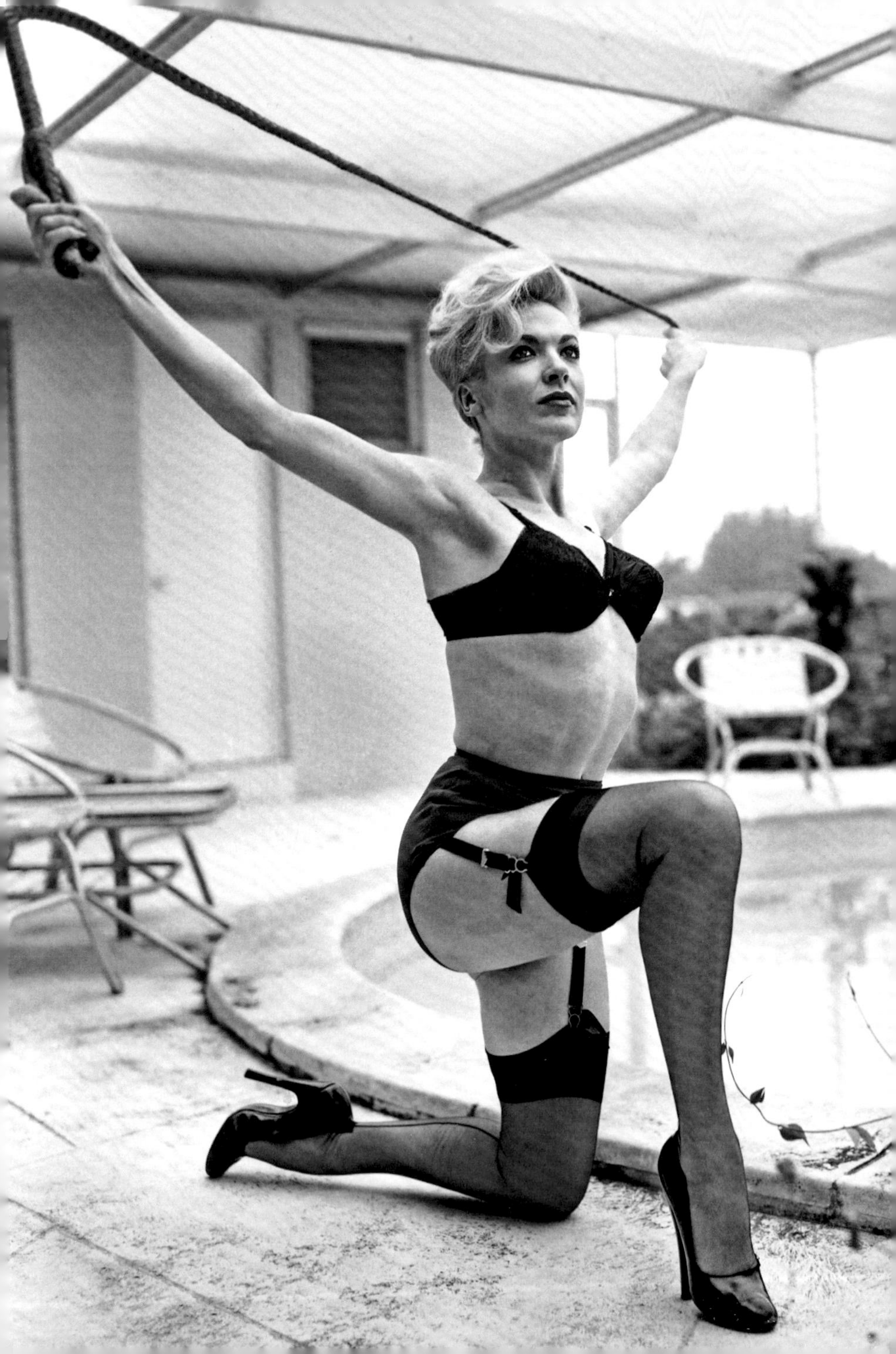

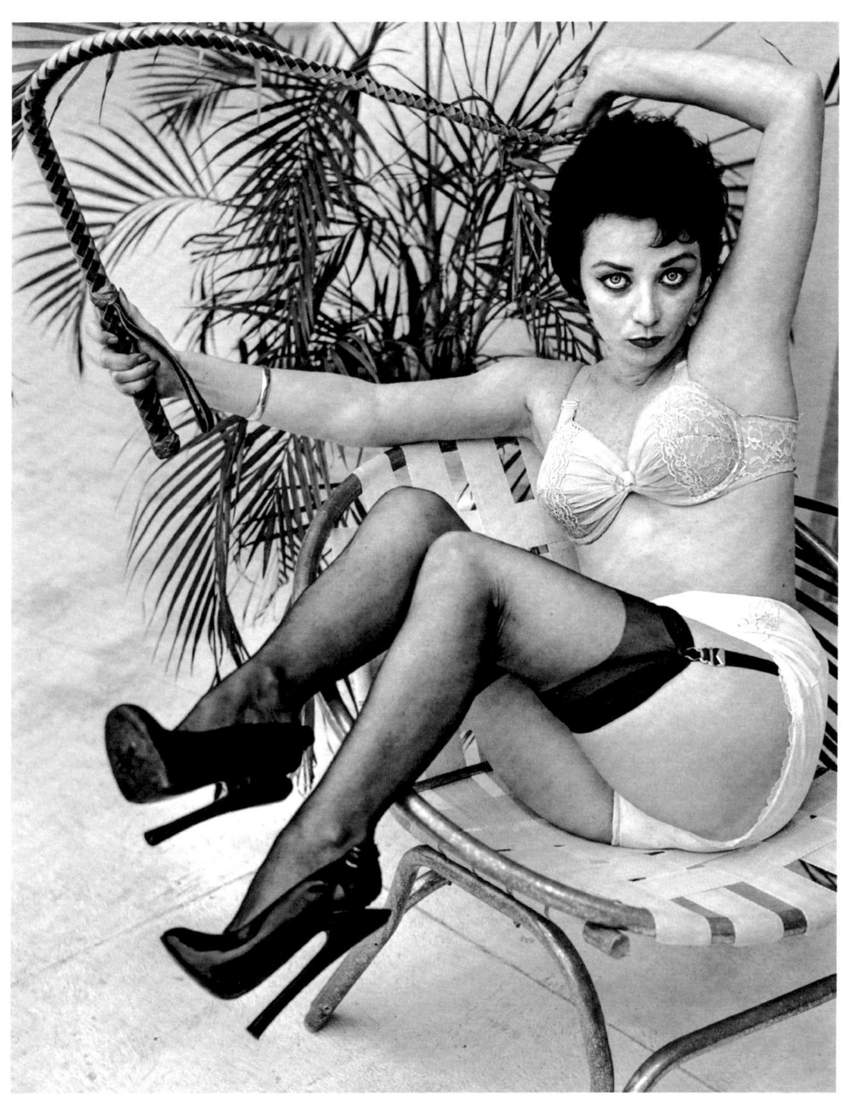

OPPOSITE AND ABOVE Unknown

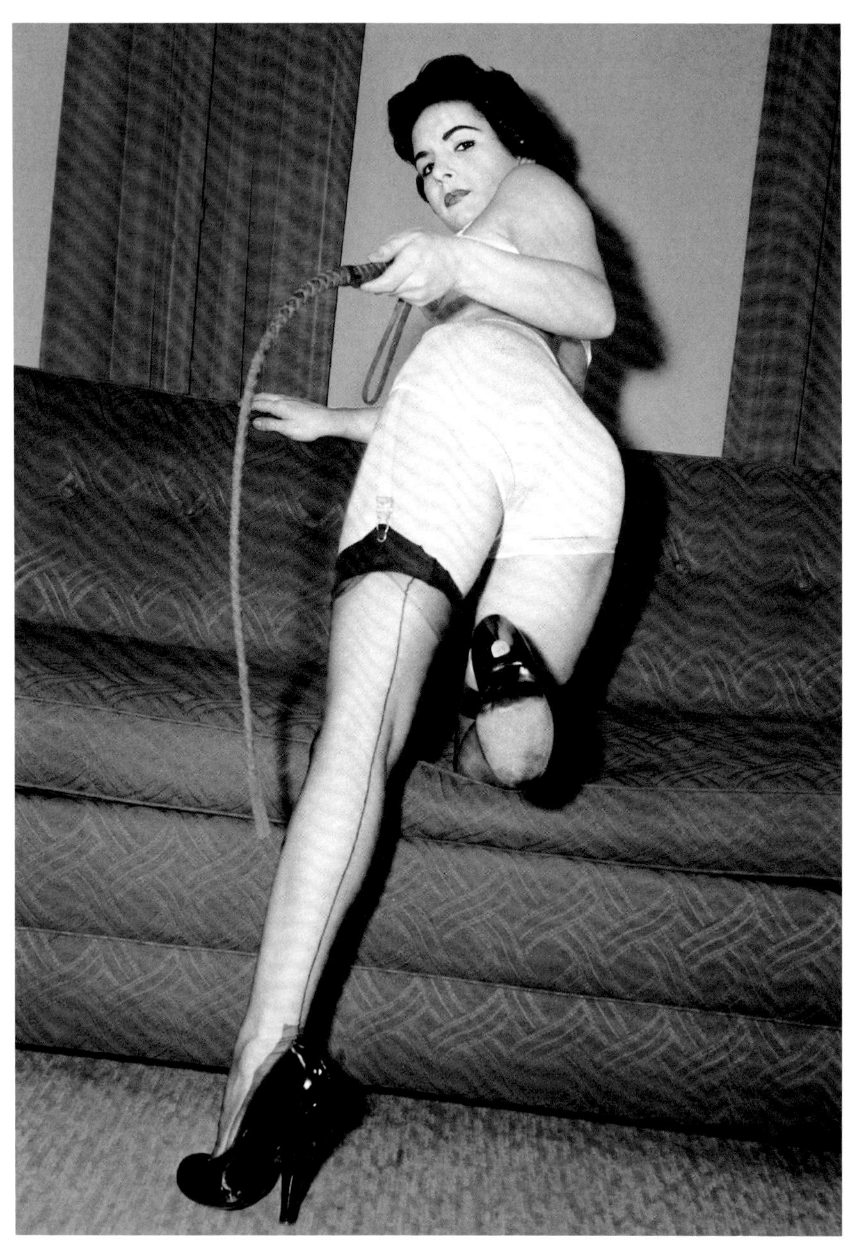

ABOVE **Desiree**, PAULA KLAW

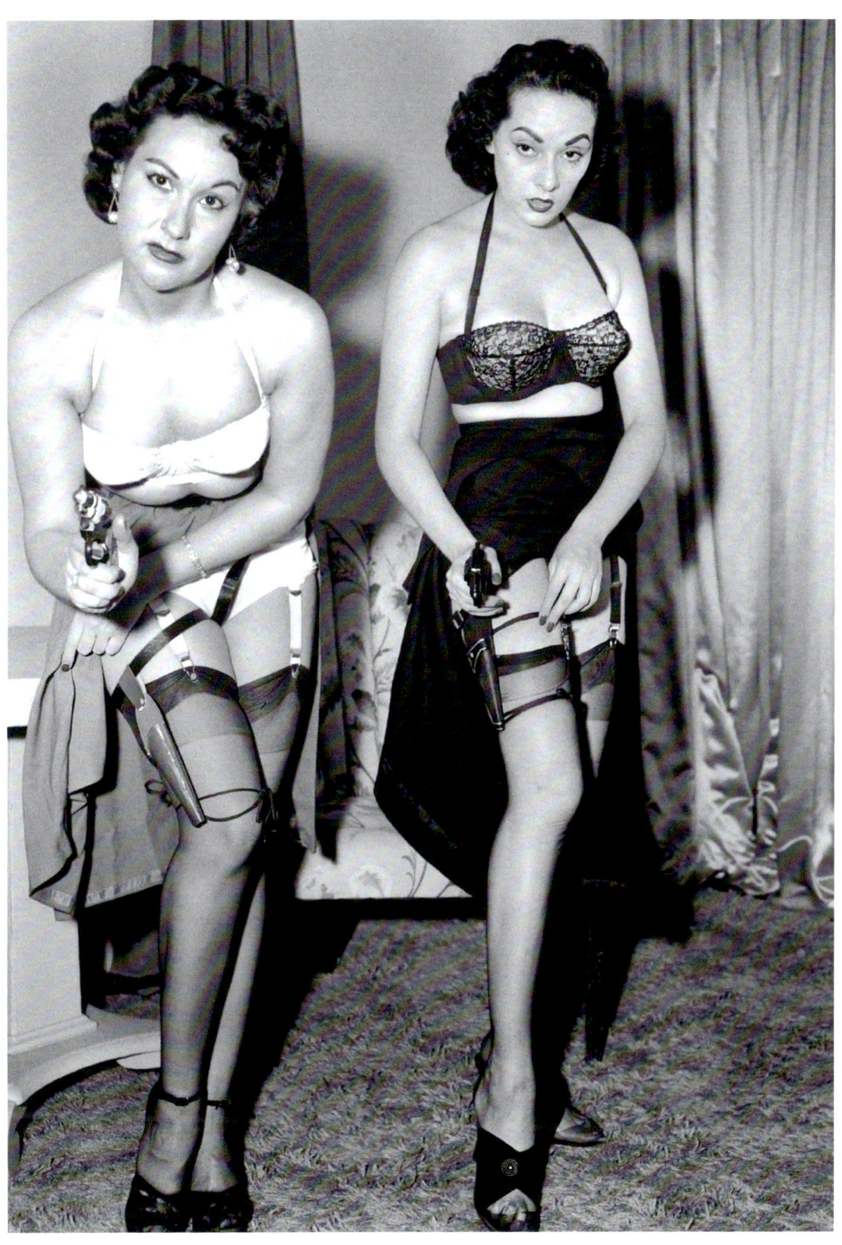

ABOVE Brandy K. and Friend, PAULA KLAW

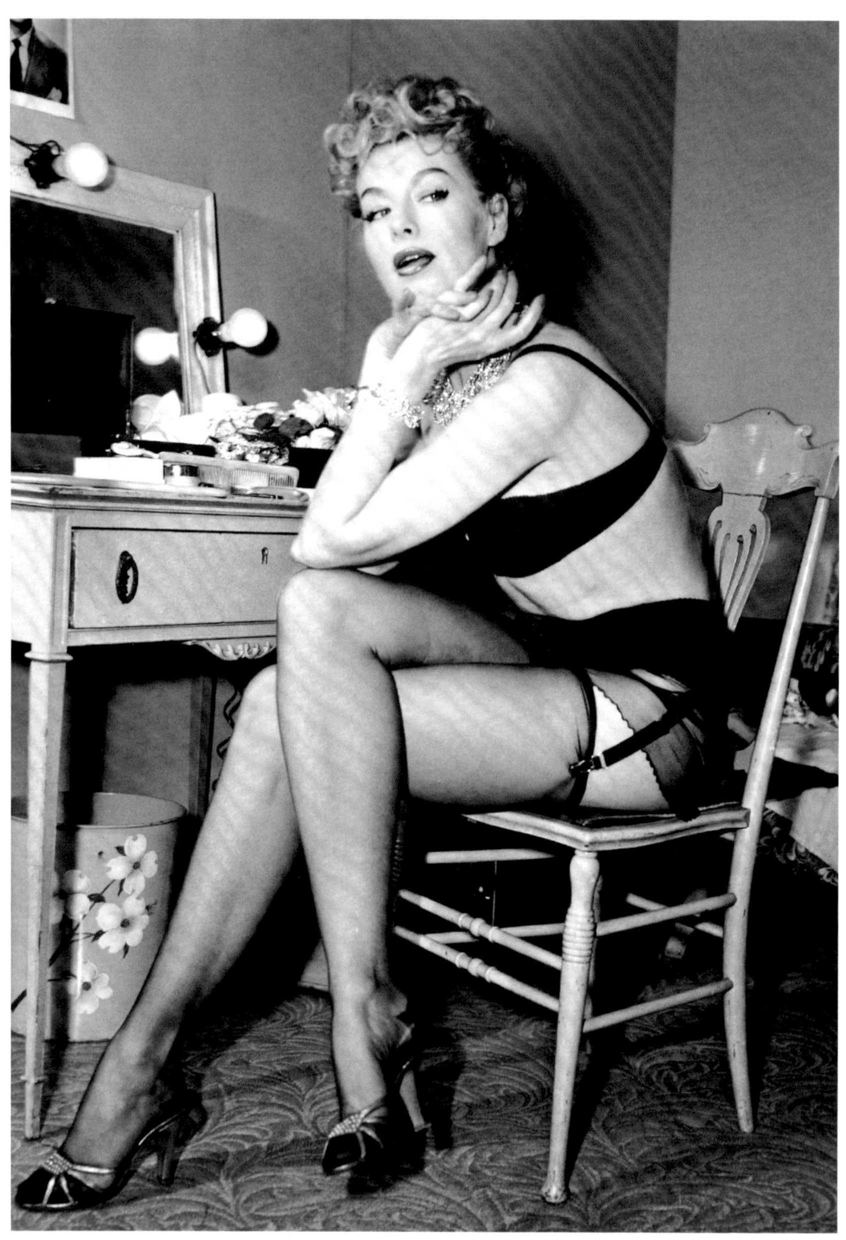

ABOVE Lili St. Cyr, PAULA KLAW   OPPOSITE Debby Dare, PAULA KLAW

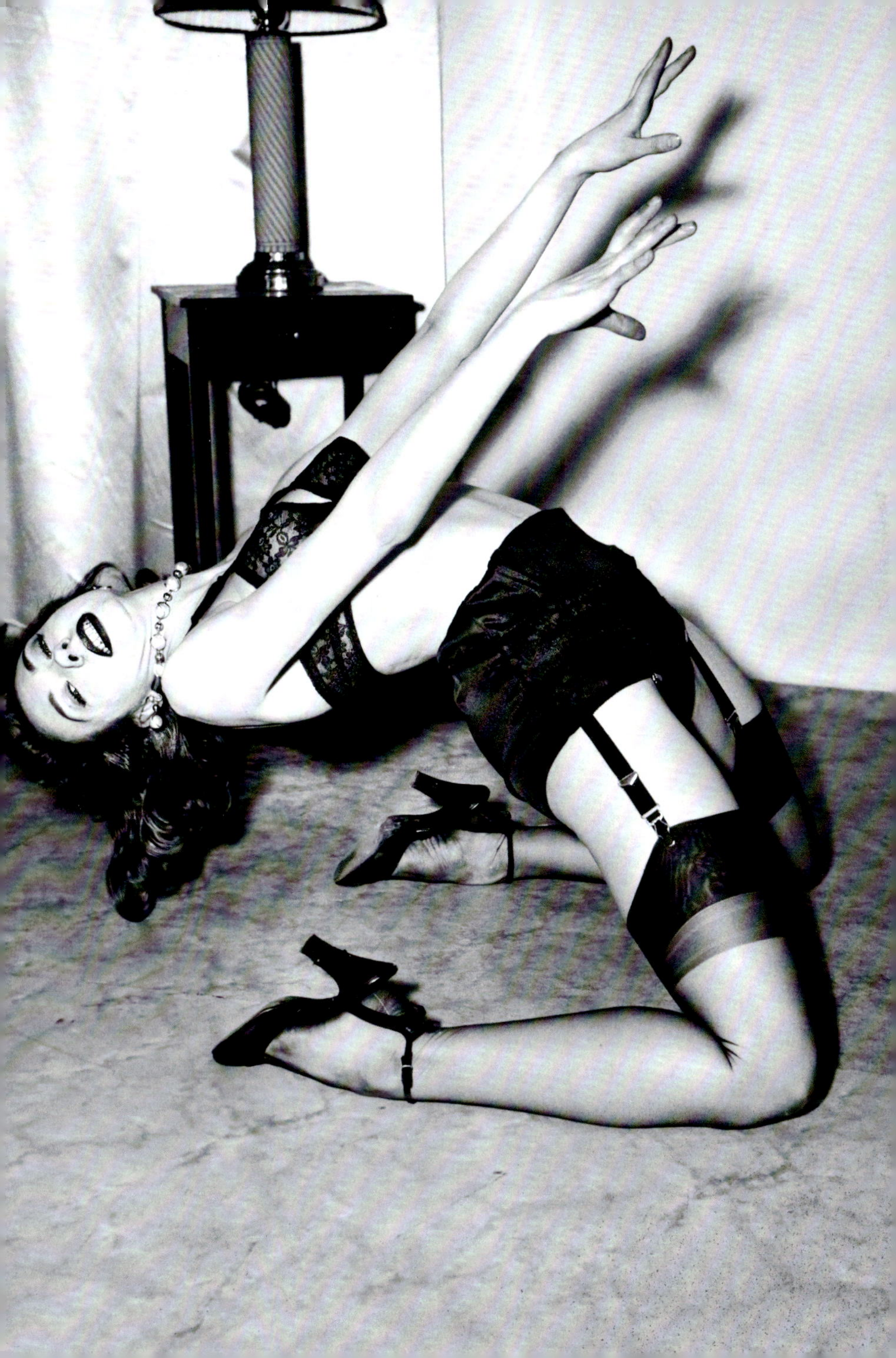

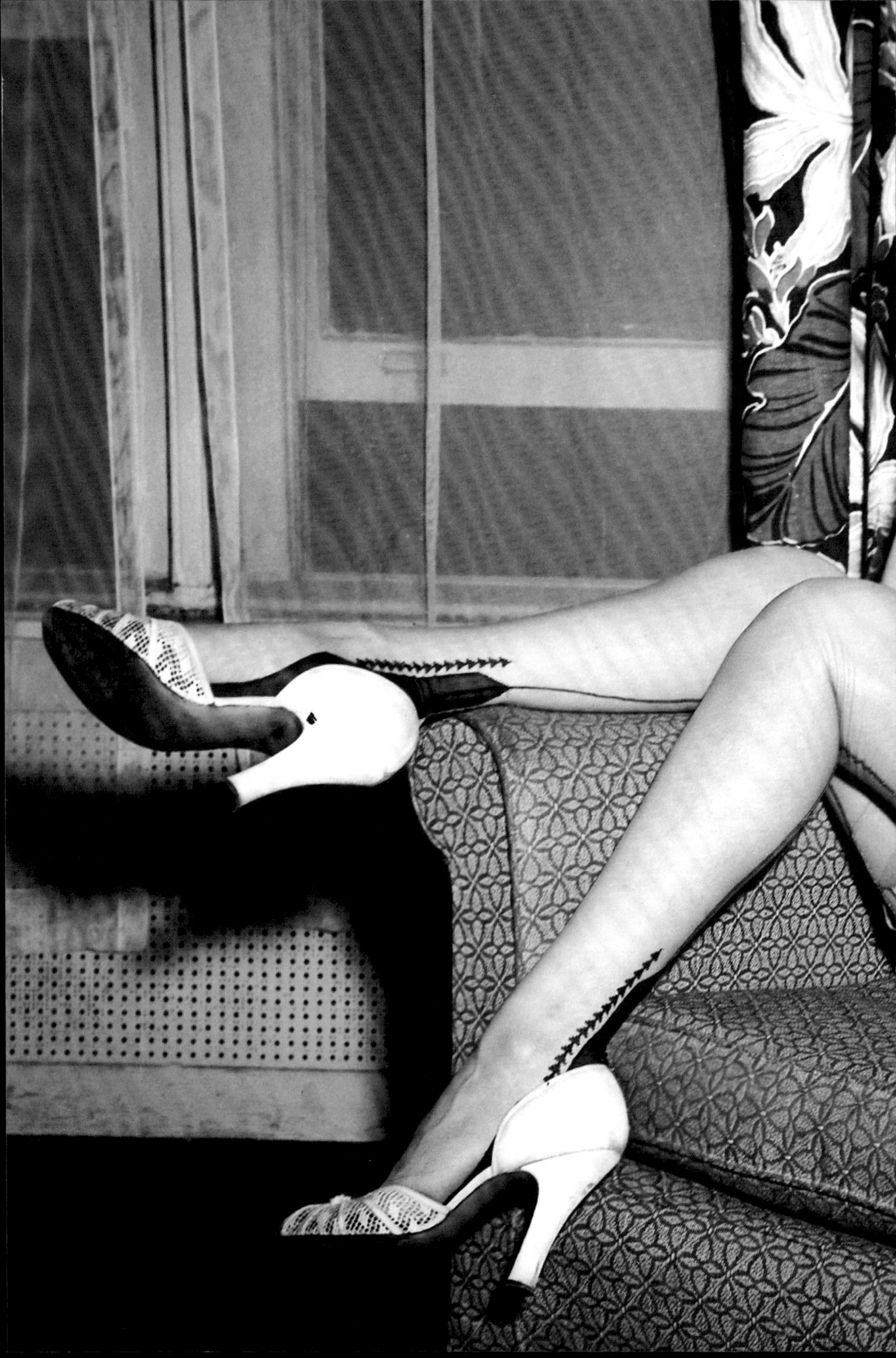

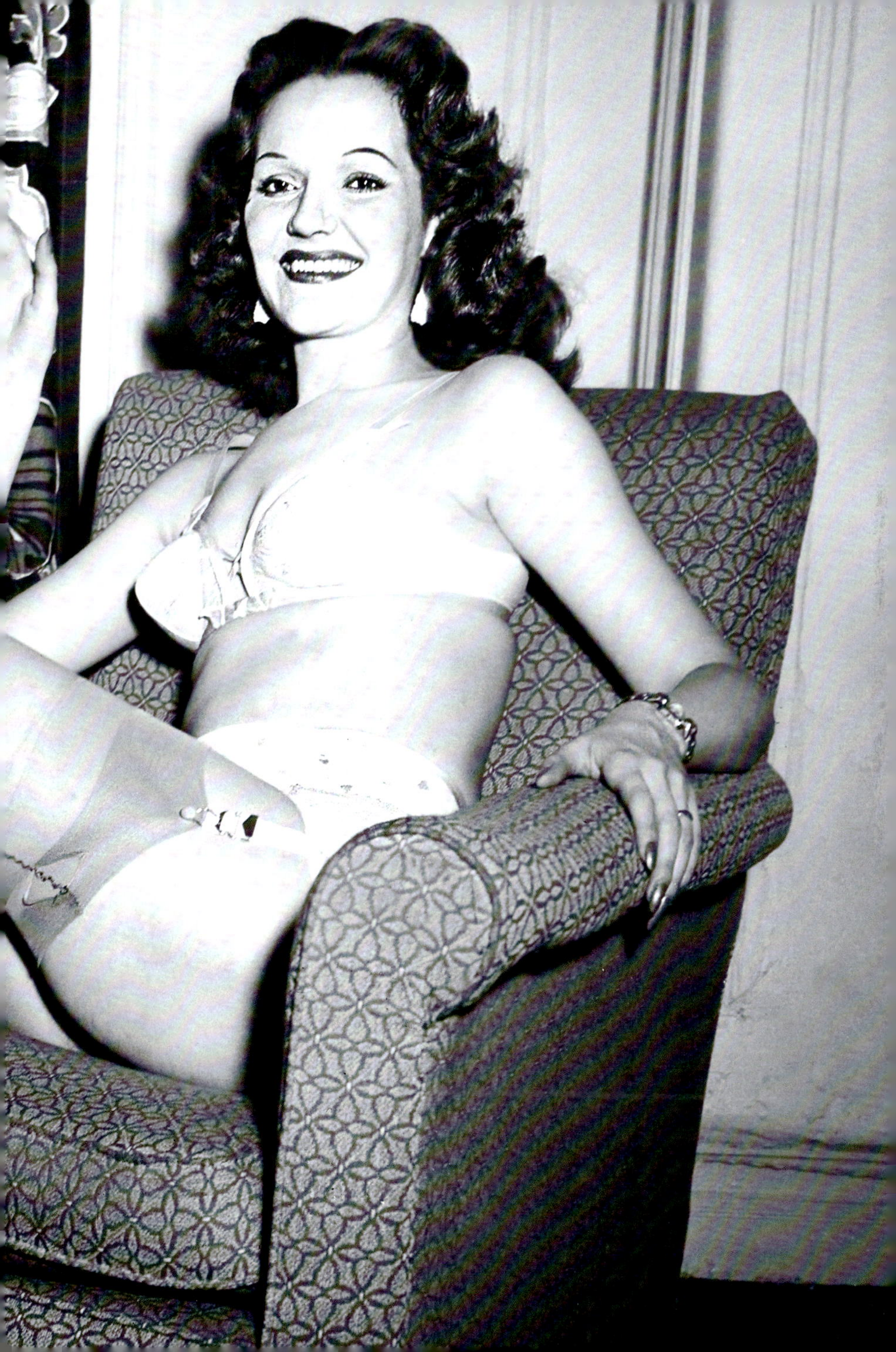

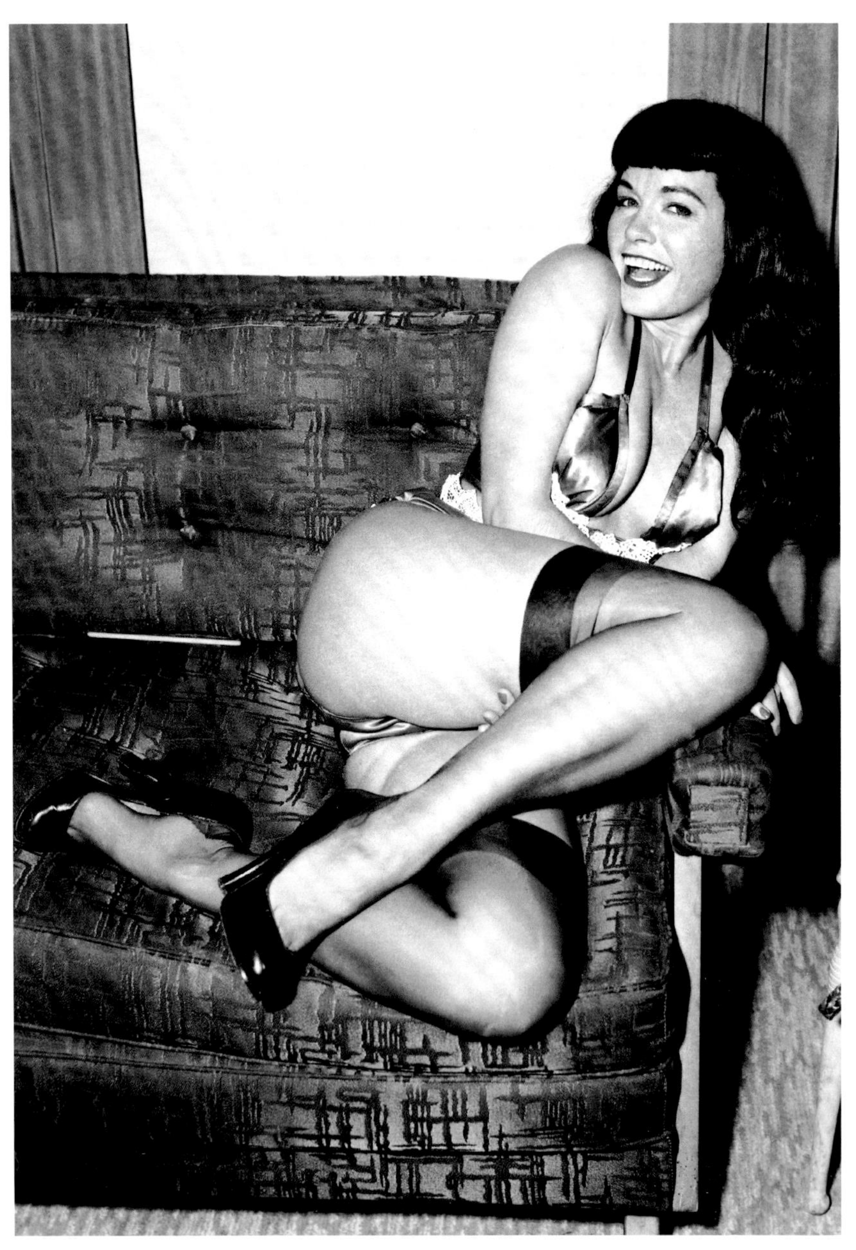

PAGES 66-67 Eleanor Vidor, PAULA KLAW   ABOVE AND OPPOSITE Bettie Page, PAULA KLAW

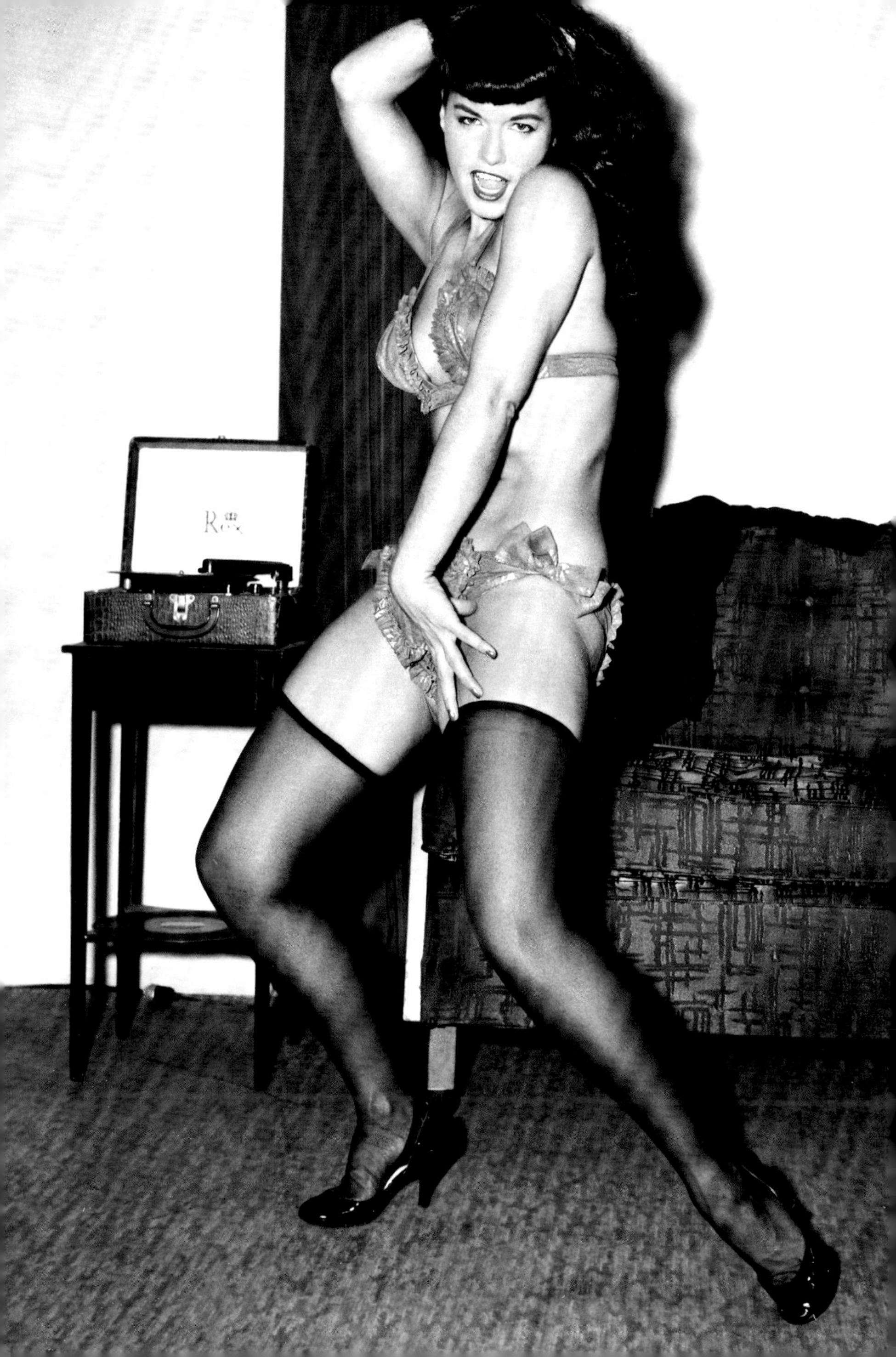

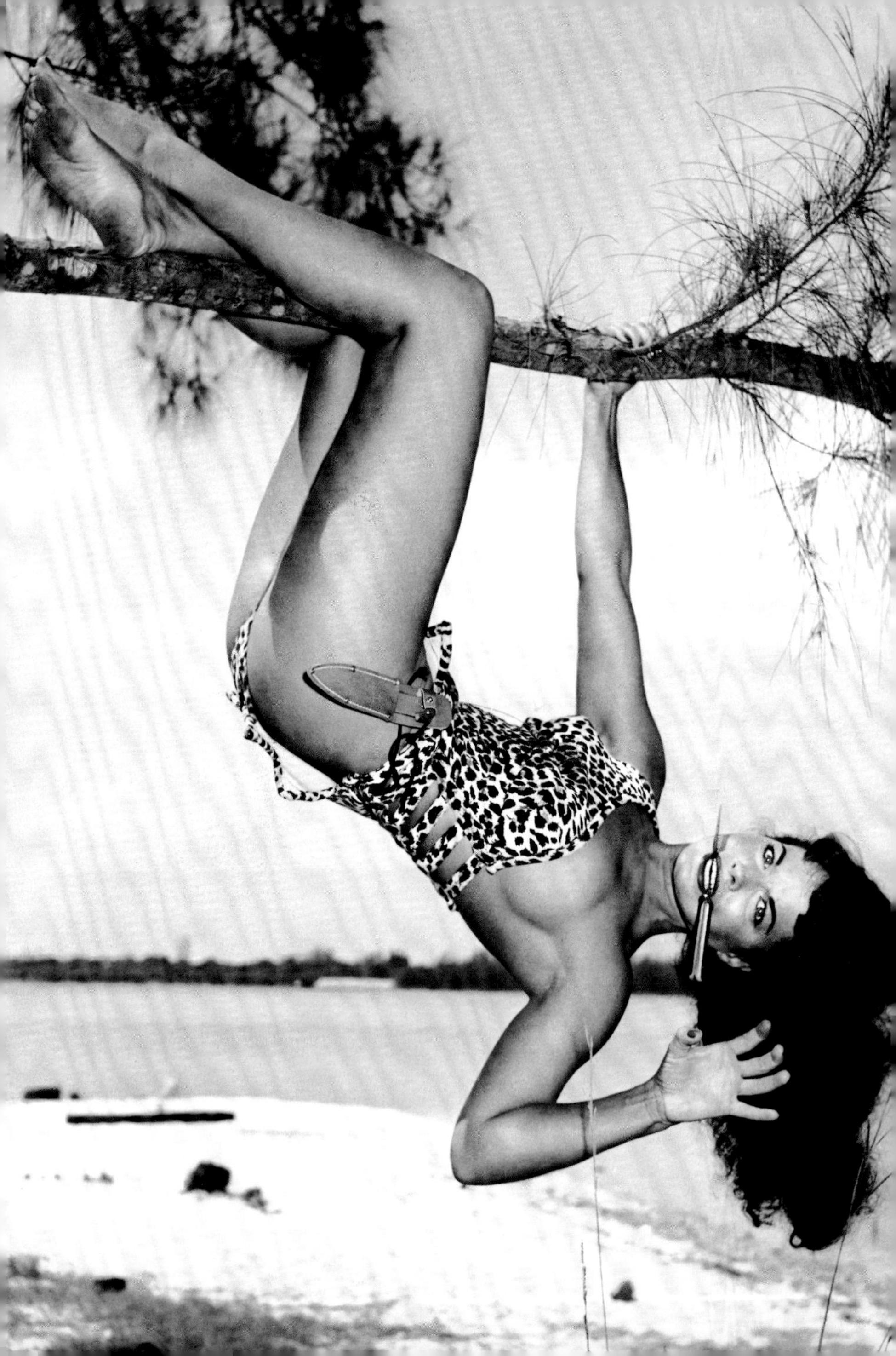

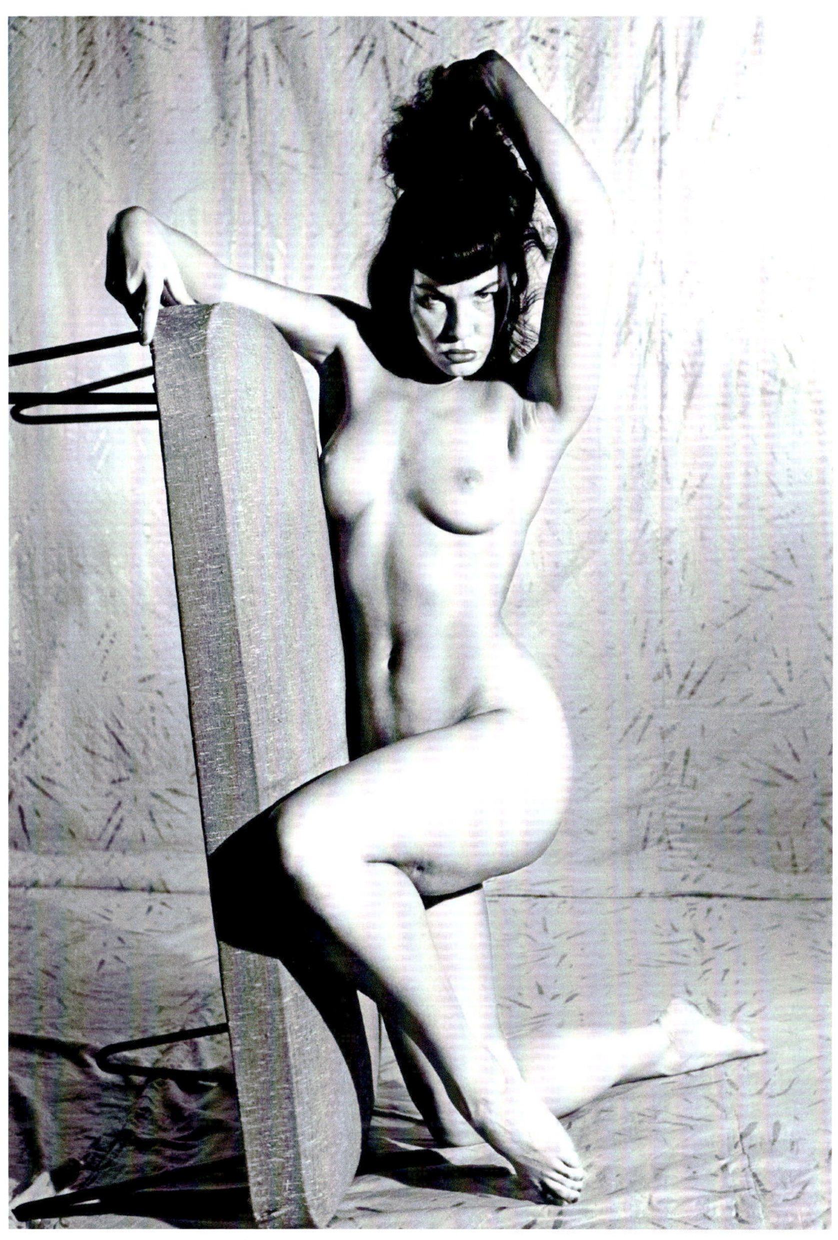

OPPOSITE AND ABOVE Bettie Page, BUNNY YEAGER

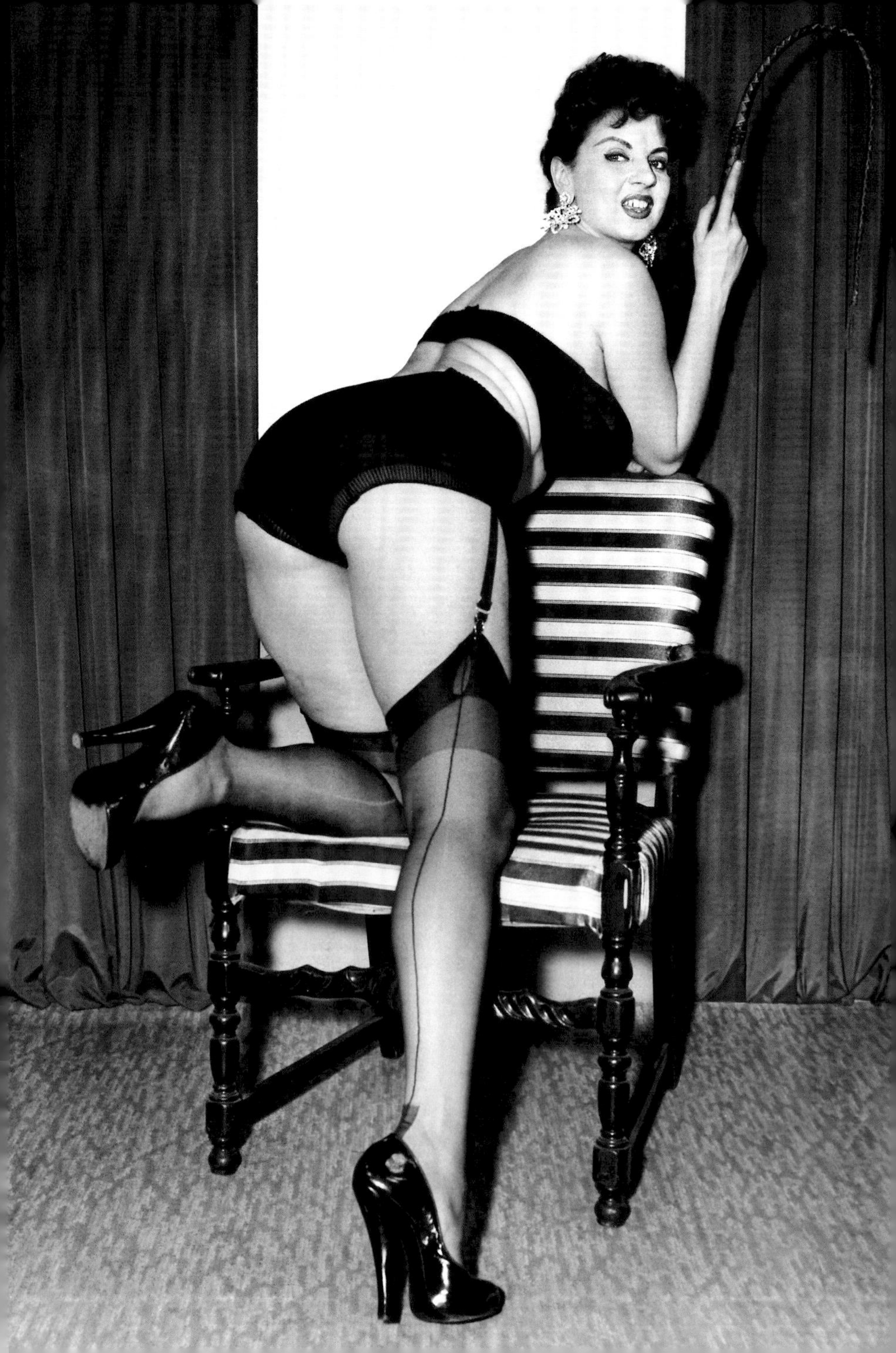

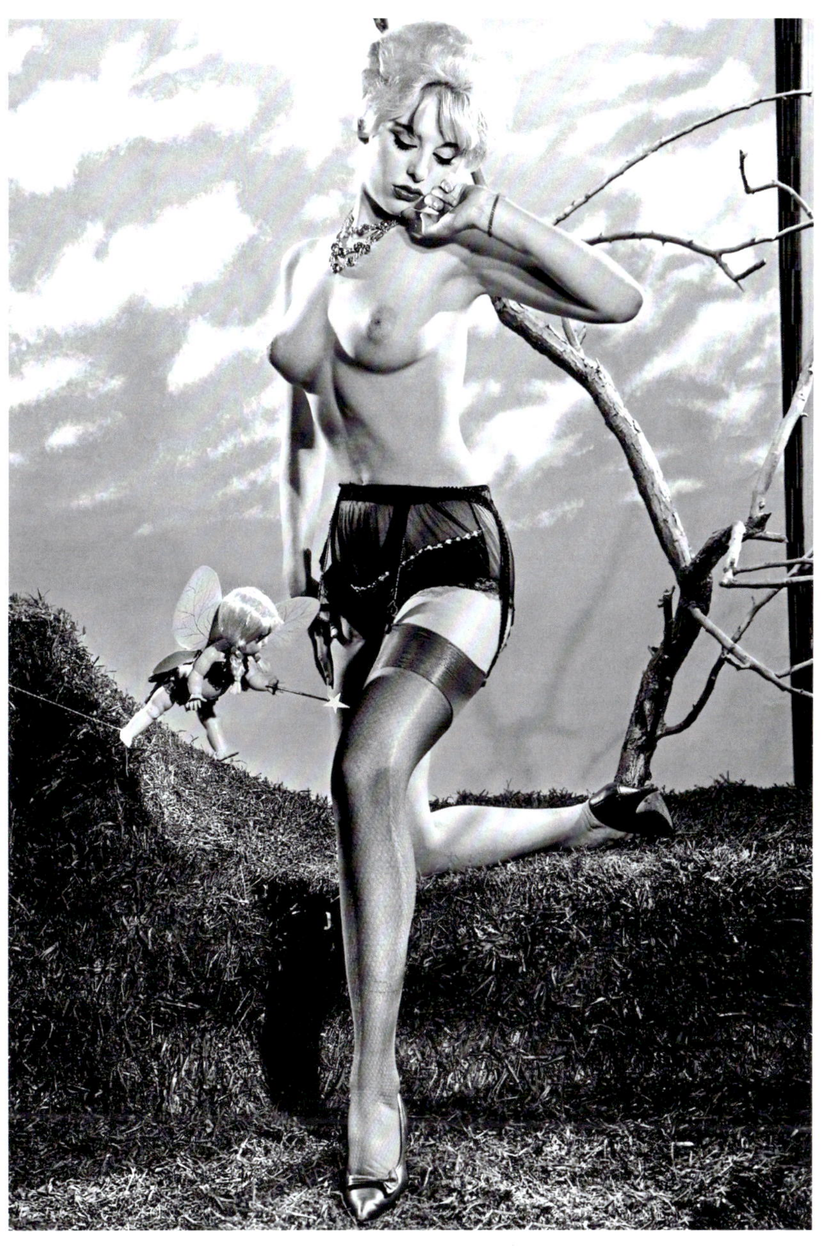

OPPOSITE Jackie Miller, PAULA KLAW   ABOVE Unknown

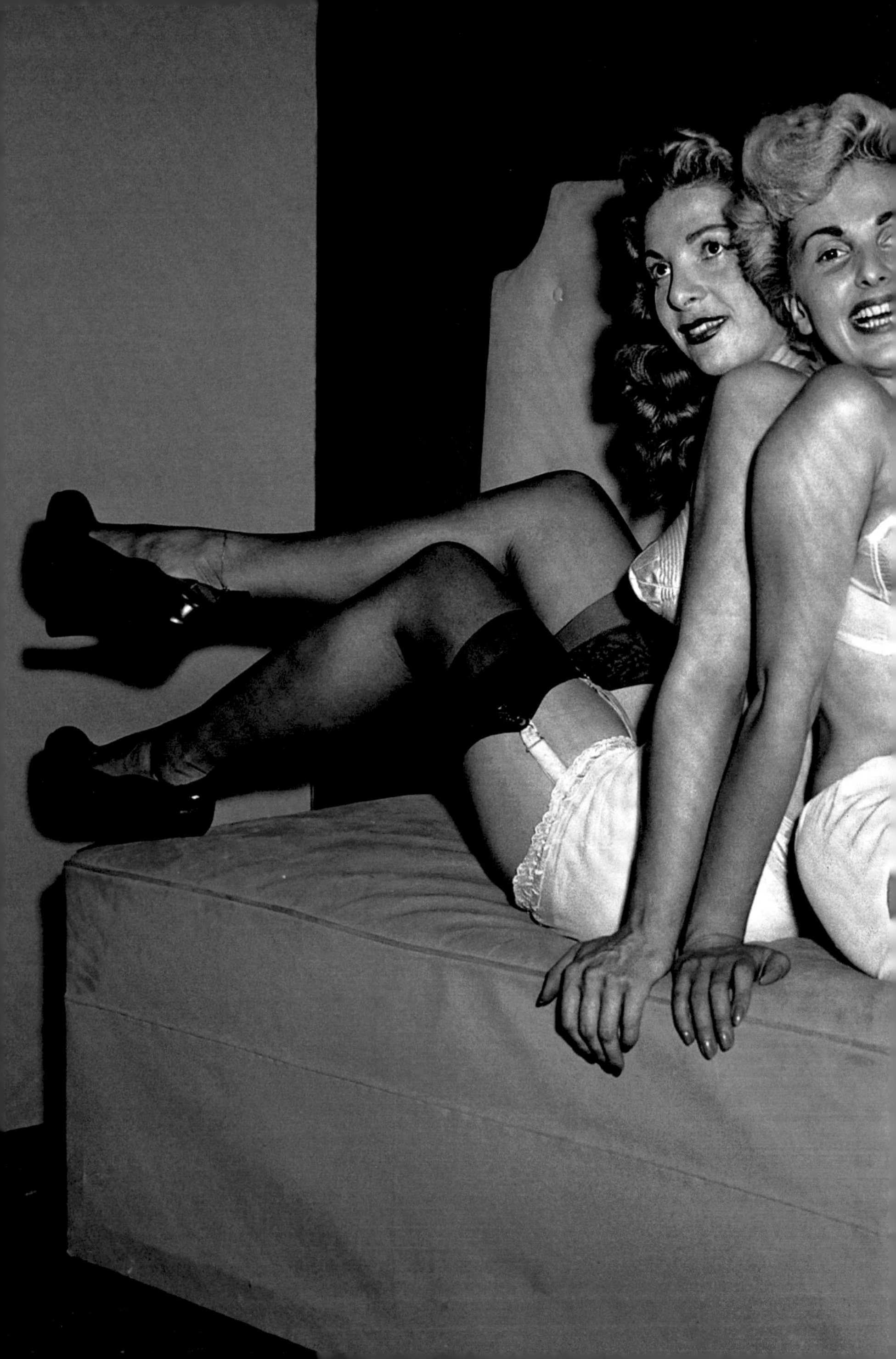

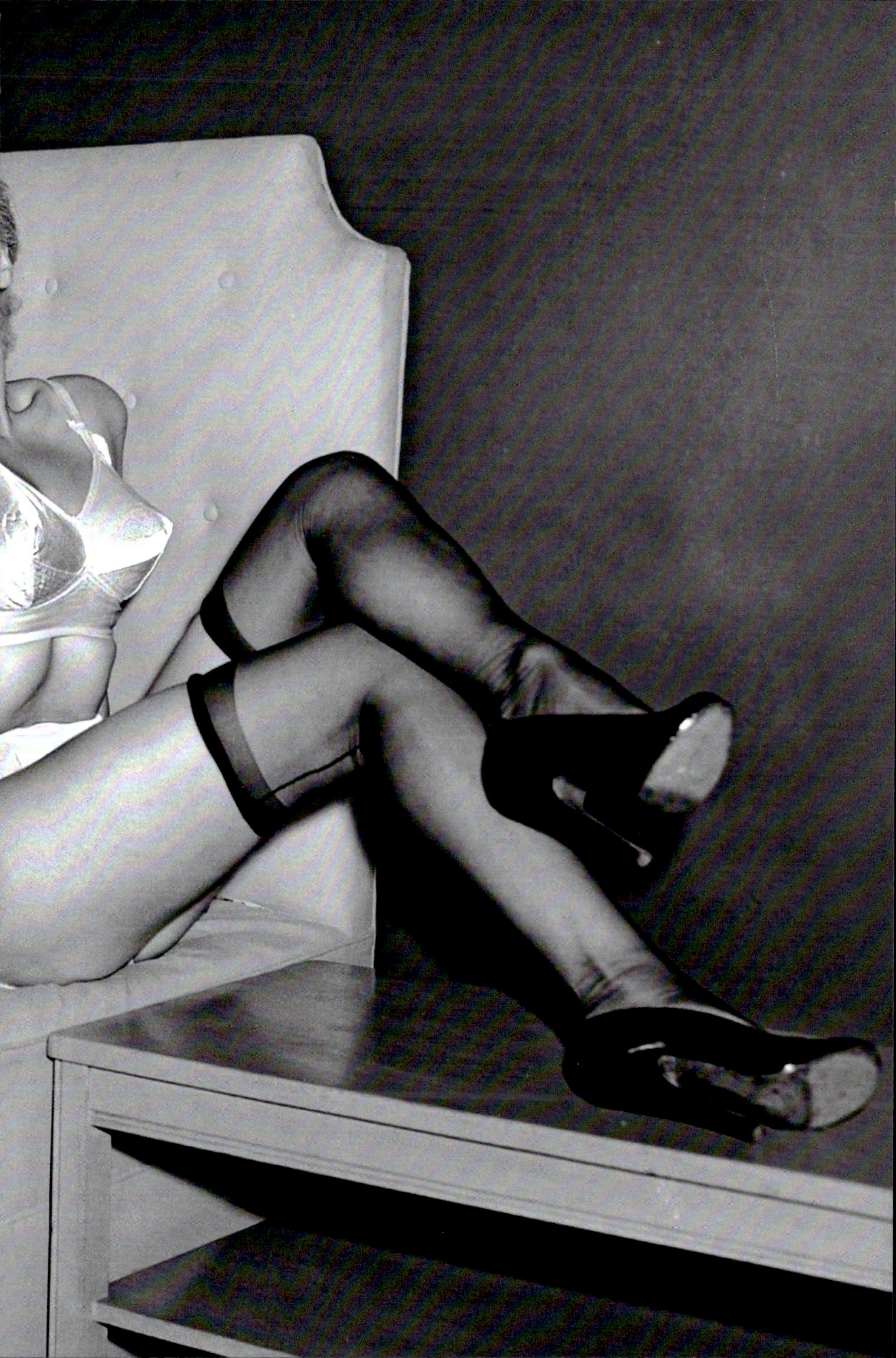

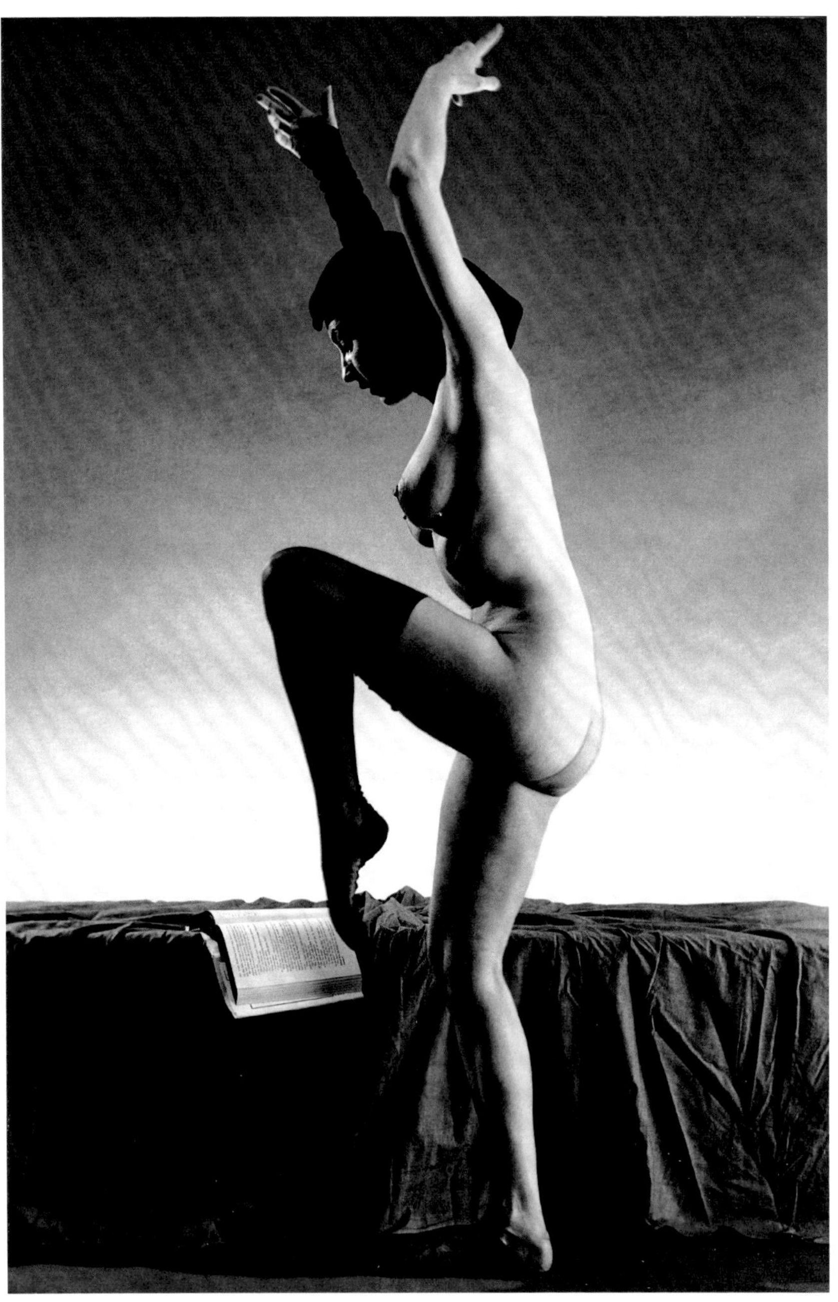

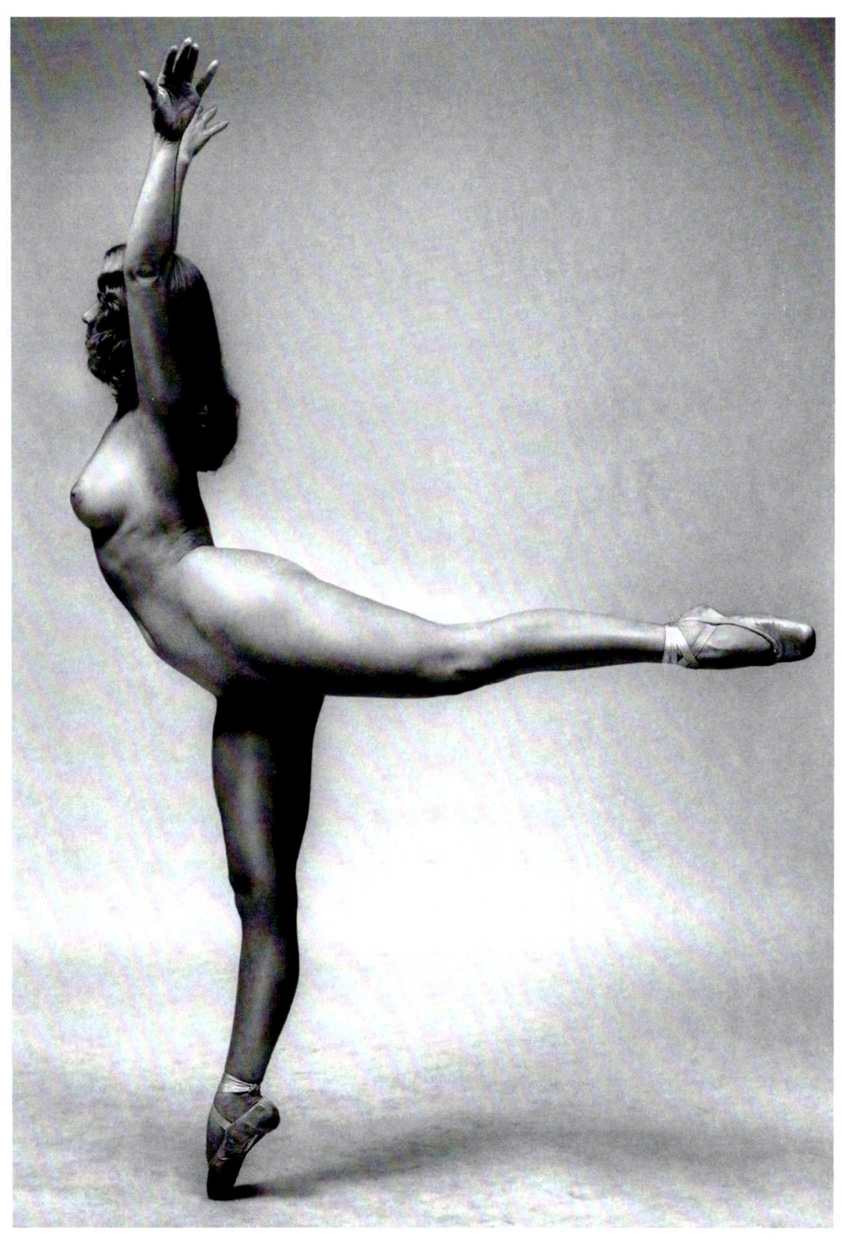

PAGES 74-75 Busty Brown and friend OPPOSITE Alice Denham ABOVE Diane Webber

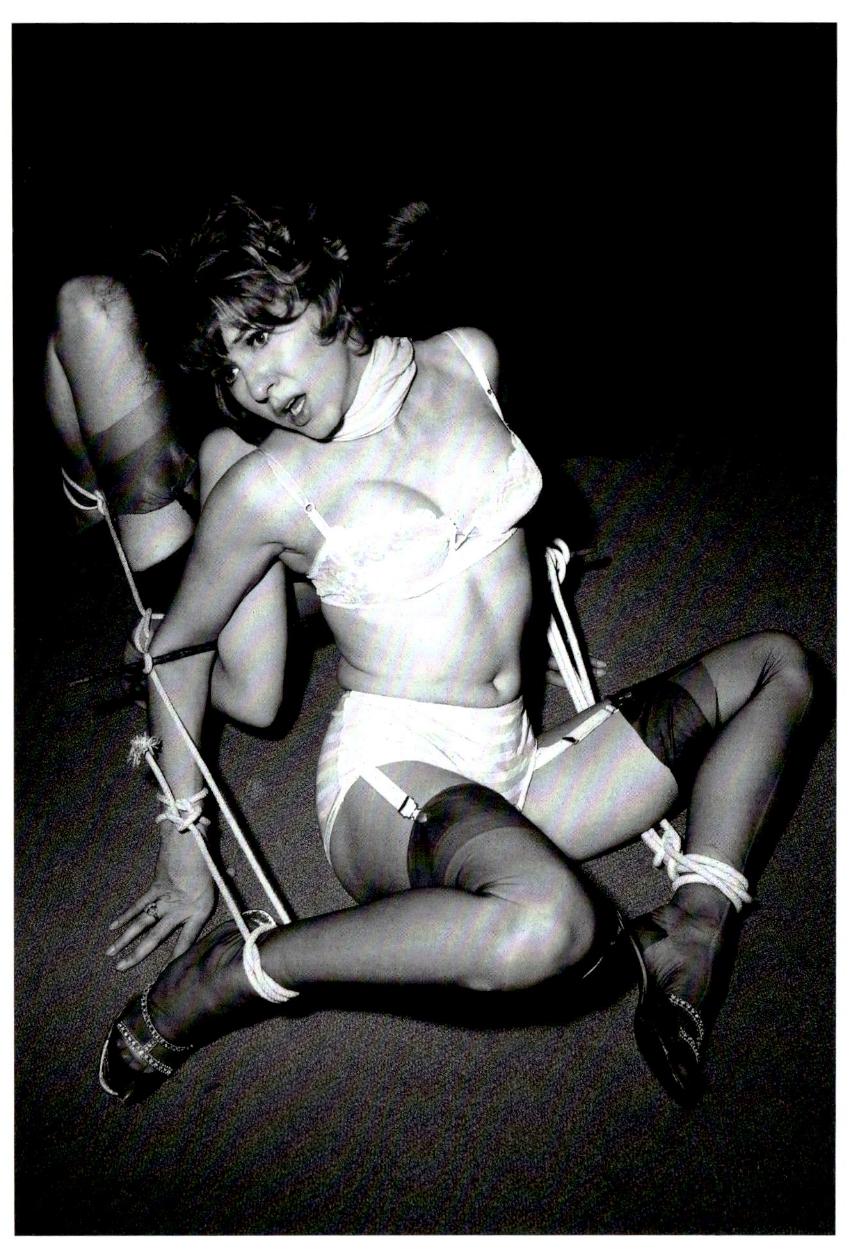

OPPOSITE AND ABOVE Unknown

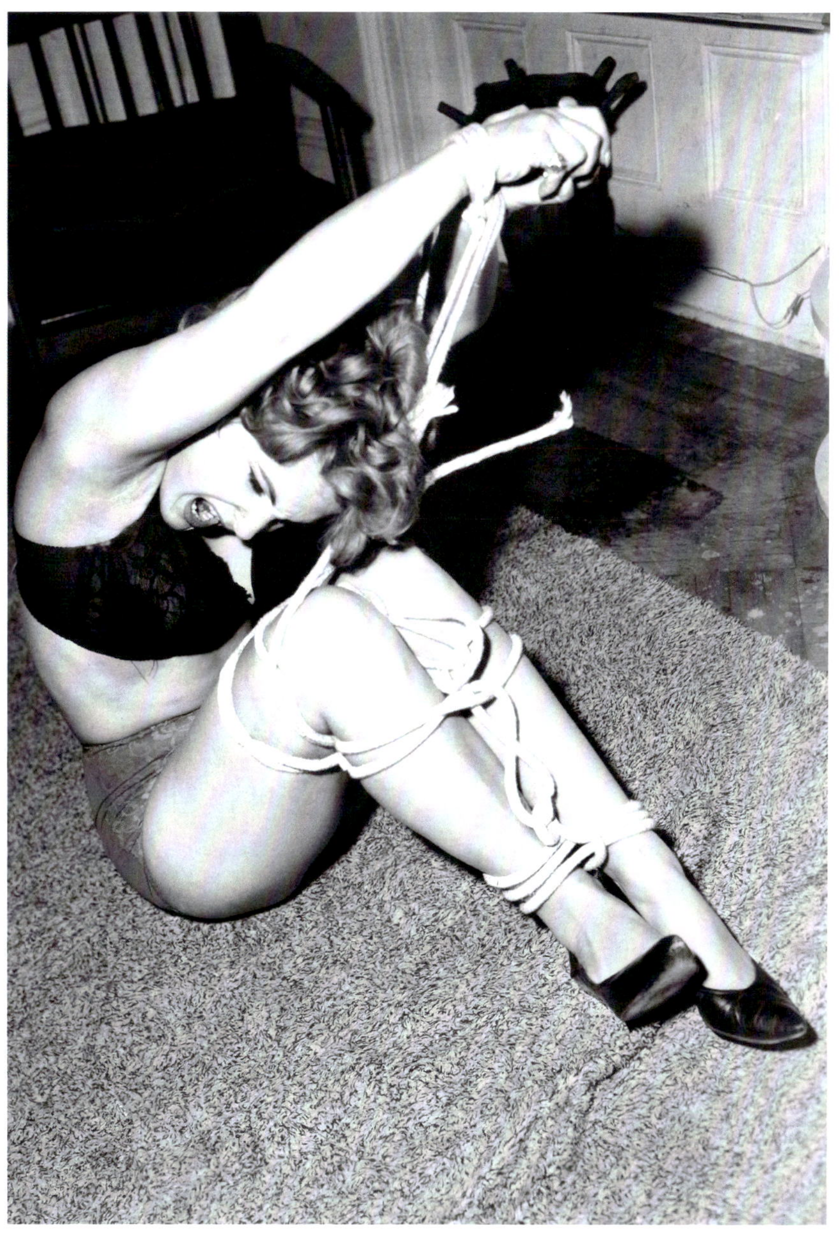

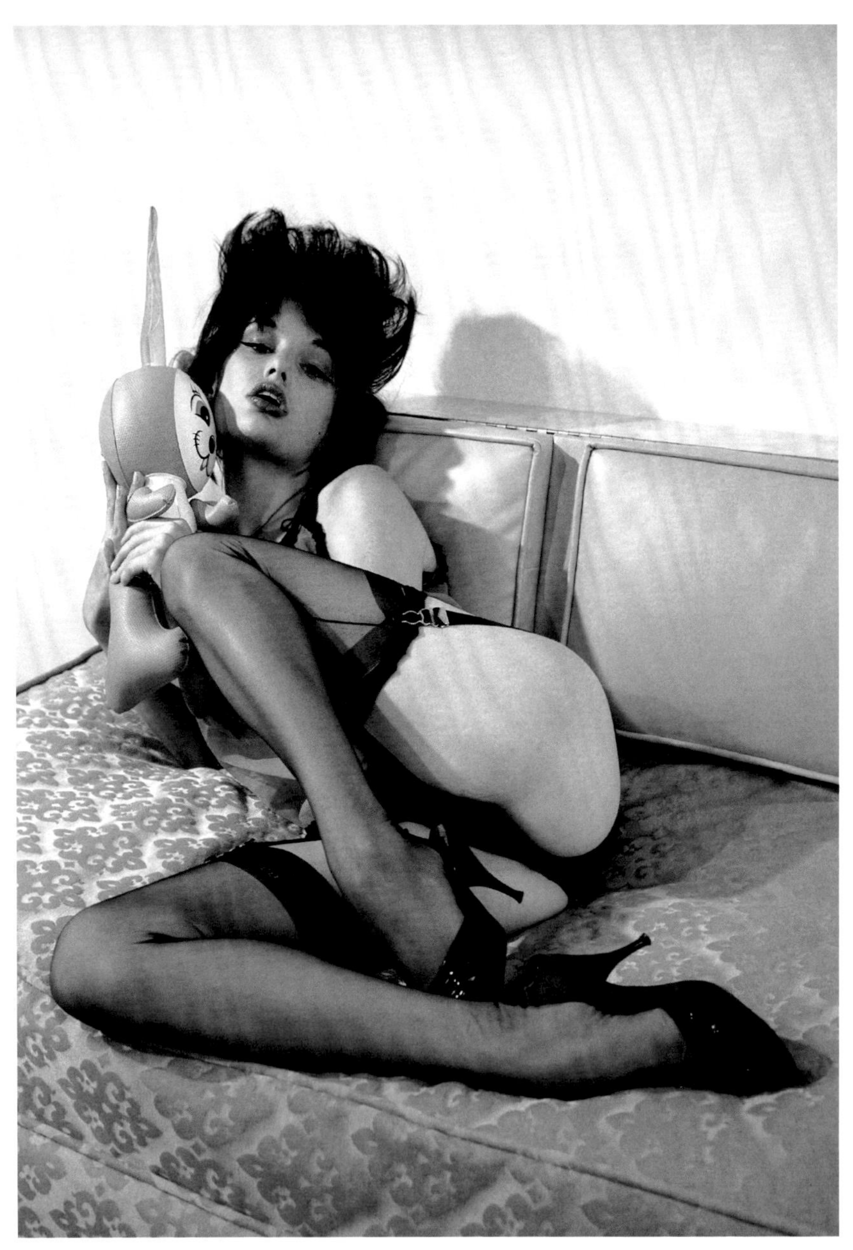

ABOVE Karen Benneto   OPPOSITE Unknown   PAGES 82-83 Unknown, ELMER BATTERS

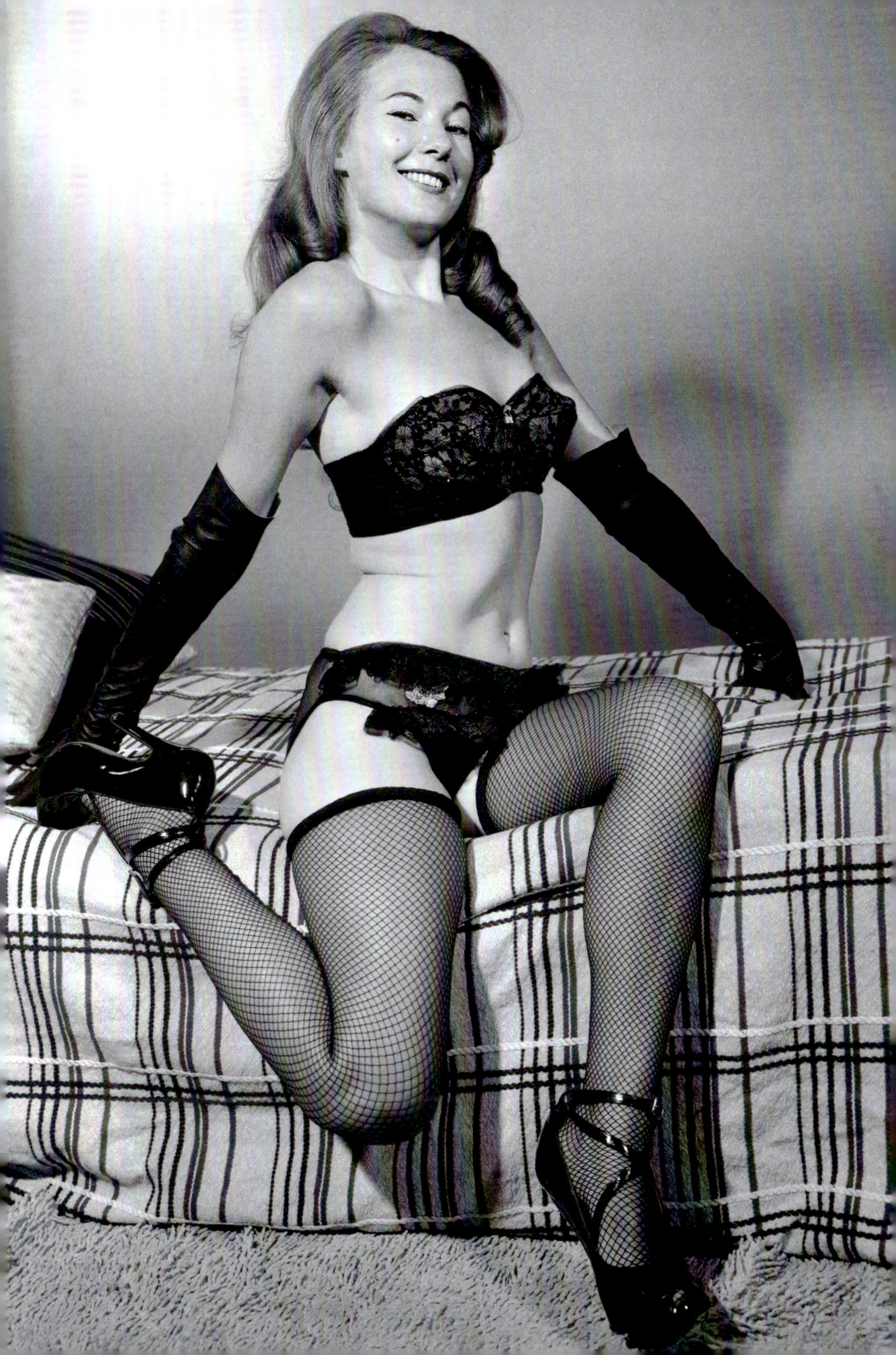

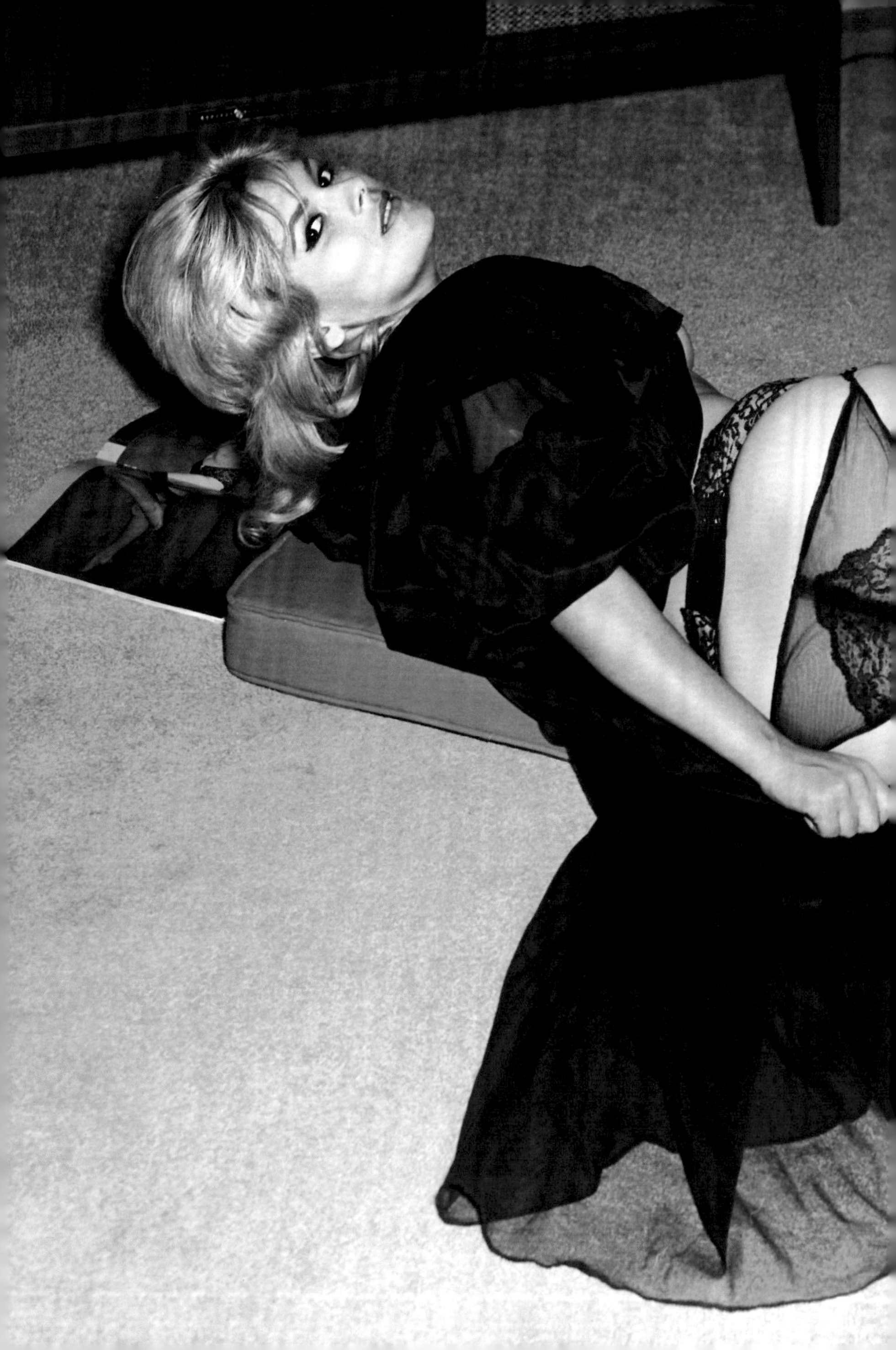

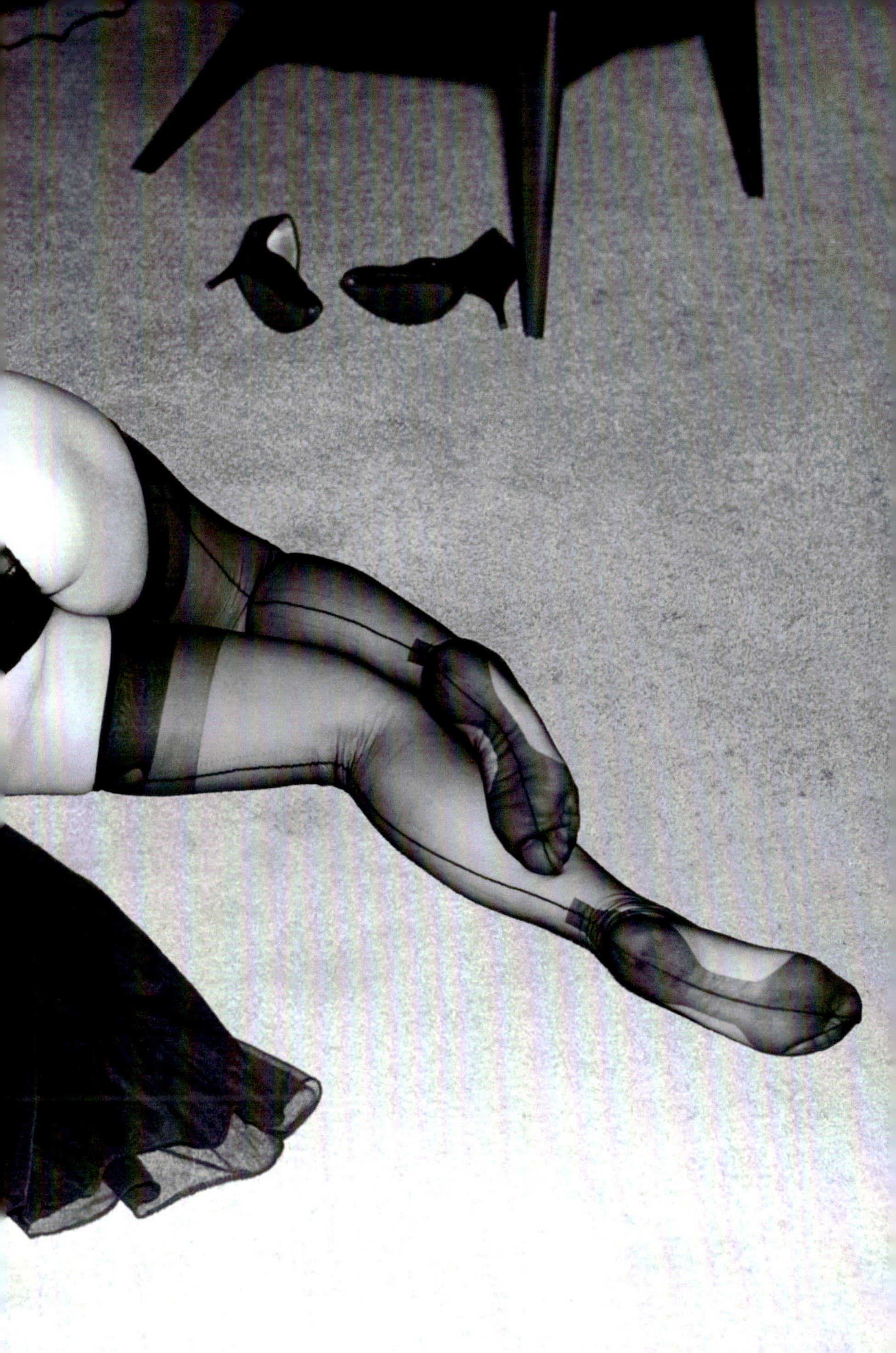

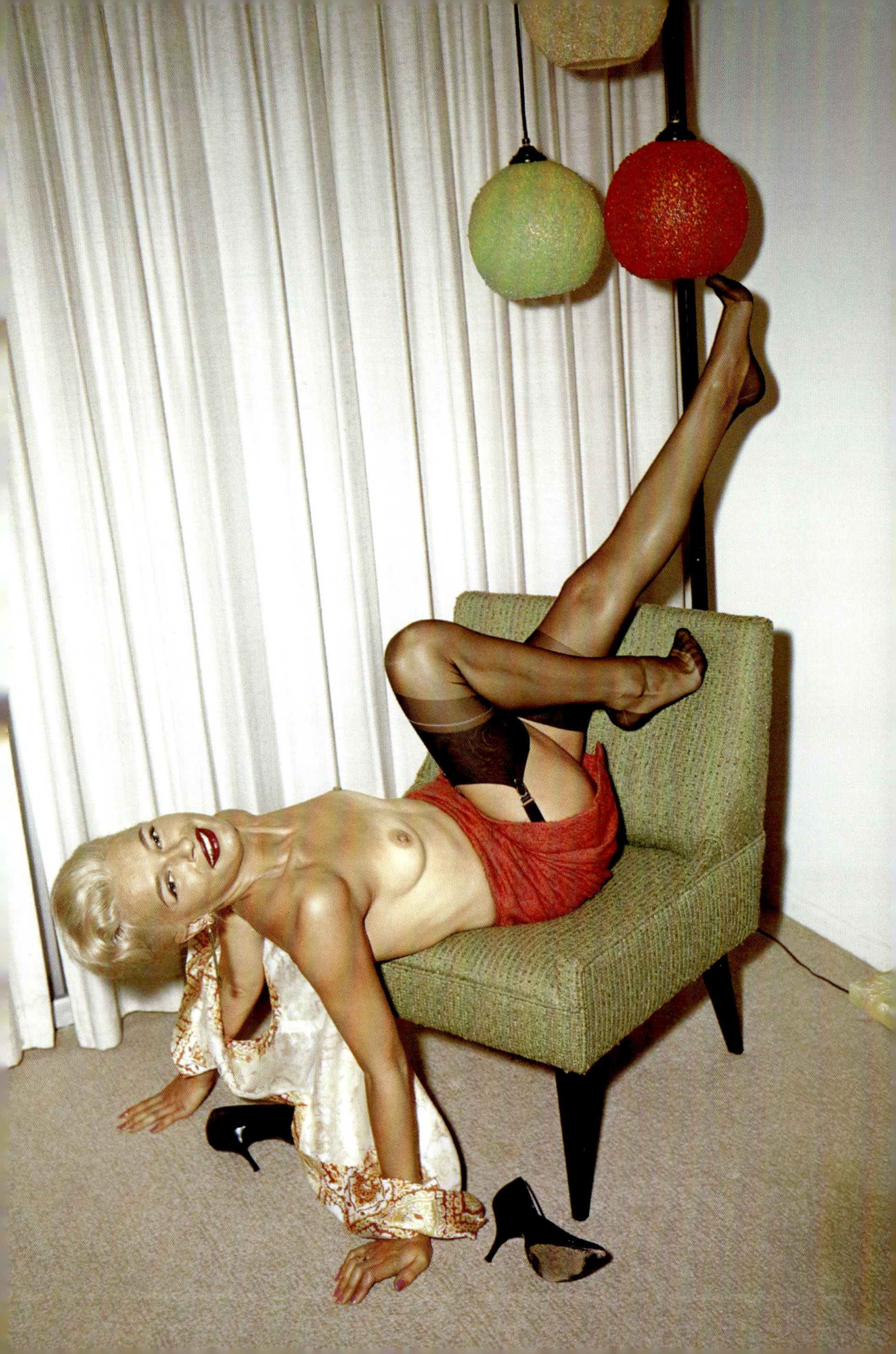

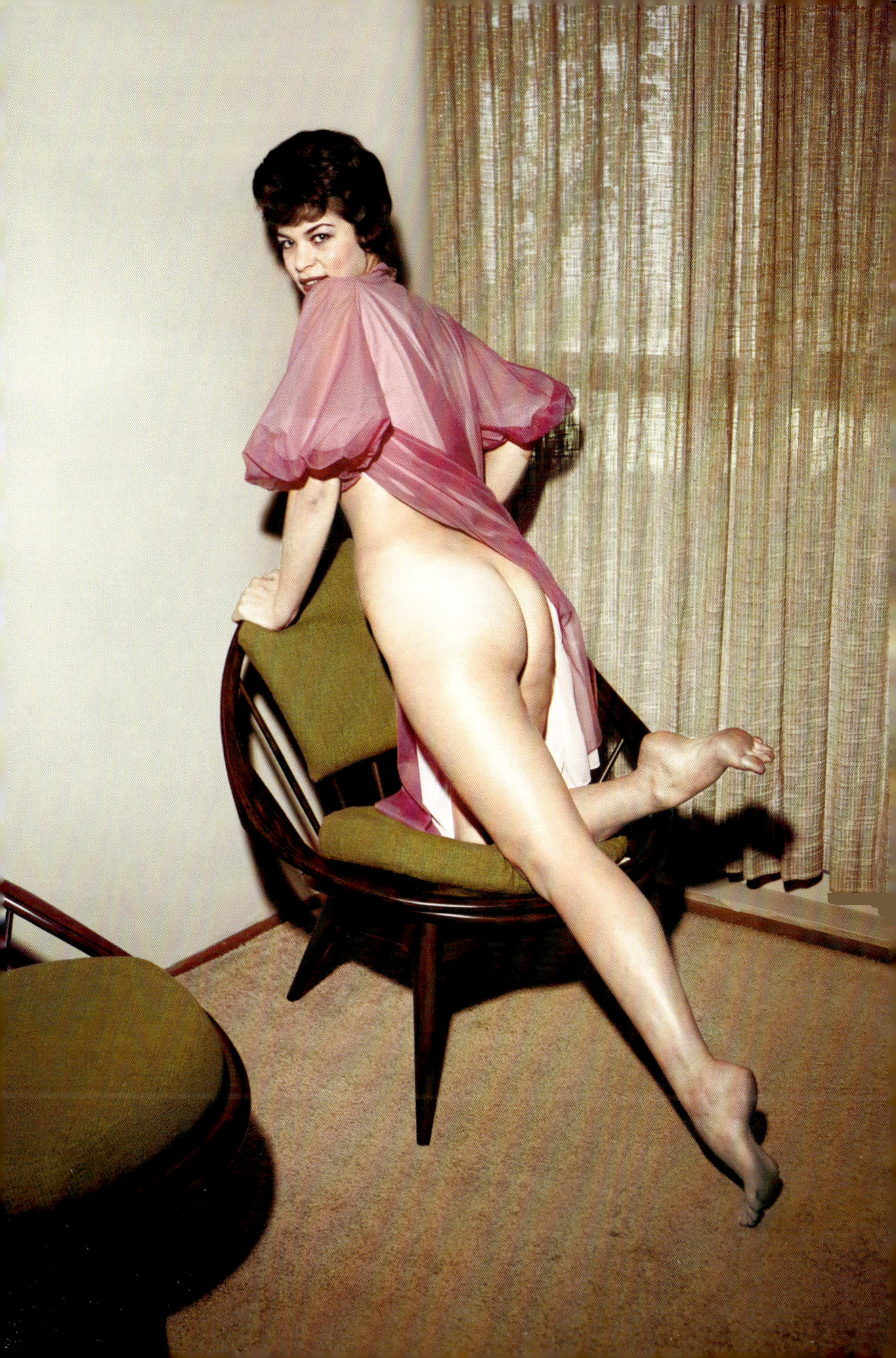

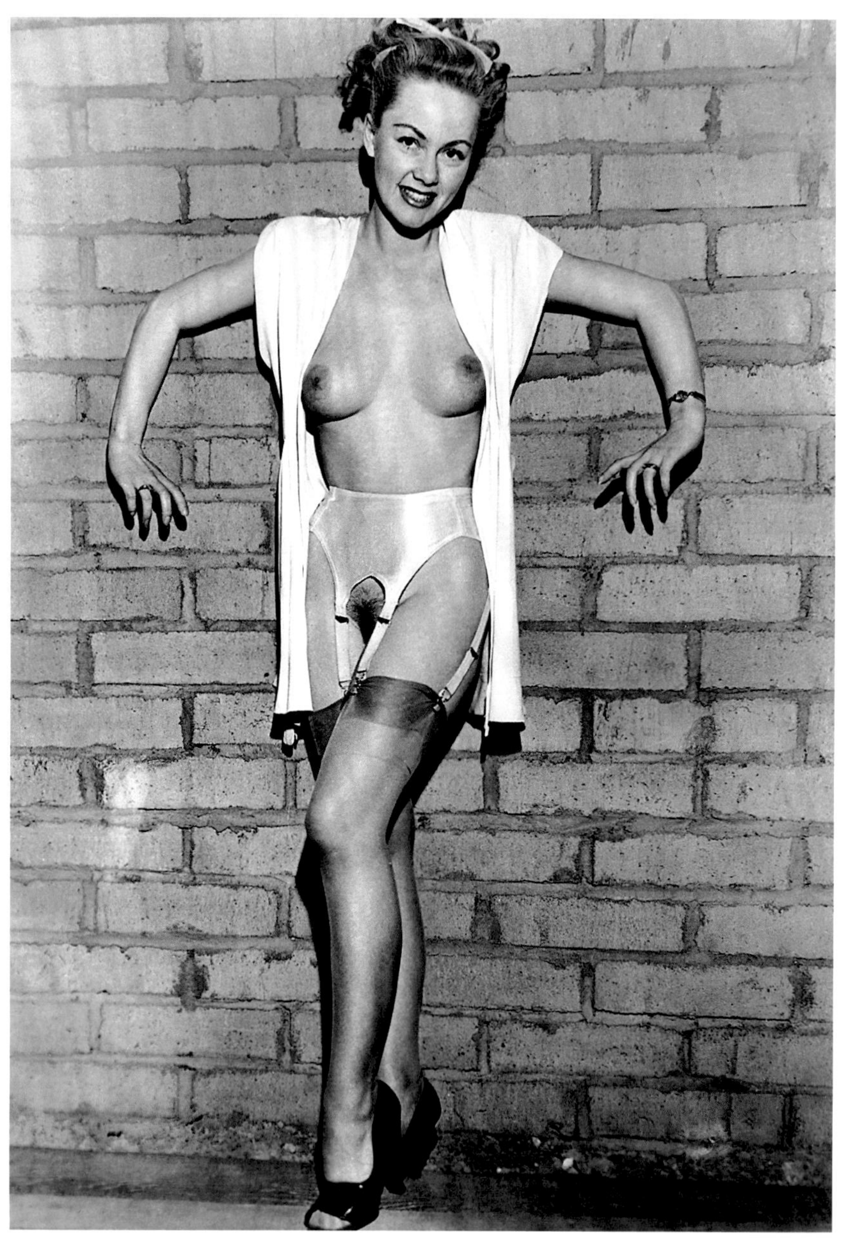

PAGES 84-85 **Both unknown**, ELMER BATTERS

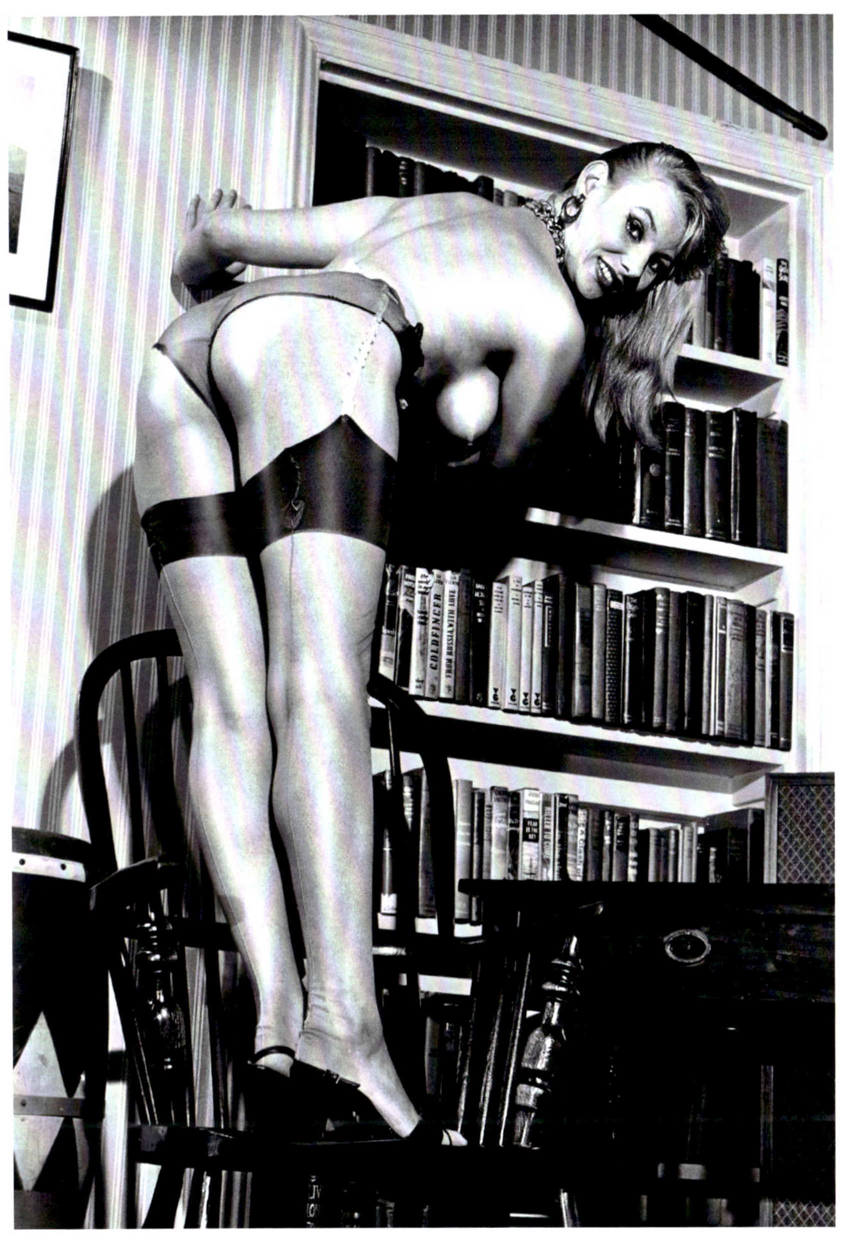

OPPOSITE AND ABOVE Unknown

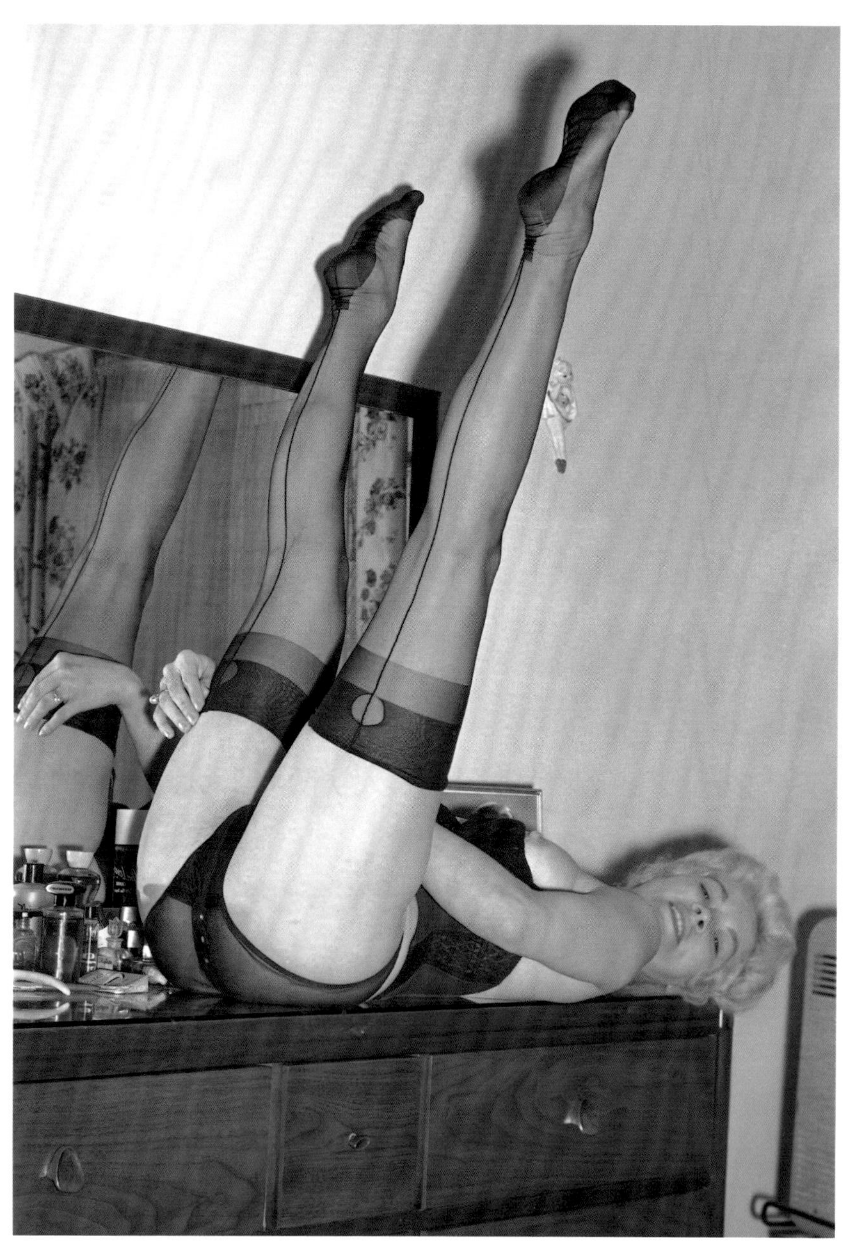

ABOVE AND OPPOSITE Unknown   PAGES 90-91 Jackie Miller, PAULA KLAW

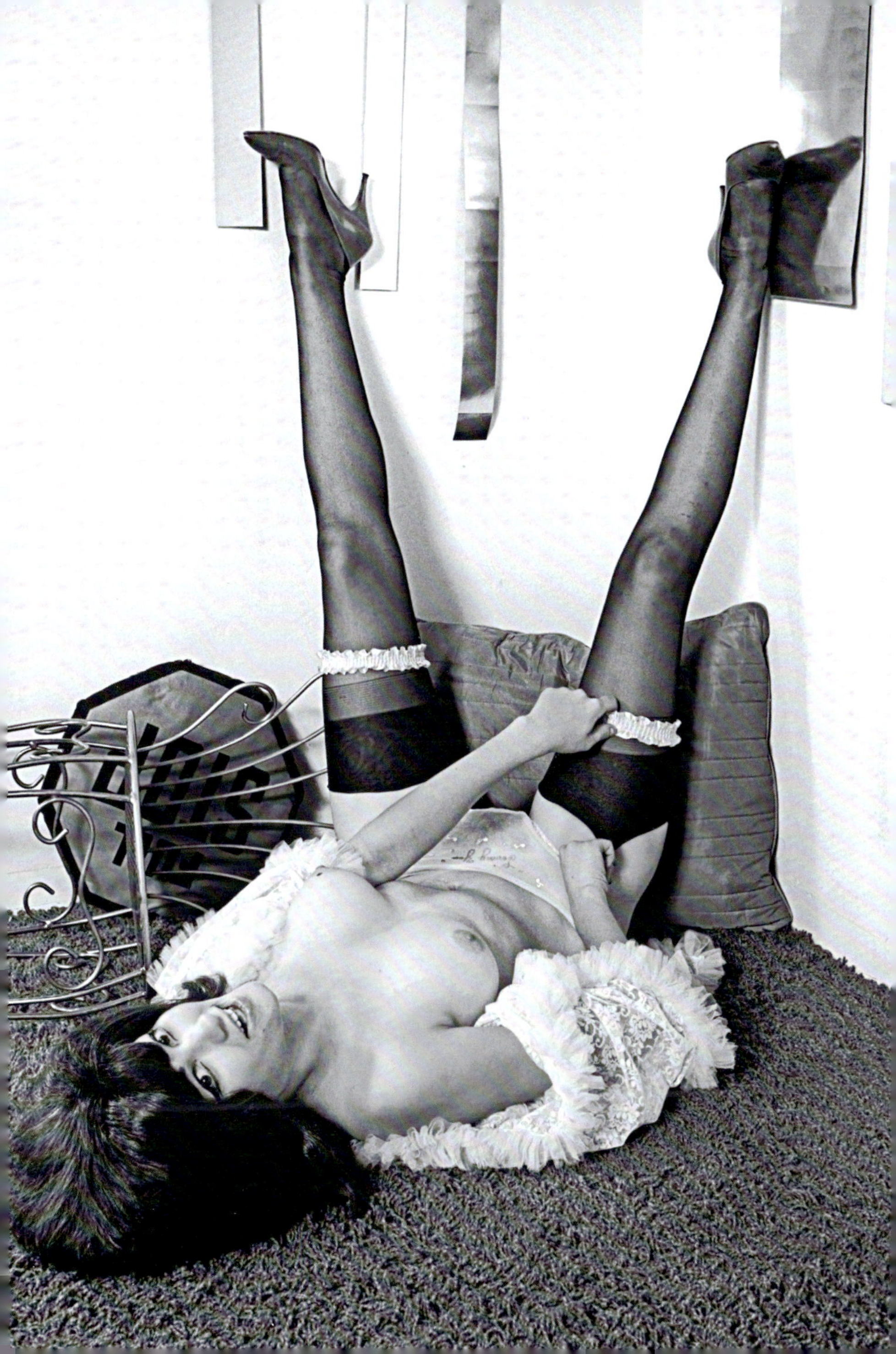

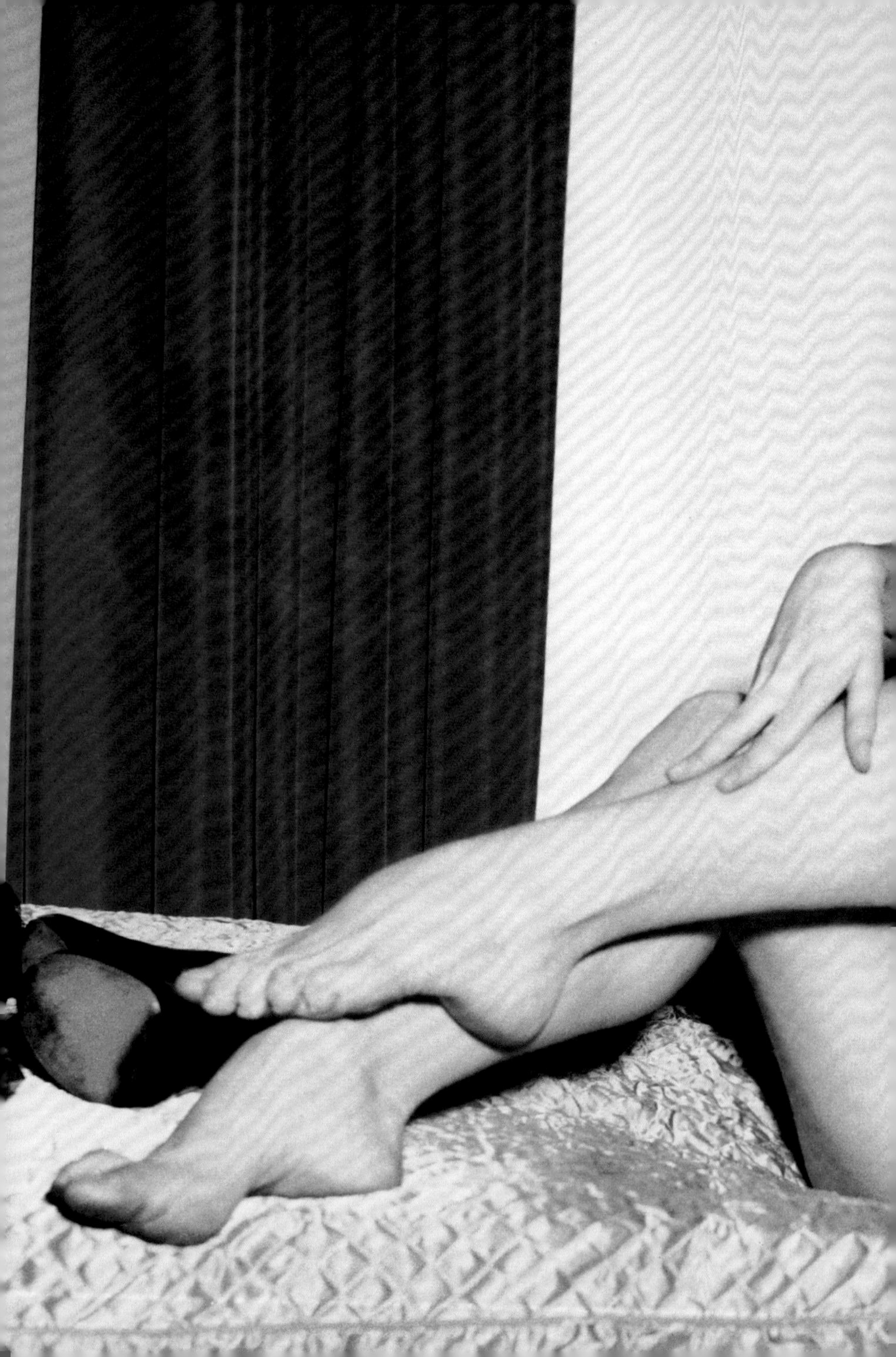

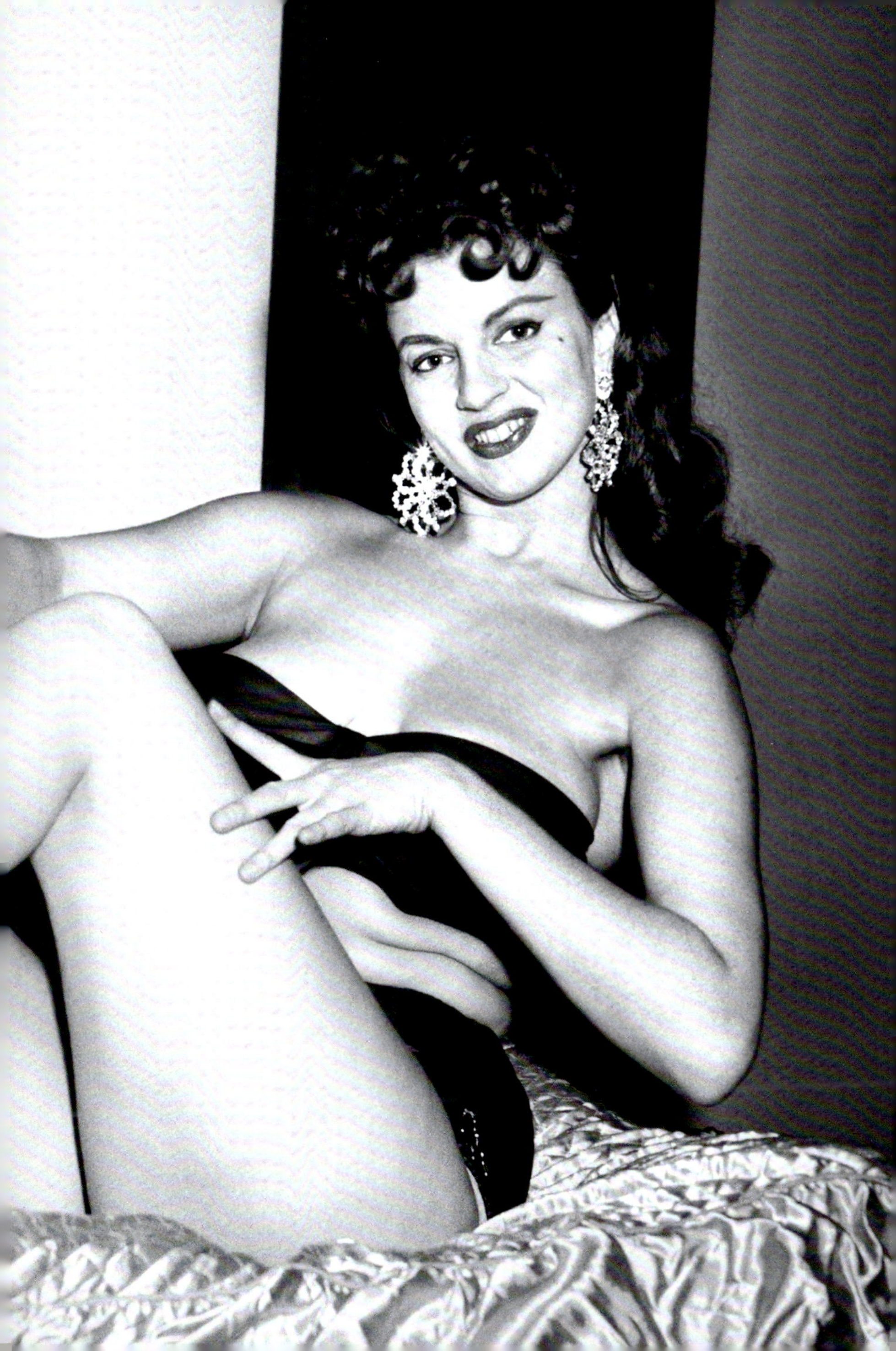

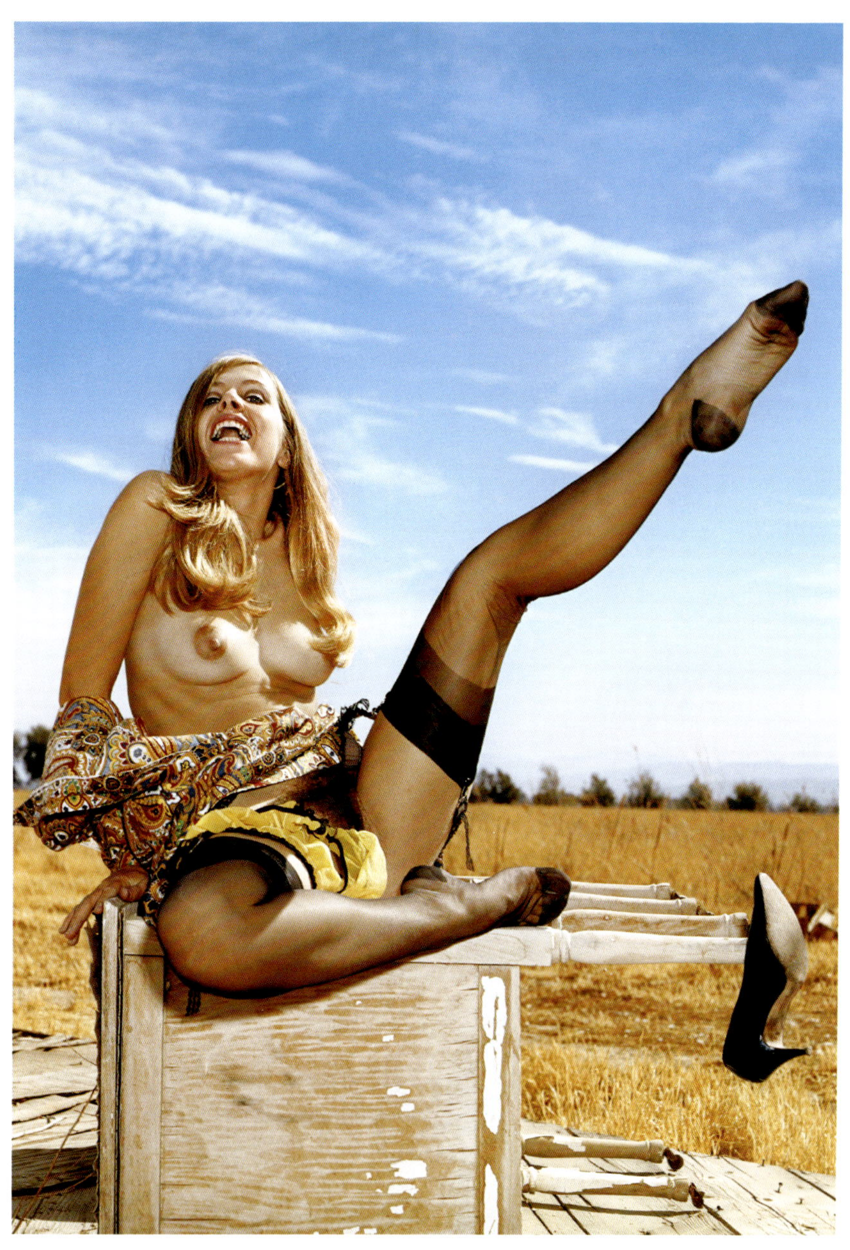

ABOVE Unknown, ELMER BATTERS   OPPOSITE Carla

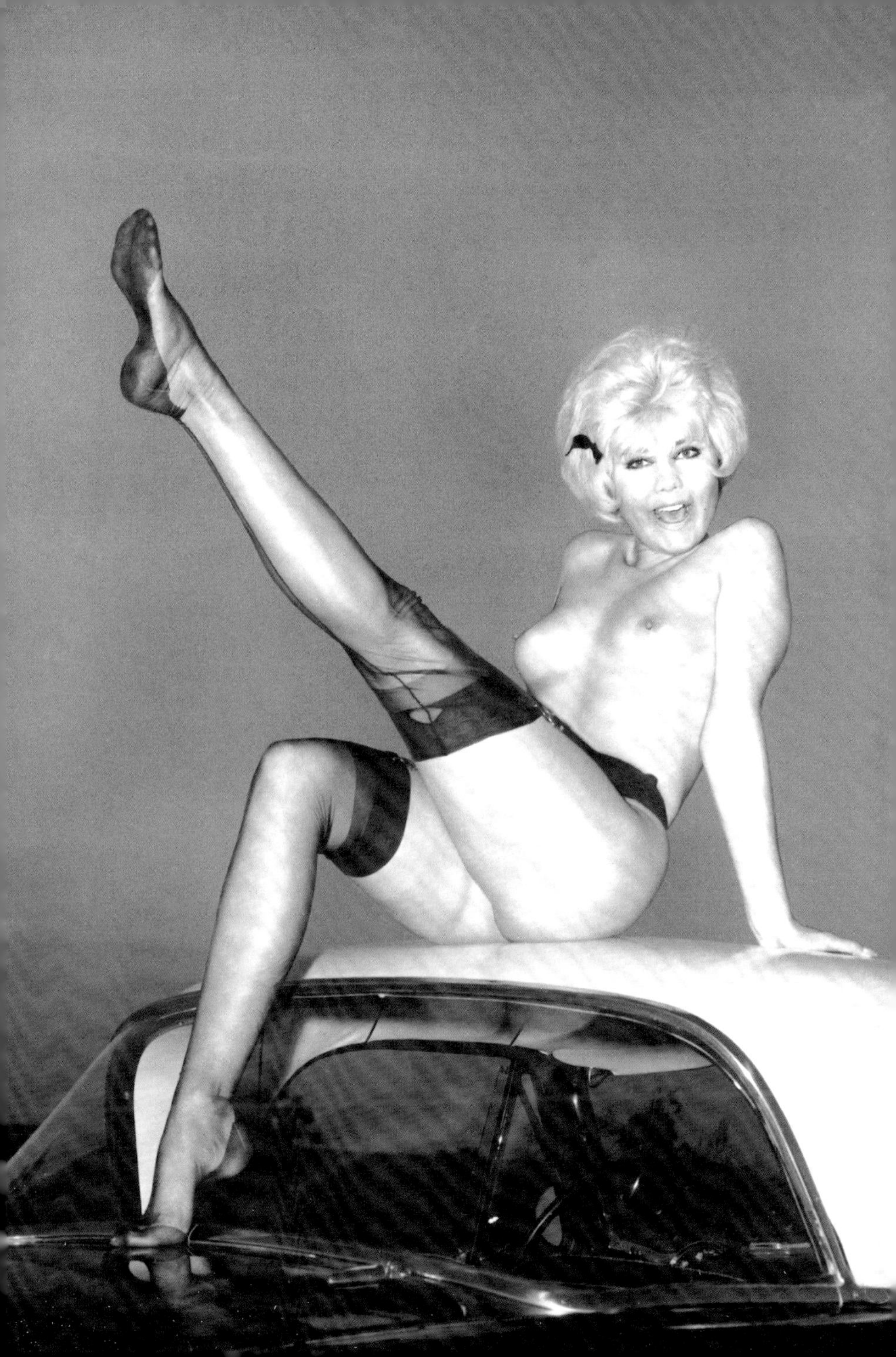

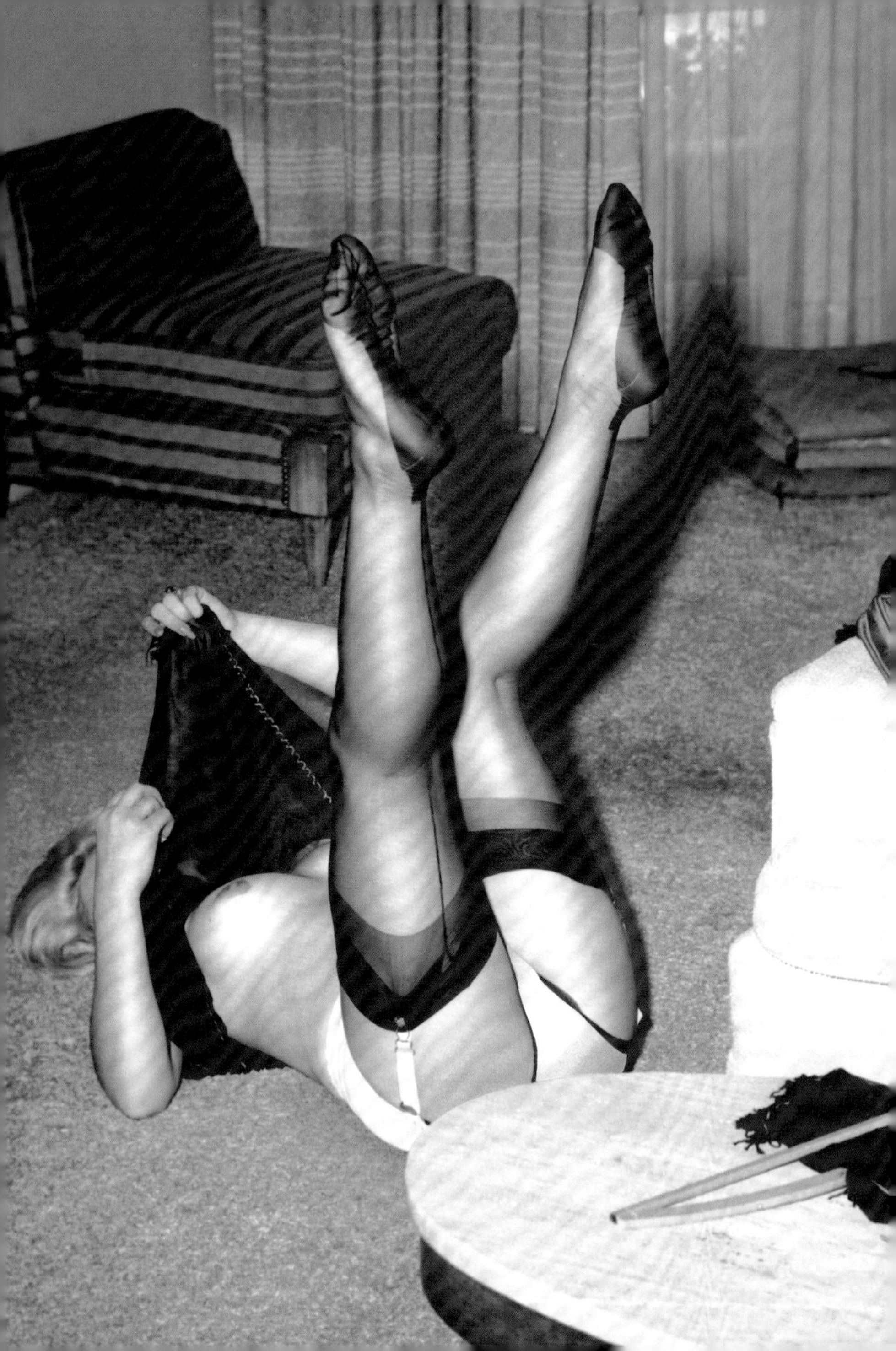

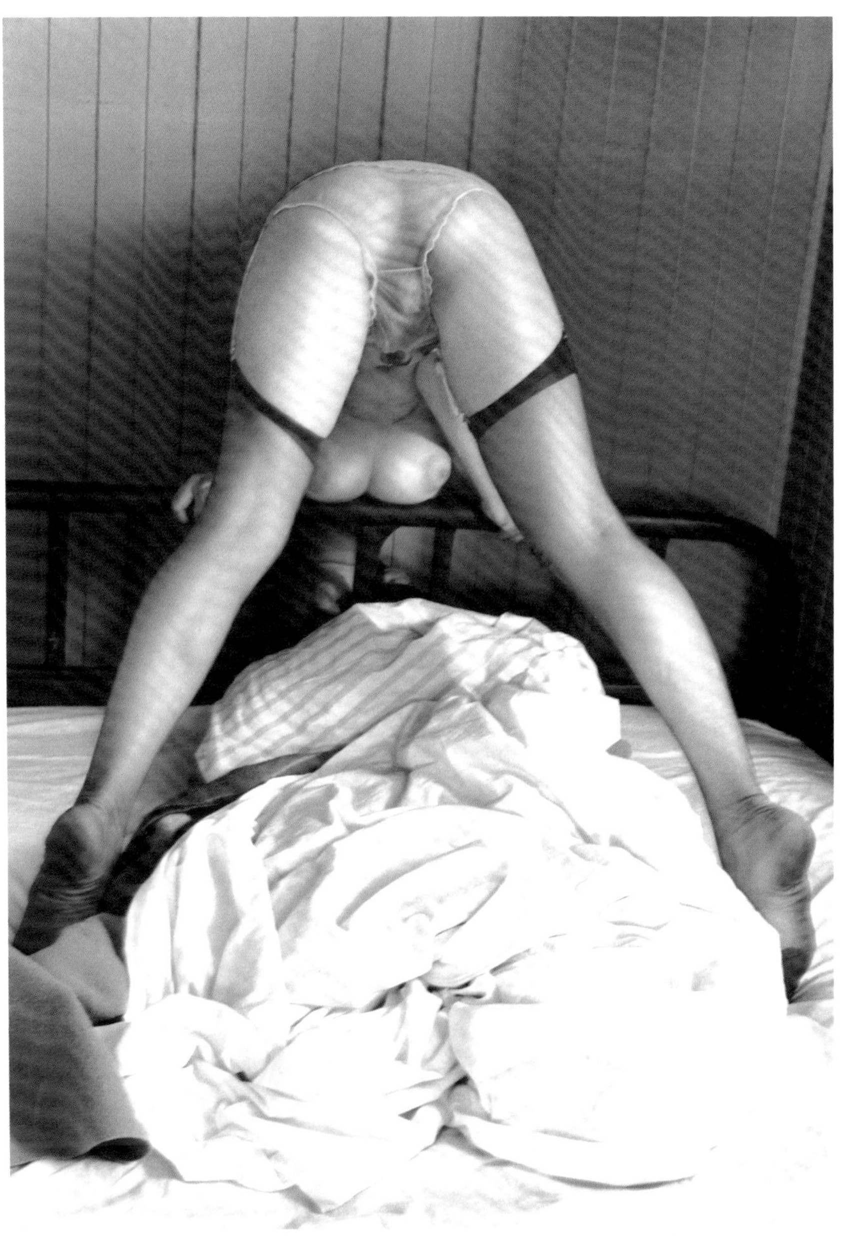

OPPOSITE Denise DuBois   ABOVE Pam McKnight   PAGES 96-97 Unknown

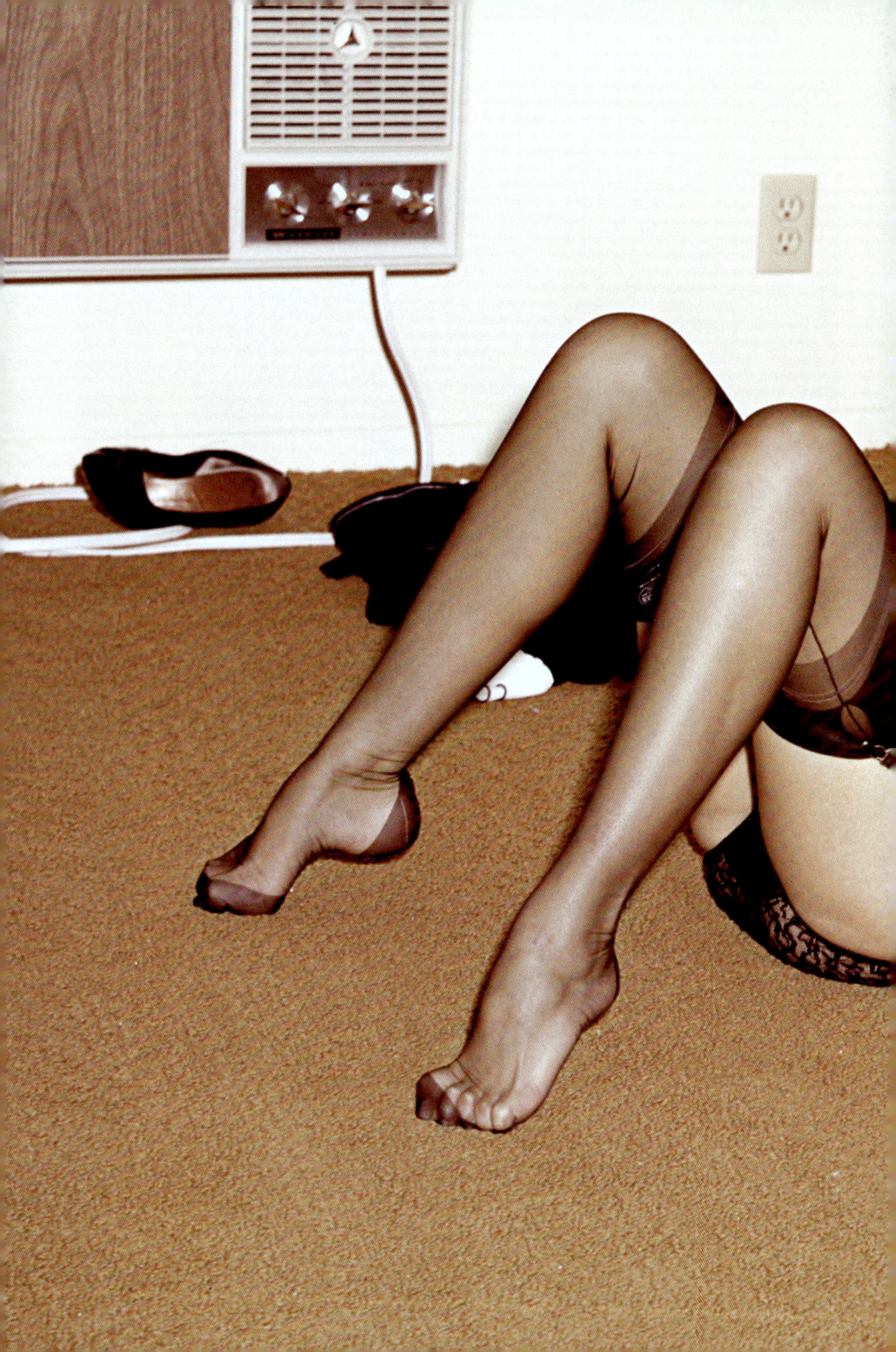

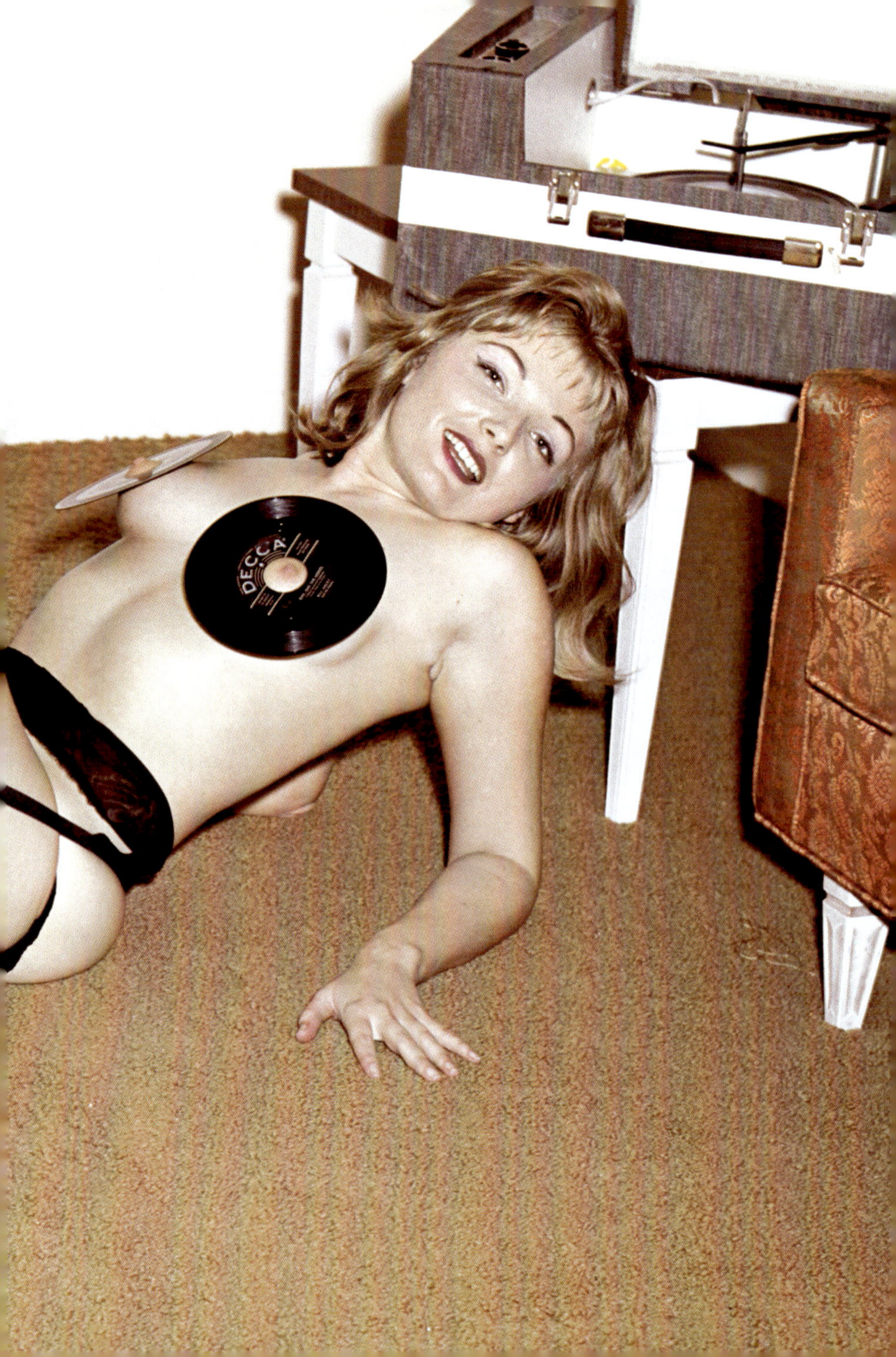

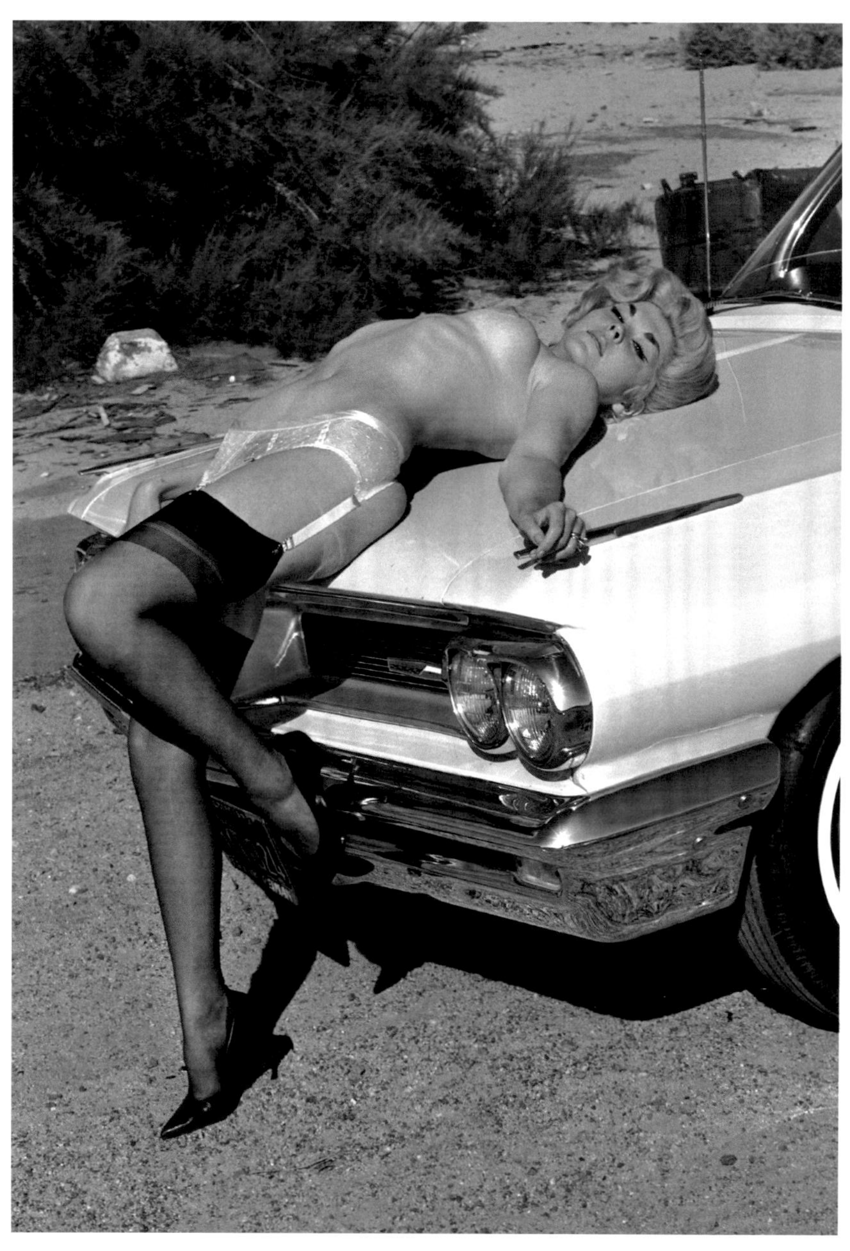

ABOVE Pam Pendergast   OPPOSITE Unknown

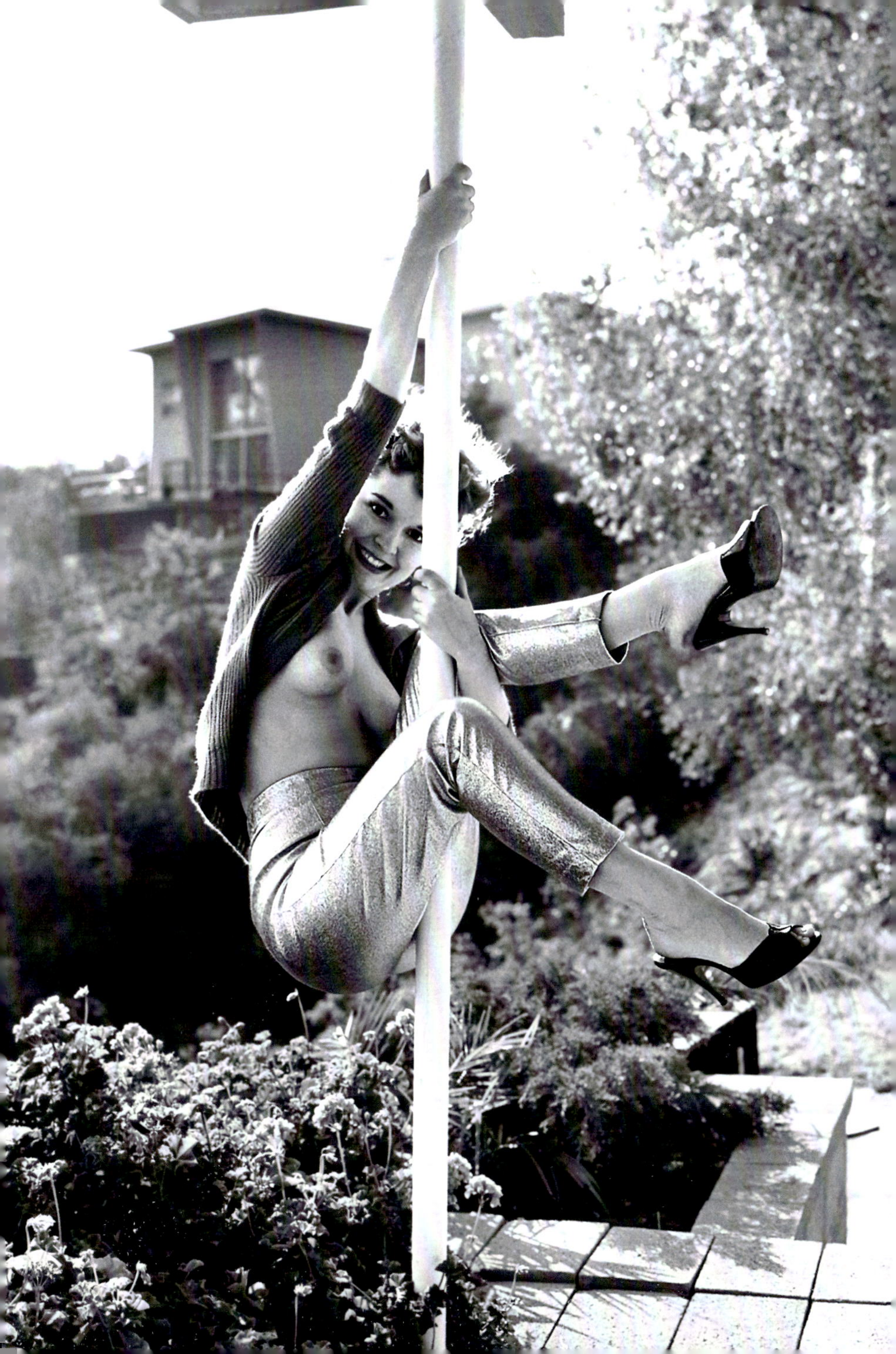

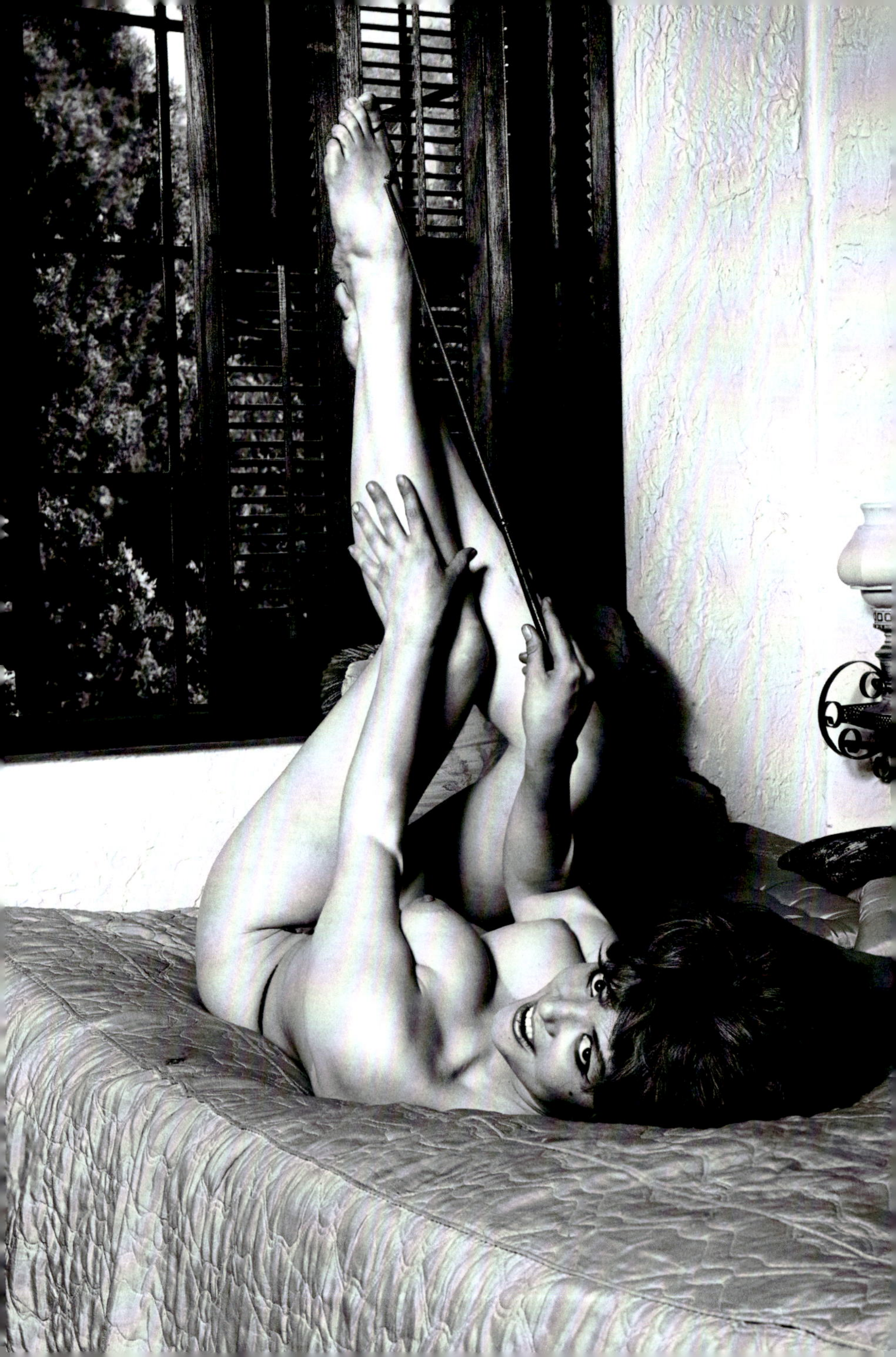

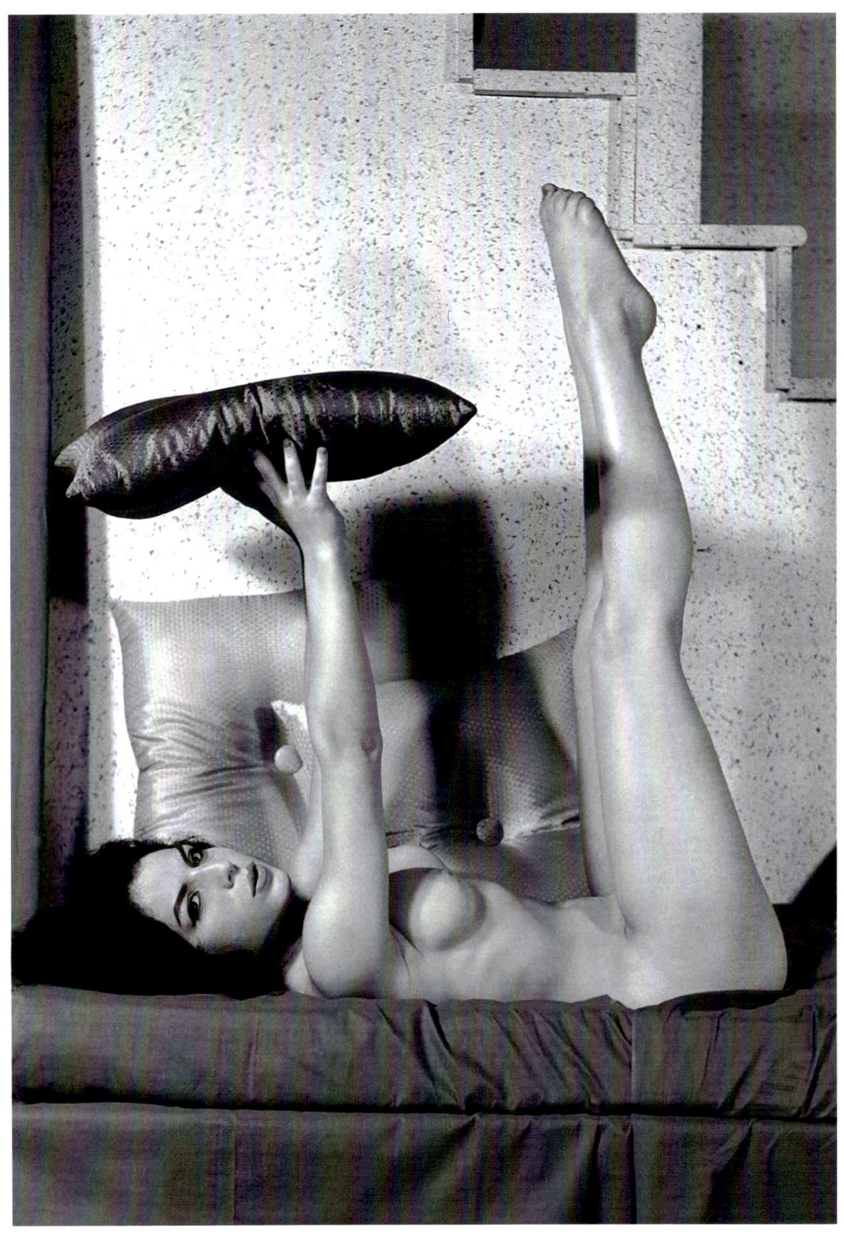

OPPOSITE AND ABOVE Unknown   PAGES 102-103 Candy Palms

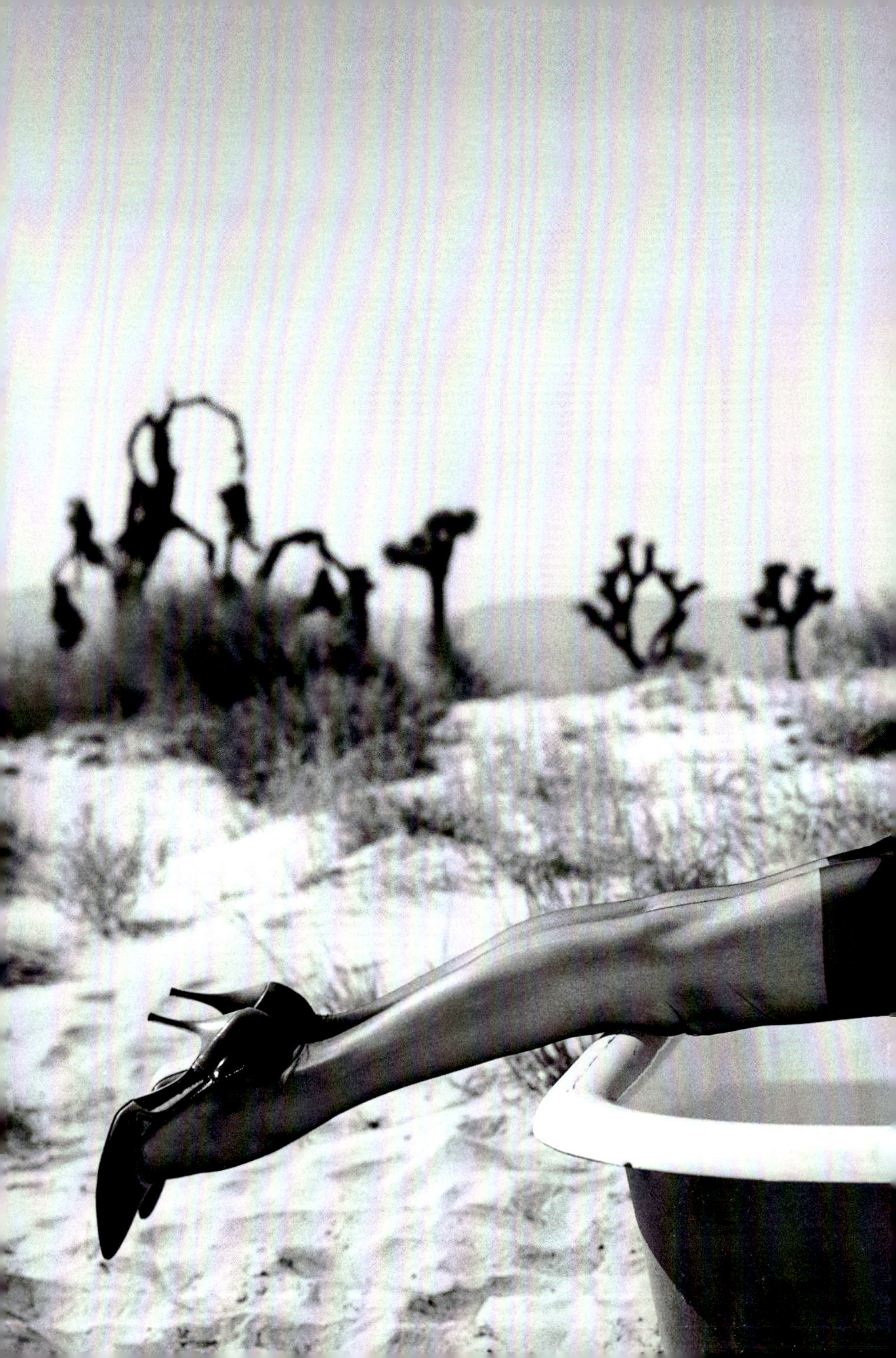

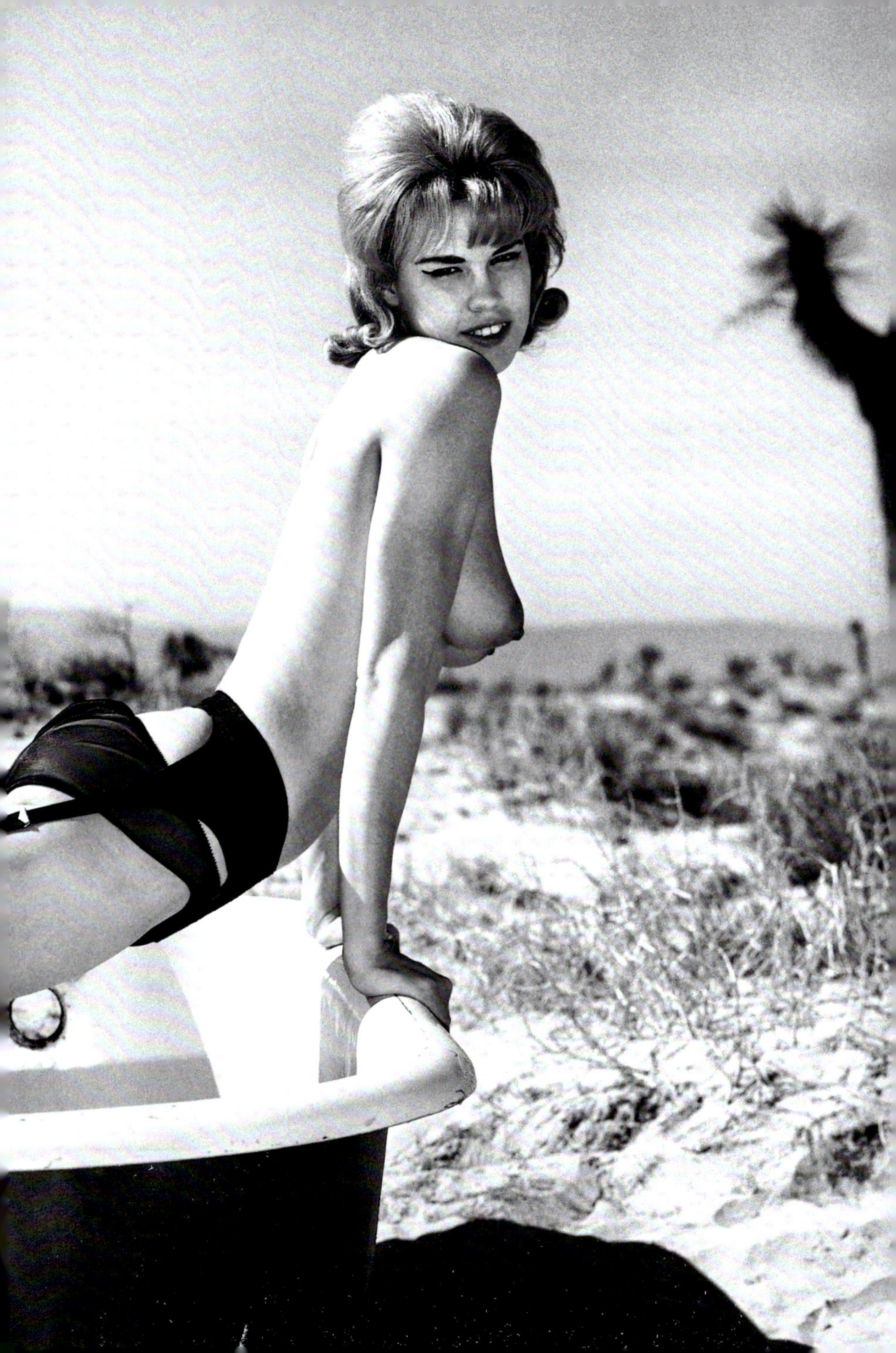

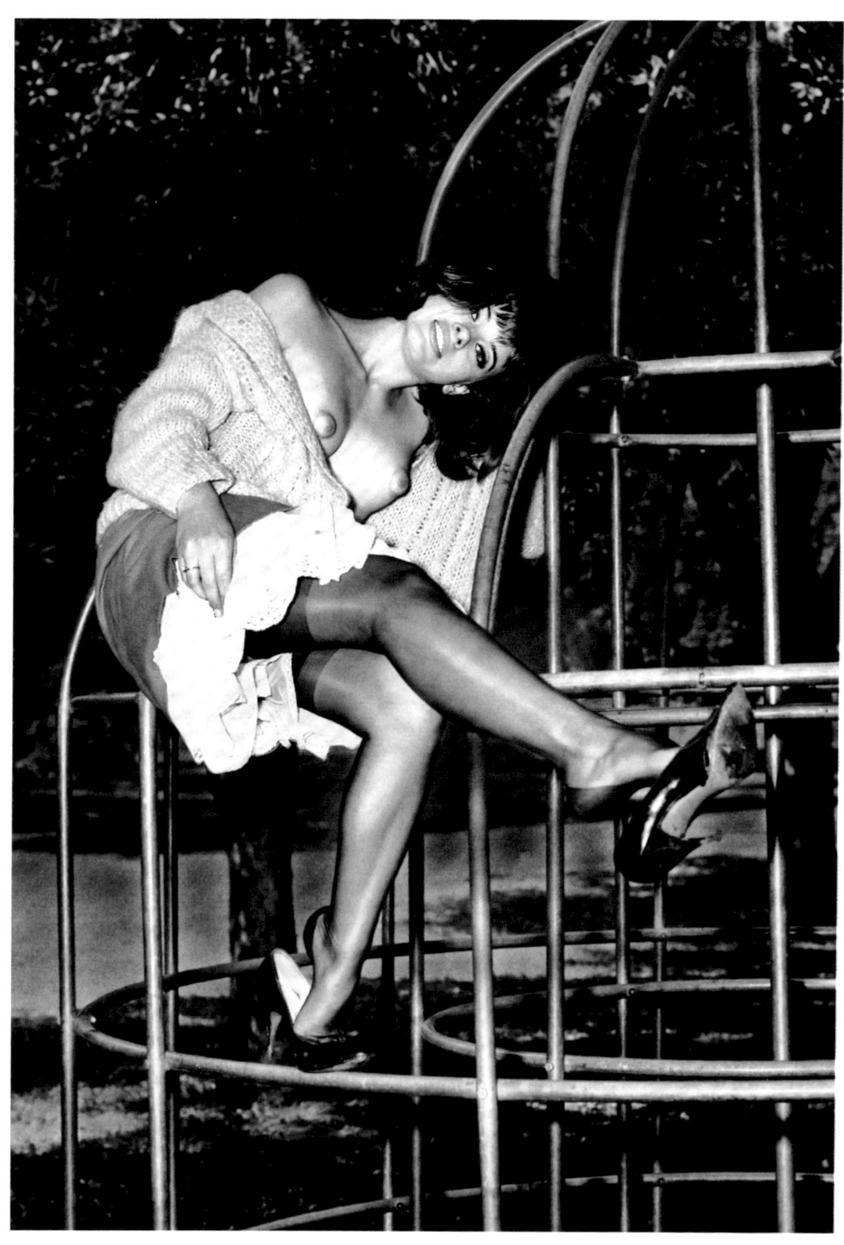

ABOVE AND OPPOSITE Kathy Johnson, ELMER BATTERS

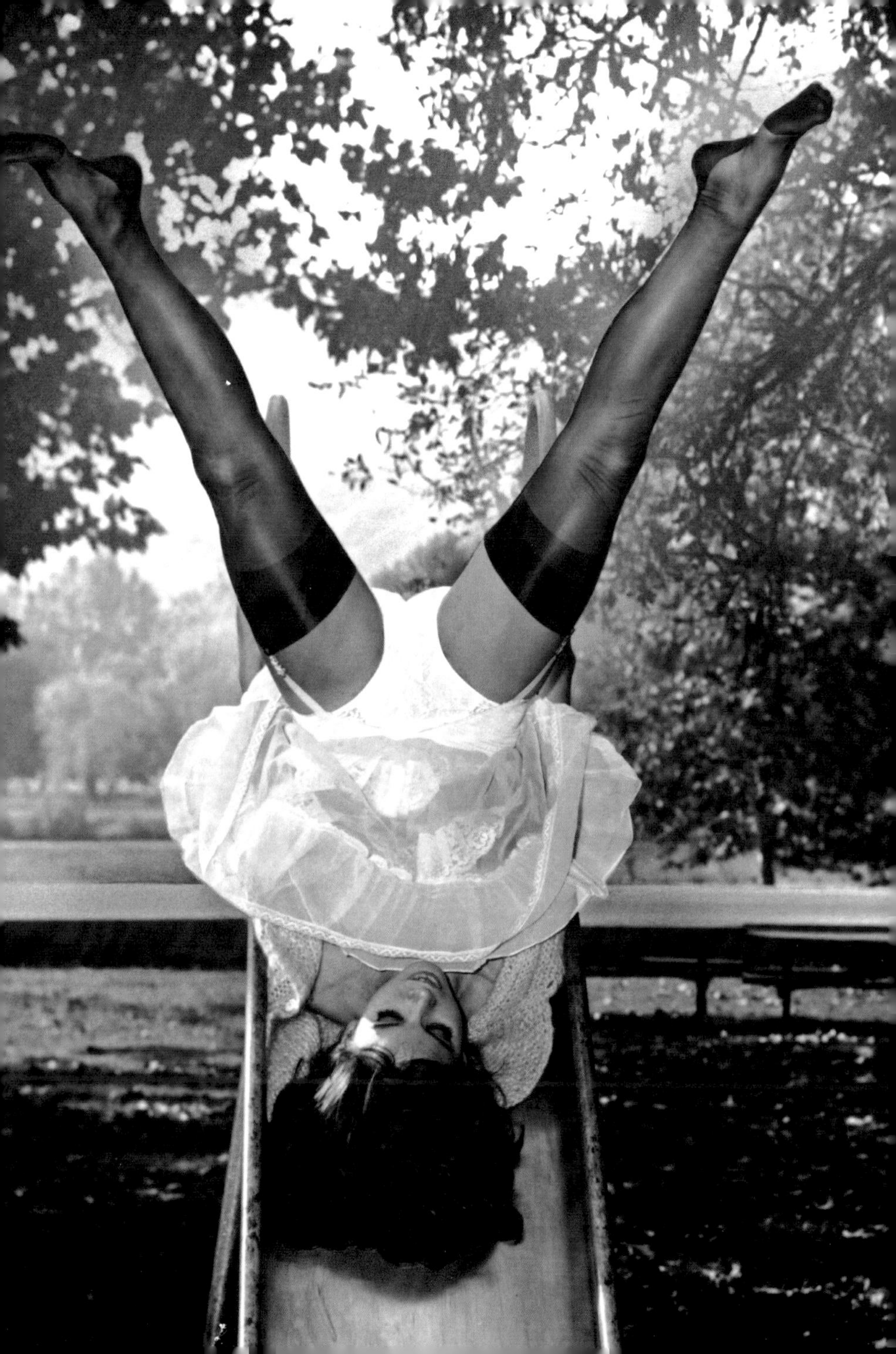

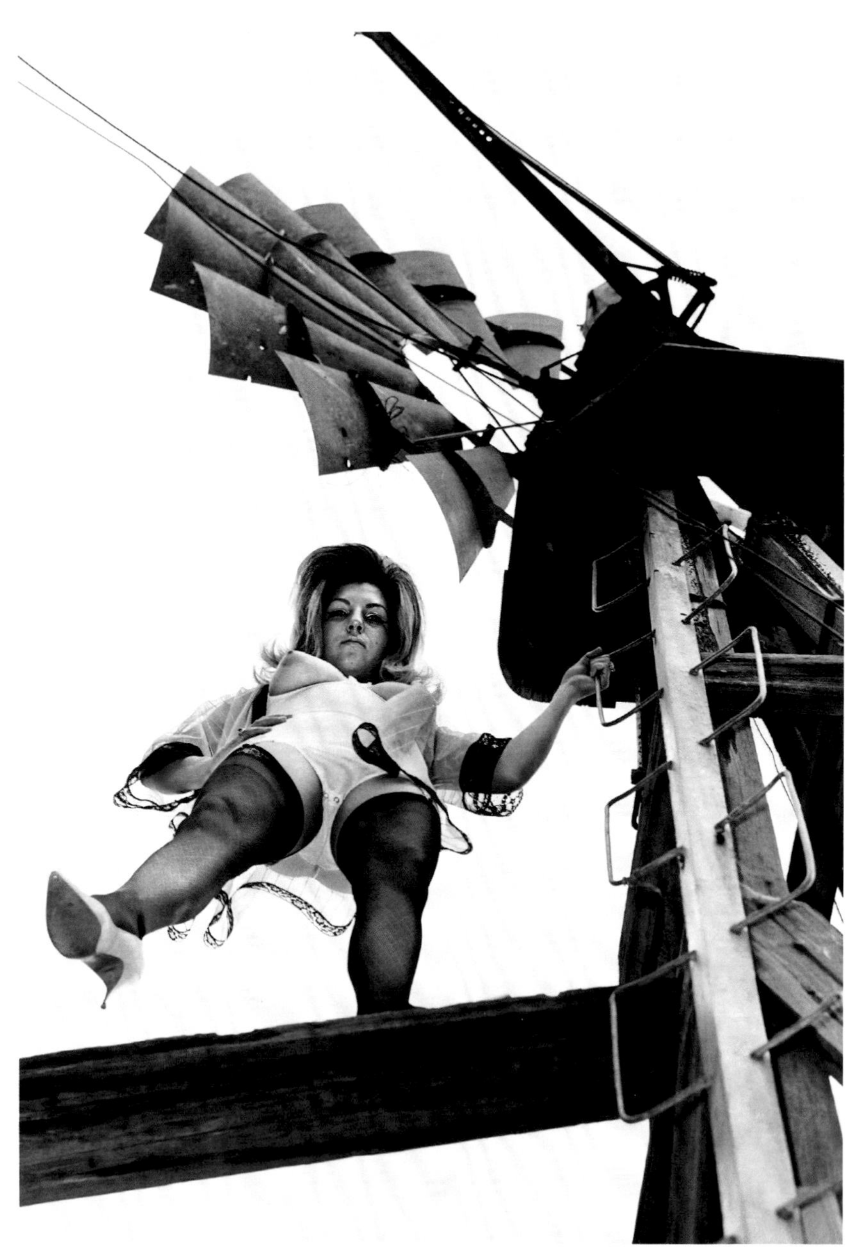

ABOVE Angela Del Vecchio, ELMER BATTERS

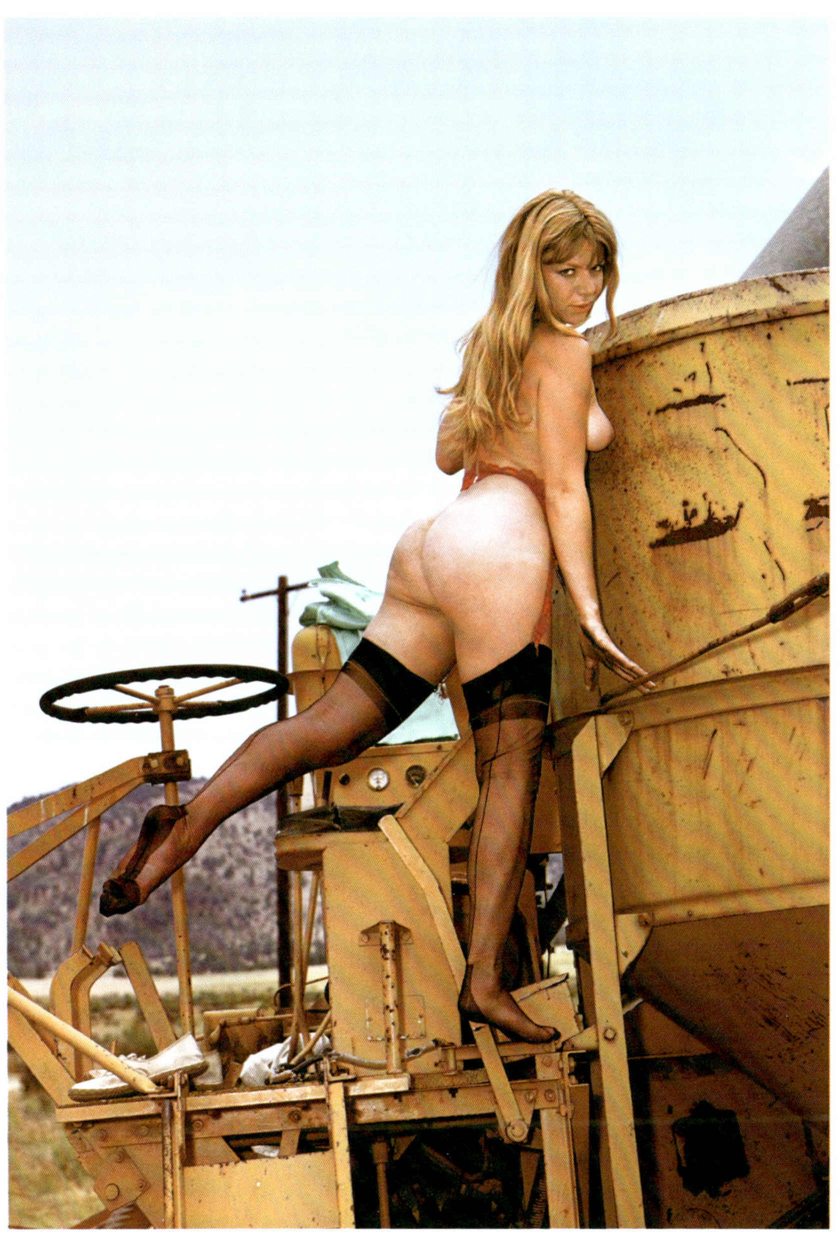

ABOVE Lilith Anderson

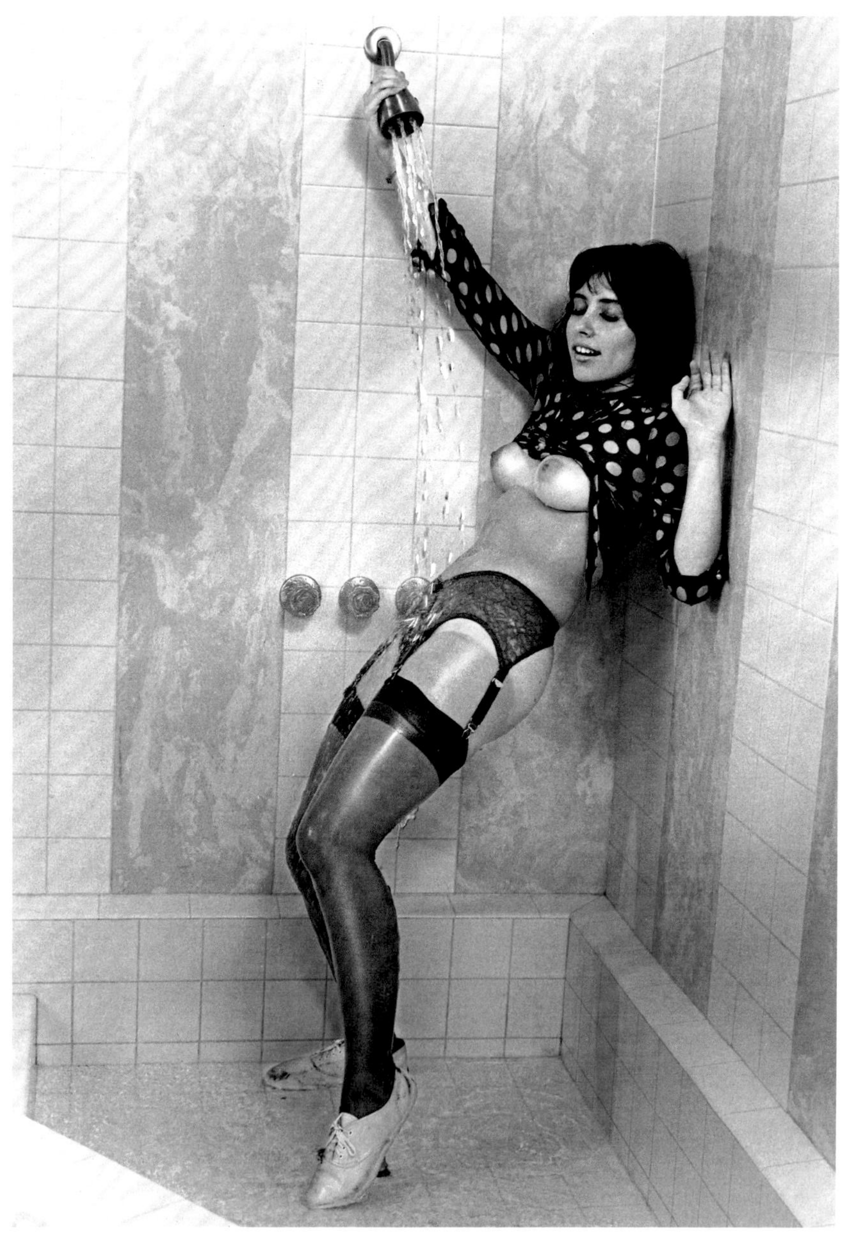

ABOVE **Unknown**

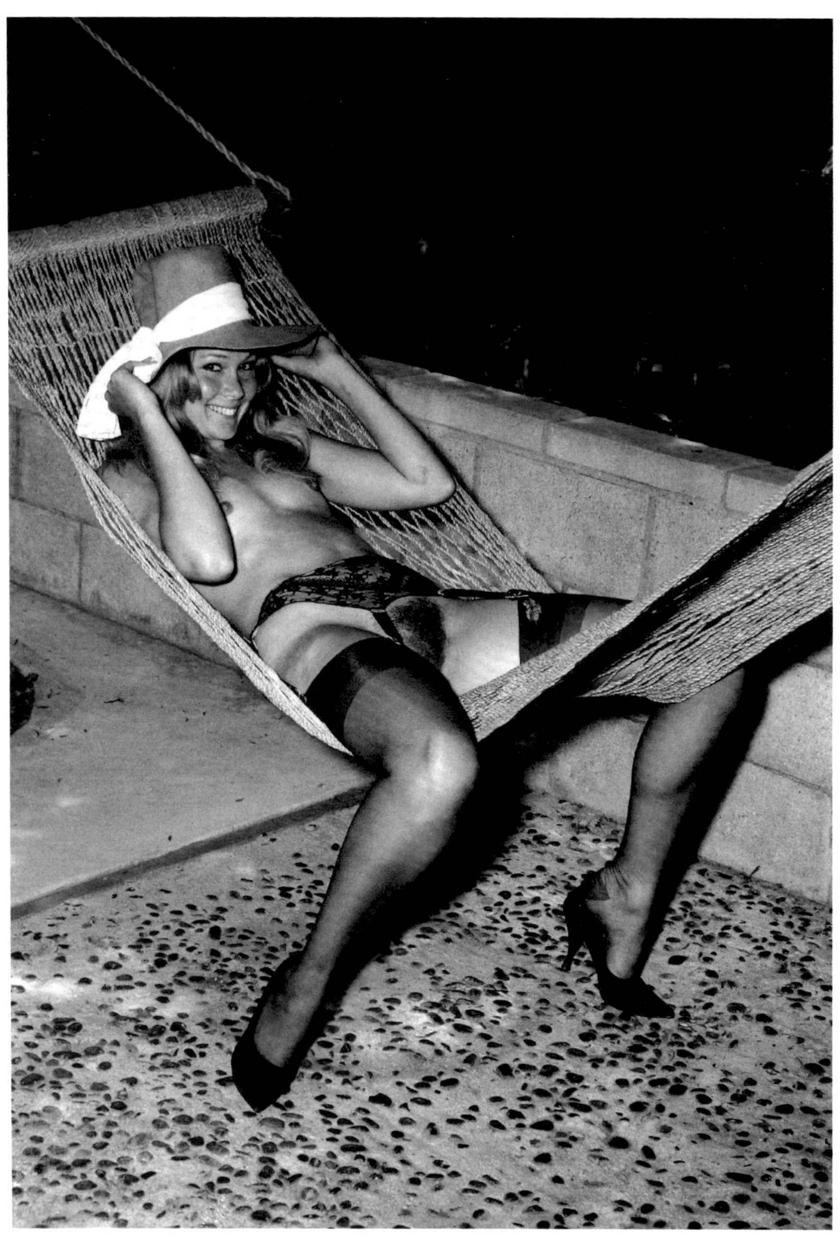

ABOVE Unknown, ELMER BATTERS

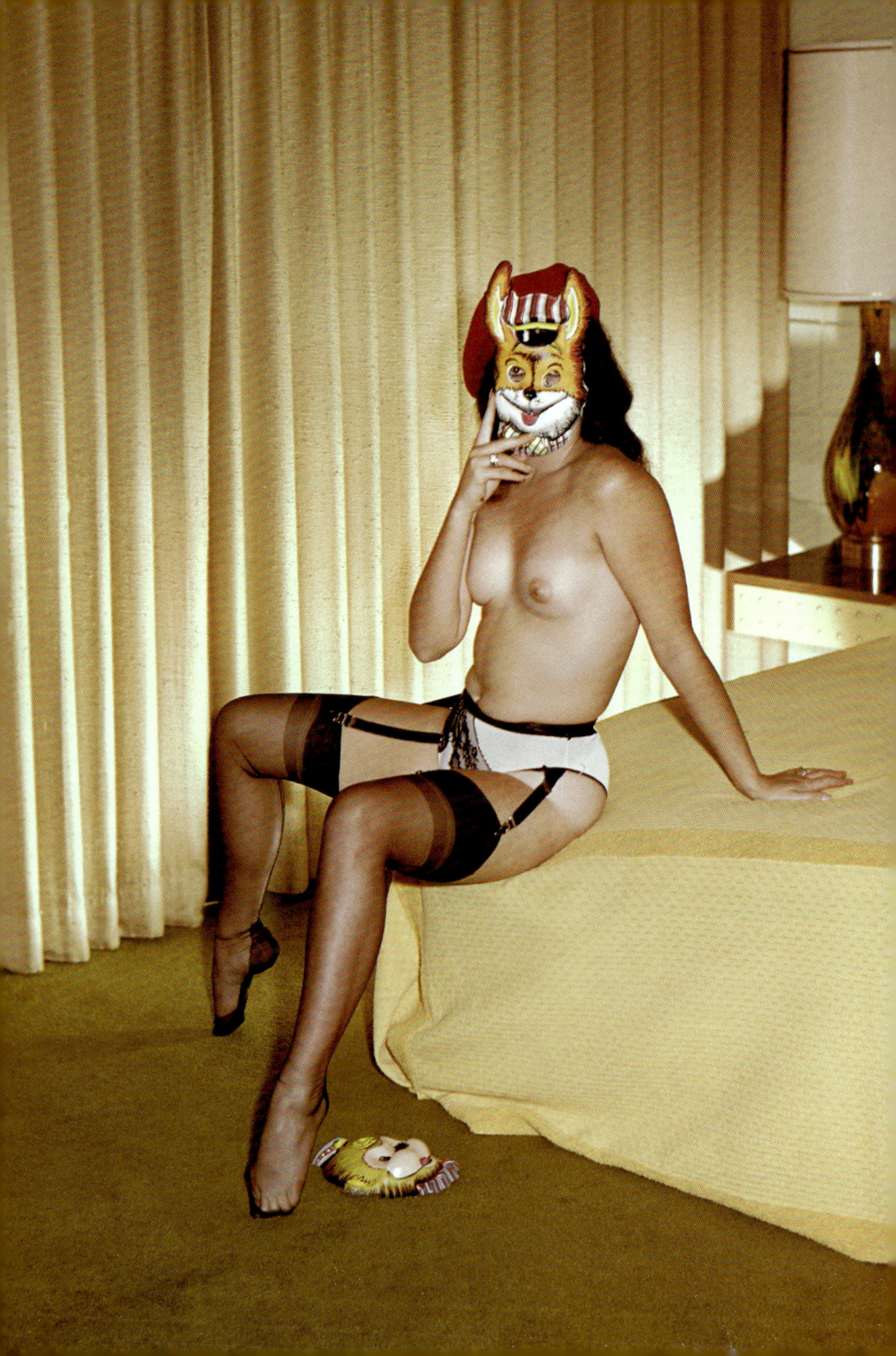

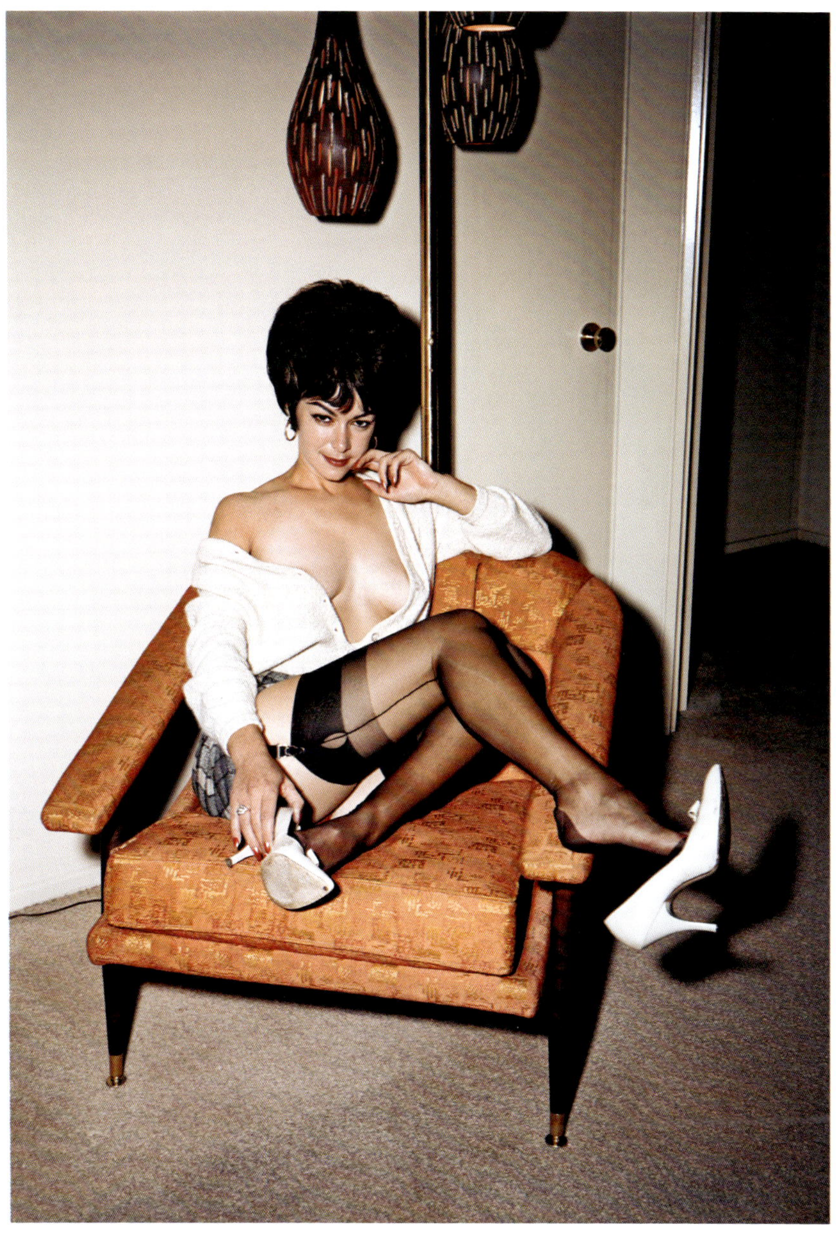

OPPOSITE Janis Moore   ABOVE Unknown   PAGES 112-113 Teisha Graham

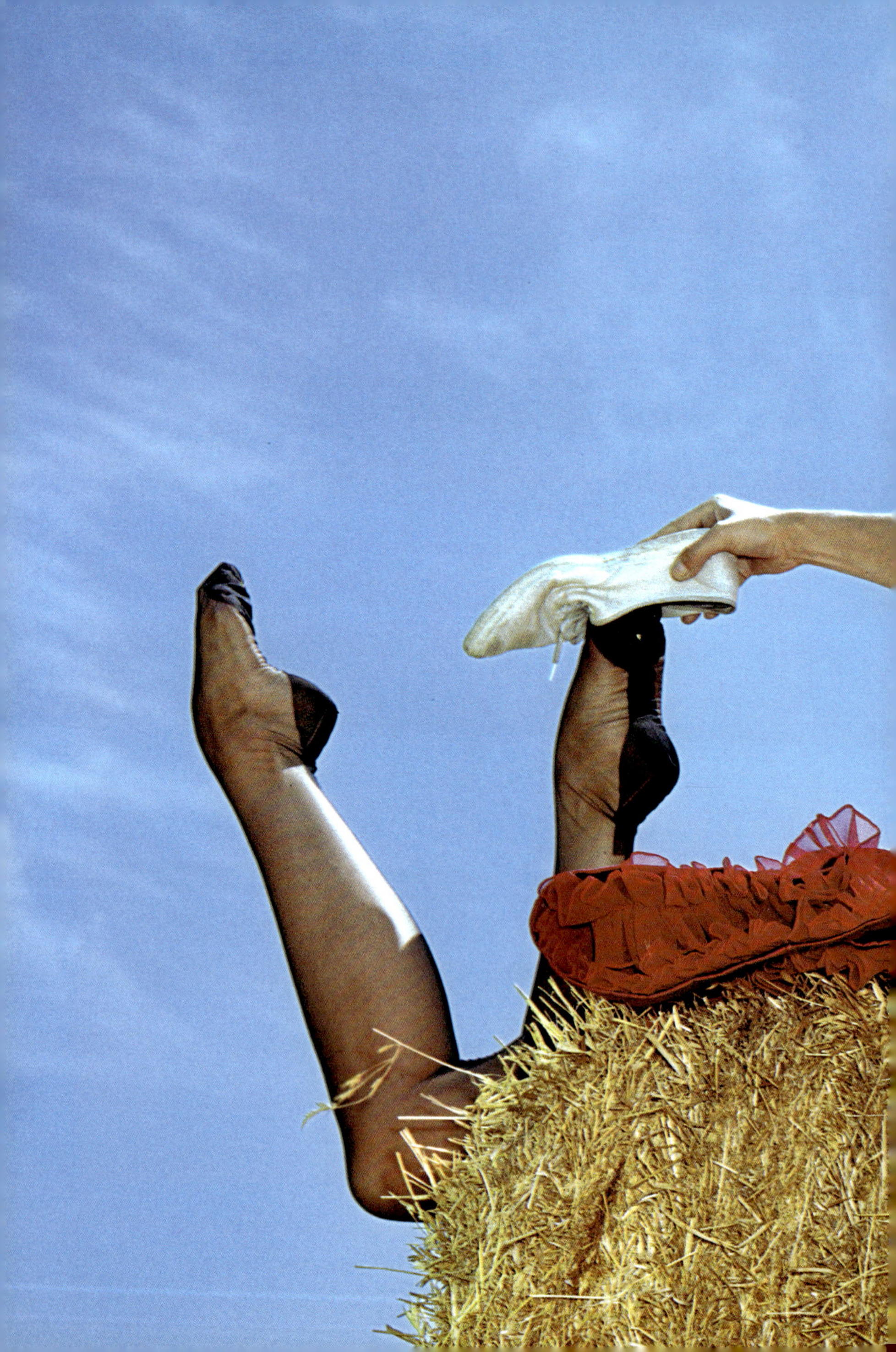

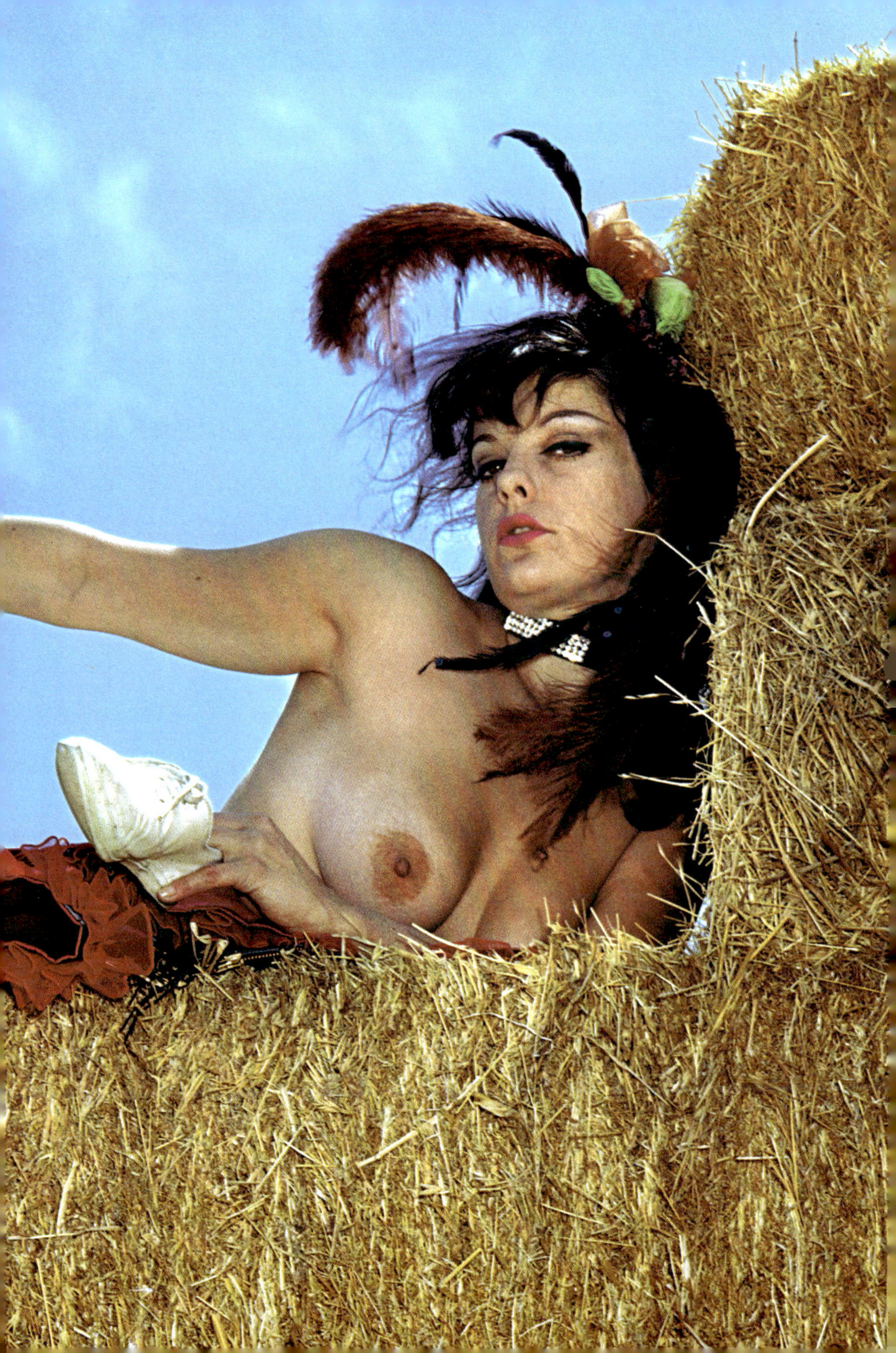

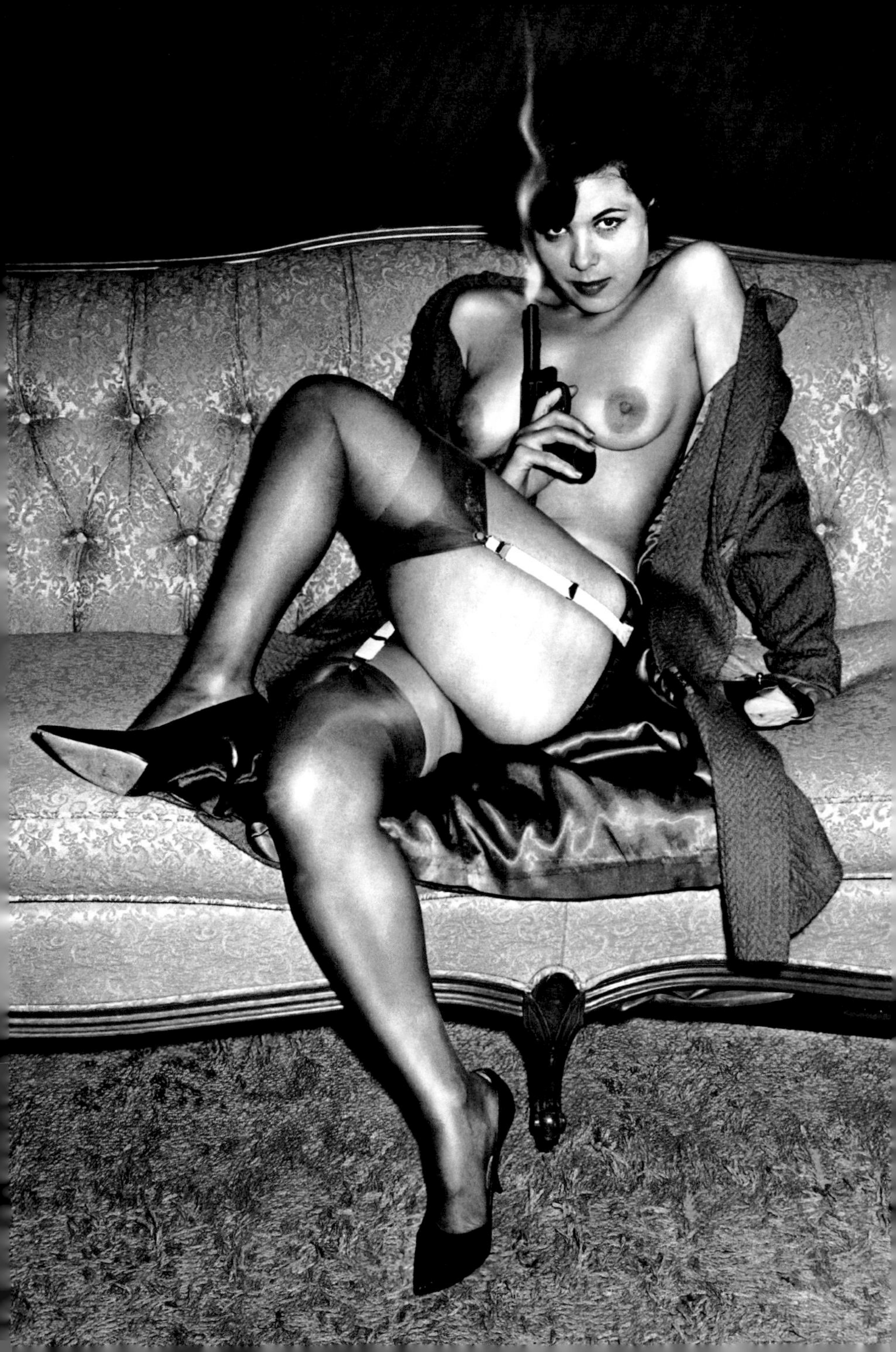

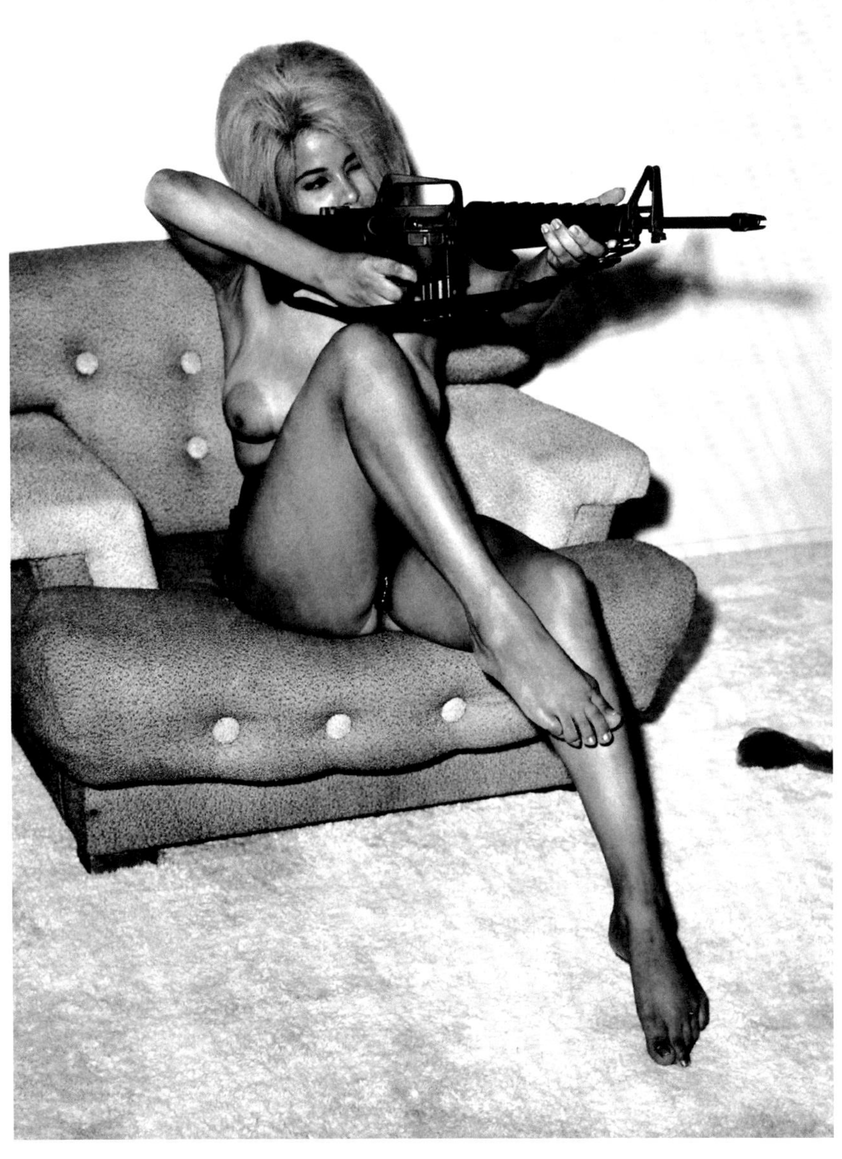

OPPOSITE Angel Carter   ABOVE Unknown

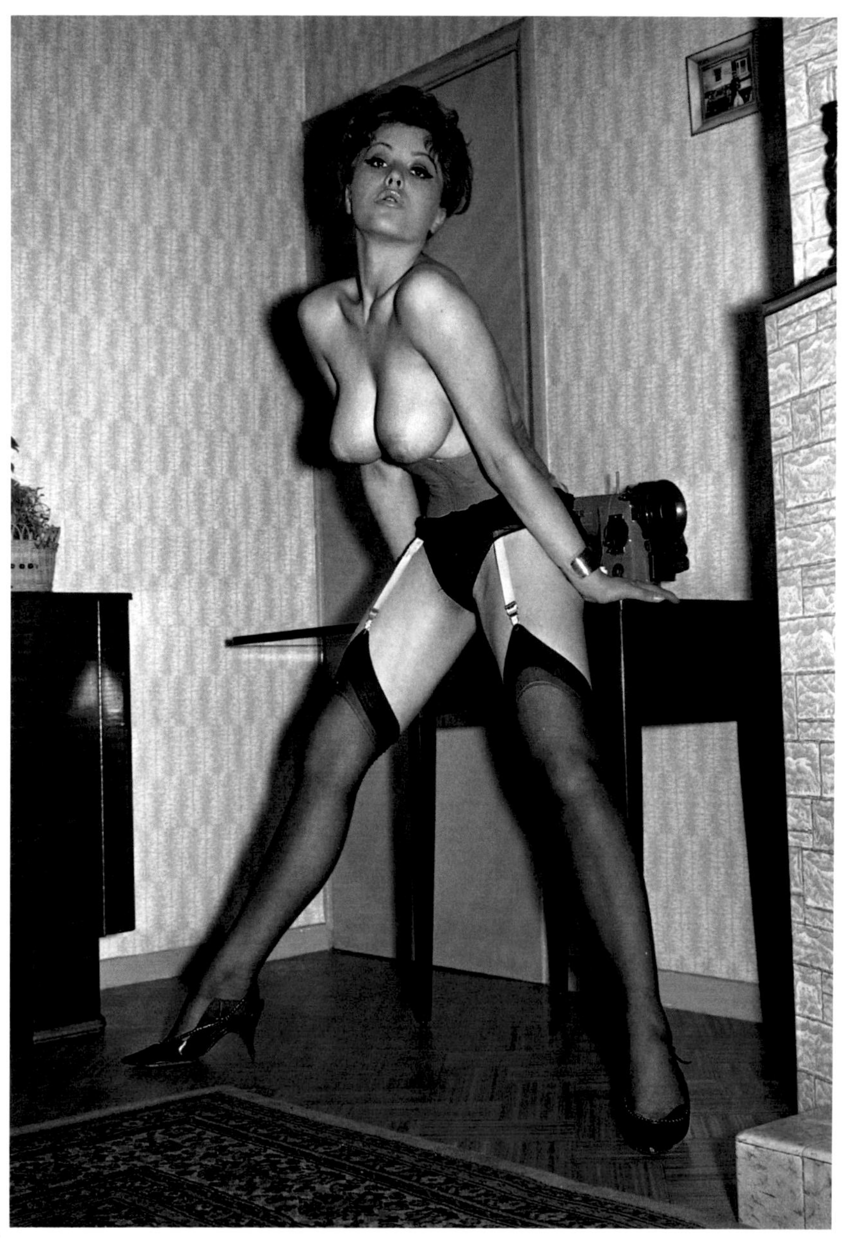

ABOVE Vicki Kennedy

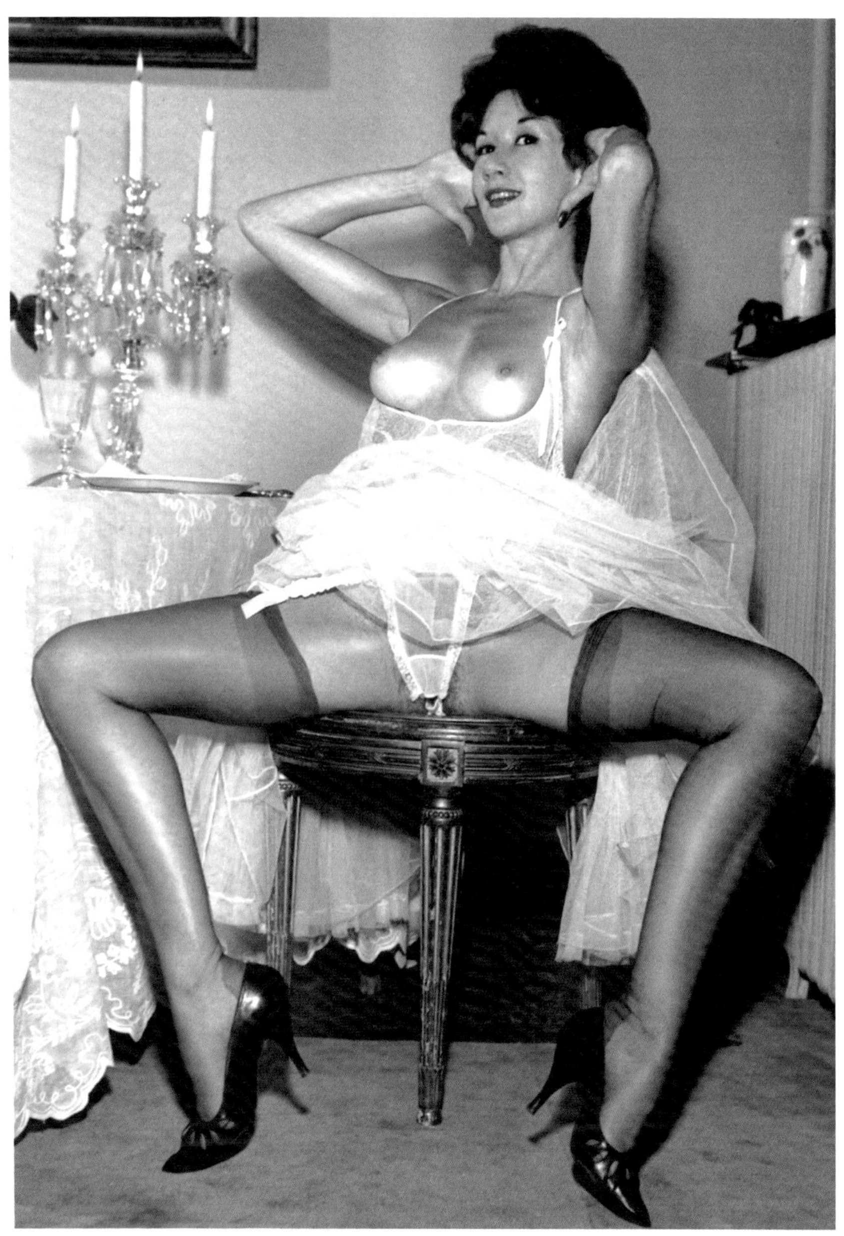

ABOVE Laural LaPir

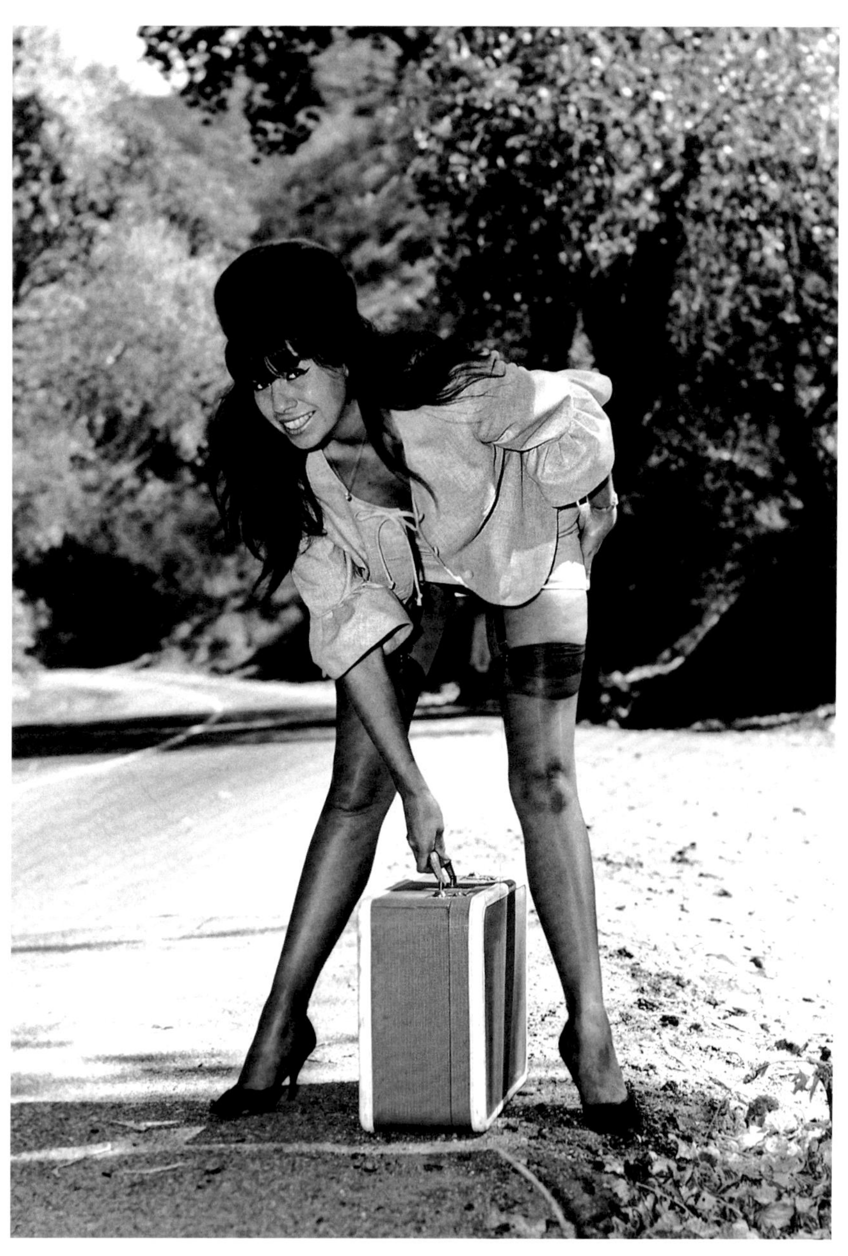

ABOVE AND OPPOSITE Unknown, ELMER BATTERS   PAGES 120-121 Betty Bosco

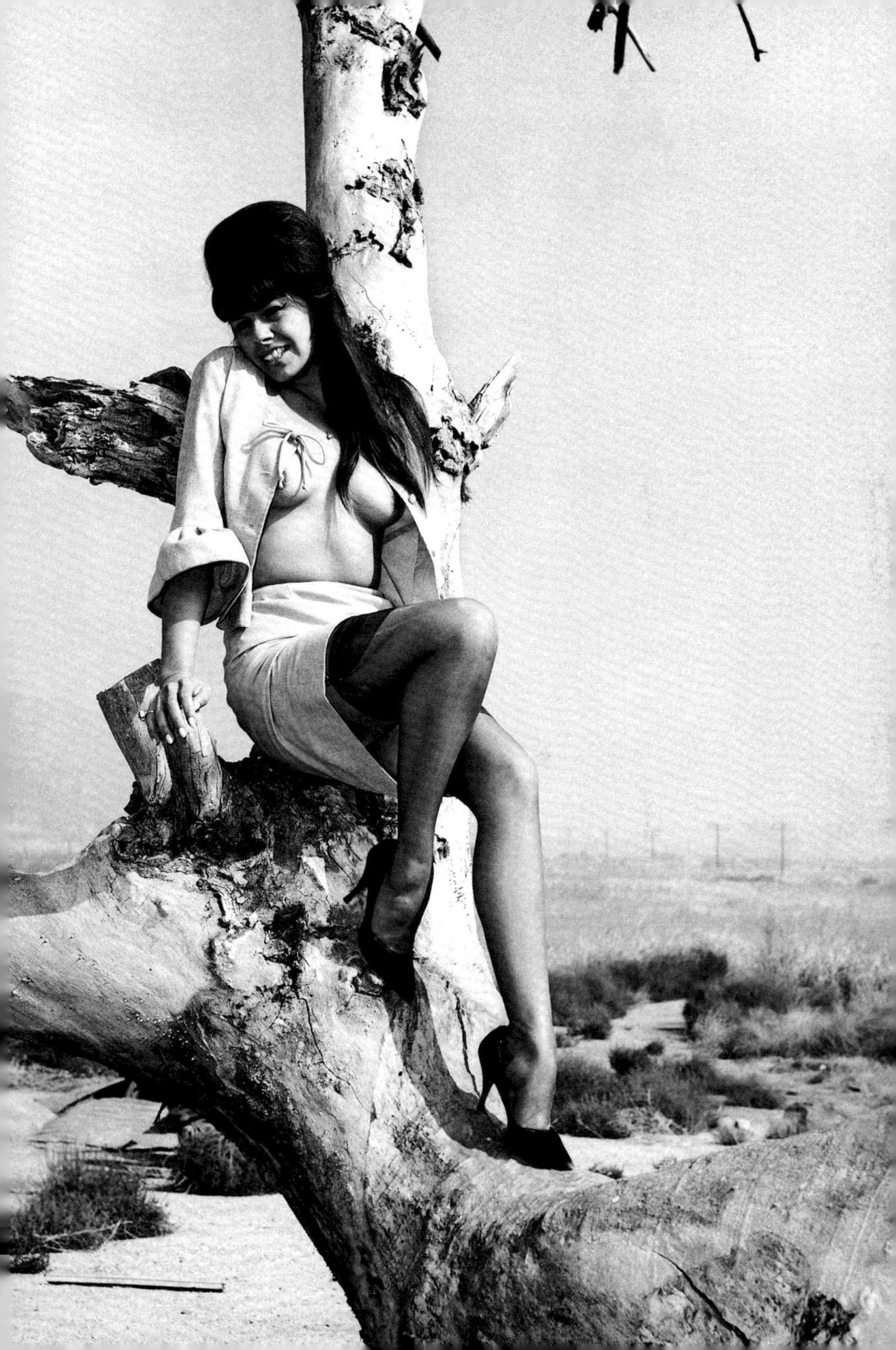

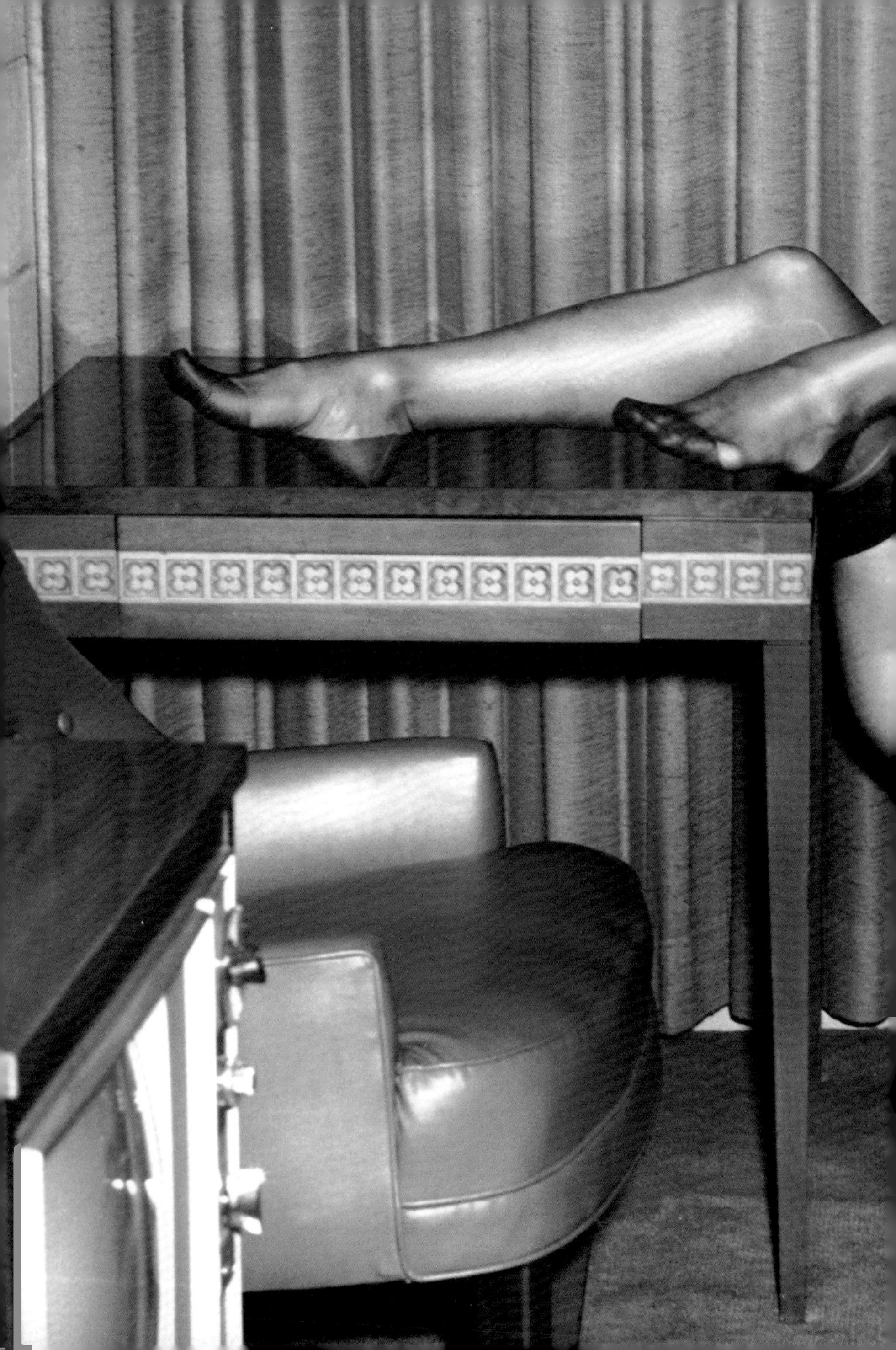

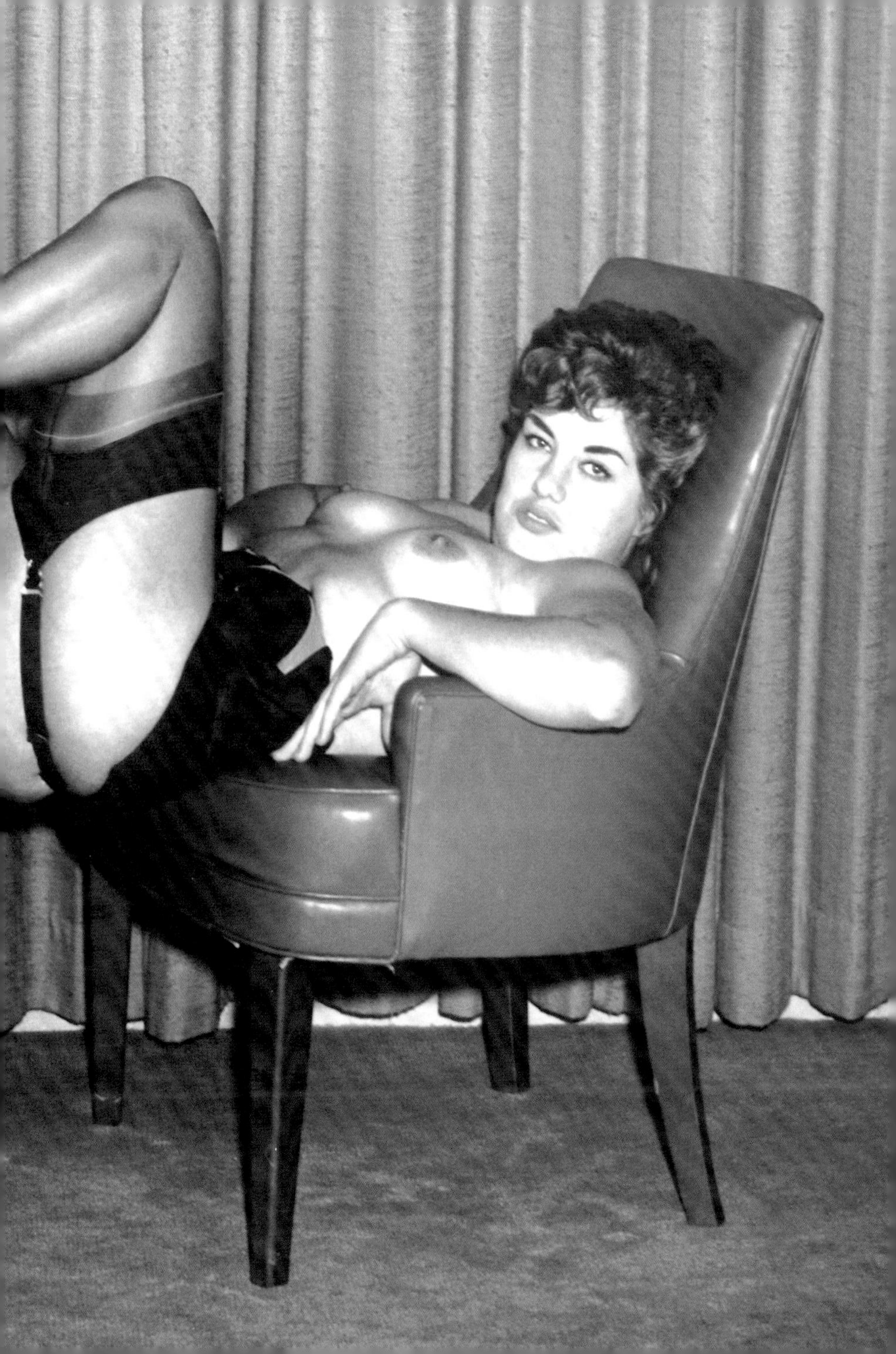

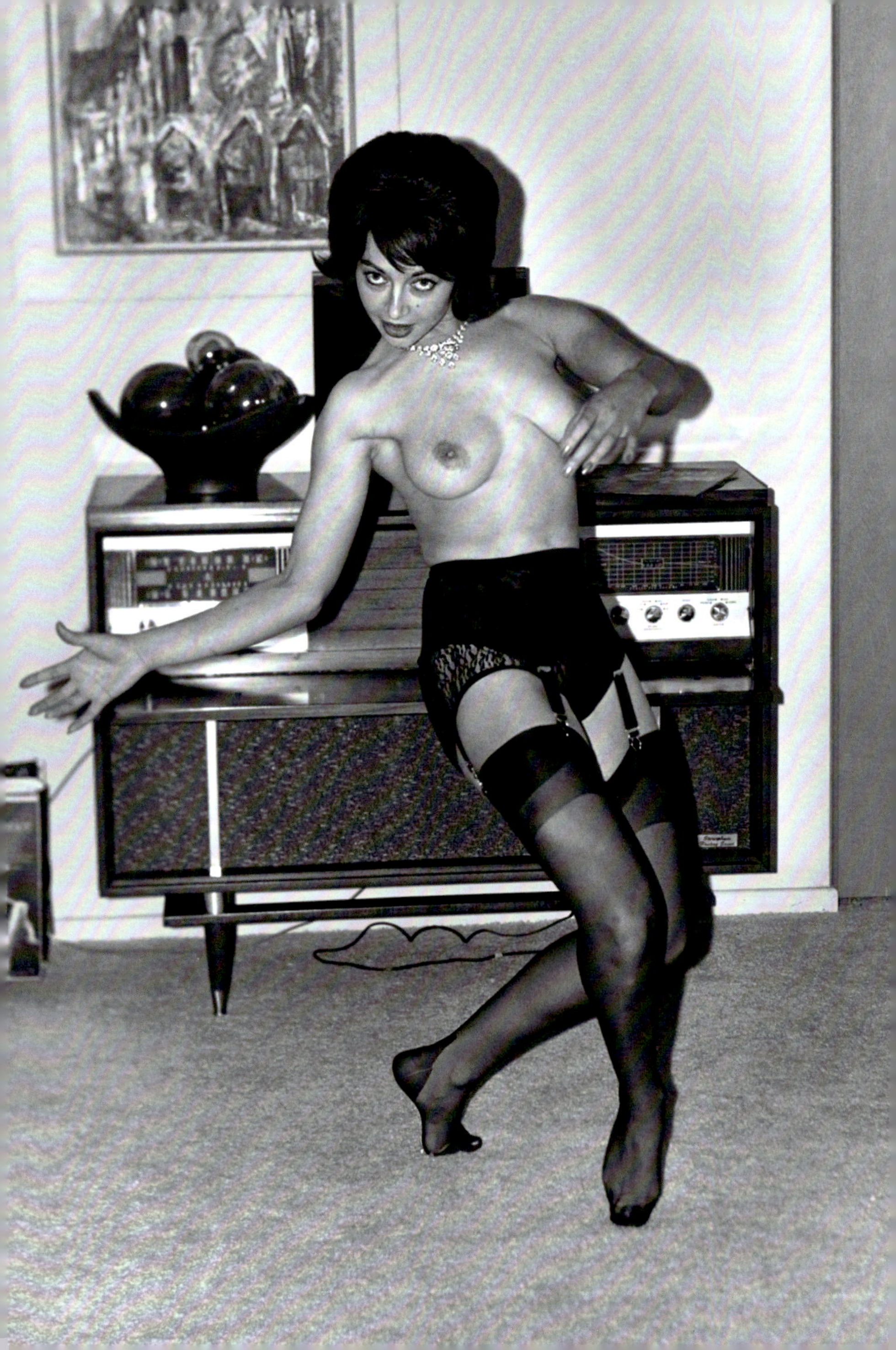

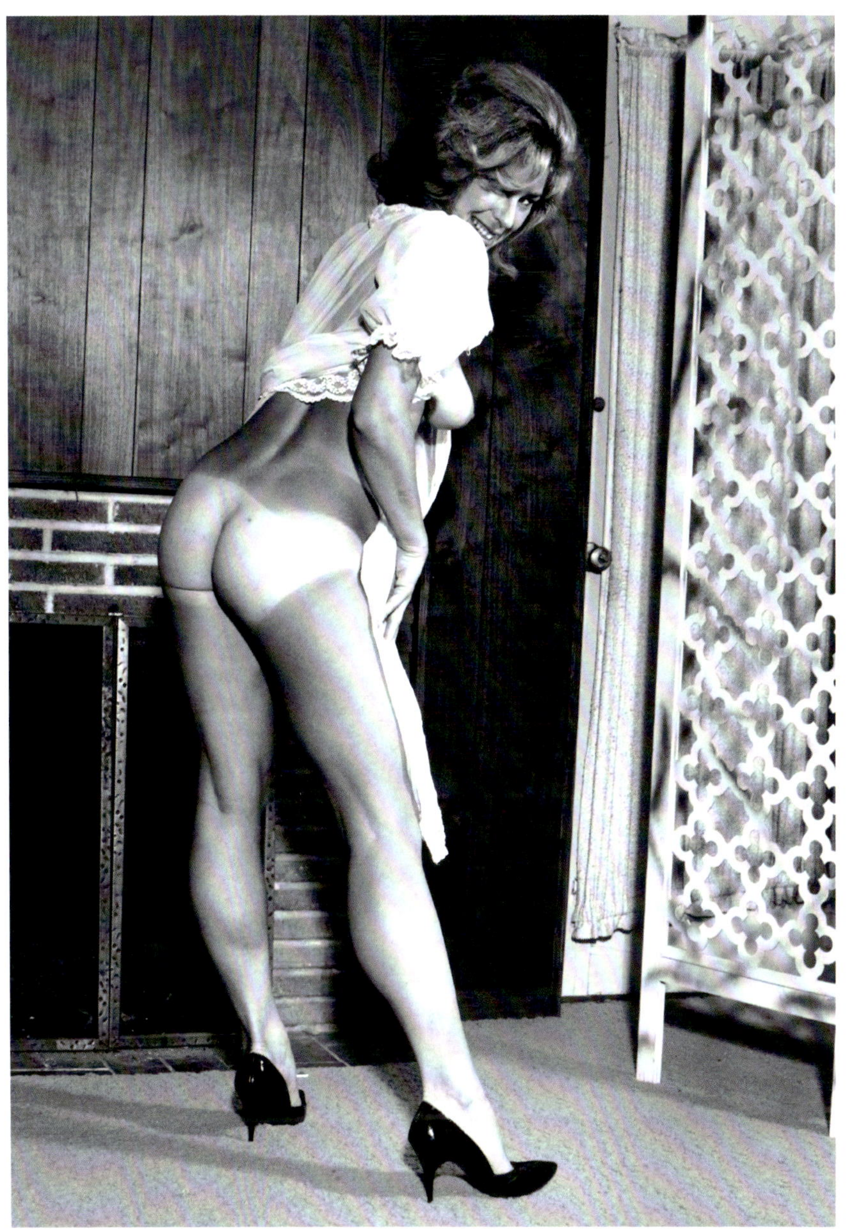

OPPOSITE Lynn Taylor   ABOVE Unknown

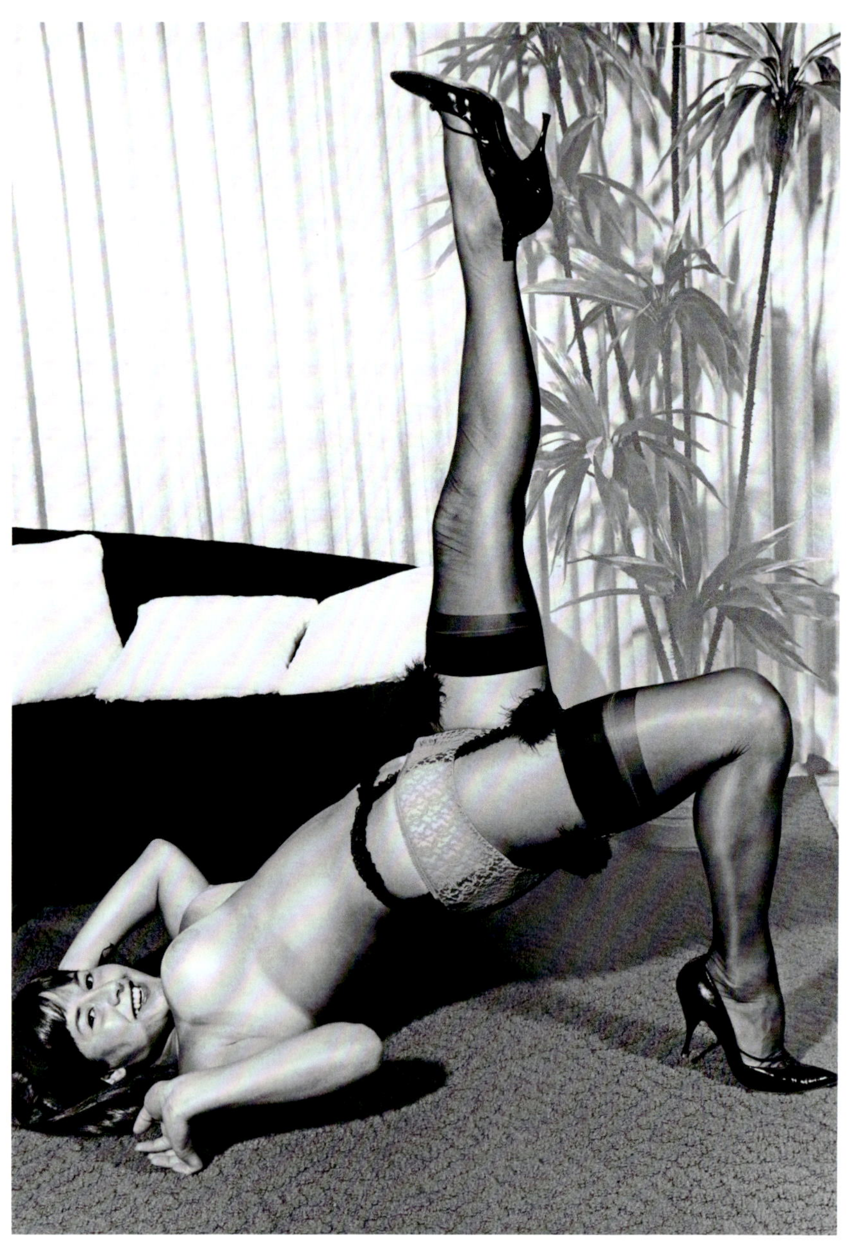

ABOVE Sharon Lee Whitlock

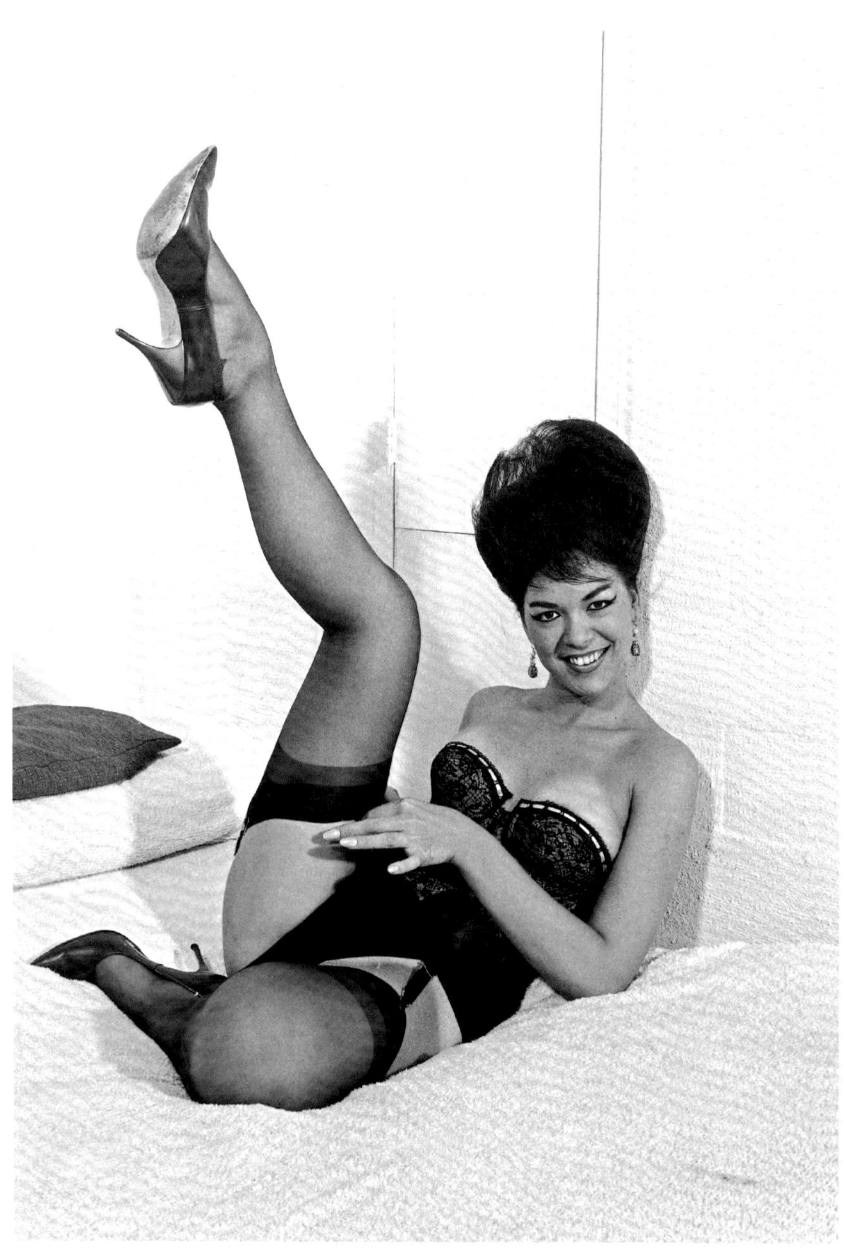

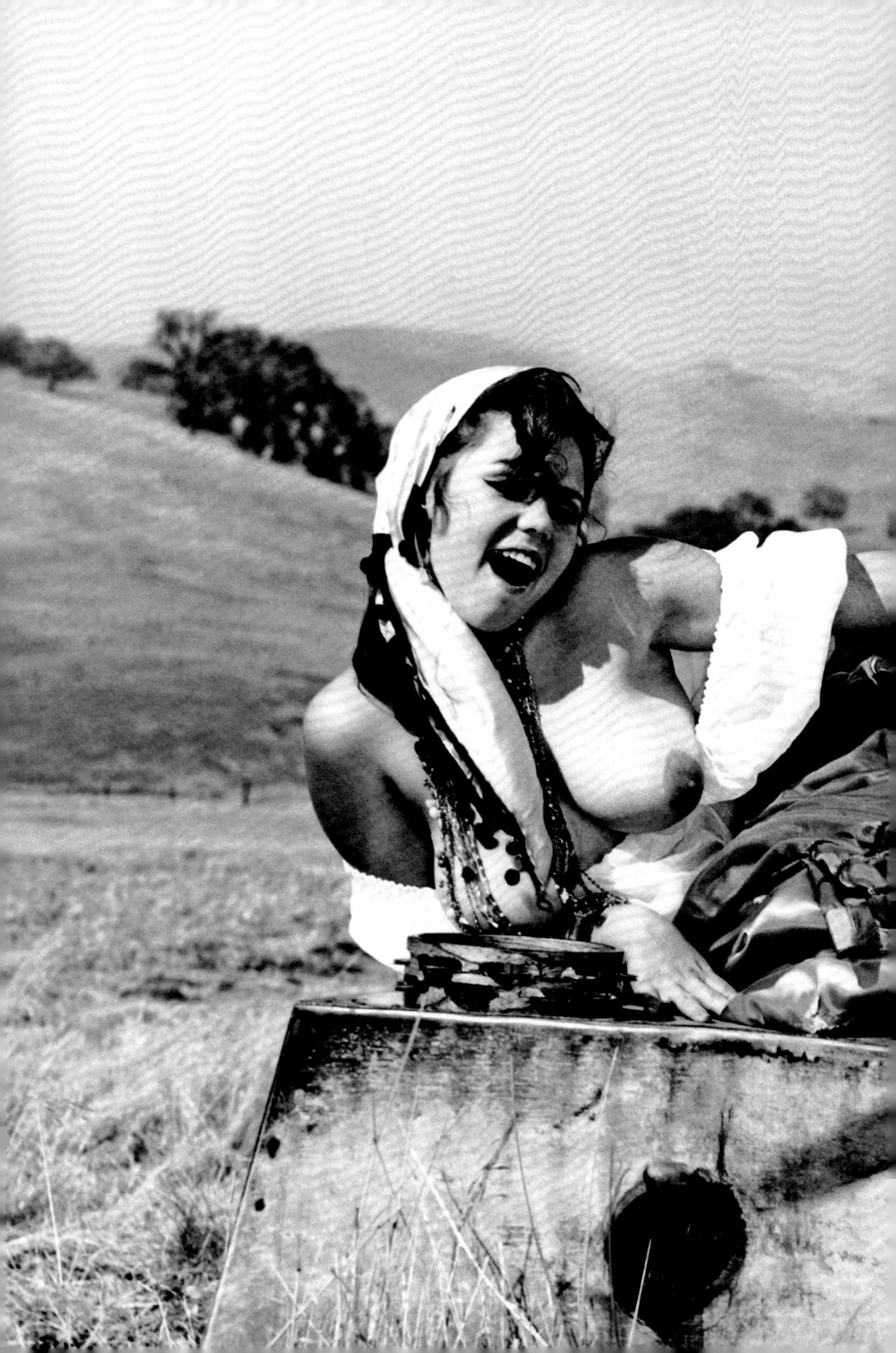

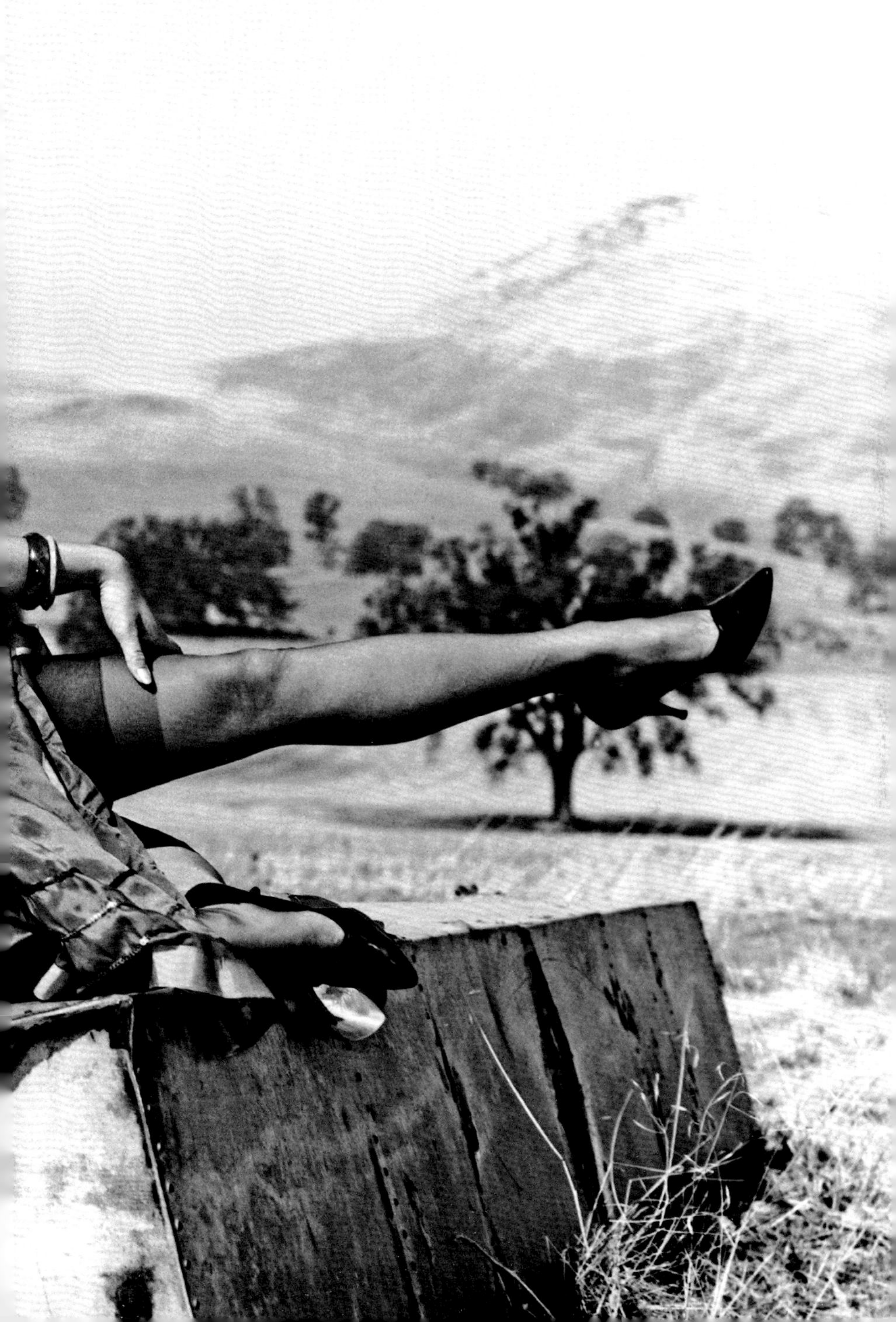

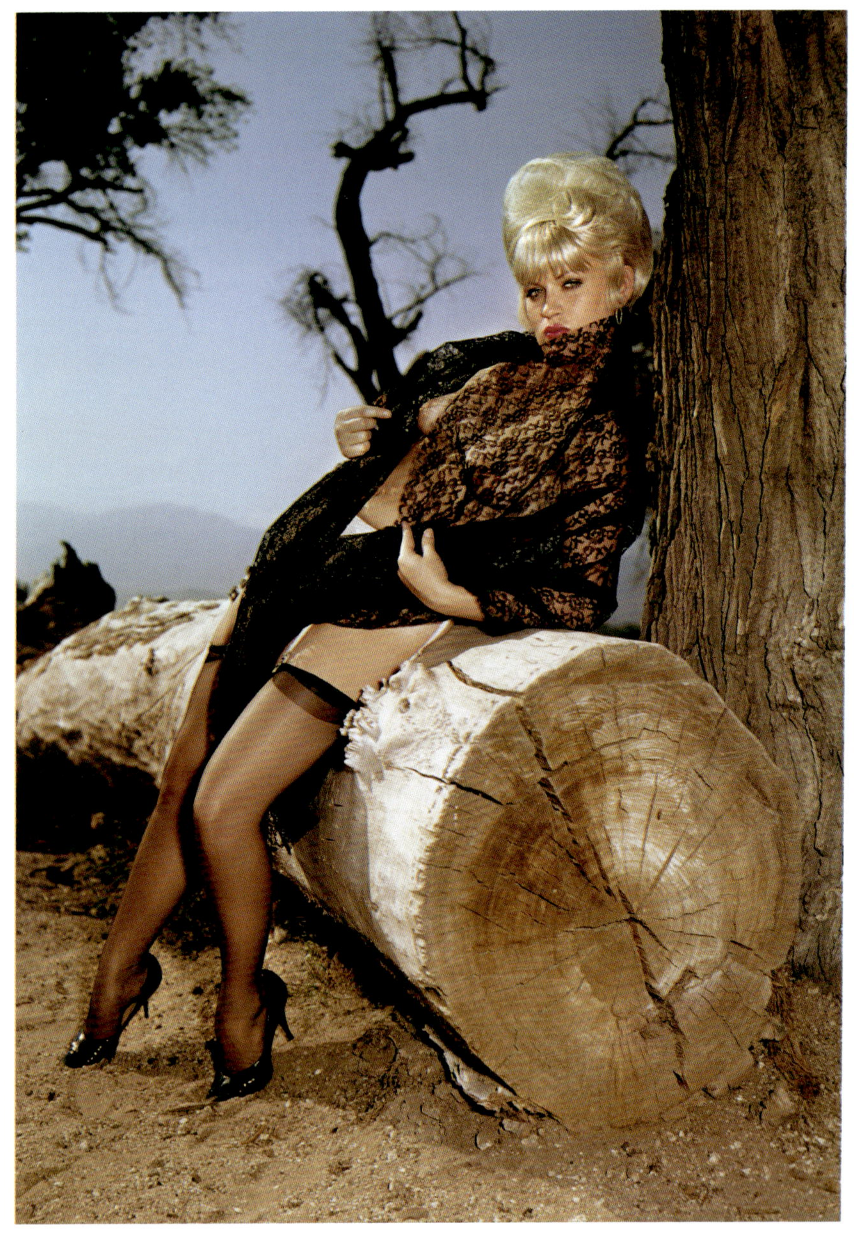

ABOVE Unknown

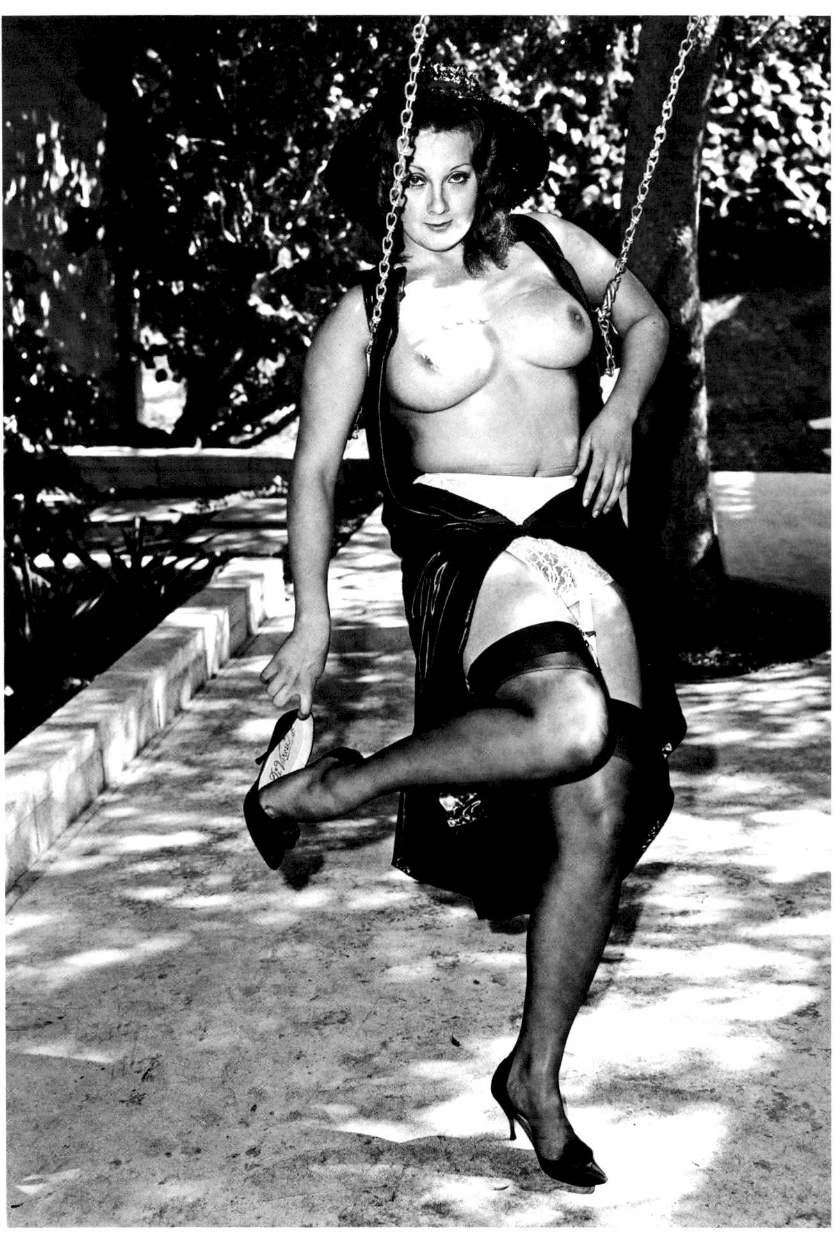

ABOVE Caruschka, ELMER BATTERS

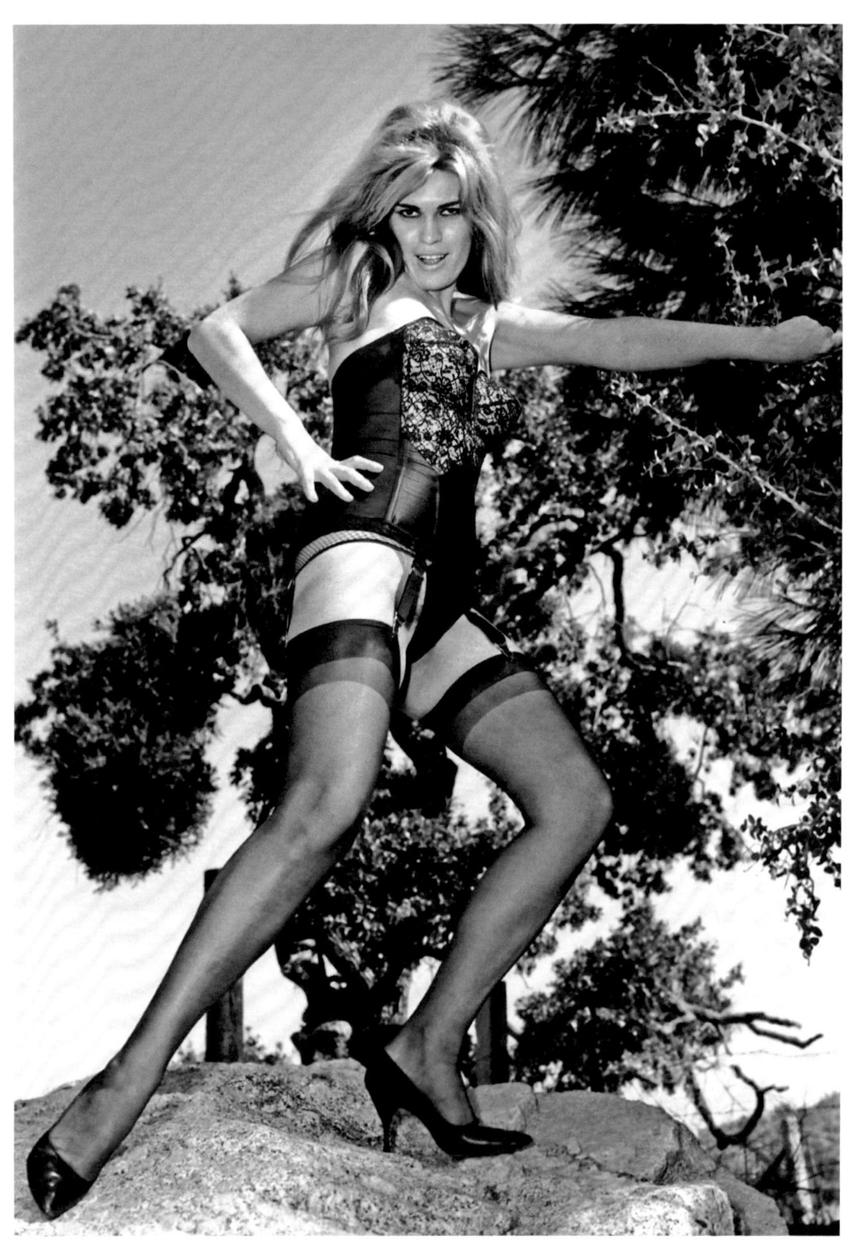

ABOVE Unknown   OPPOSITE Yvette Marne

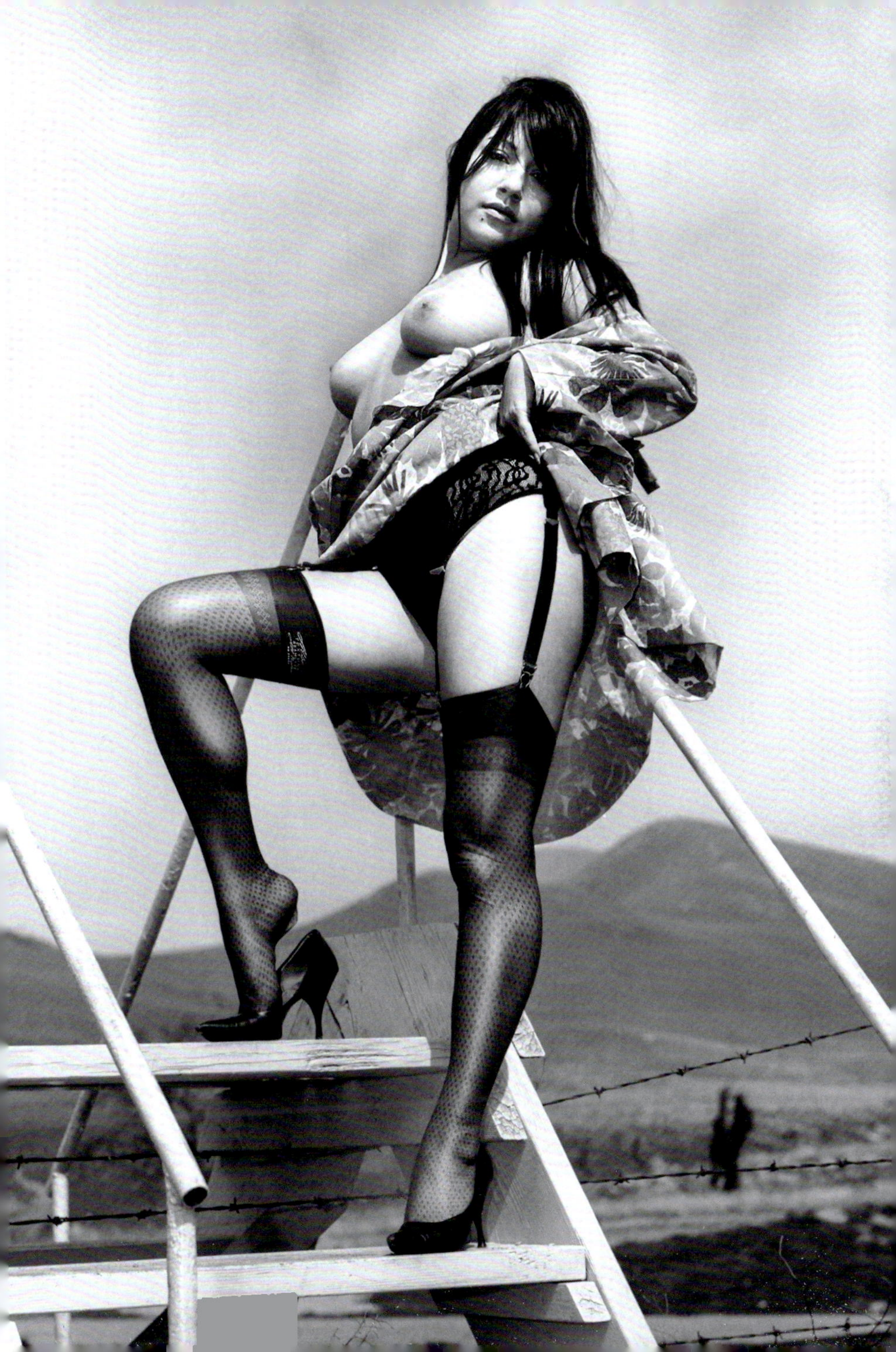

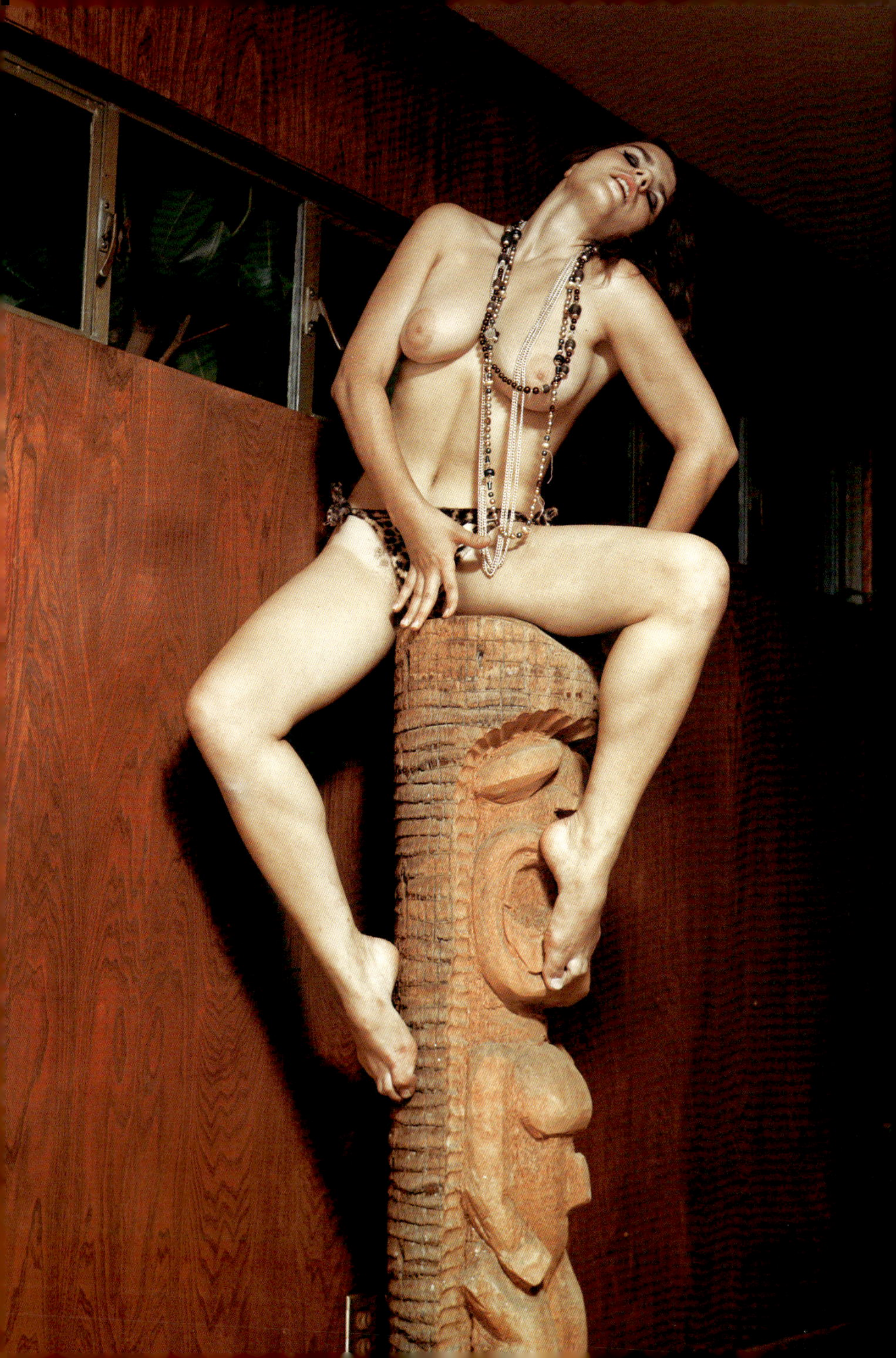

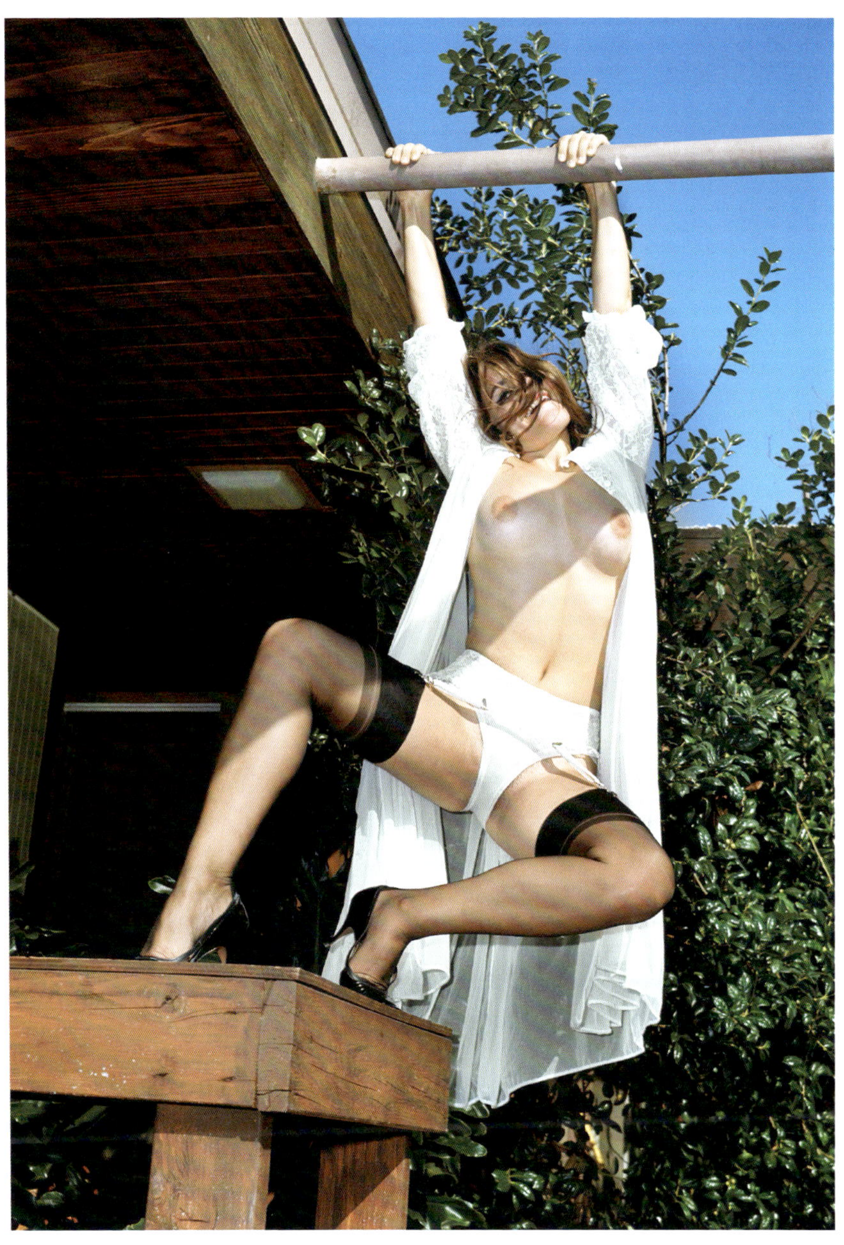

OPPOSITE AND ABOVE Barbara Trent   PAGES 134-135 Unknown

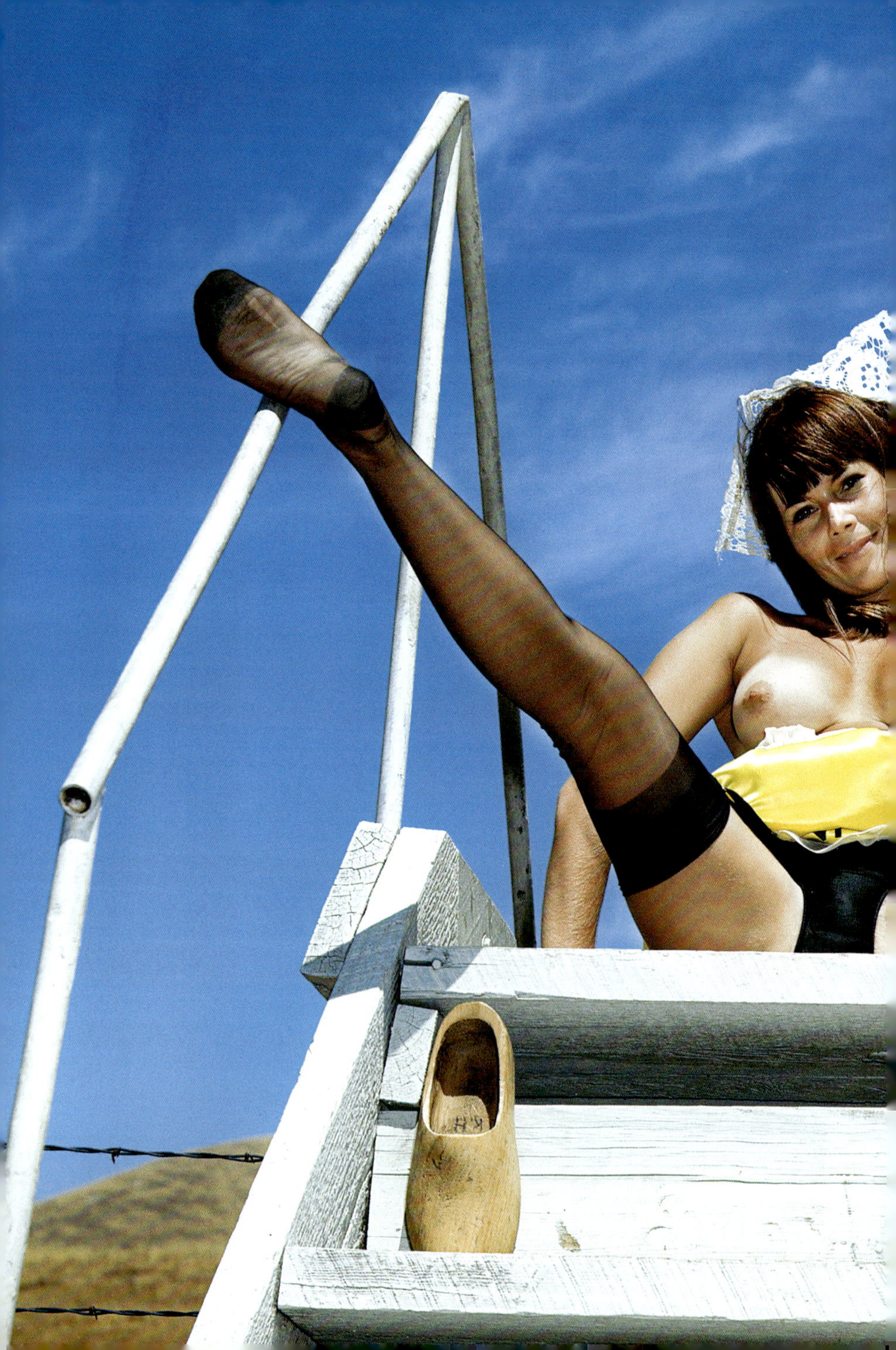

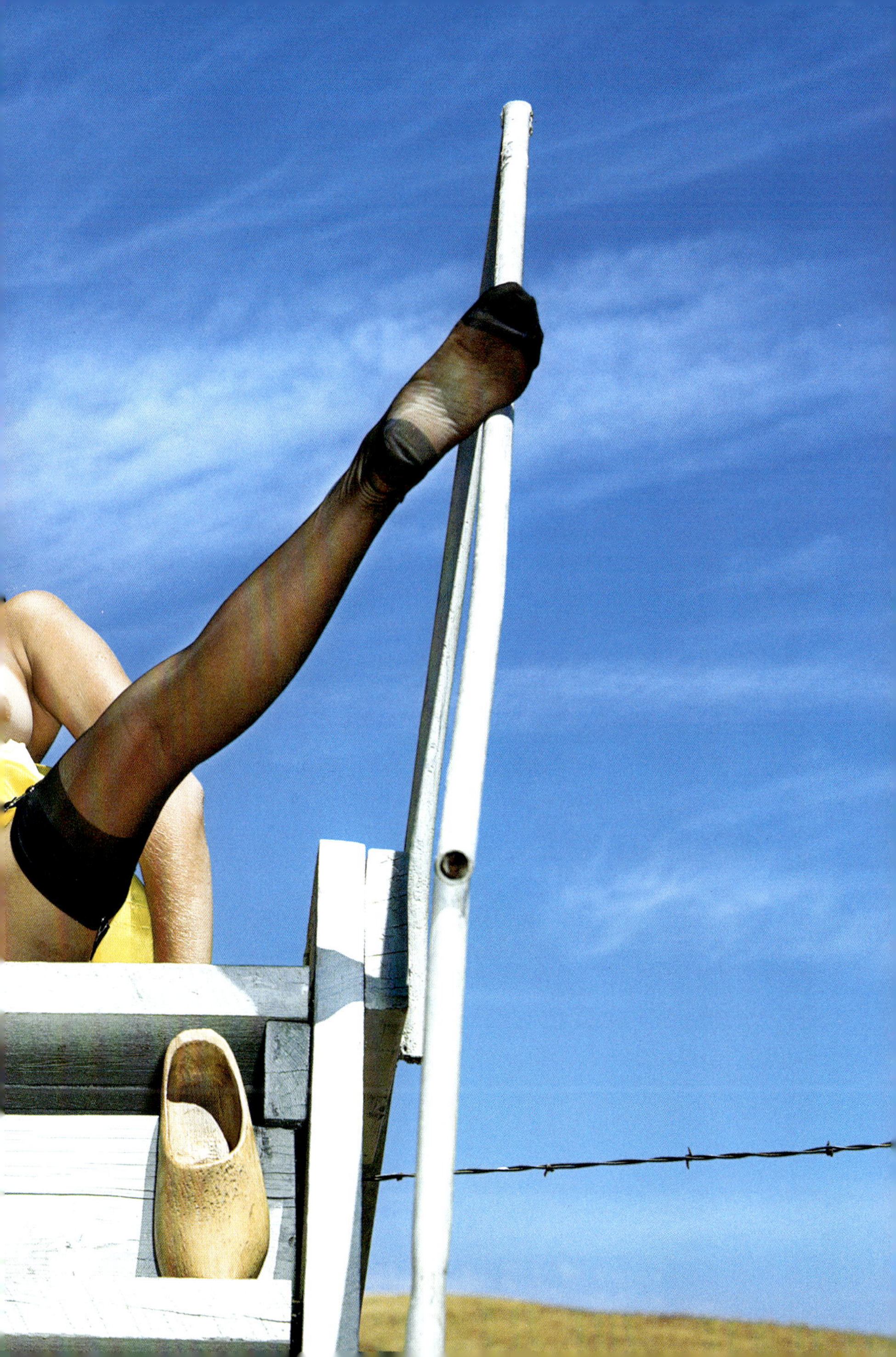

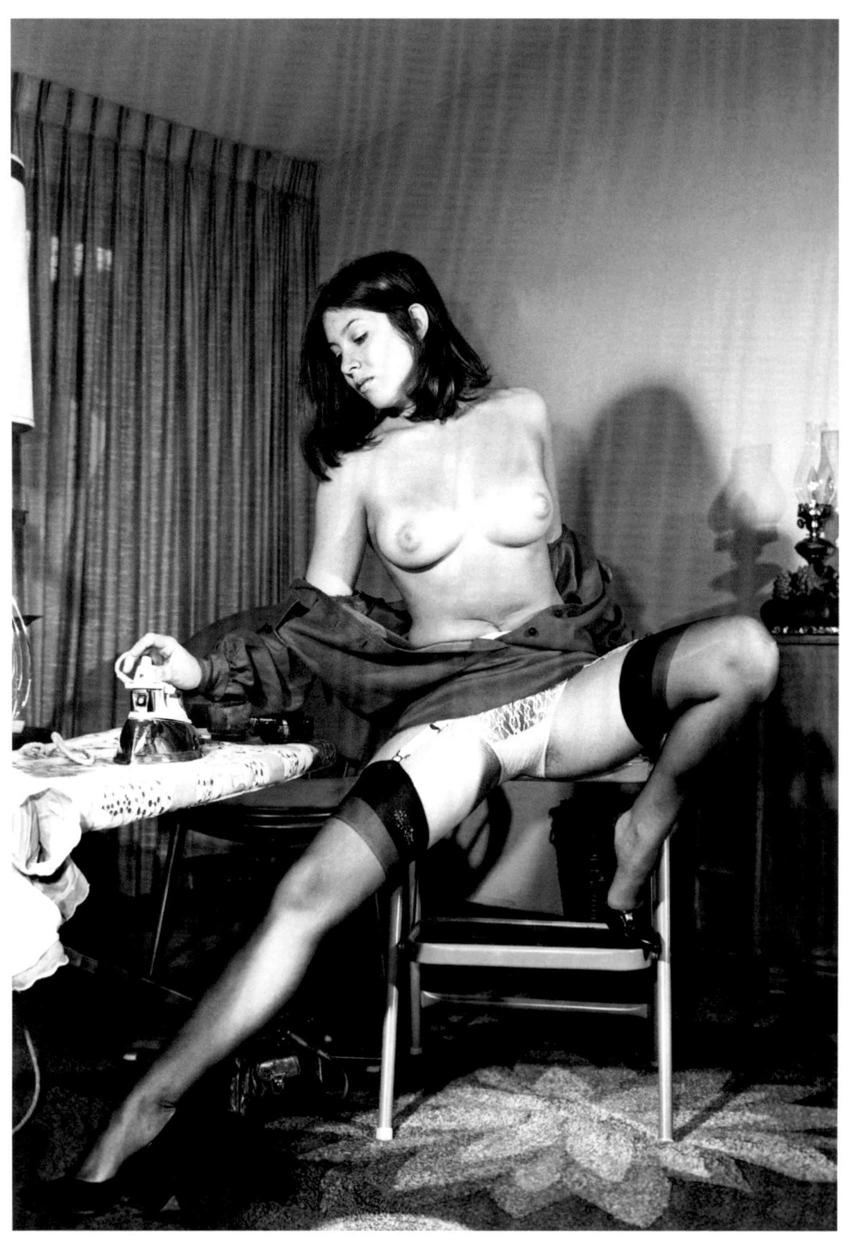

ABOVE **Unknown**, ELMER BATTERS

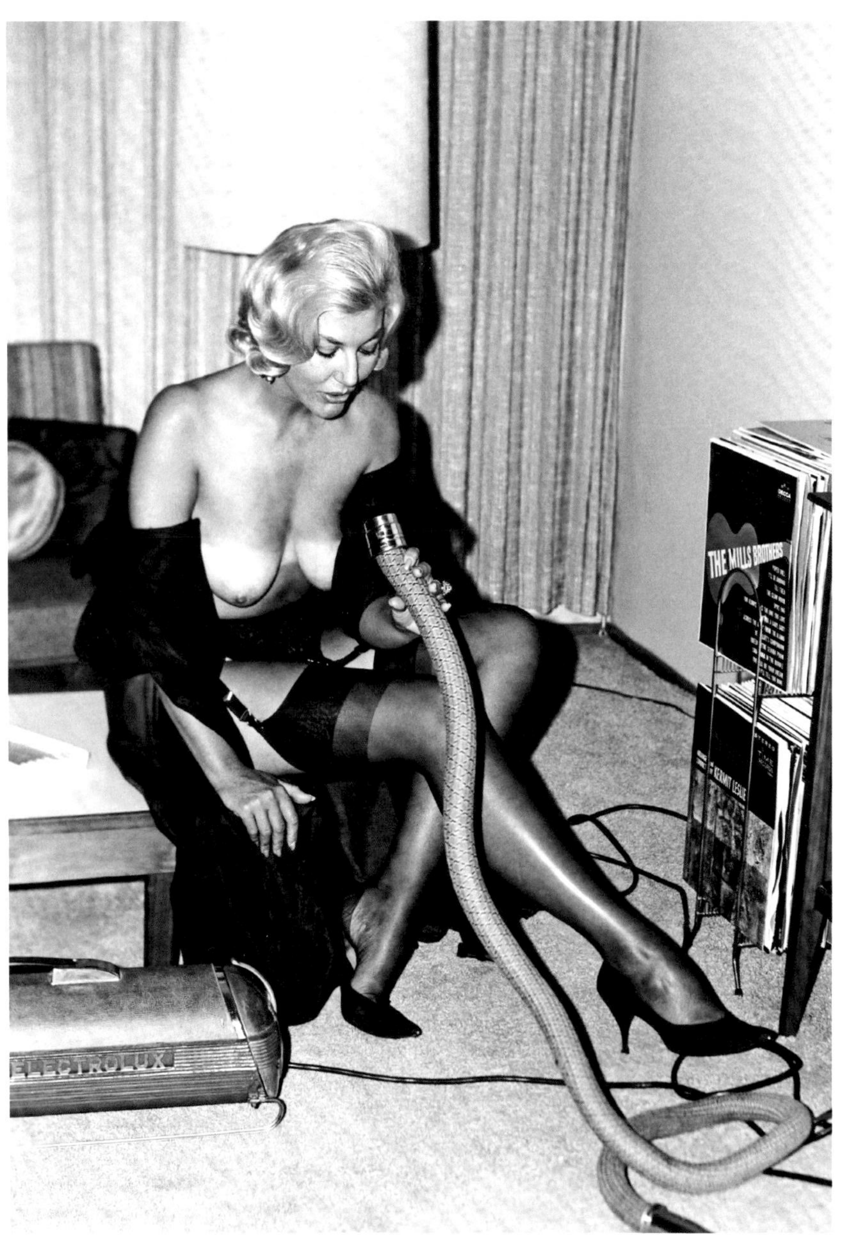

ABOVE **Kimberly Kimble**, ELMER BATTERS

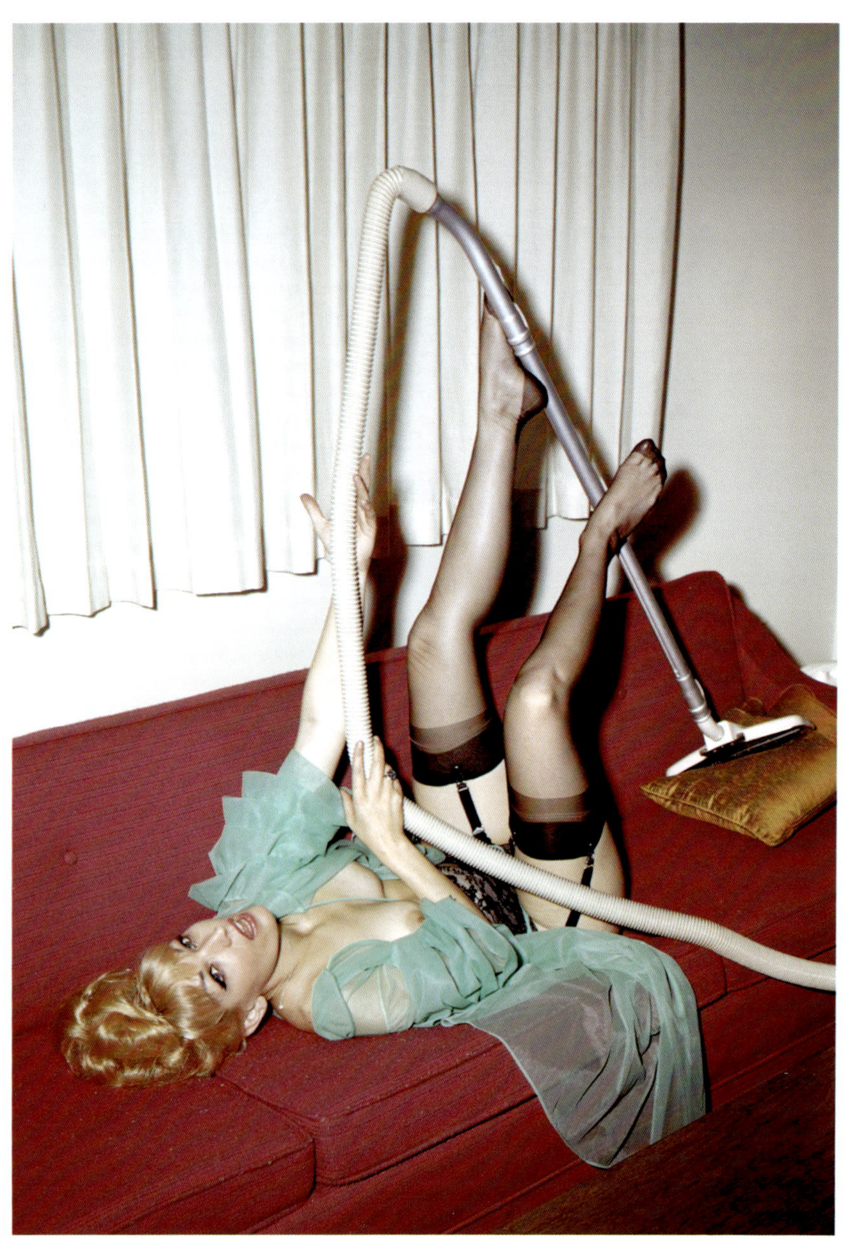

ABOVE Unknown, ELMER BATTERS   OPPOSITE Unknown

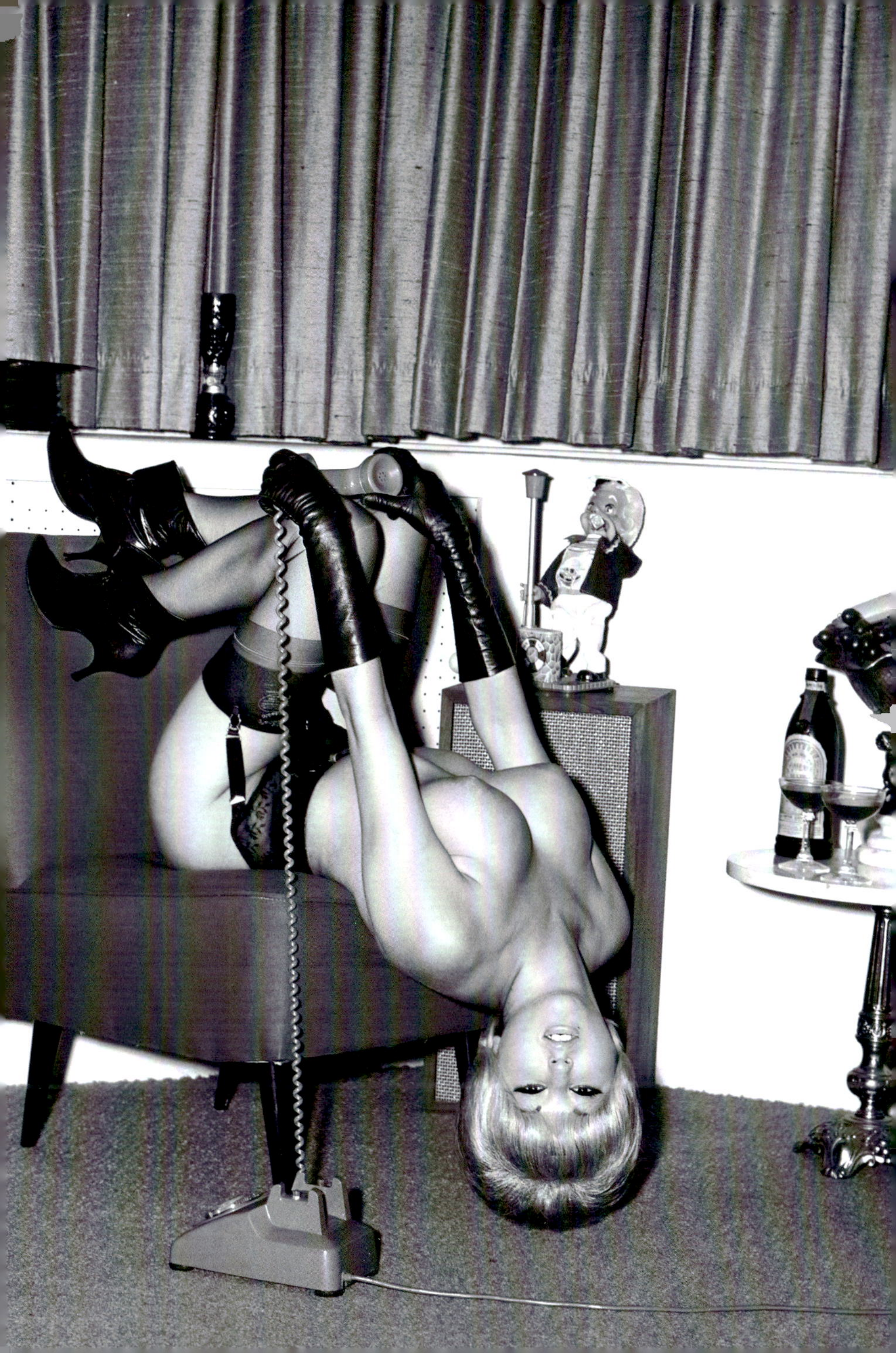

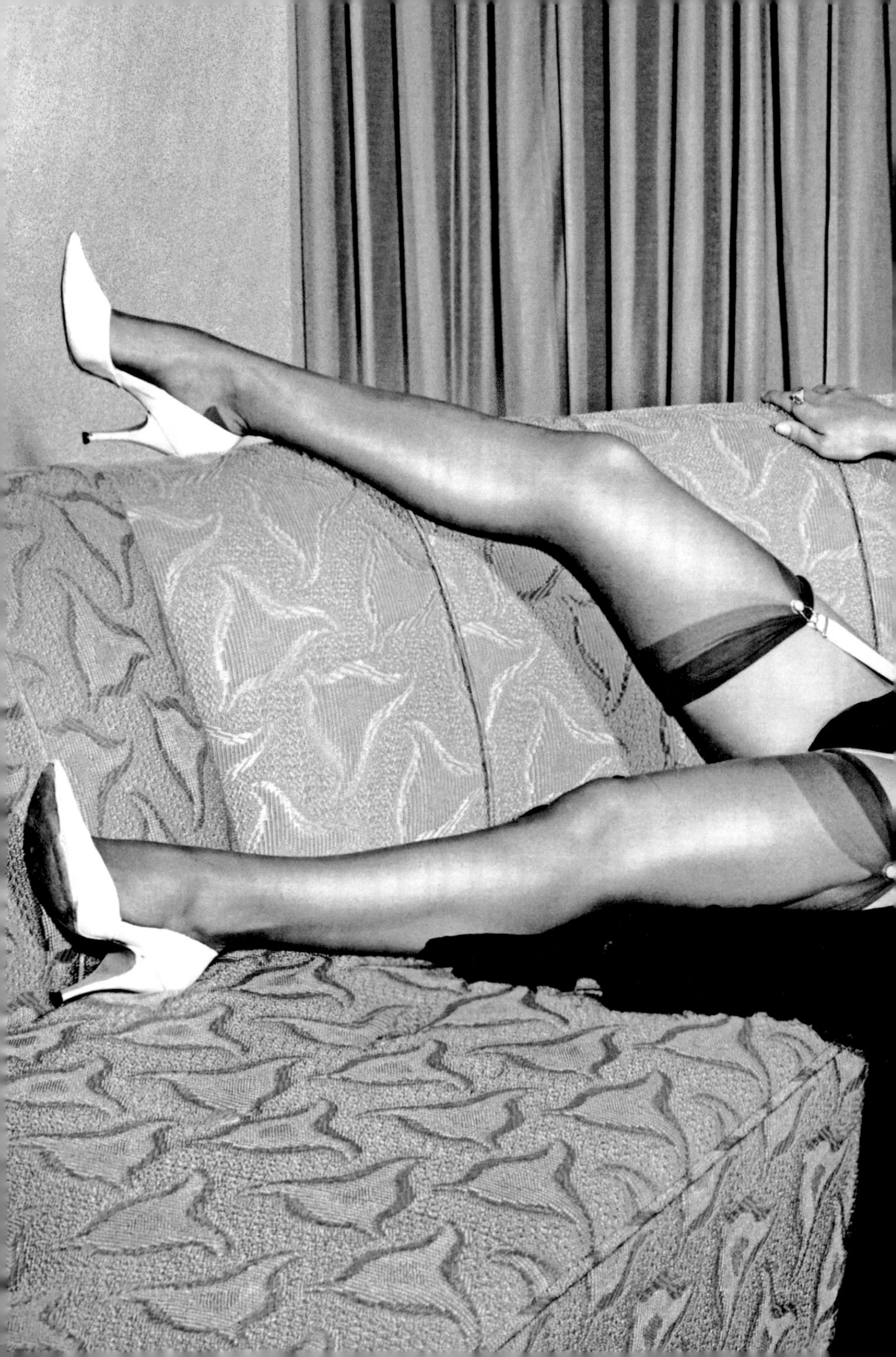

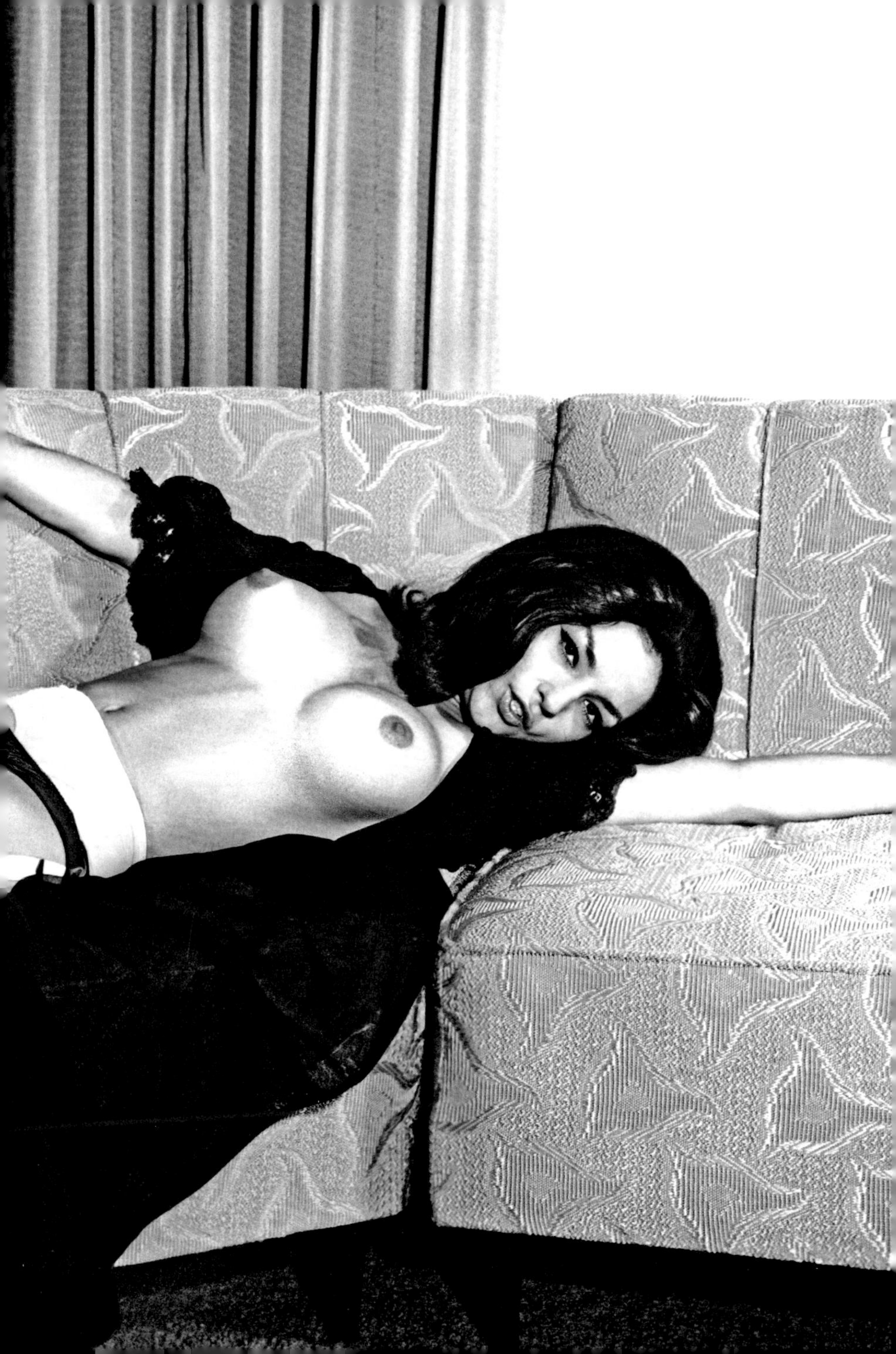

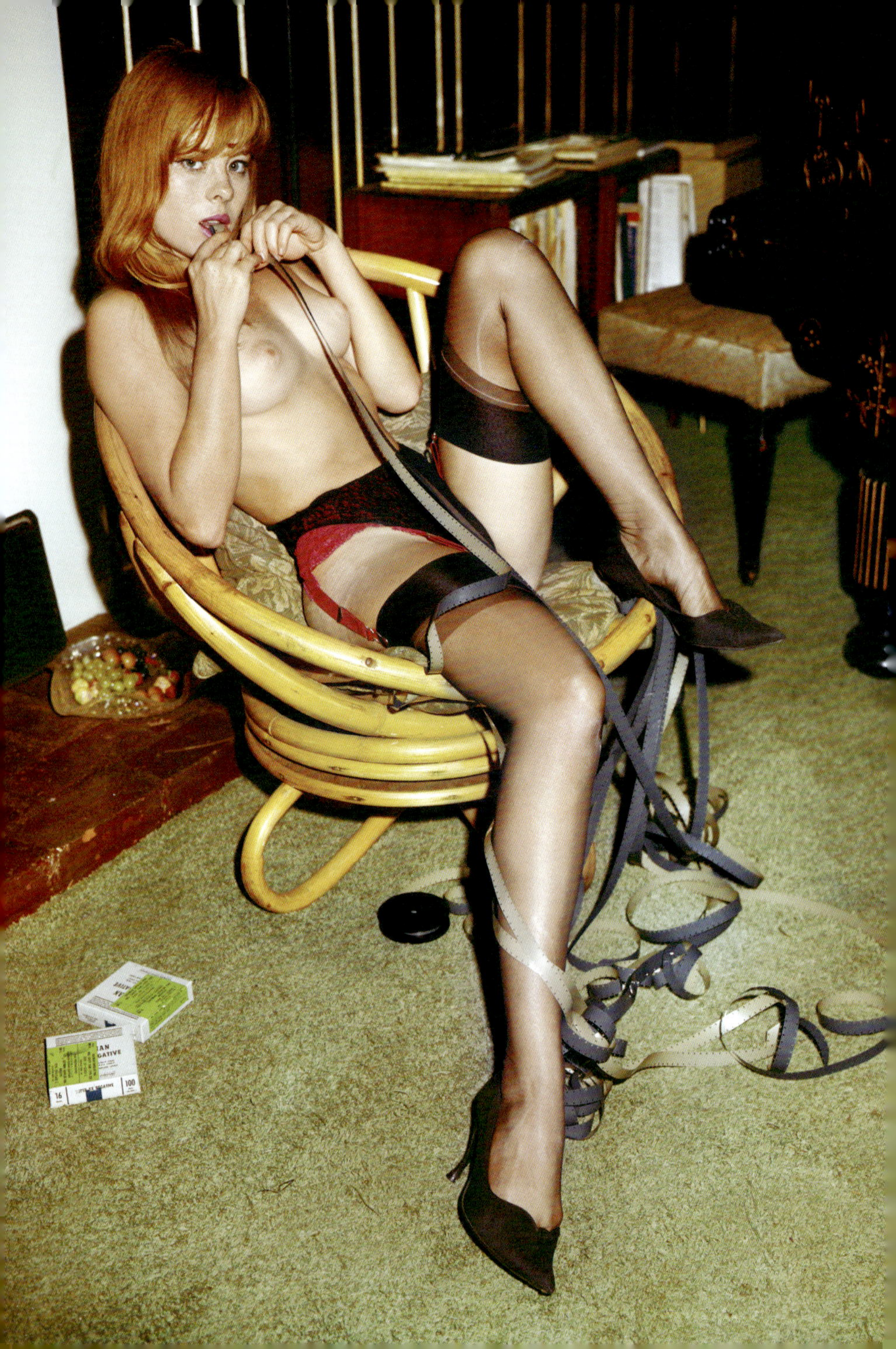

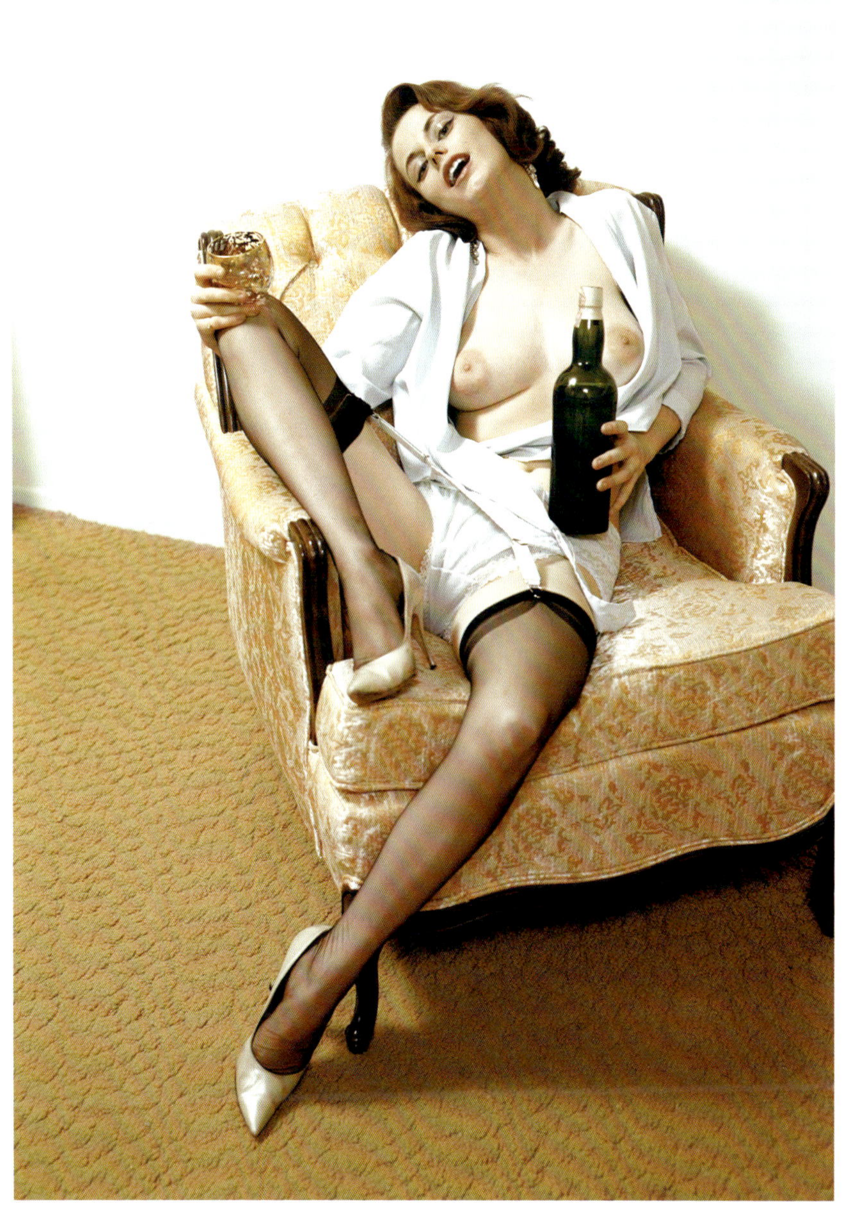

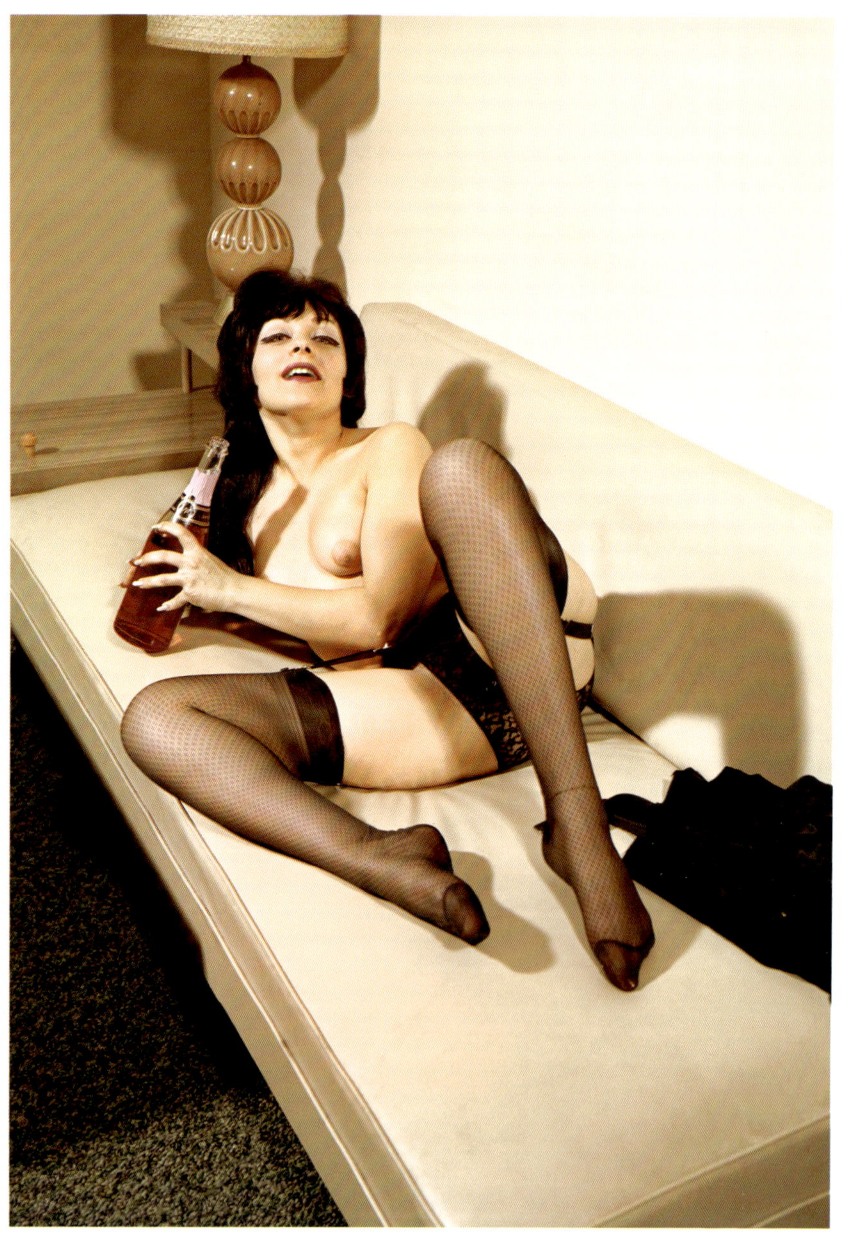

ABOVE Terrie Martin

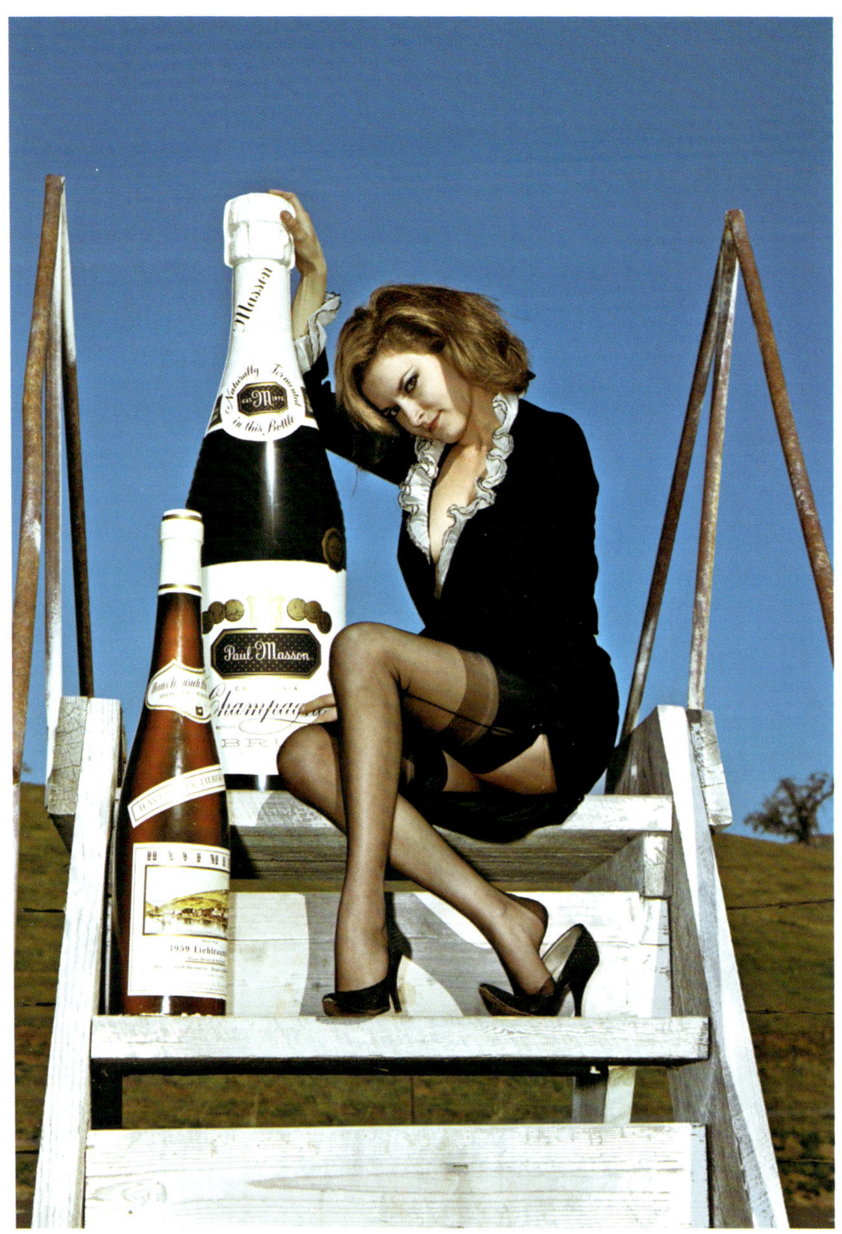

ABOVE Unknown

ABOVE Unknown   OPPOSITE Cynthia Bond   PAGES 148-149 Gayle Glenn in Elmer's car

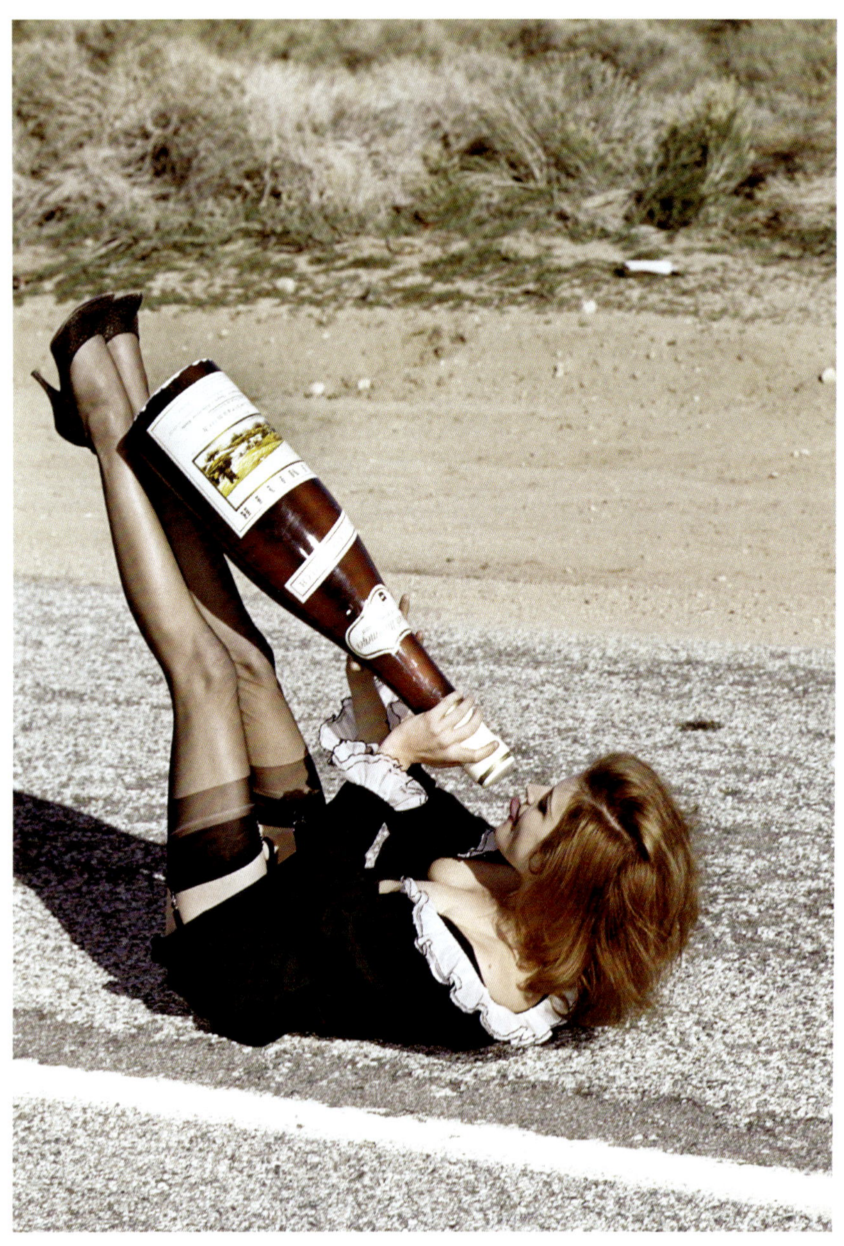

146

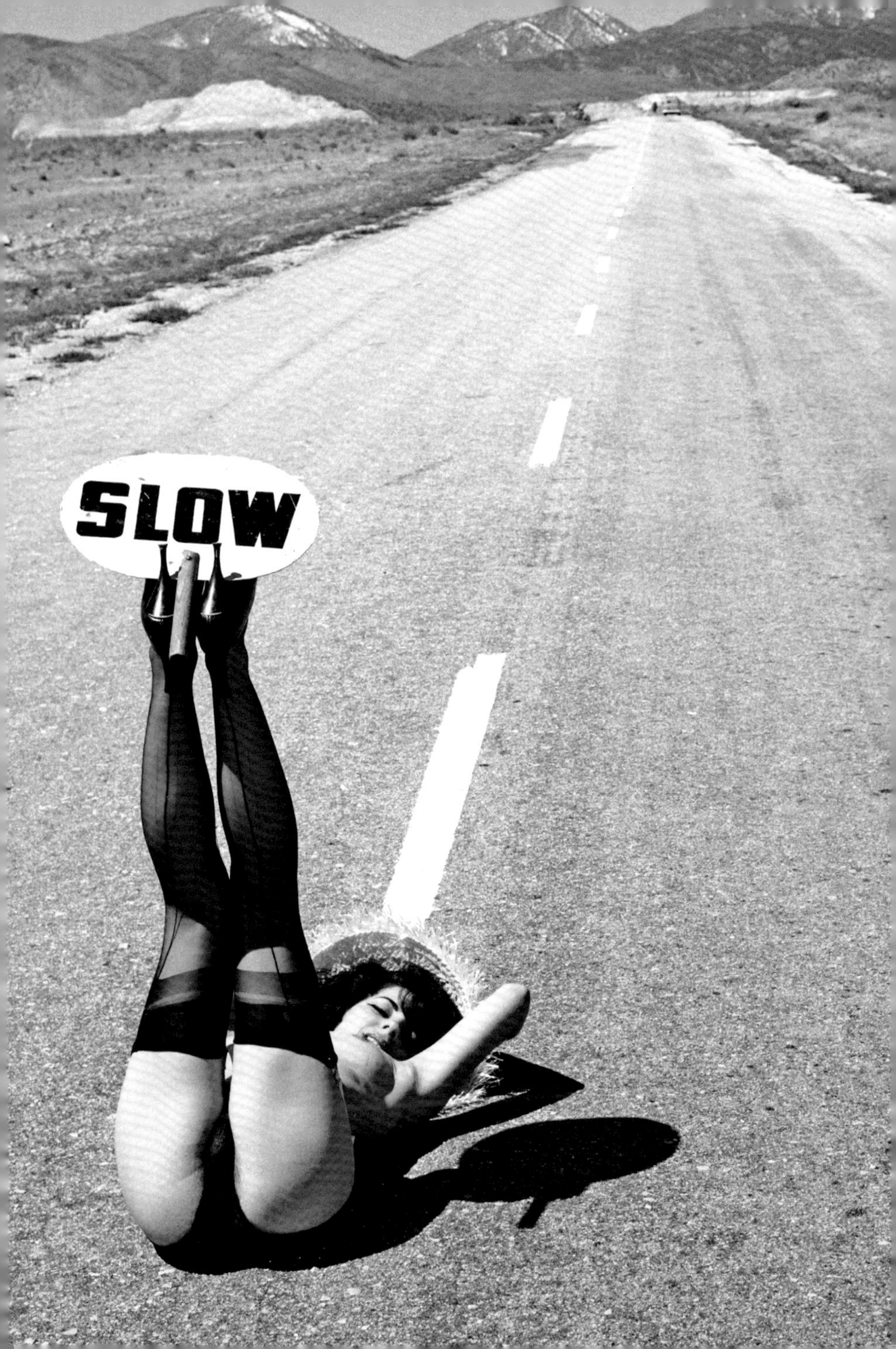
SLOW

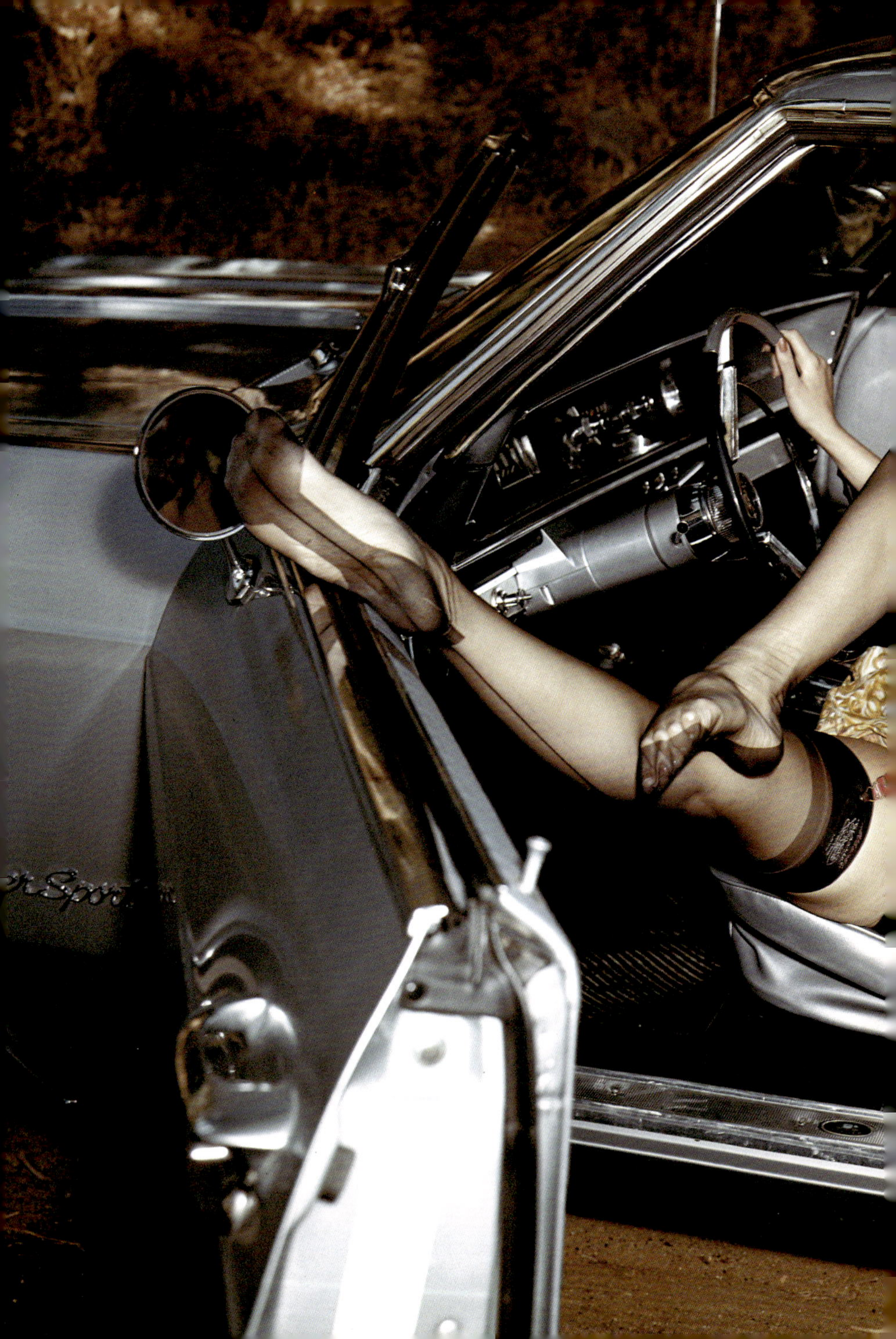

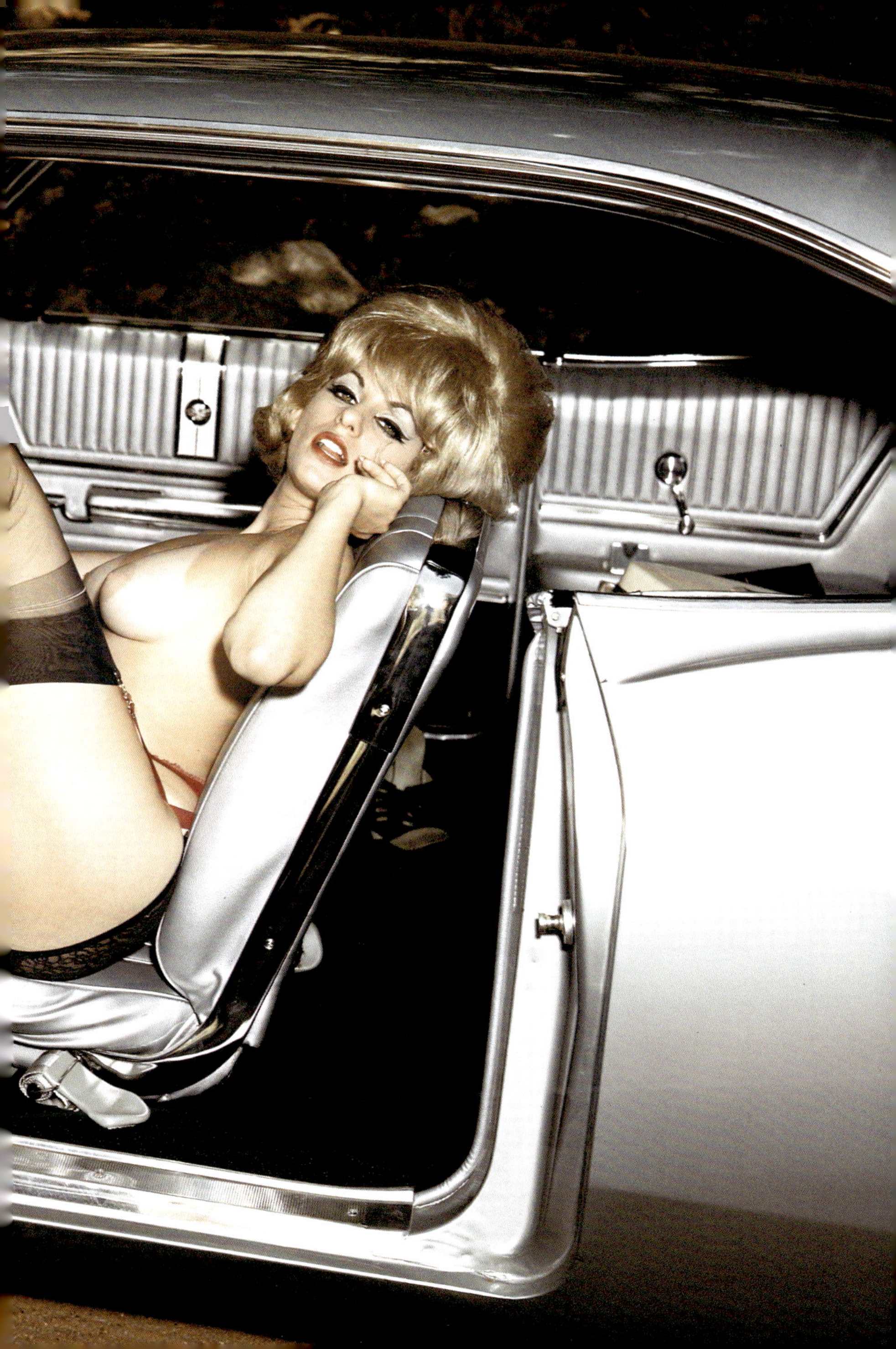

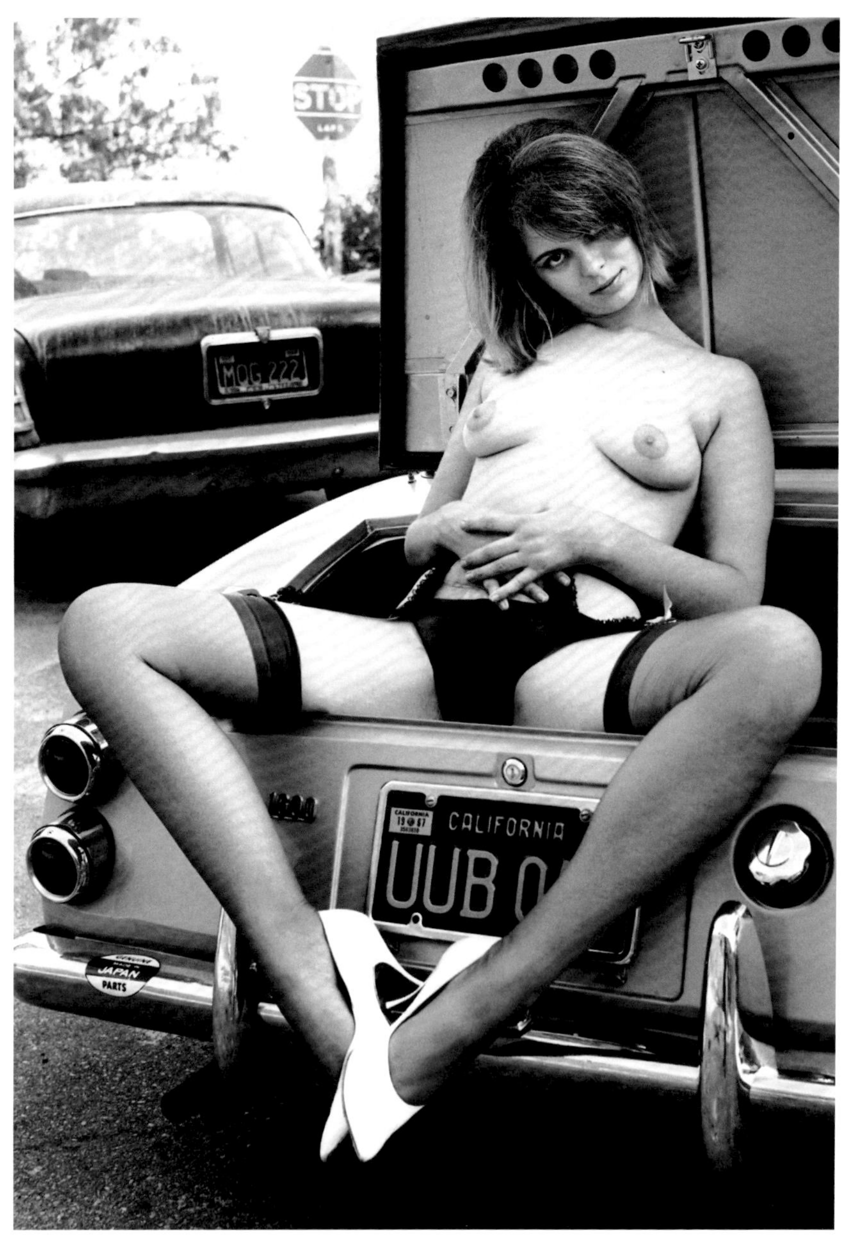

ABOVE Unknown

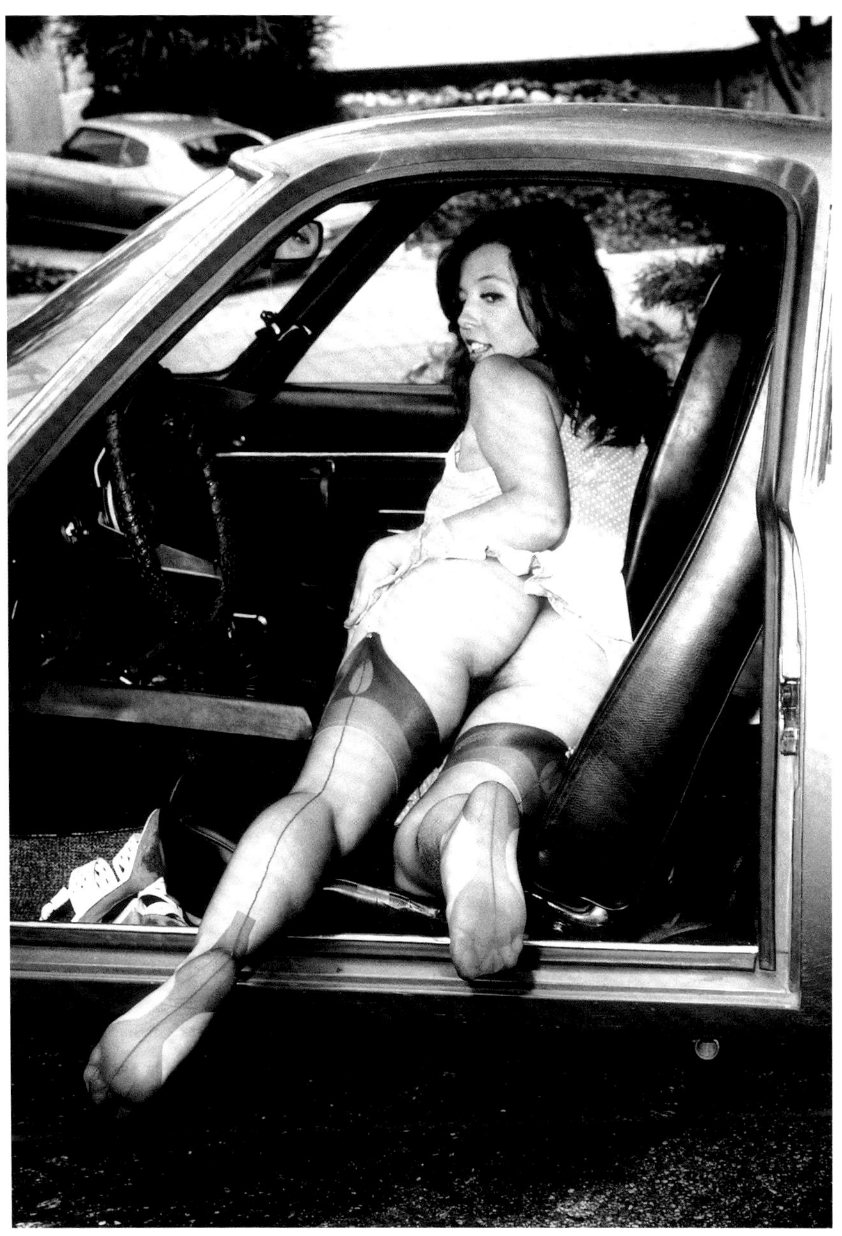

ABOVE Rene Bond, ELMER BATTERS

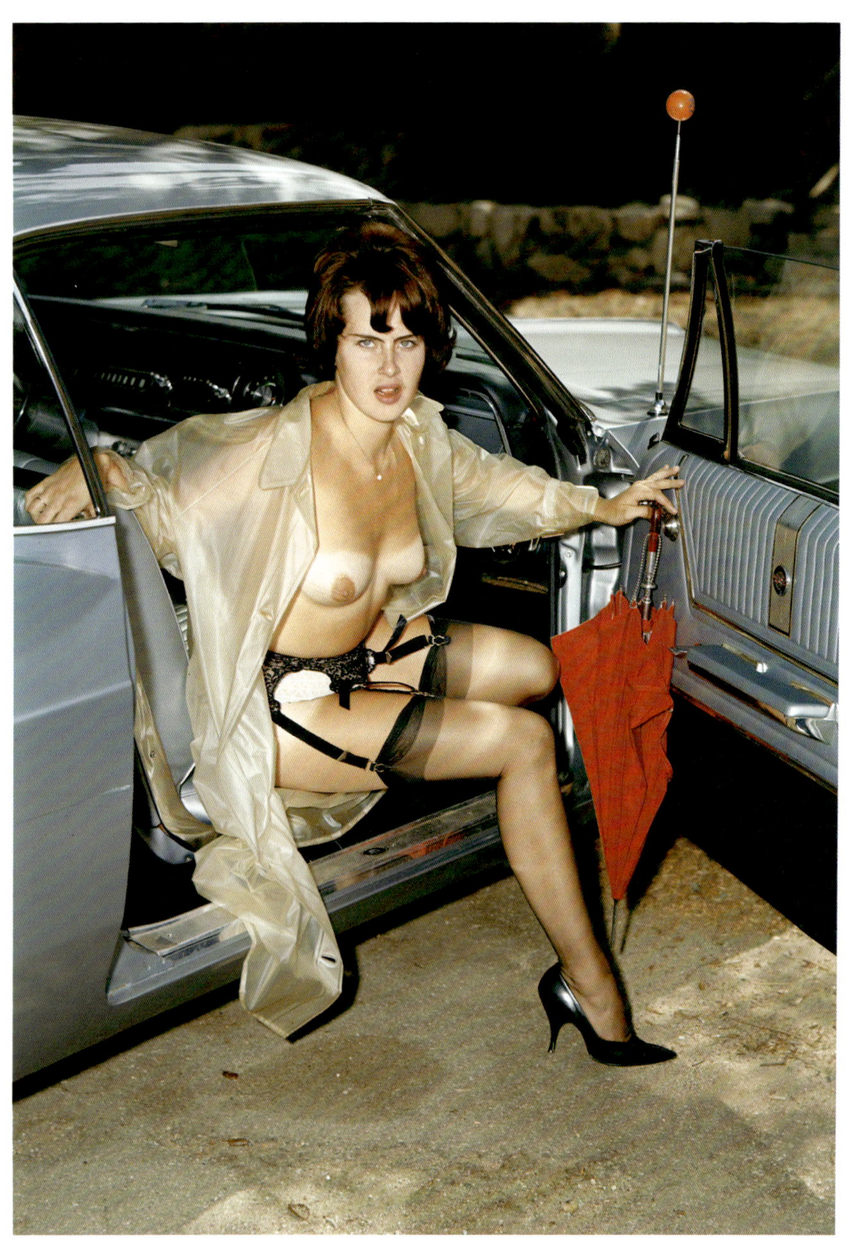

ABOVE Unknown, ELMER BATTERS

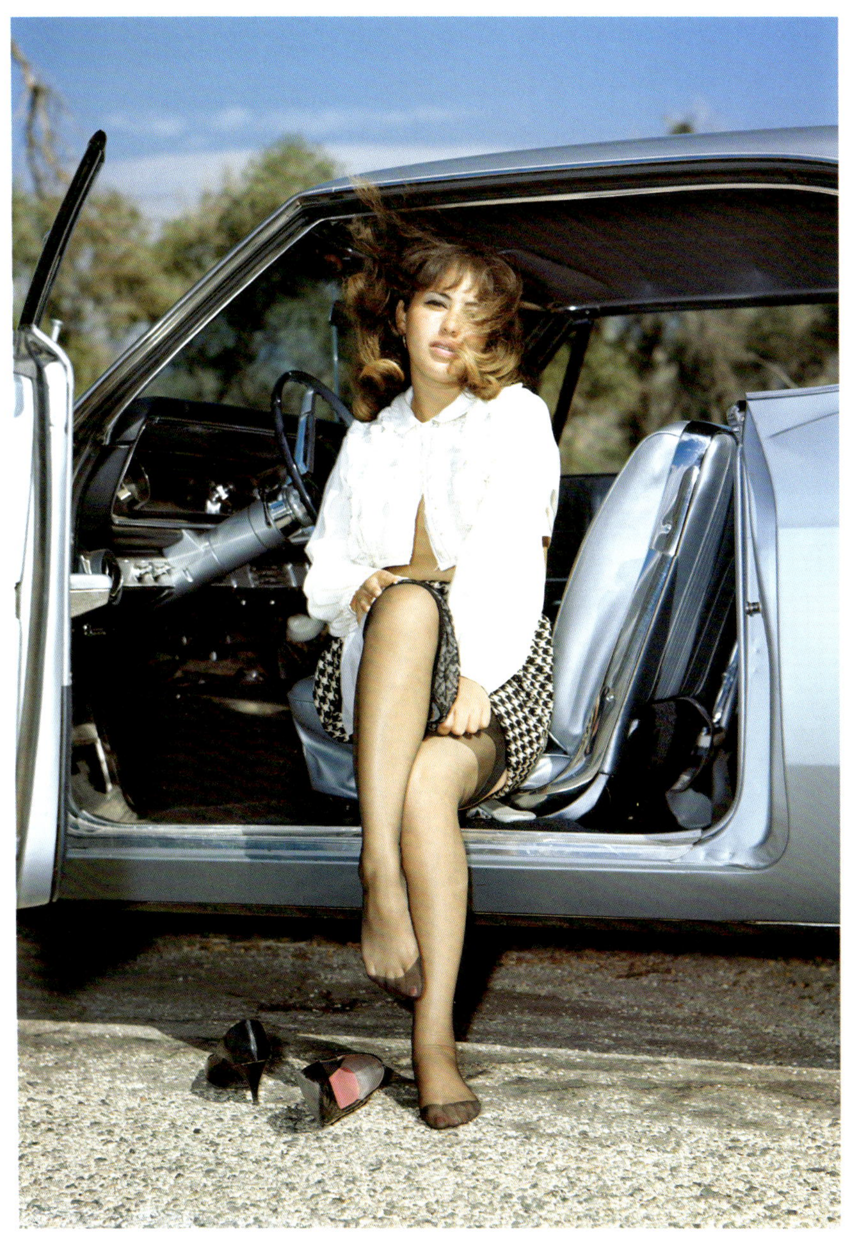

ABOVE Unknown, ELMER BATTERS

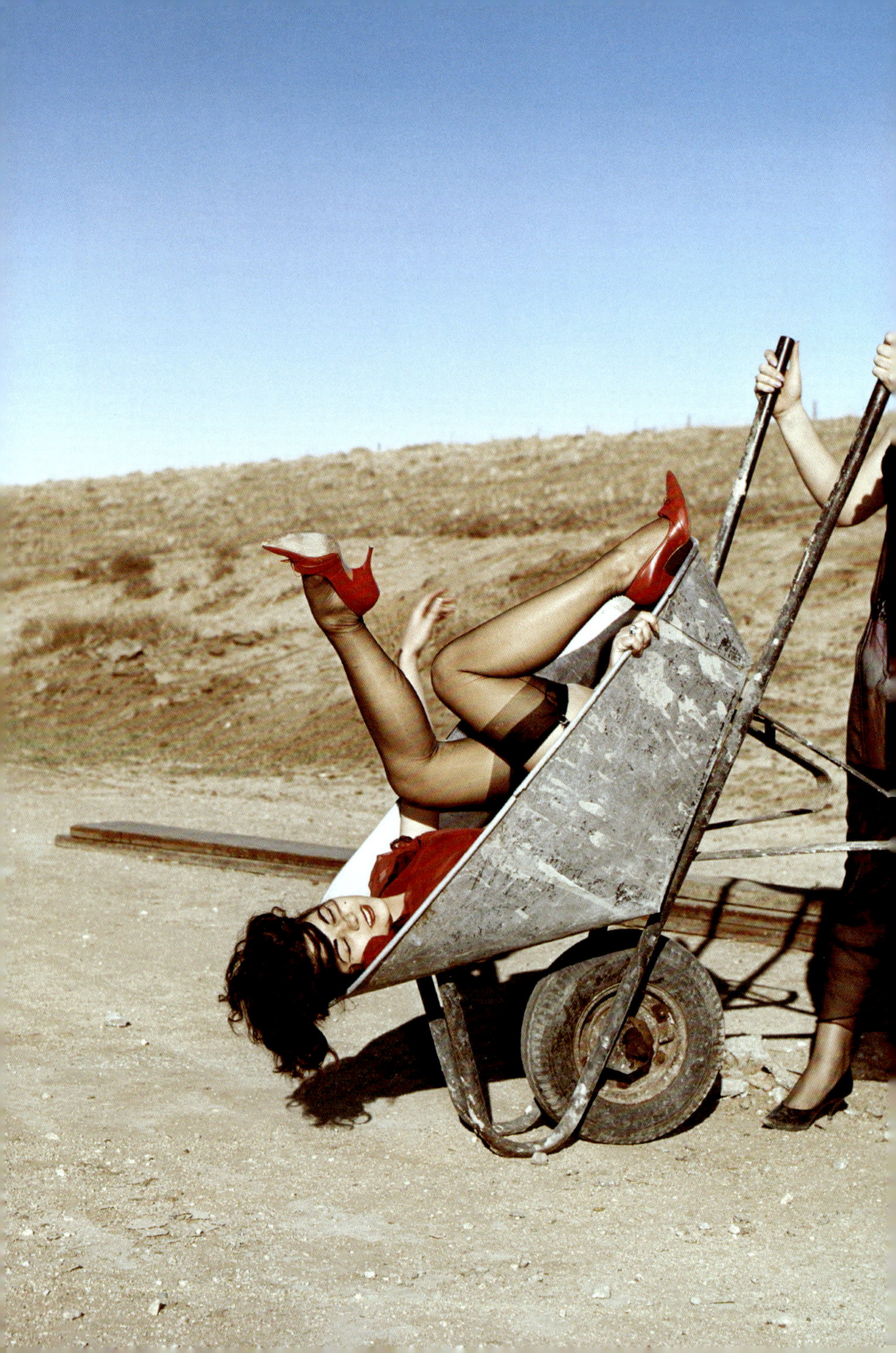

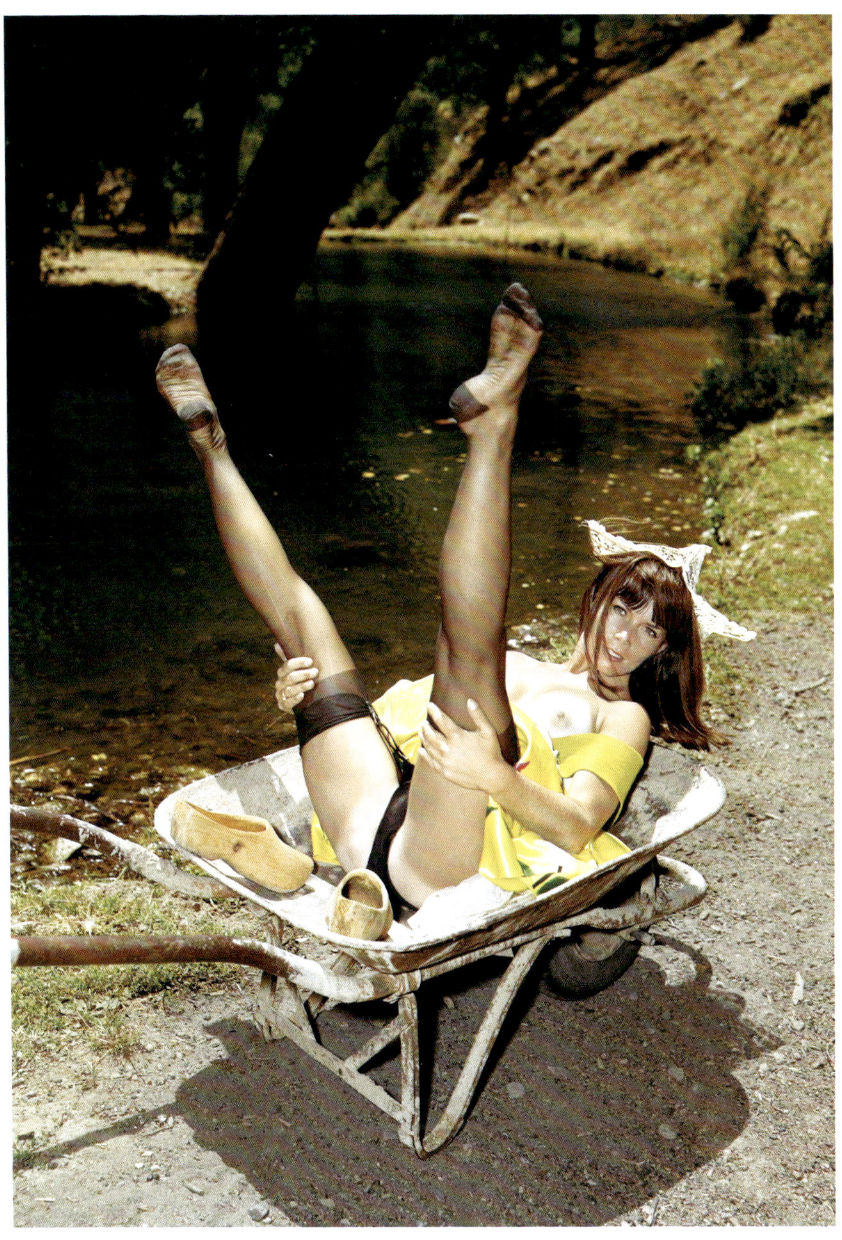

OPPOSITE **Unknown** ABOVE **Brandy Lane**, ELMER BATTERS

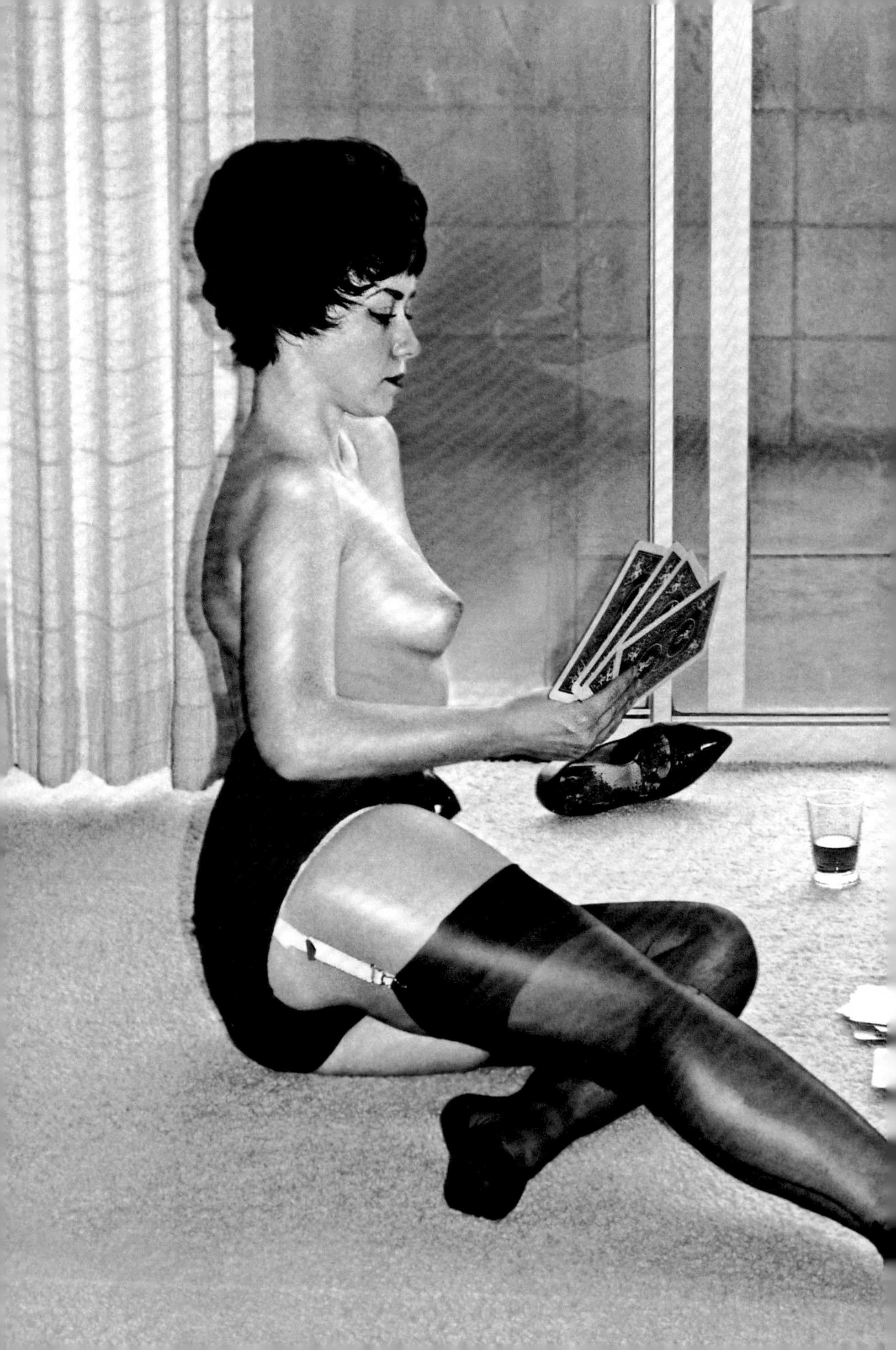

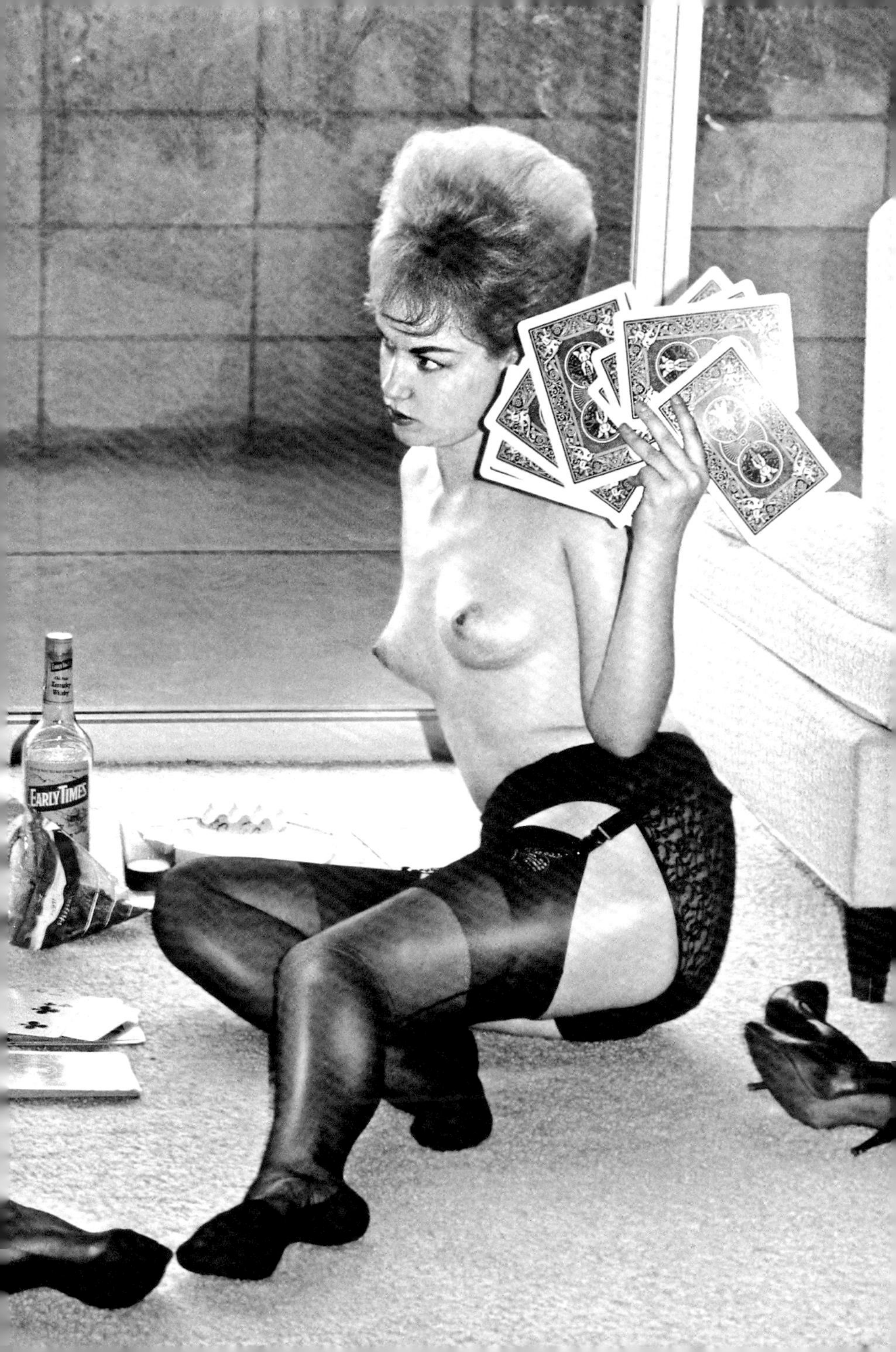

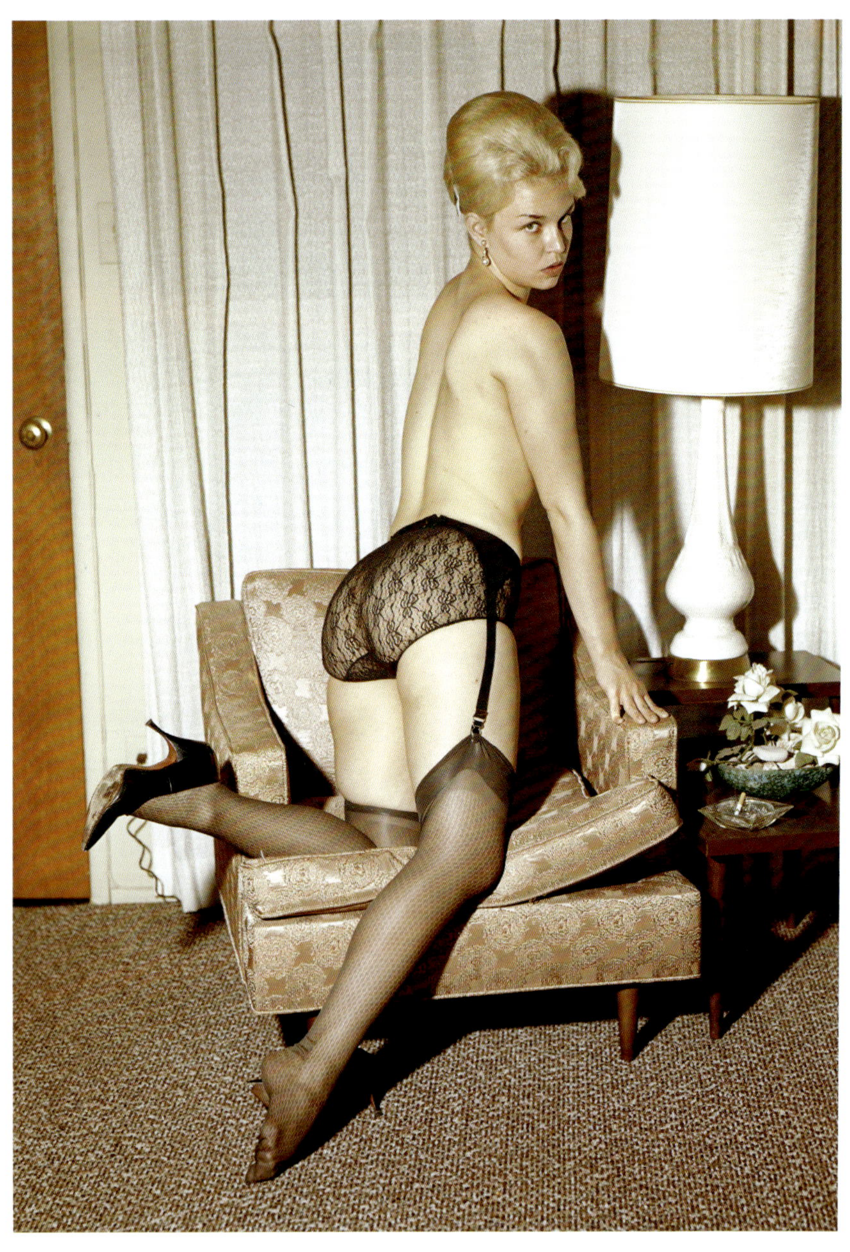

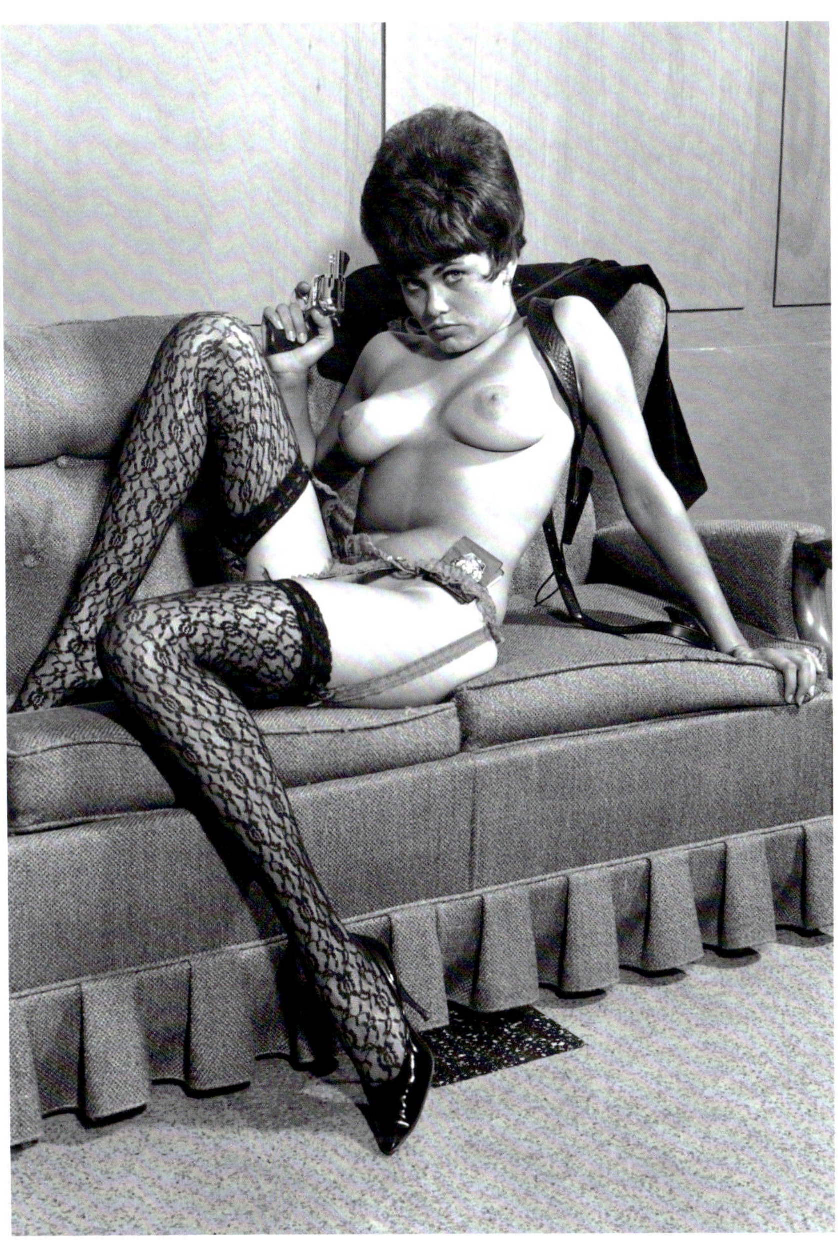

ABOVE Lydia Farrell

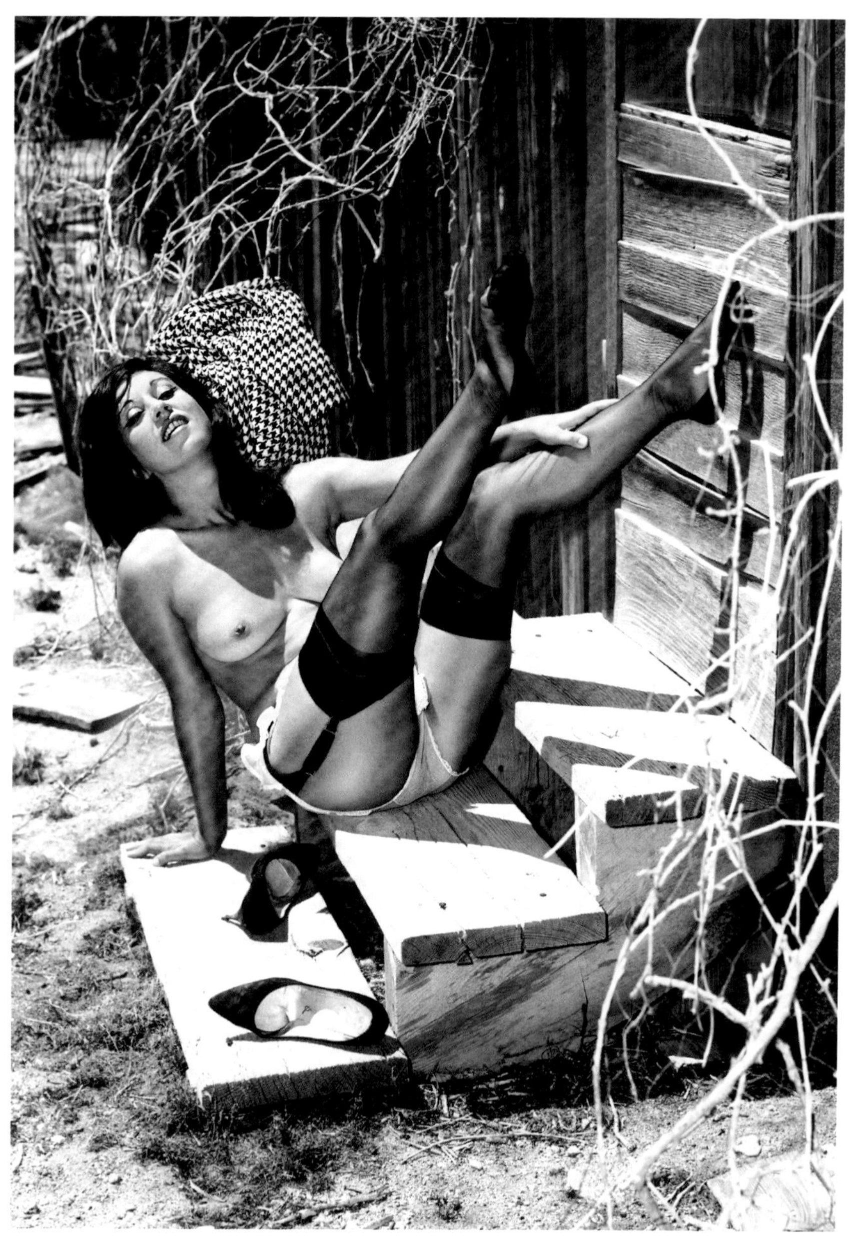

ABOVE Cora Lee, ELMER BATTERS   OPPOSITE Randy Glen, ELMER BATTERS

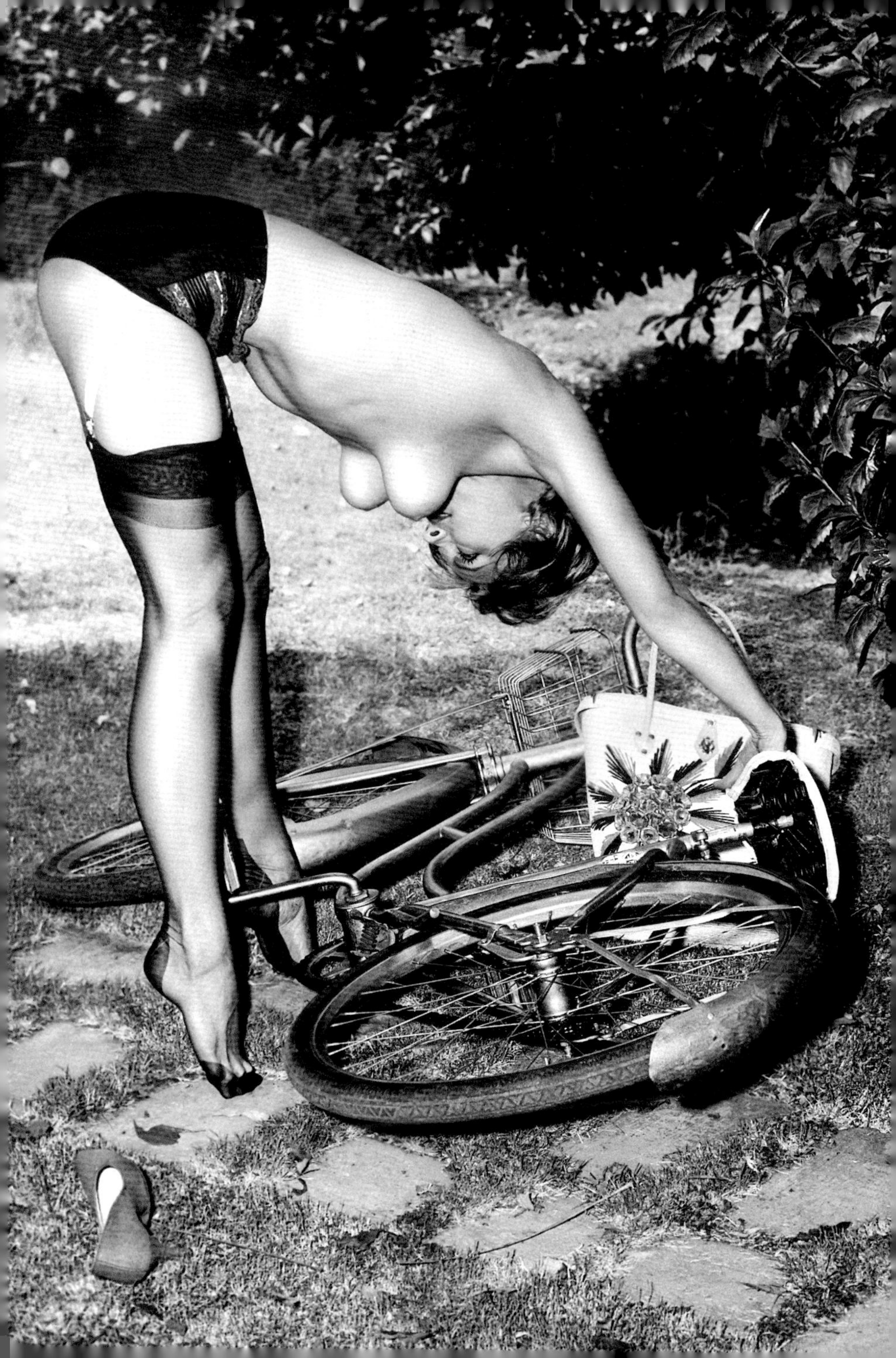

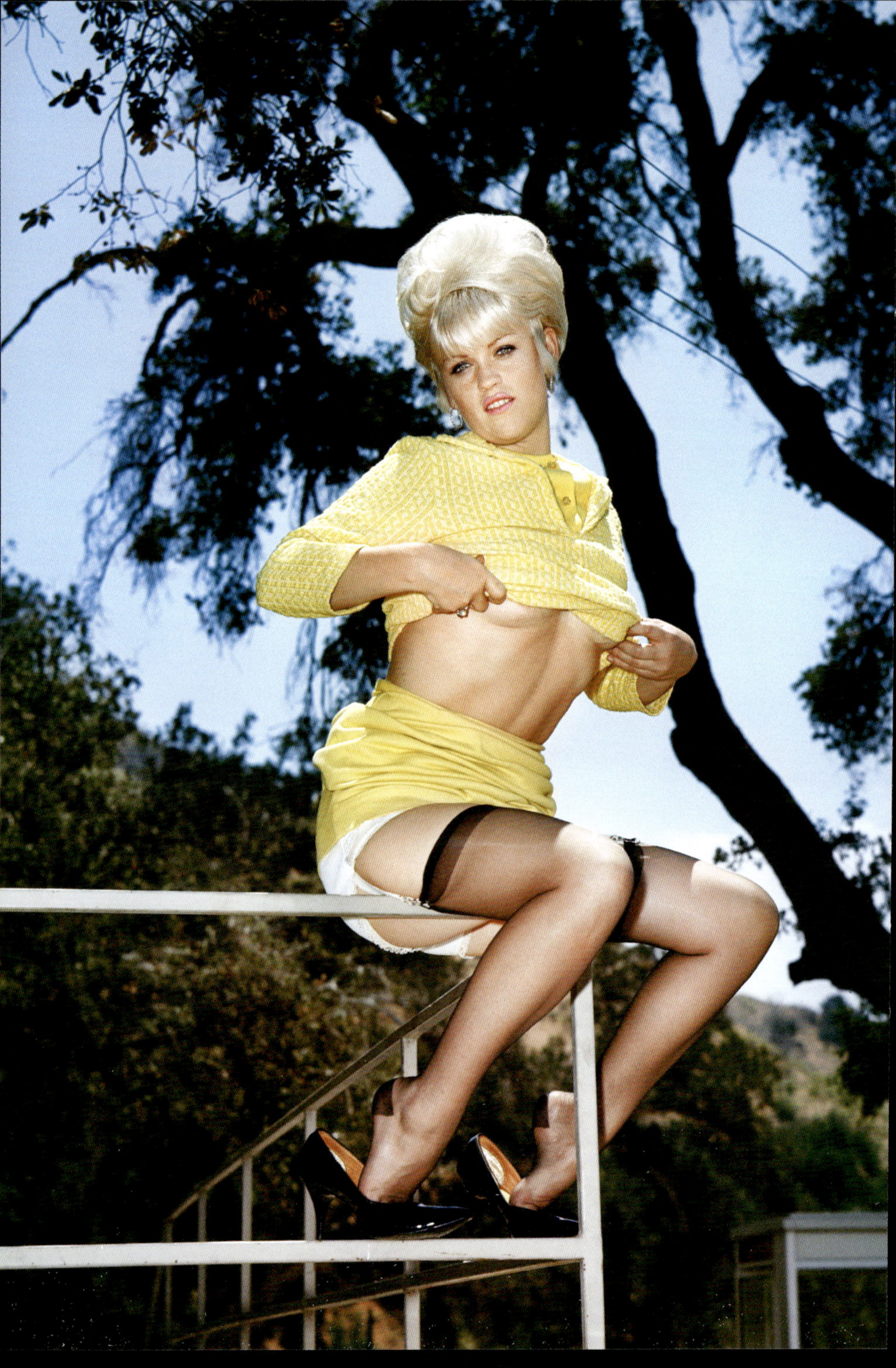

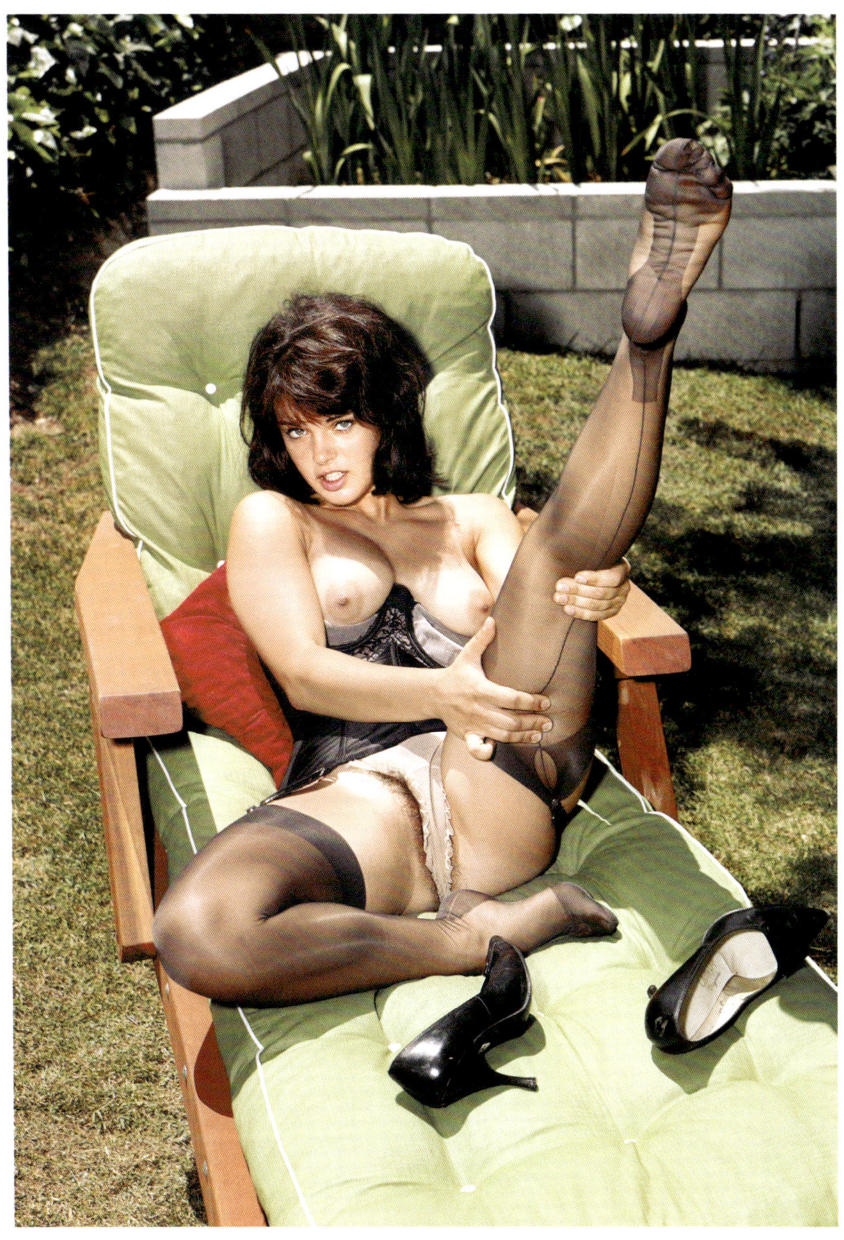

OPPOSITE **Unknown**   ABOVE **Carol Baughman**, ELMER BATTERS

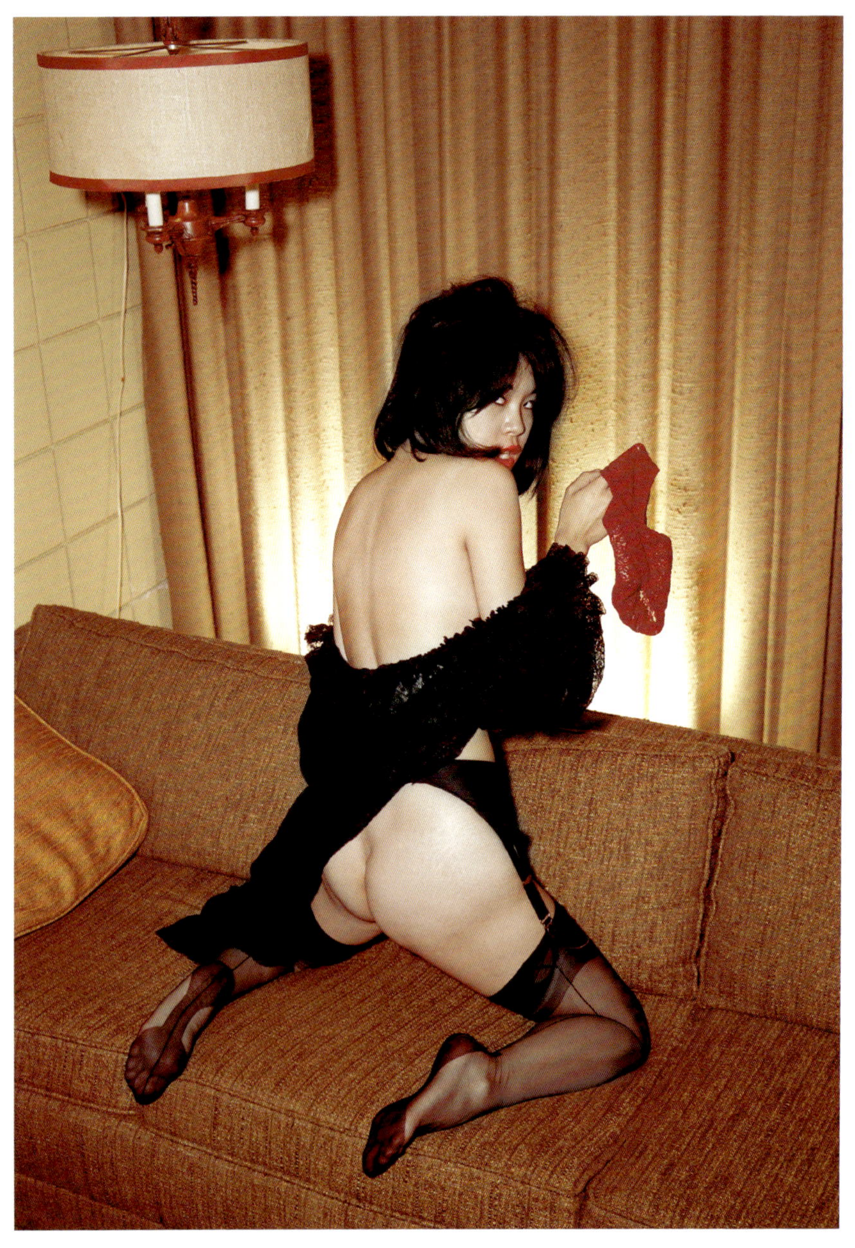

ABOVE Janis Moore

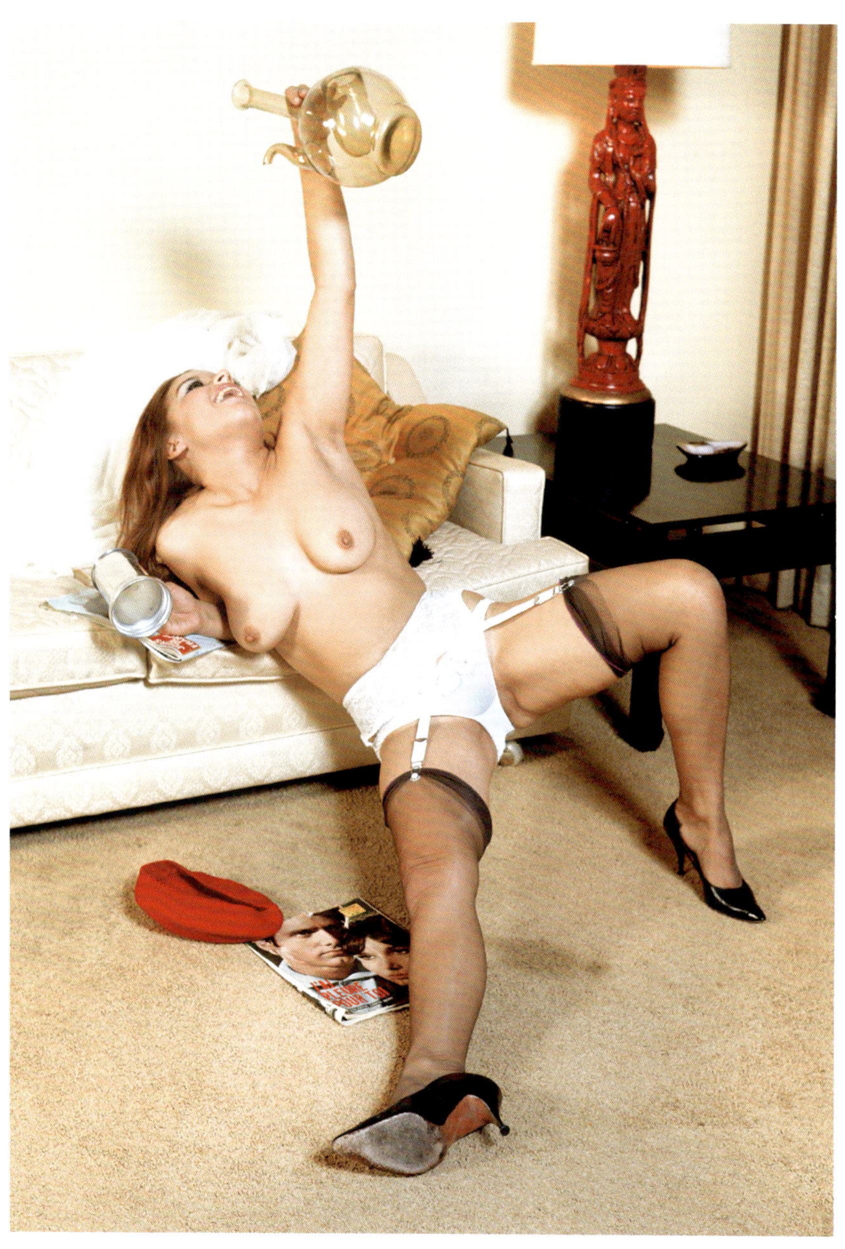

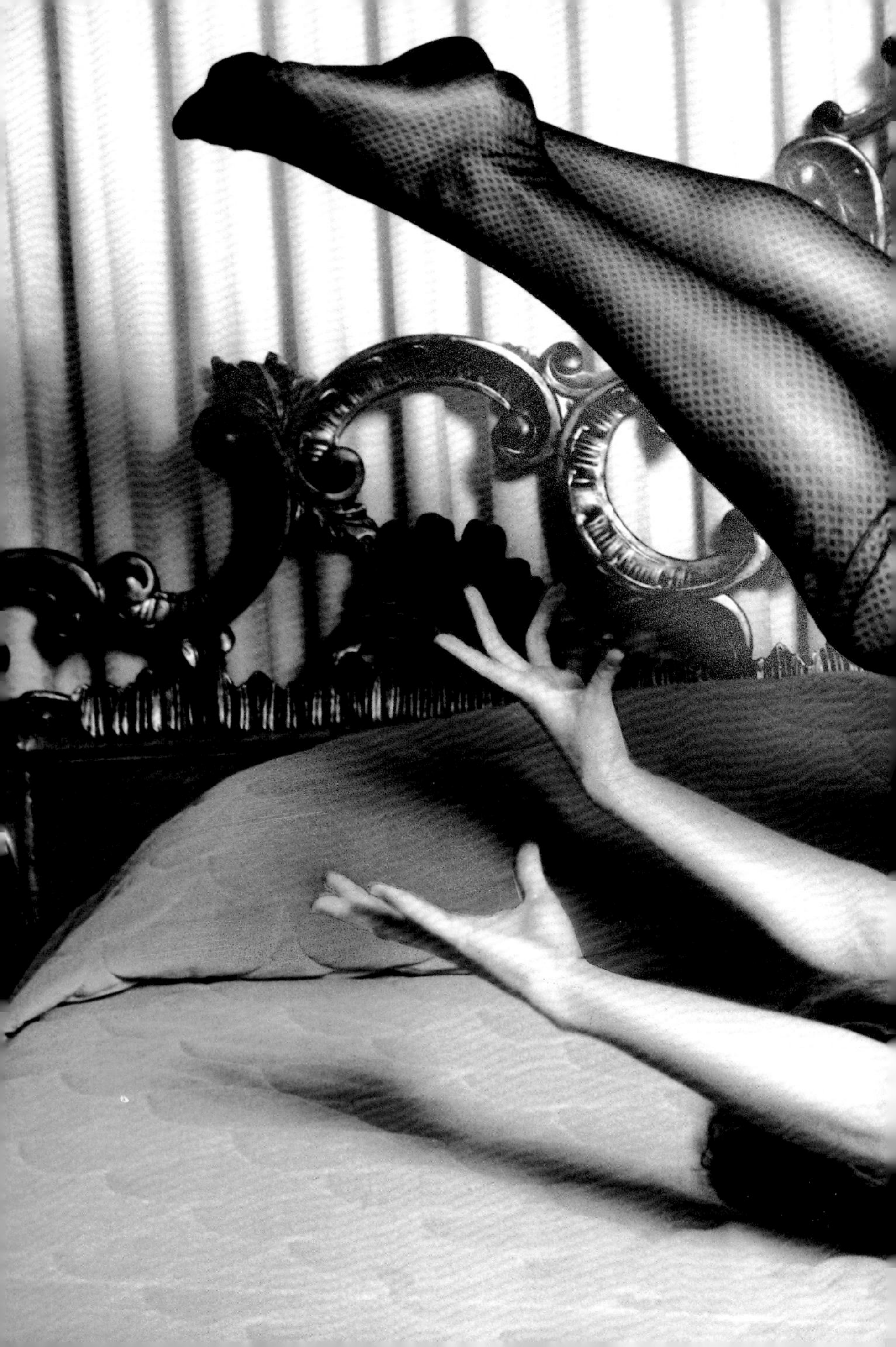

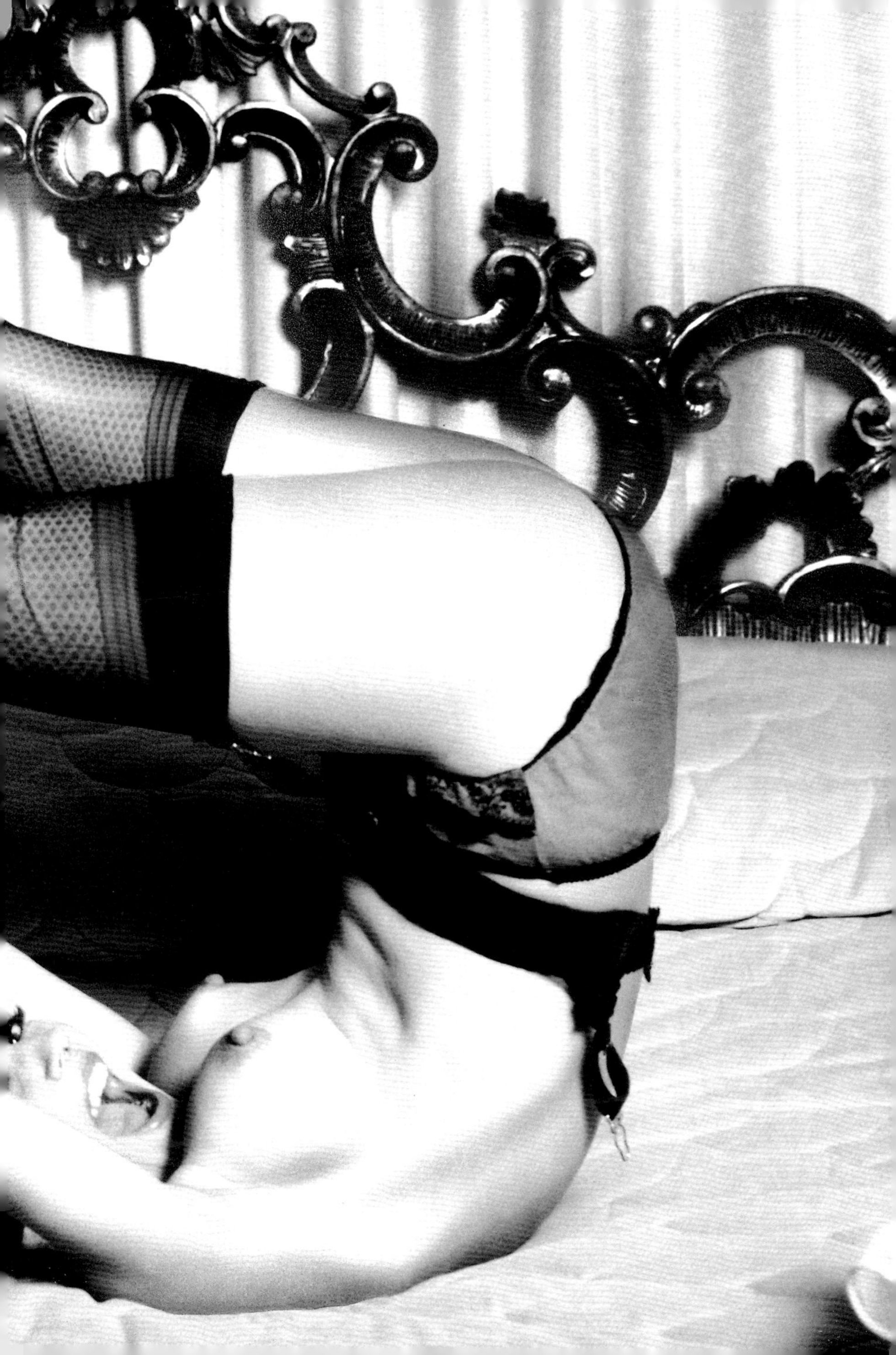

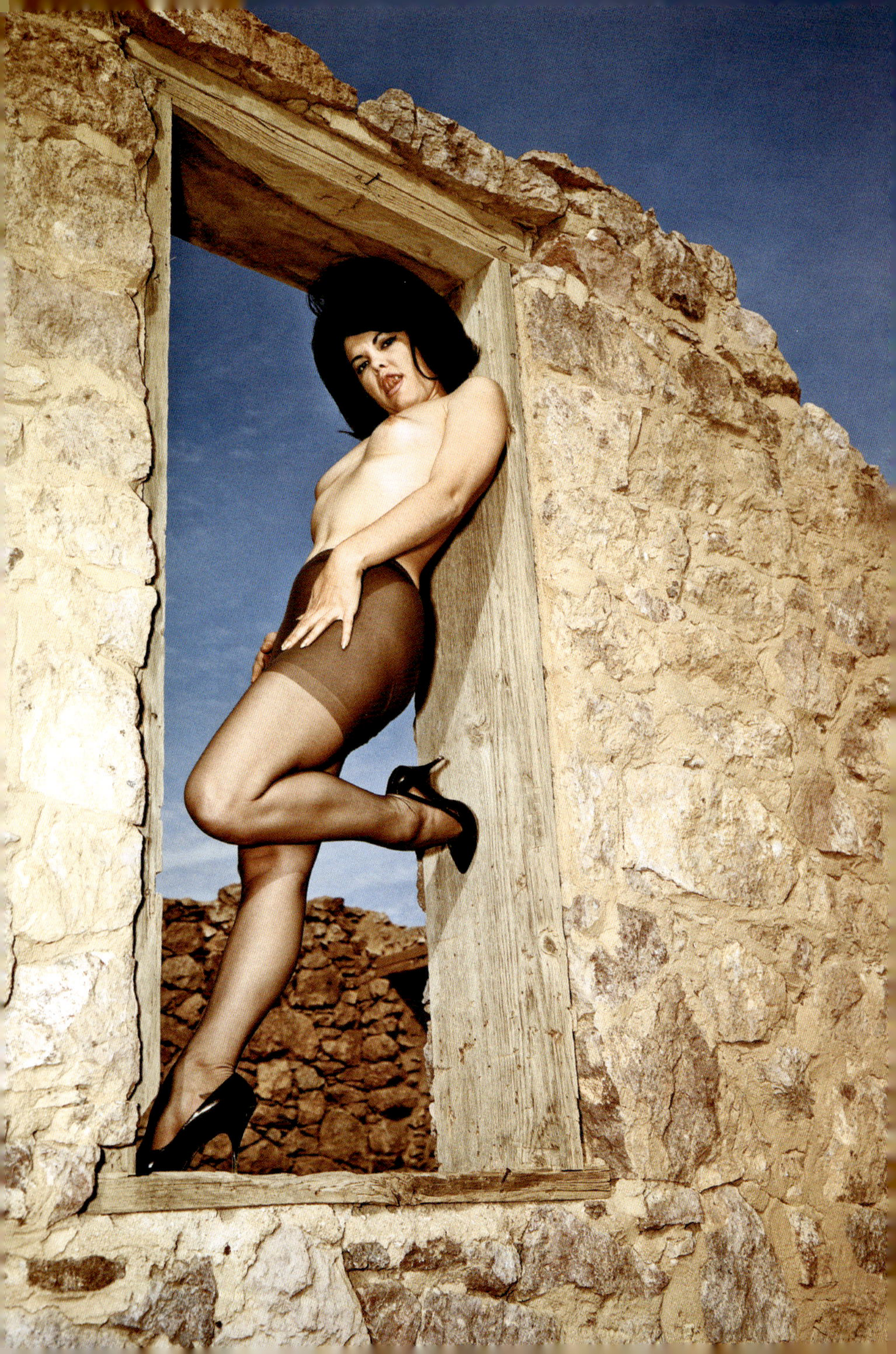

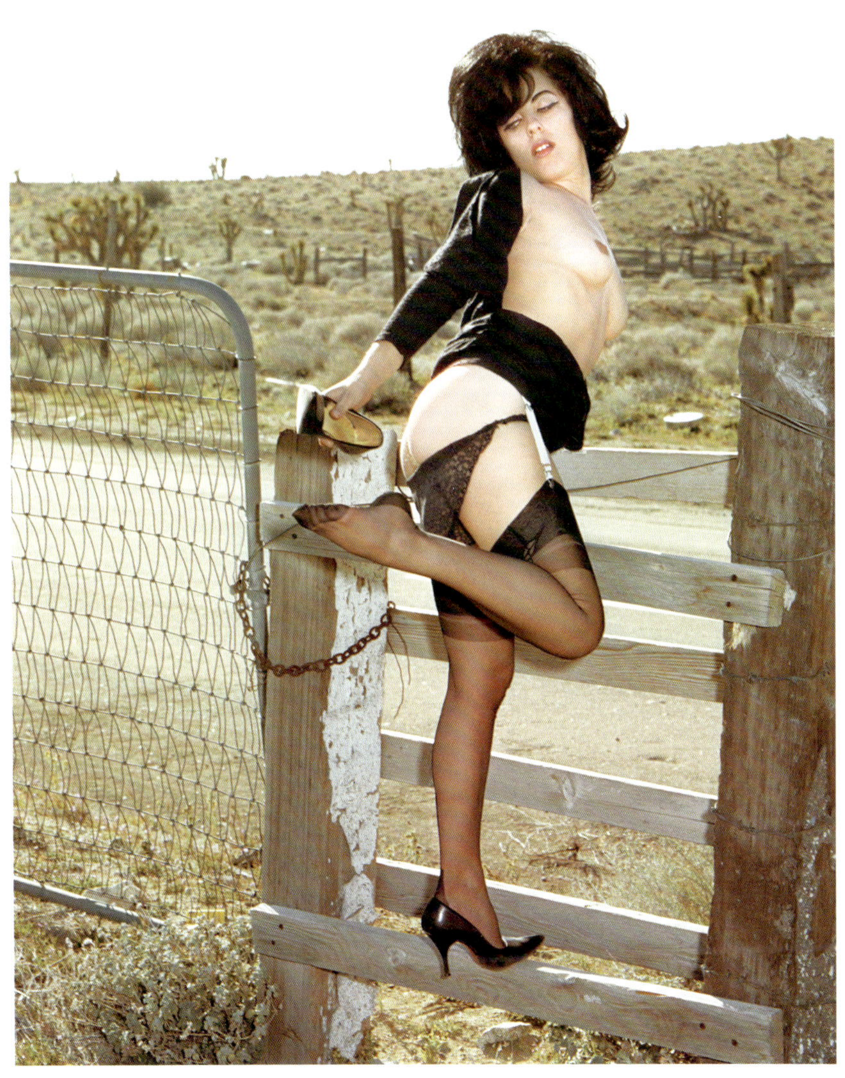

OPPOSITE **AND** ABOVE Cynthia Bond, ELMER BATTERS

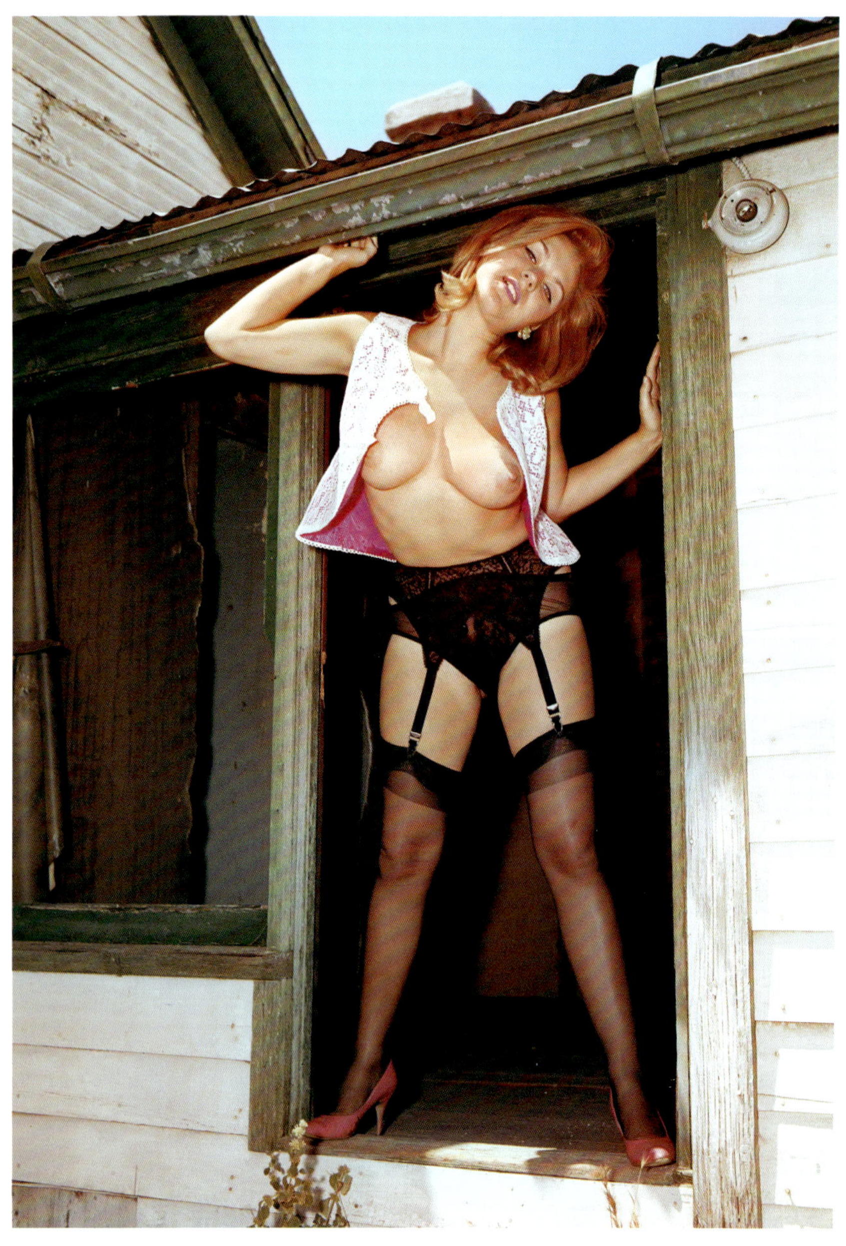
ABOVE Sandy Oliver, ELMER BATTERS

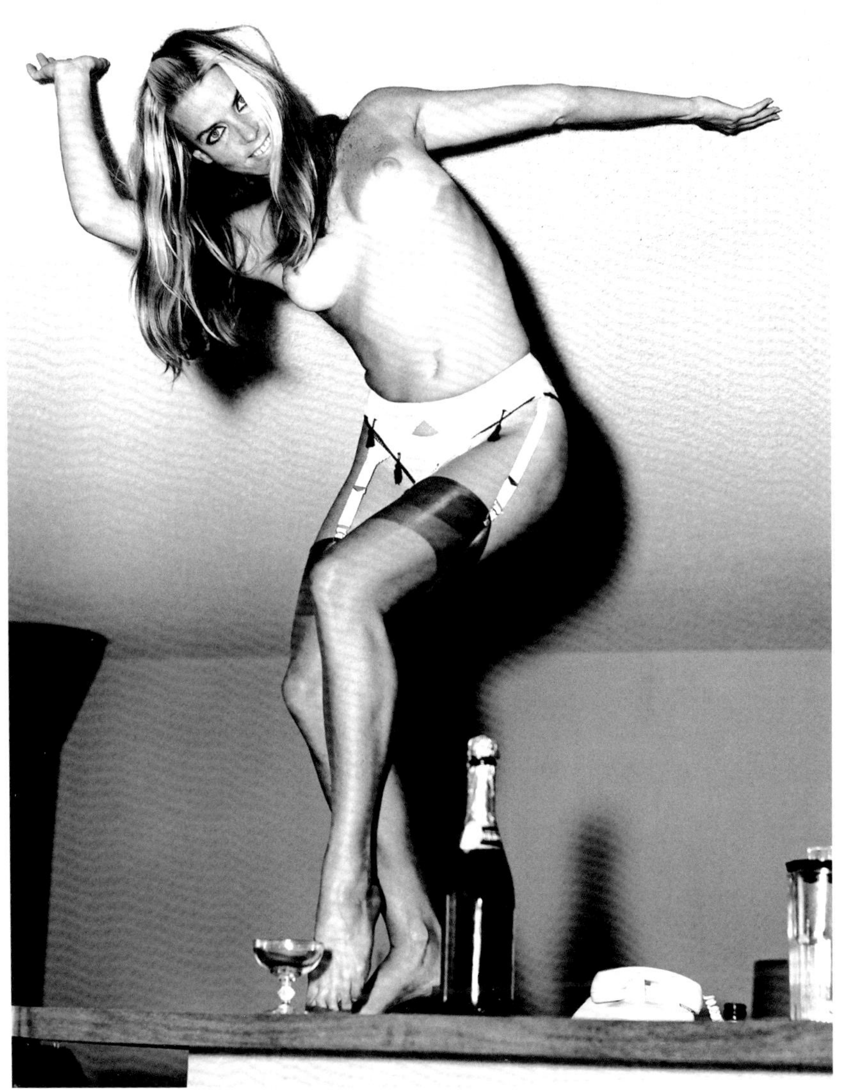

ABOVE Unknown

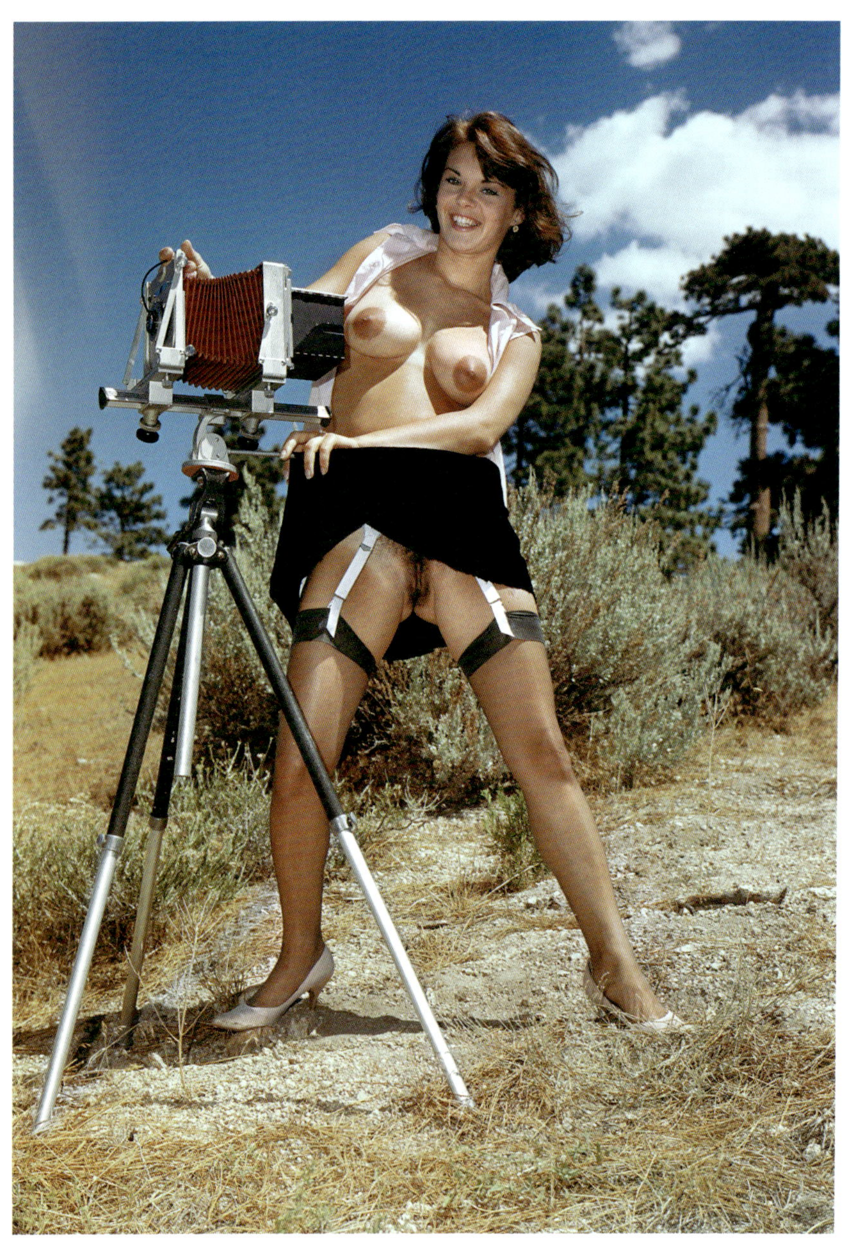

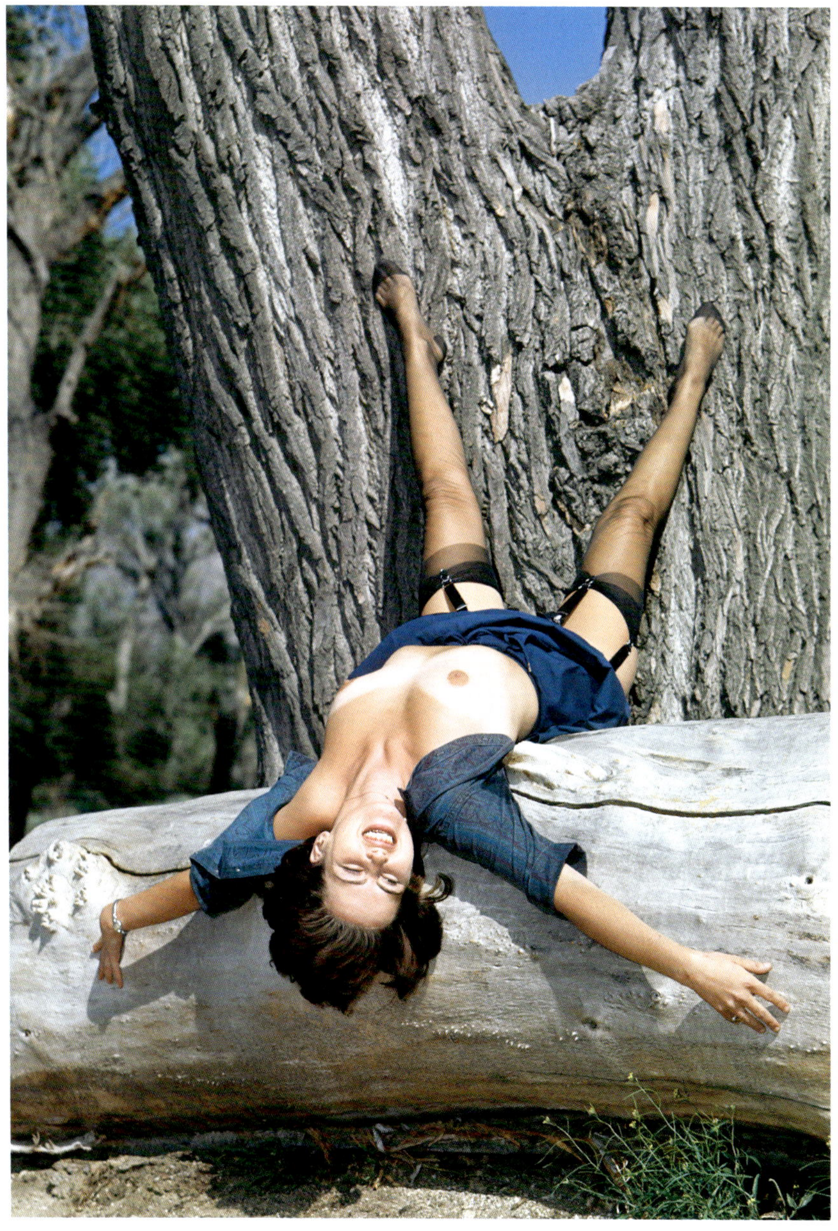

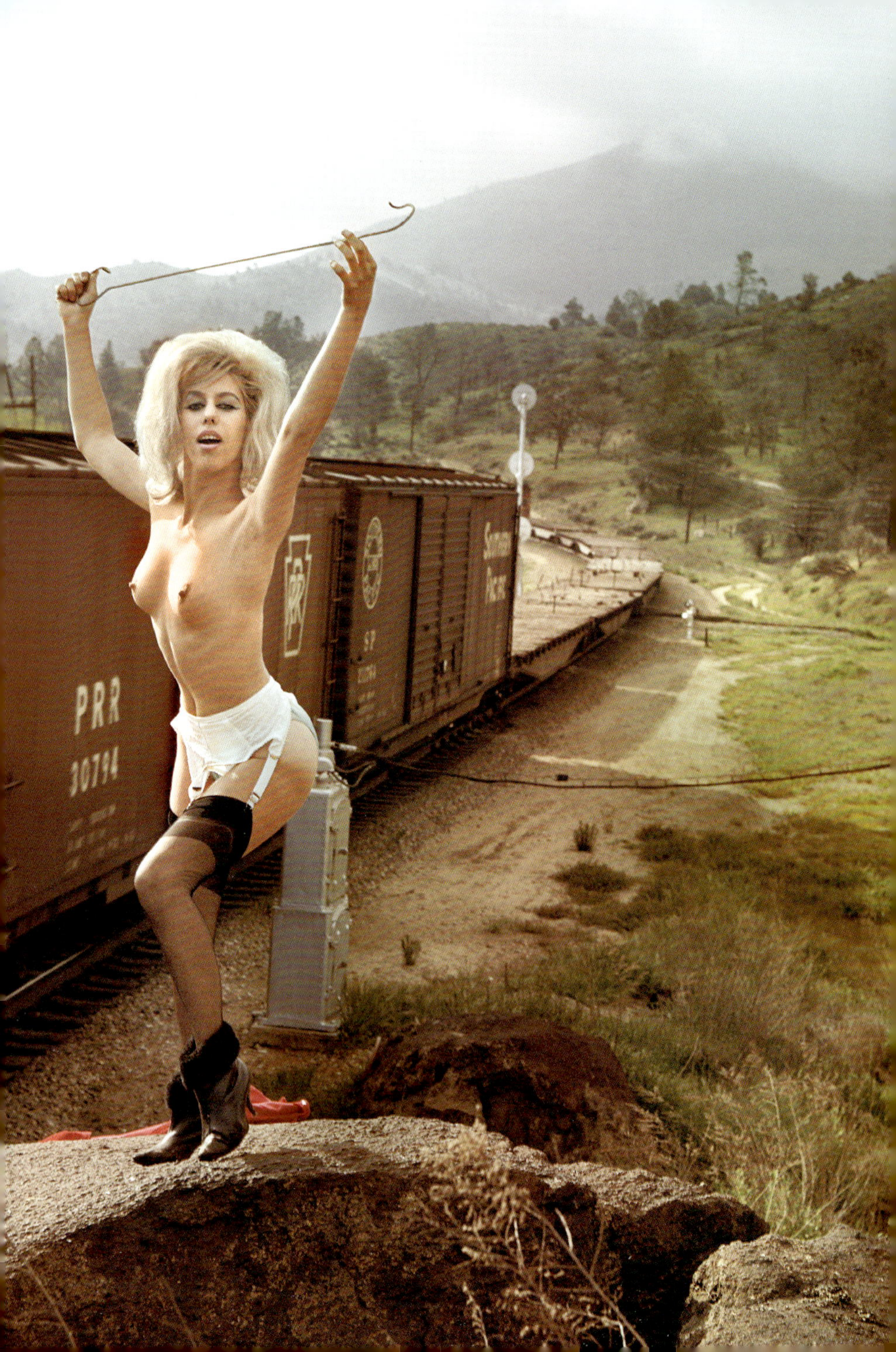

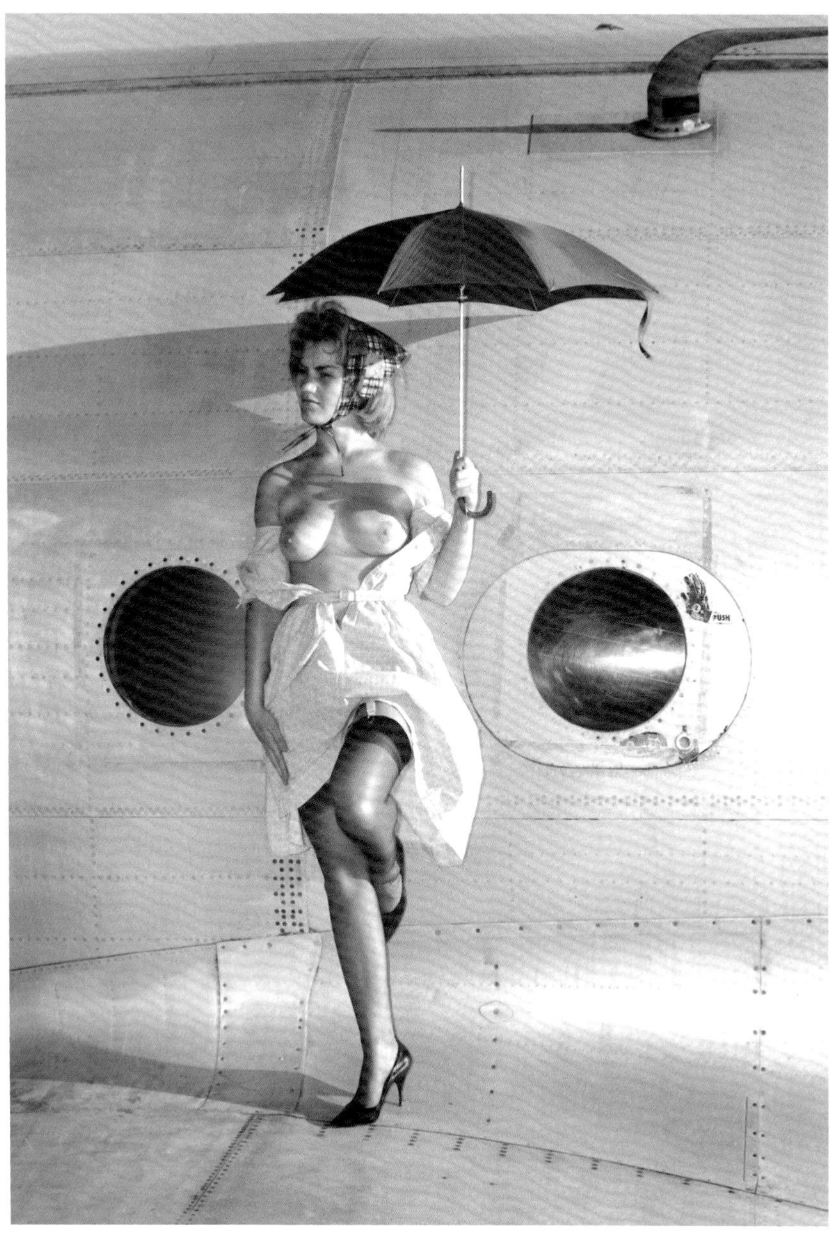

OPPOSITE Unknown   ABOVE Sandy Bottom   PAGES 176-177 Gloria Dawn

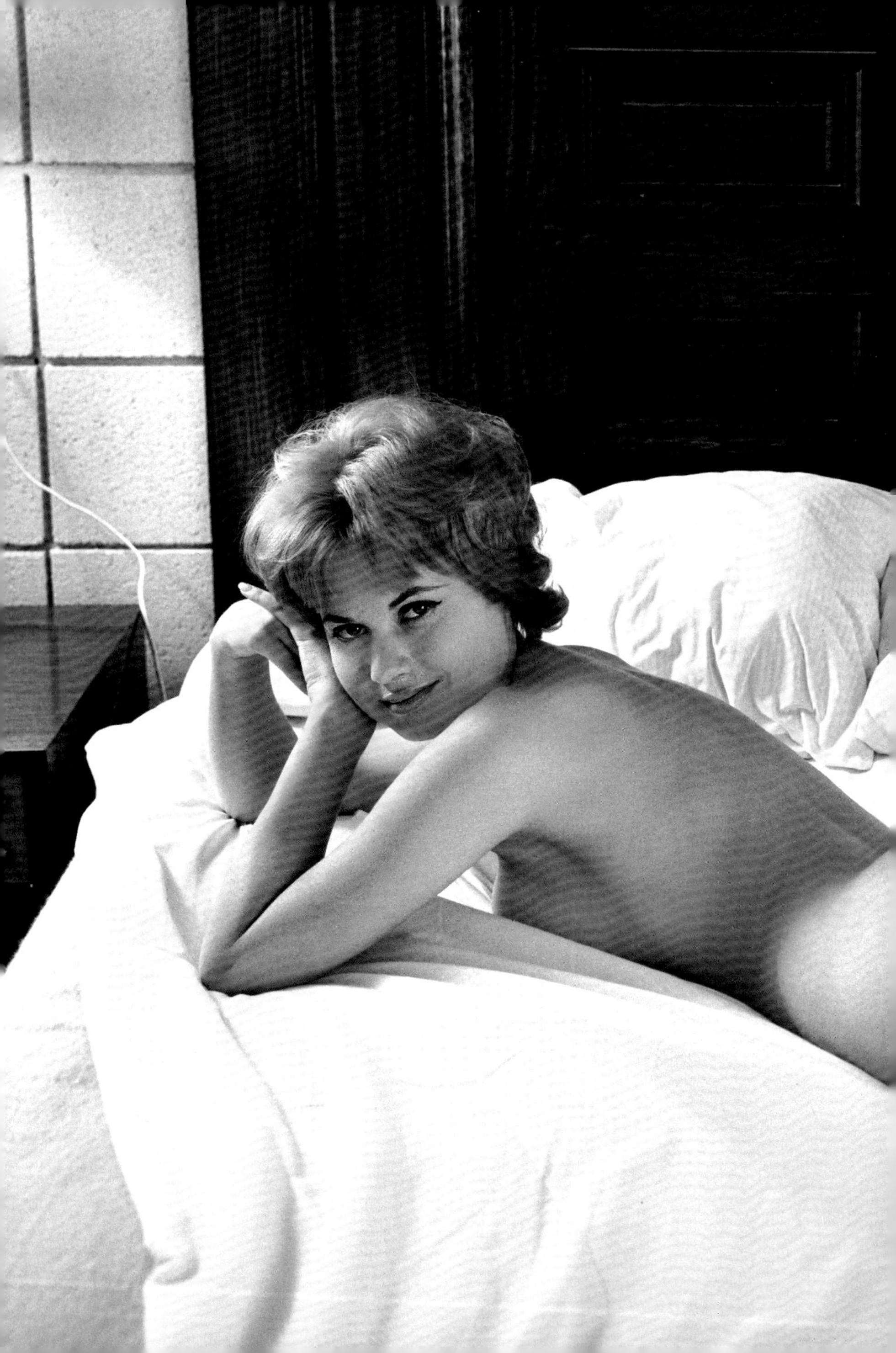

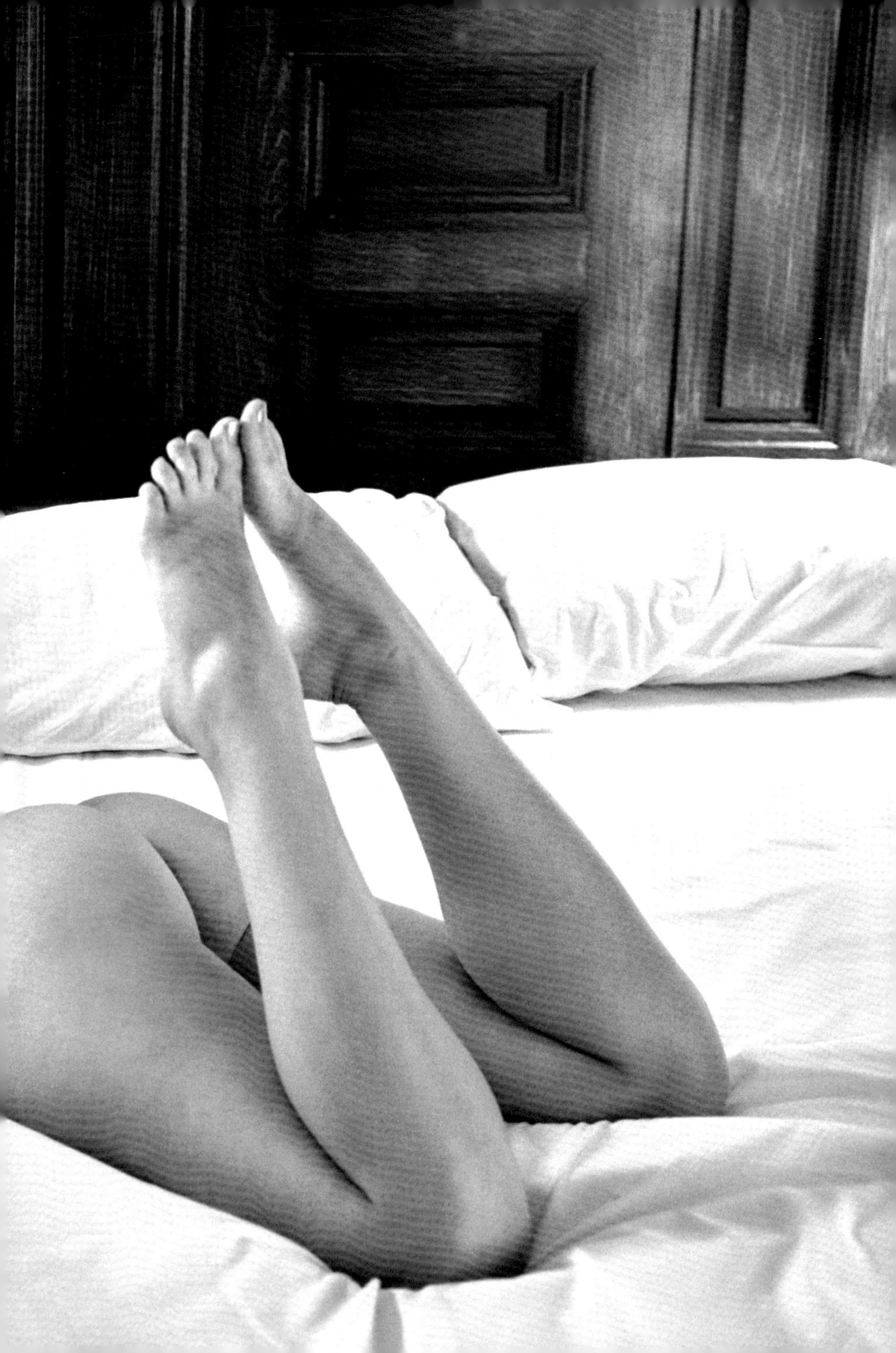

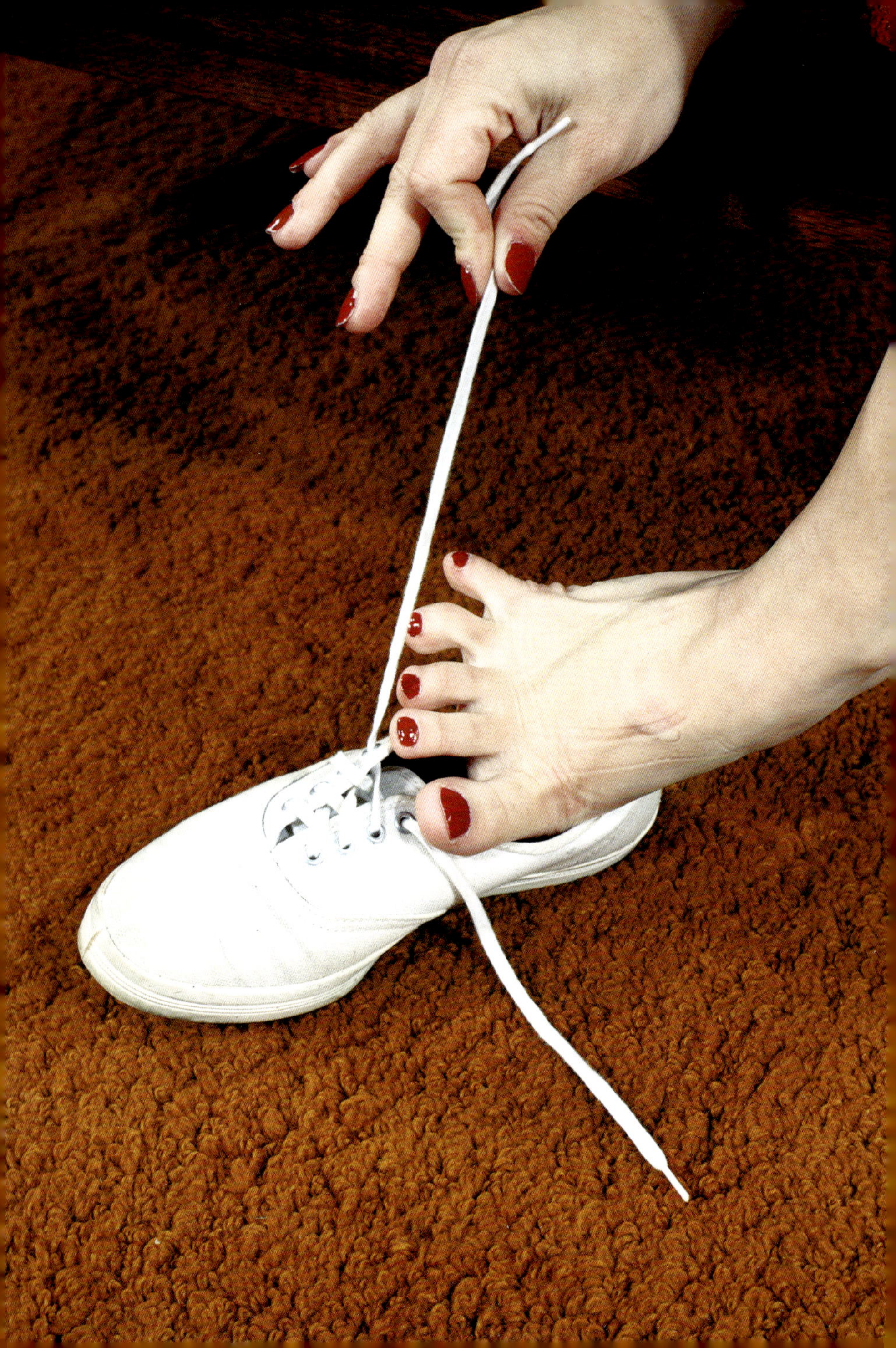

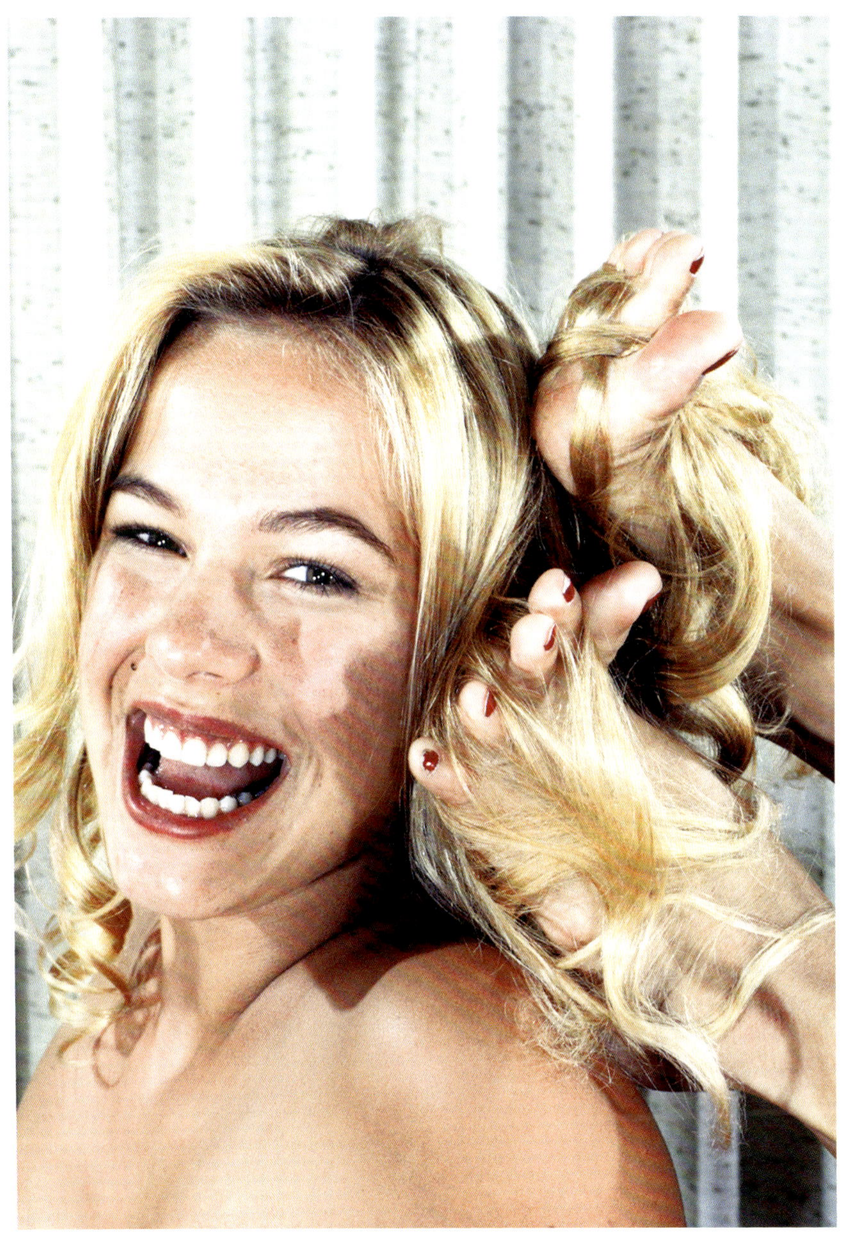

OPPOSITE AND ABOVE Unknown, ELMER BATTERS

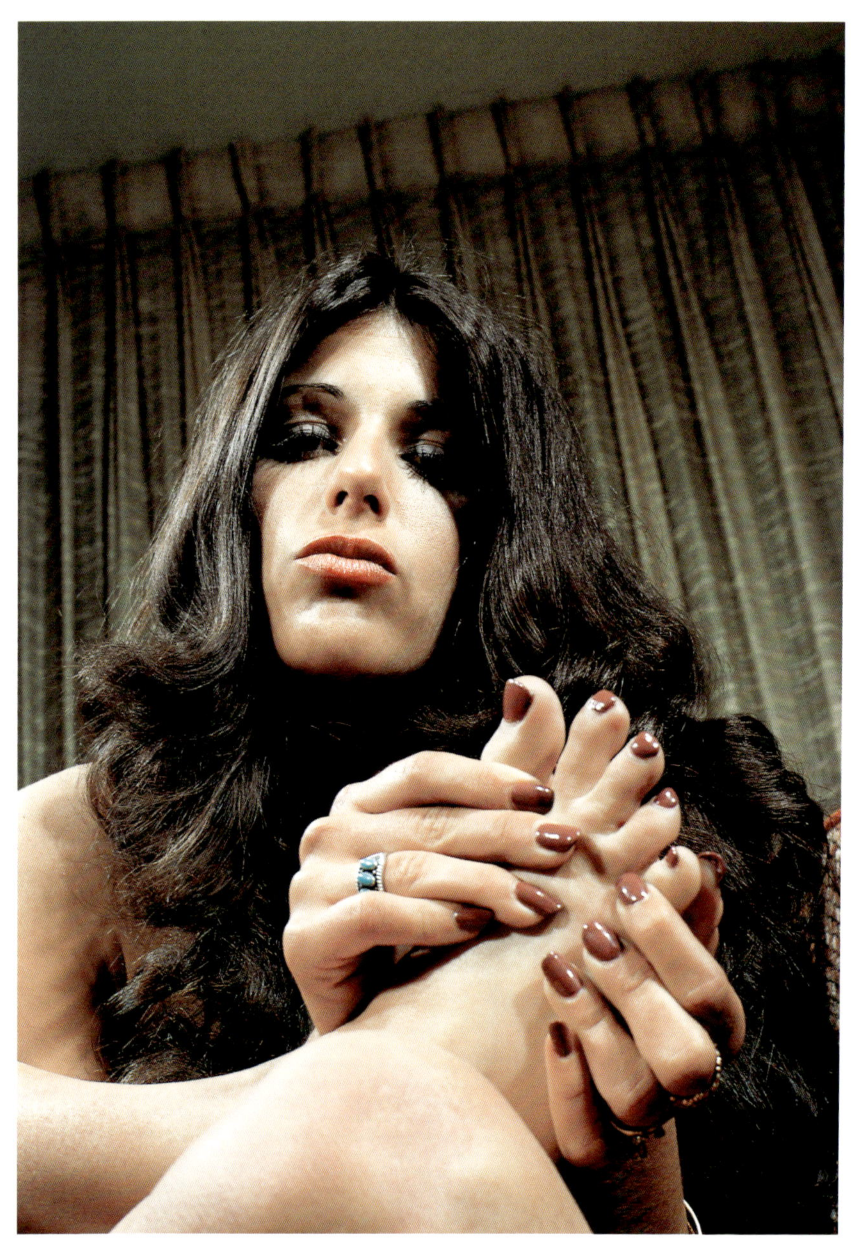

ABOVE **Unknown**, ELMER BATTERS

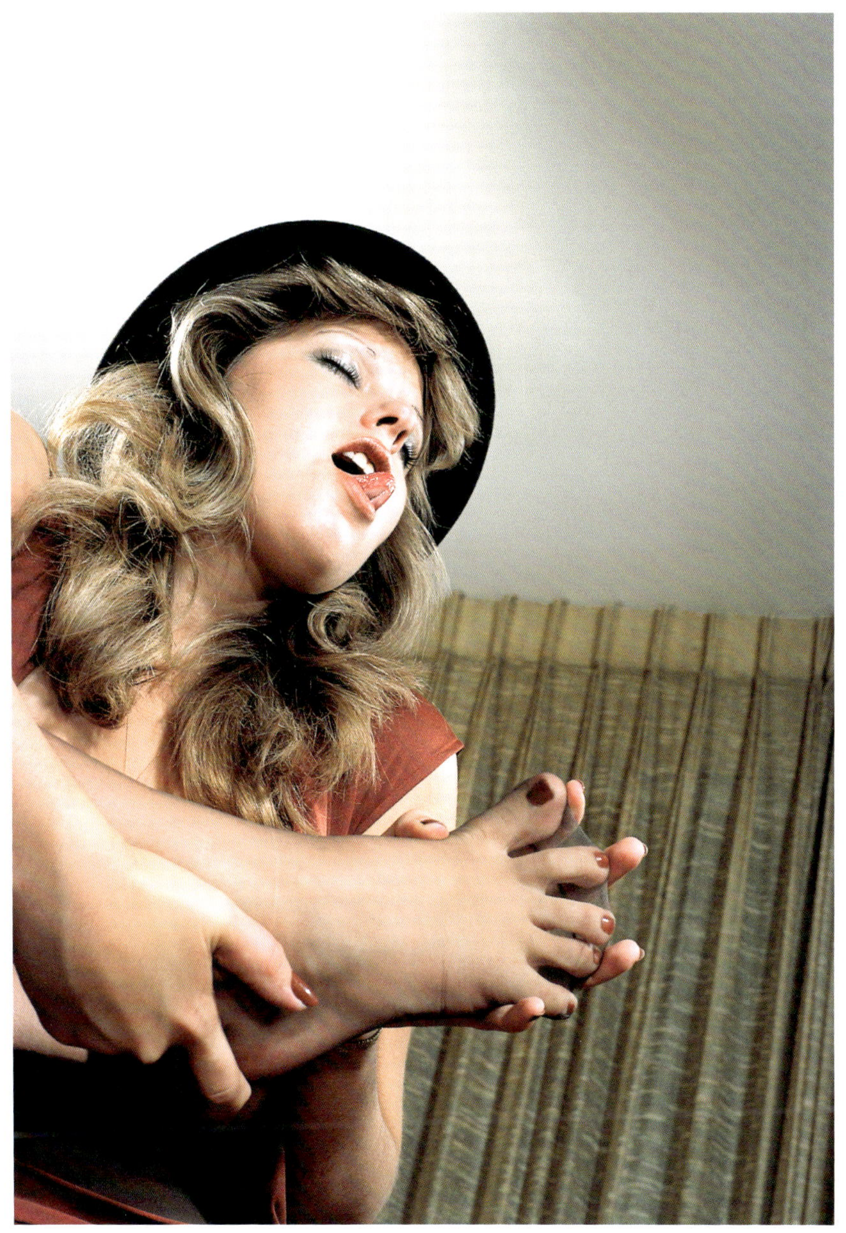

ABOVE Denise, ELMER BATTERS

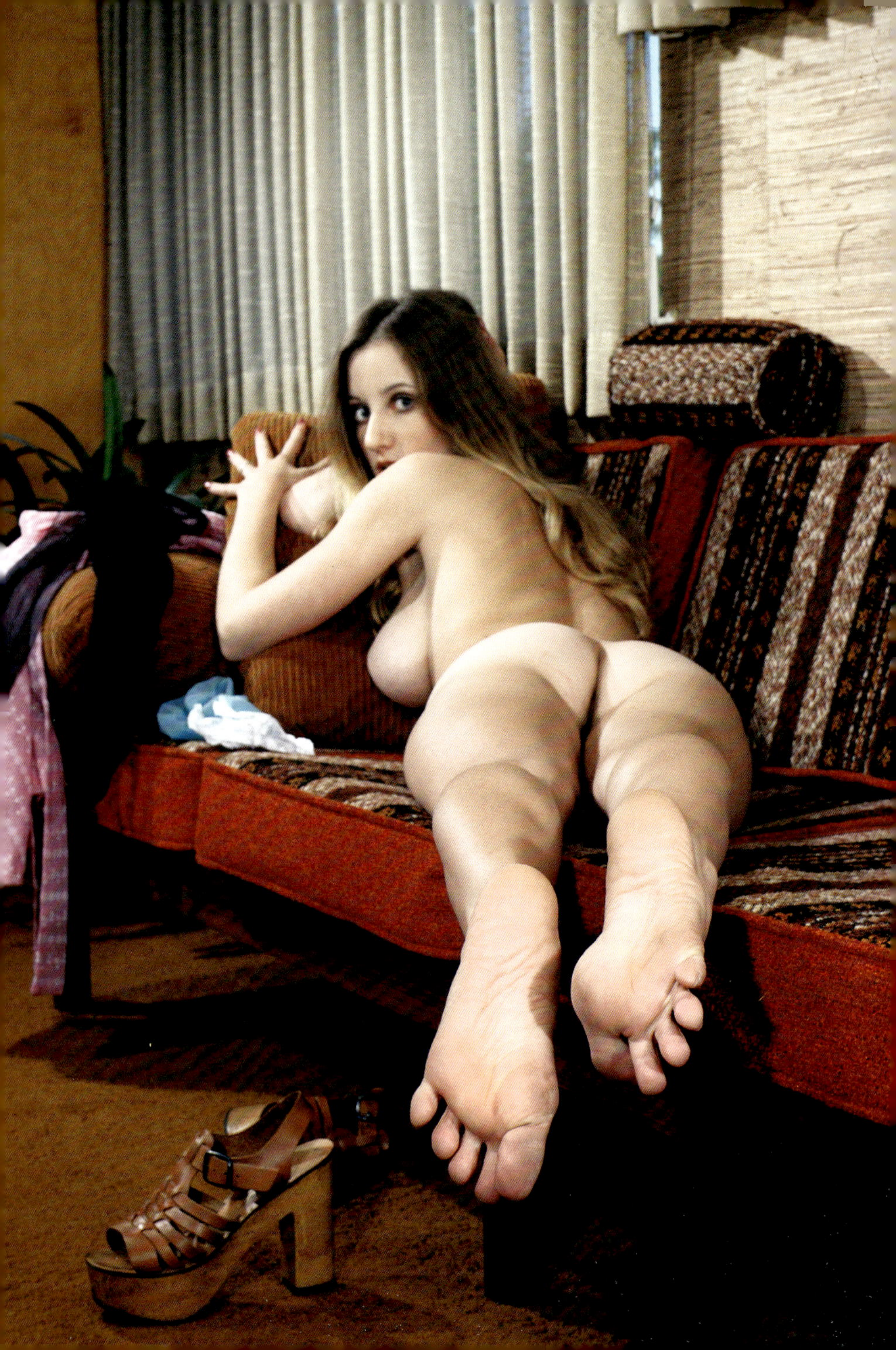

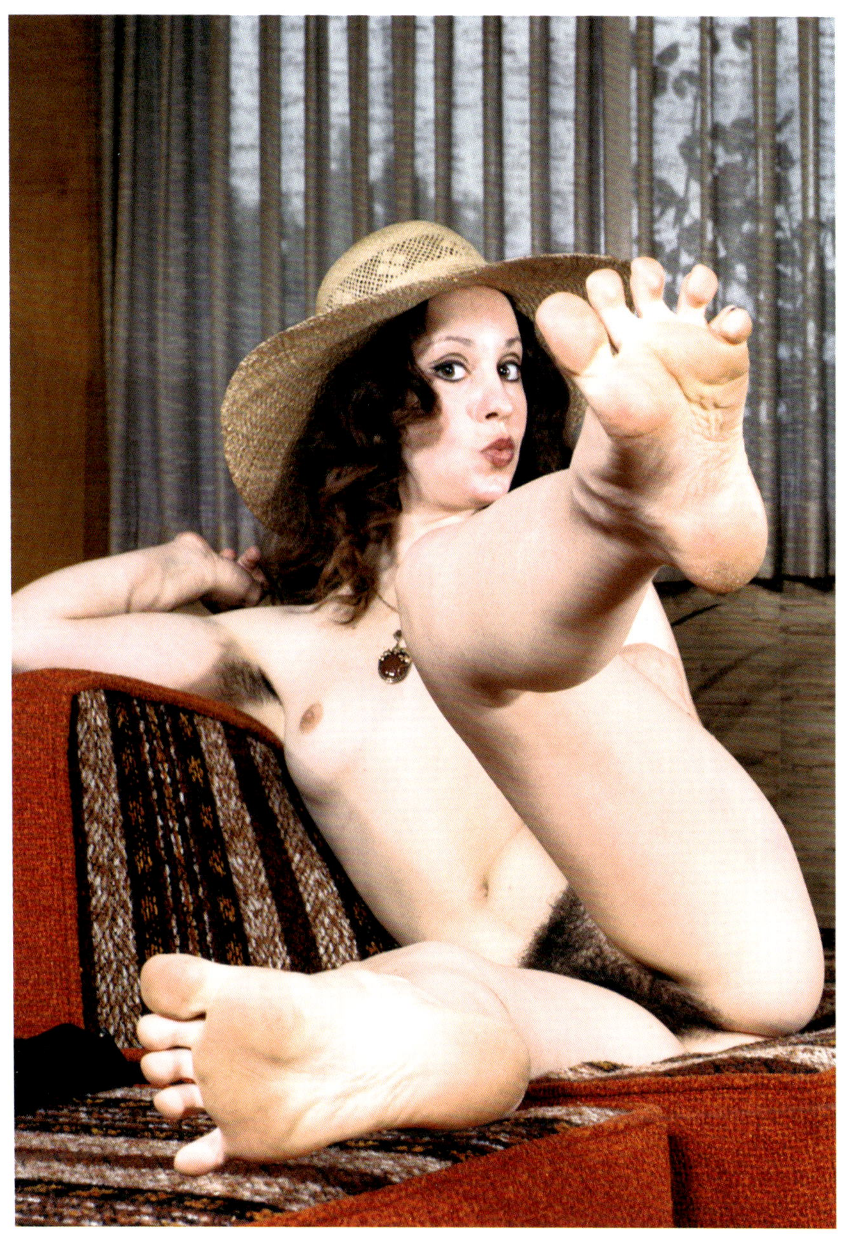

OPPOSITE, ABOVE AND, PAGES 184-185 Unknown, ELMER BATTERS

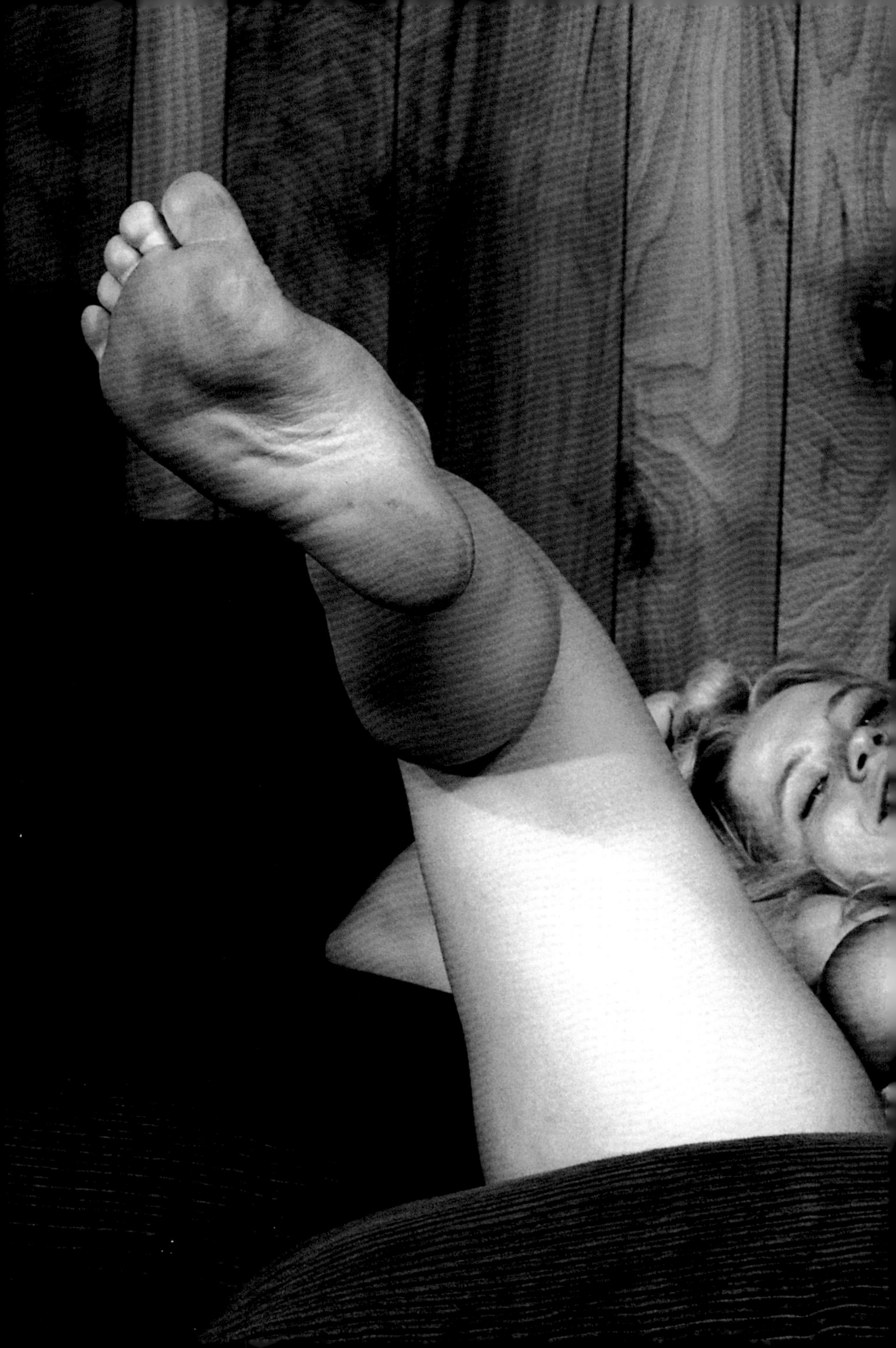

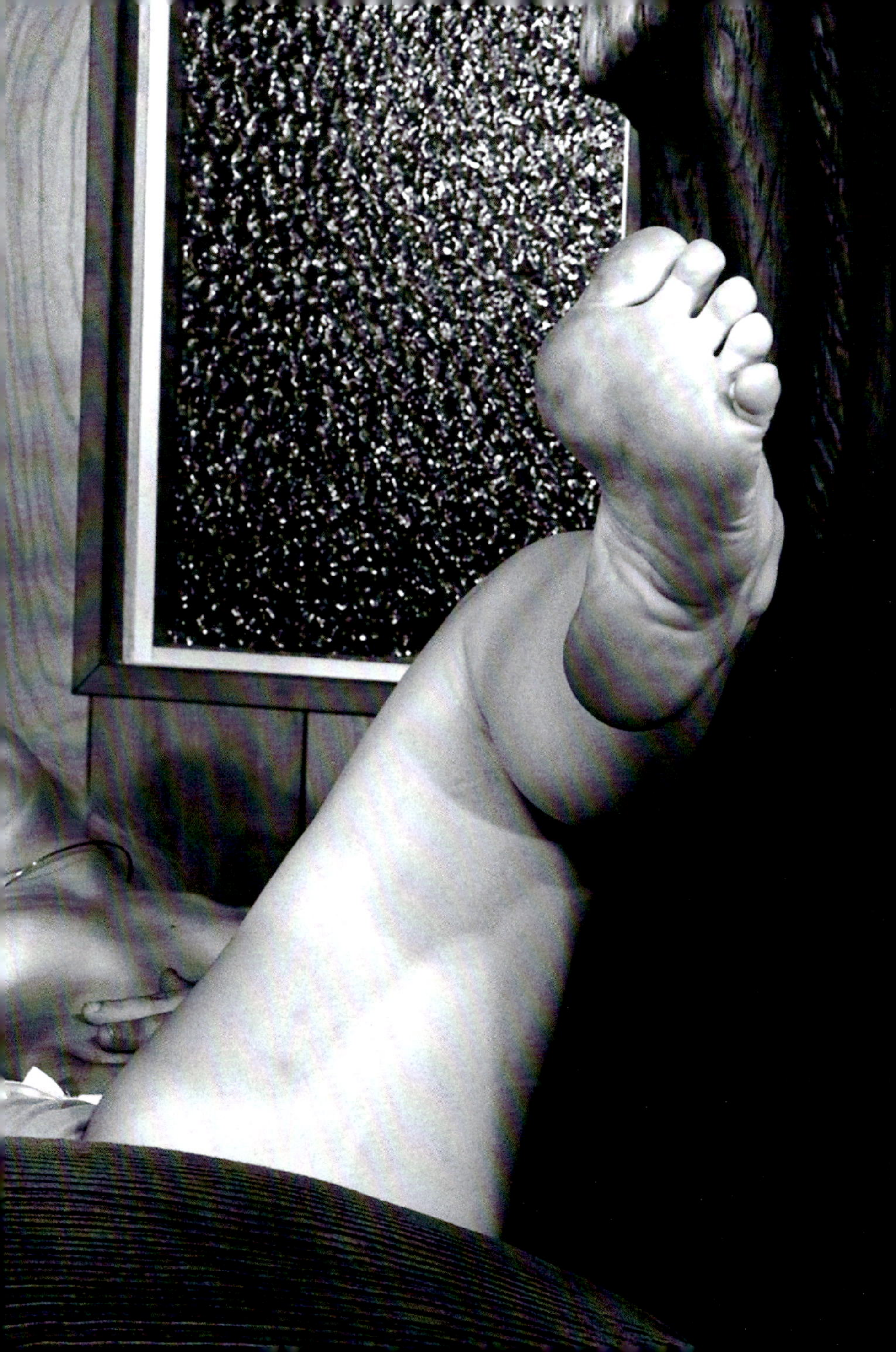

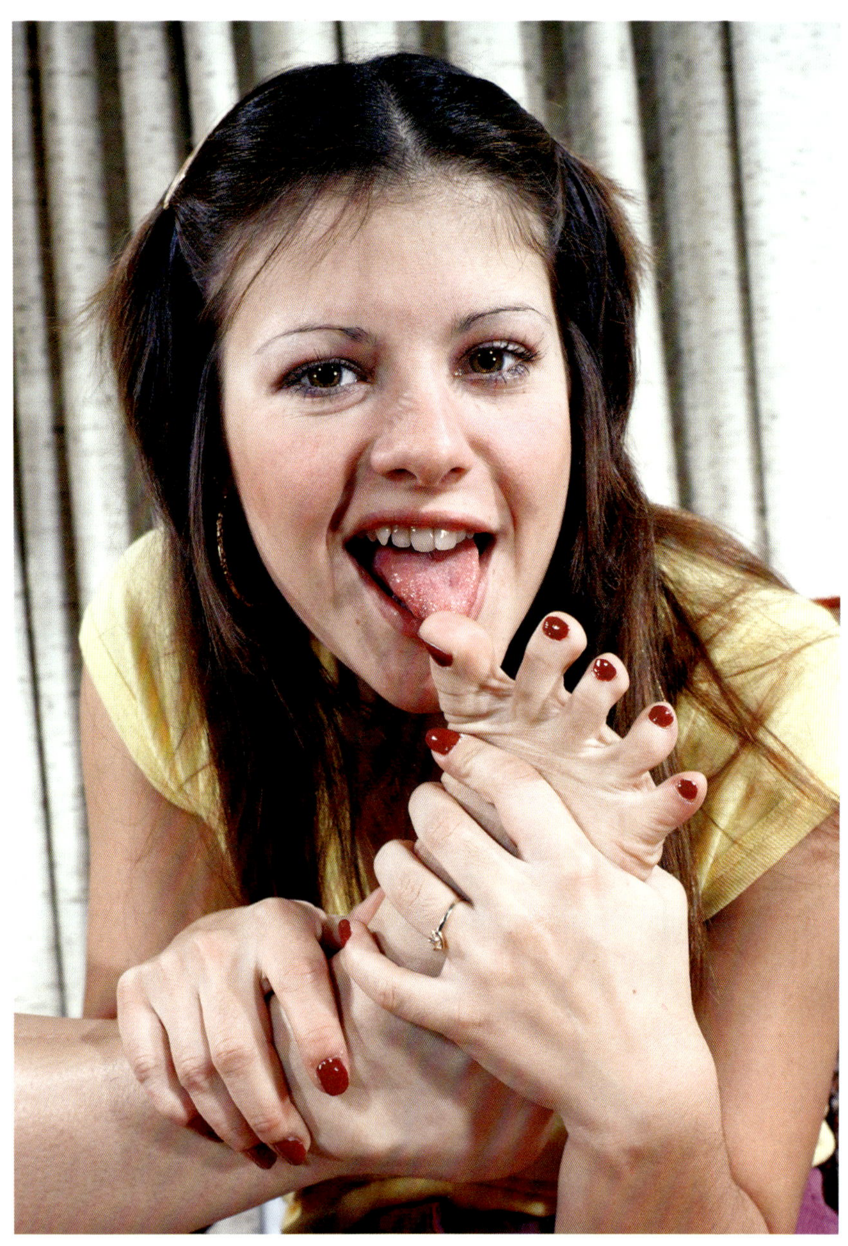

ABOVE AND OPPOSITE Unknown, ELMER BATTERS

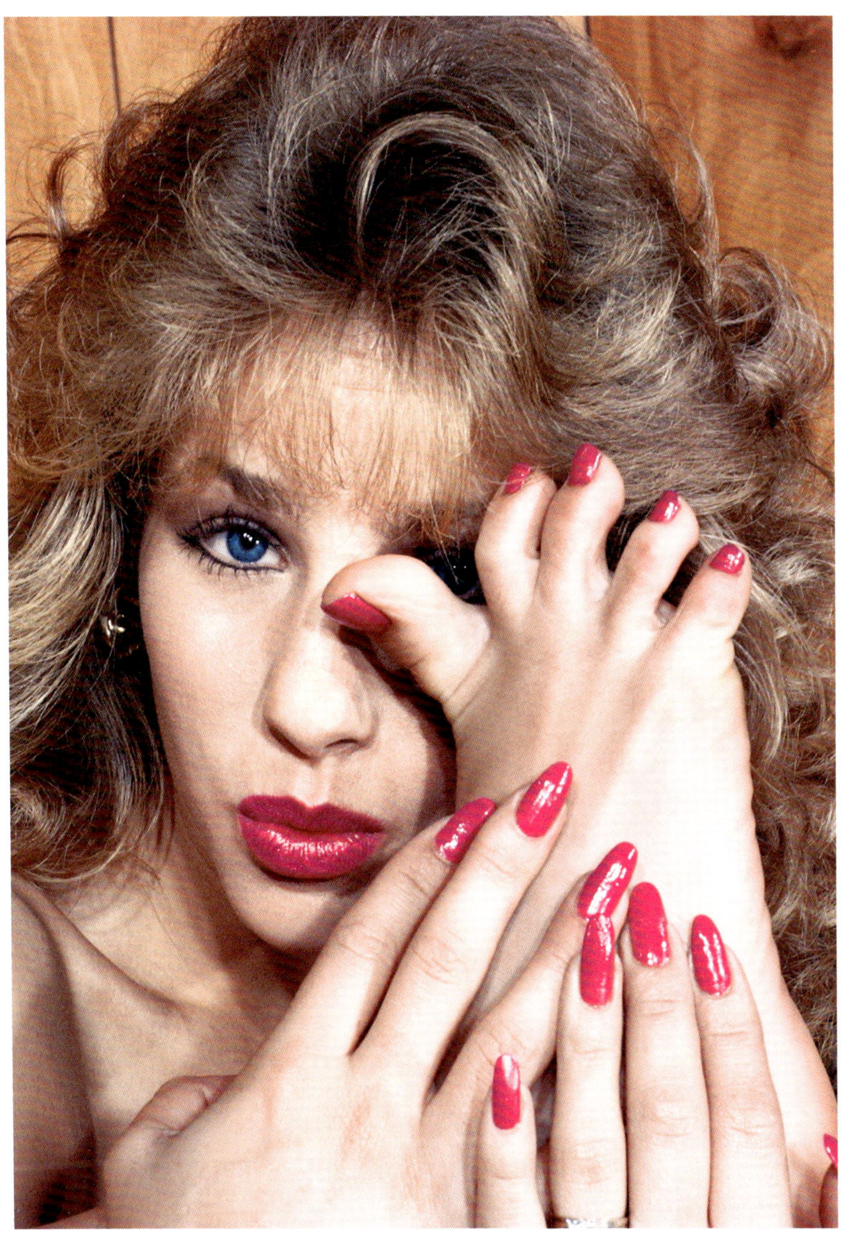

PAGES 188-189 Unknown, ELMER BATTERS

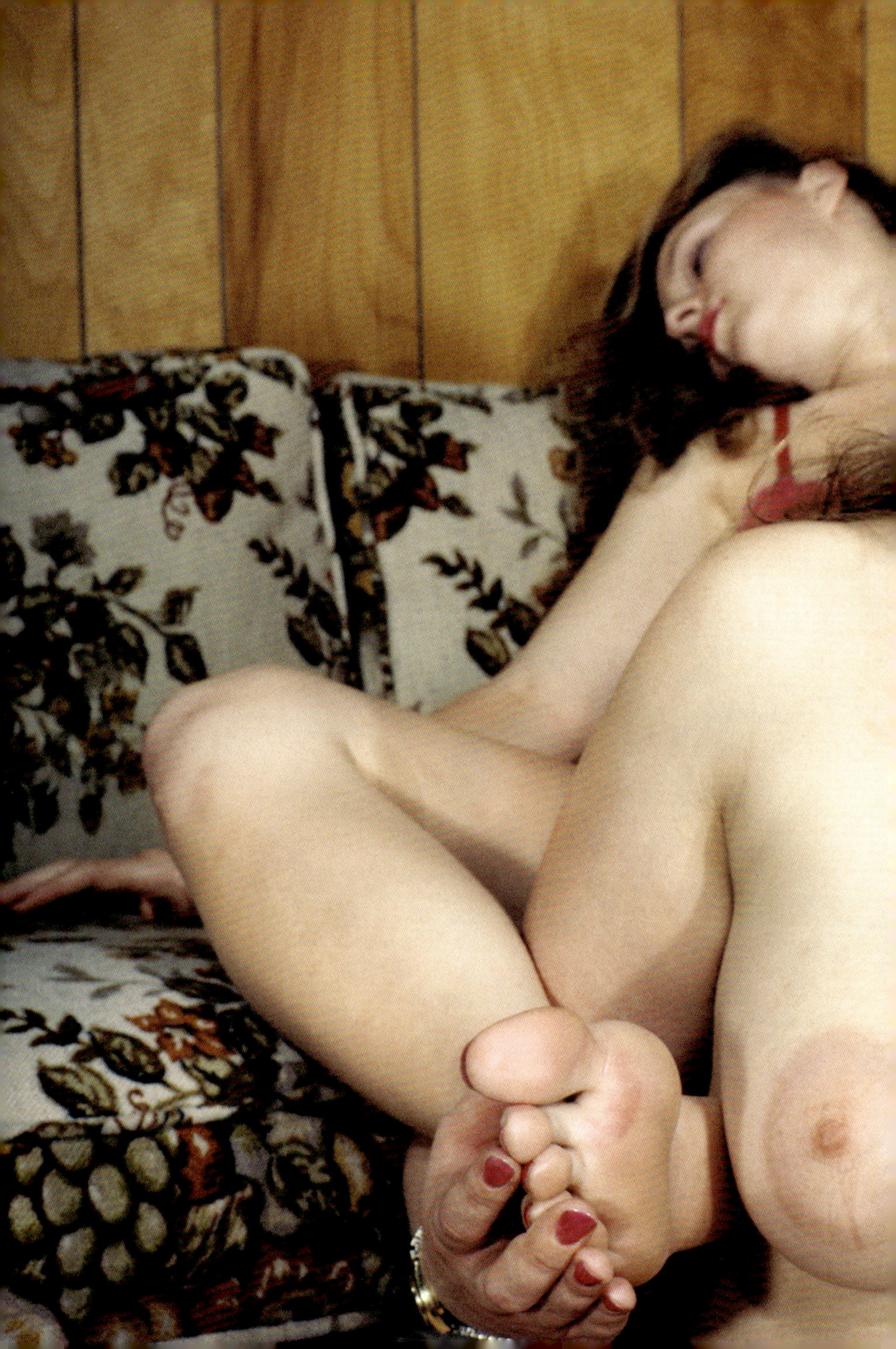

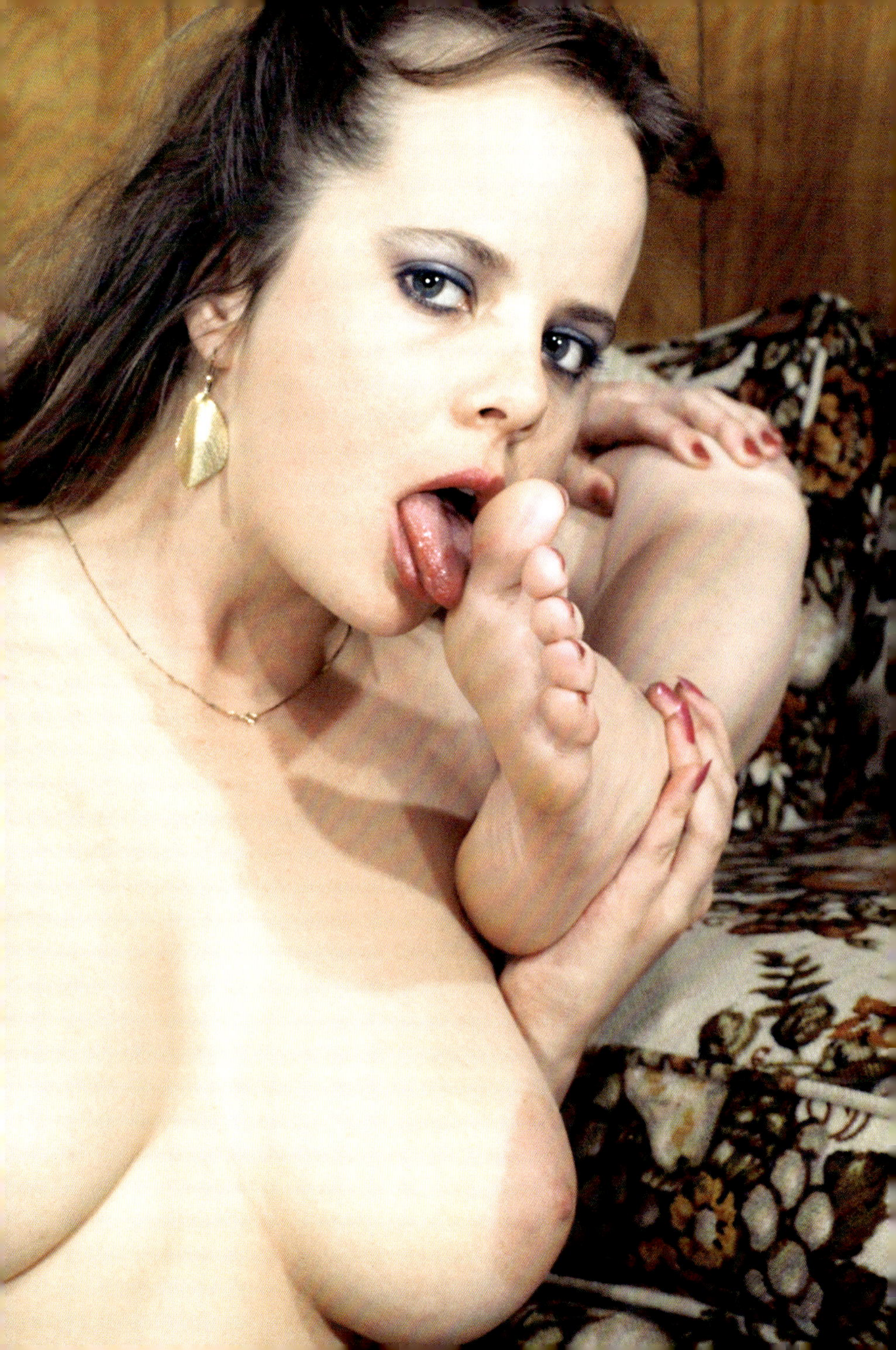

Acknowledgments

Most of the photographs in this book were obtained from the massive archive of A. R. S. Inc., sellers of vintage erotica for over 25 years. They may be contacted by email at yesgirls@yesterdaygirls.com. Photographs on pages 30, 39, 40, 41, 42, 78, 79, 108, 115, 123, 171, and 191 are from the Erosarchives.com collection. The photograph from the DuPont archive on page 13, right, is property of the Hagley Museum and Library. Magazines on pages 14, and 15 are property of Eric Godtland. Photographs on pages 6,7, 12, 13, left, 16, 21, 22, 23, 33, 34, 35, 36, 37, 43, 85, 89, 109, 118, 119, 125/126, 129, 130, 136, 151, 178, 179, 180, 181, 182, 183, 186, 187, and 188/189 are the property of Dian Hanson. Photographs on pages 10, 48, 54/55, 56, 57, 60, 61, 62, 63, 64, 65, 66/67, 68, 69, 72, 74/75, and 90/91 are by Paula Klaw and Movie Star News www.moviestarnews.com. Contact Movie Star News to purchase these and other vintage prints. The endpapers are from The Kobal Collection. The Gil Elvgren print, page 1, is courtesy of Louis K. Meisel Gallery. Photographs on pages 70, and 71 are © Bunny Yeager. The song lyrics on page 5 are the property of the listed artist and his representatives.

Special thanks to Ed Fox for his front and back cover photos of the astounding Ryan Keely. Thanks as well to Josh Baker, Cara Walsh and Jessica Sappenfield for design, Martin Holz for editorial coordination, Jennifer Patrick for production, and RP Digital for scanning.

Any credit omissions are unintentional, and appropriate credit will be given in future editions if such copyright holders contact the publisher.

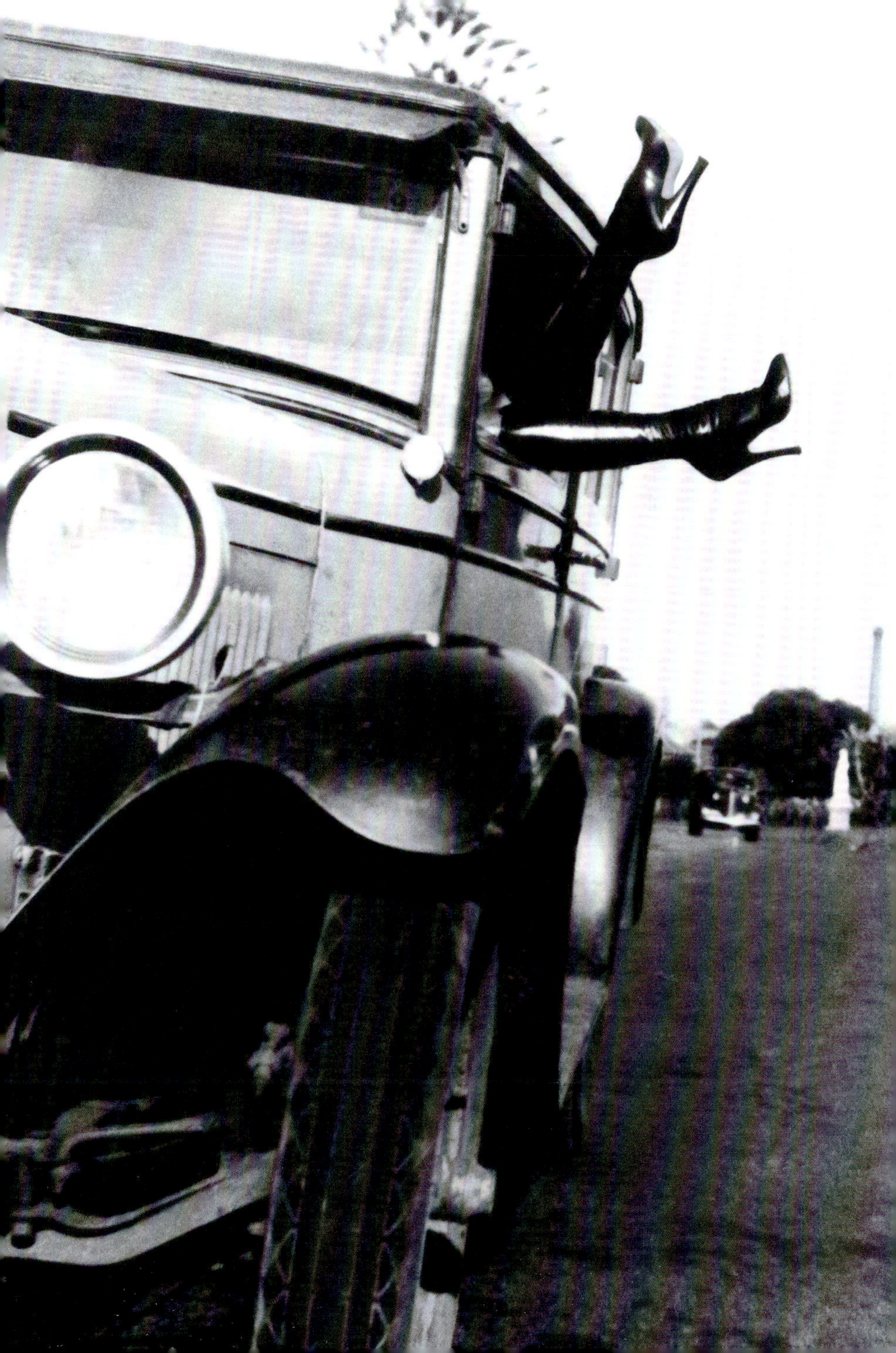

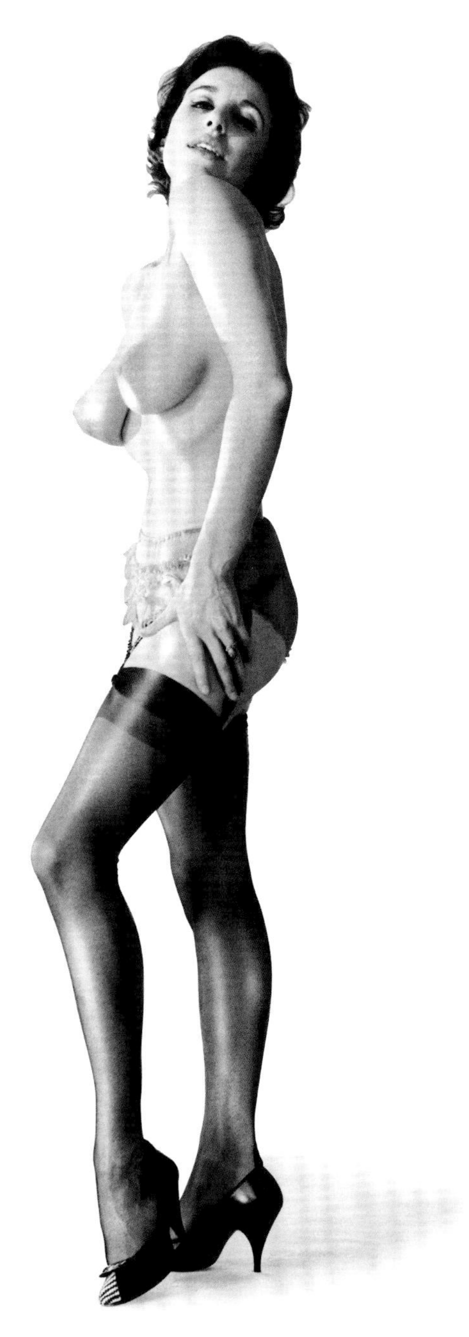

FRONT AND BACK COVER Ryan Keely by Ed Fox
ENDPAPERS 20th Century Fox issued this Manual of Arms
starring Bettie Grable during World War II. The Kobal Collection.
PAGE 1 Station Wow by Gil Elvgren, courtesy of Louis K. Meisel Gallery
PAGE 2 Angel Carter, circa 1965
PAGE 191 John Willy, circa 1945, originally featured in *Bizarre* magazine
LEFT Vergie Brown, circa 1965

EACH AND EVERY TASCHEN BOOK PLANTS A SEED!
Each year, we offset our annual carbon emissions with carbon credits at the Instituto Terra, a reforestation program in Minas Gerais, Brazil, founded by Lélia and Sebastião Salgado. To find out more about this ecological partnership, please check: www.taschen.com/institutoterra.
Inspiration: unlimited. Carbon footprint: (almost) zero.

Want to see more? Visit taschen.com to view our current publications, browse our latest magazine, and subscribe to our newsletter.

© 2026 TASCHEN GmbH
Hohenzollernring 53, D–50672 Köln
www.taschen.com

German translation by Ronit Jariv, Cologne
French translation by Bernard Clément, Paris

Printed in Italy
ISBN 978-3-8365-8036-6

Manual of *Arms*

(AND LEGS)

ARMS *by U. S. Army*
LEGS *by Betty Grable,*
20th Century-Fox Star

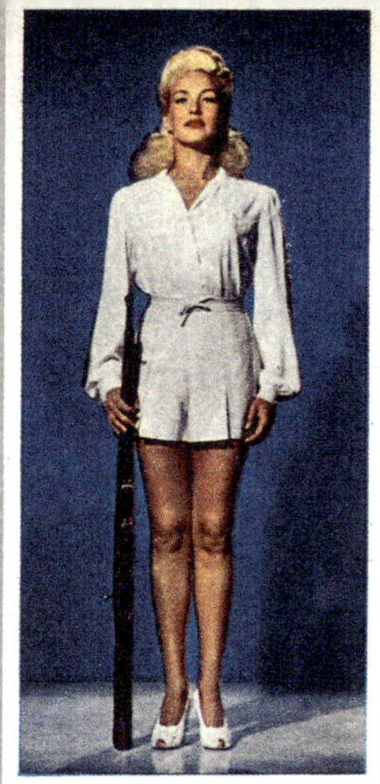

1. ORDER ARMS:
The butt of the rifle
Rests on the ground,

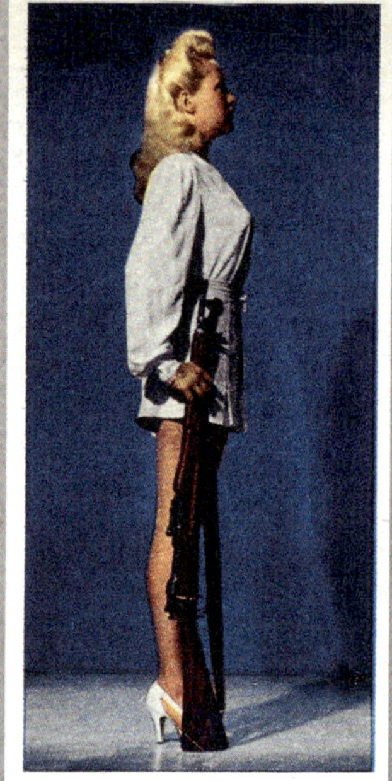

Eyes straight ahead—
Don't look—honor bound!

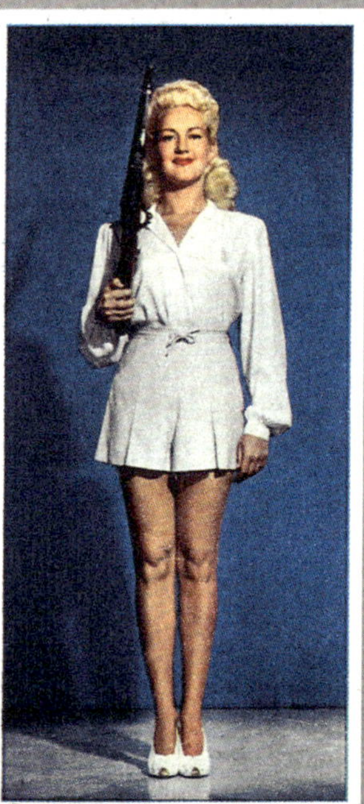

Regrasp it, right hand
This time on the butt,

Now place the rifle
At shoulder. Don't strut!

3. PORT ARMS:
Now raise the rifle
With your right hand